German Census Records 1816–1916

The When, Where, and How of a Valuable Genealogical Resource

Roger P. Minert, Ph.D., A.G.

Research Assistants
Jeanne G. Minert
Jilline Maynes

Printed in the United States of America by Family Roots Publishing, Orting, WA.
First Edition

Library of Congress Control Number: 2016934482

German census records from 1816 to 1916 / Roger P. Minert

       p.   cm.
       Includes index.
       ISBN-10: 1-62859-077-7 (soft bound)
       ISBN-13: 978-1-62859-077-7 (soft bound)
       ISBN-10:1-62859-078-5 (hard bound)
       ISBN-13:978-1-62859-078-4 (hard bound)
1.   German History – German Census.   2. Genealogy – German Research.

Family Roots Publishing Co. LLC
PO Box 1682
Orting, WA 98360
www.familyrootspublishing.com

Table of Contents

Acknowledgements

For some reason, I cannot recall precisely when the idea of creating a book about German census records became a necessity in my mind. Like other professionals who had worked for decades in the field of German family history and genealogy, I knew of and had studied only a few census records created in only a few states in Germany before the establishment of the German Empire in 1871. I too had wondered if there were any more in those states or in other states. It seemed likely somehow, even though I had never seen any original census records in Germany and had never heard or read of them when dealing with archivists and researchers all over the German-language territory. If census records were compiled and had survived, why were we not using them more often for genealogical research on either side of the Atlantic Ocean? By early 2014, a hypothesis had been born and a plan took shape very quickly.

Thanks to the assistance and encouragement of many individuals, my quest to learn about German census records has reached a successful conclusion. This enormous undertaking would not have been possible without the contributions of many individuals and groups. Perhaps the first of these were my friends and colleagues in the Family History Library. Marion Wolfert, Sonja Nishimota, and Fritz Juengling were immediately enthusiastic about the prospects that something important would emerge from this investigation. Indeed, my search for records began in that library and positive results were immediate.

Because I felt that conducting census research from a distance would simply not suffice, I formulated a plan for a sabbatical semester in Europe. My department chair, Richard Bennett, and college dean, Brent Top, both accepted the research design and goals and expressed their confidence that I could make the program a success. The Religious Studies Center at Brigham Young University provided some funding for housing in Europe and the University's Kennedy International Center made a donation for travel in Germany. Those grants were crucial as we considered the enormous costs that would be incurred when my wife, Jeanne, and I planned to live and travel in Europe for six months.

Research assistant Jilline Maynes volunteered to help in the initial investigation into German census records found in the collection of the Family History Library in Salt Lake City. Her superb examination of the Library's catalog revealed perhaps one hundred collections of census documents microfilmed under relatively sporadic circumstances in unpredictable areas of Germany. She discovered many of those records under key words other than "census." The first several hundred emails sent to German archives during this study emanated from her keyboard. Without her assistance, I could not have completed the book during my stay in Europe.

Three of my family history students contributed in significant ways to the completion of this book. Annie Leishman was my office manager during the initial investigation into this topic. By assuming additional tasks, she allowed me to devote more and more time to pre-sabbatical preparations. Her successor, Lauren Wake, was equally helpful, keeping the office in order during my absence and working with me on the completion of the book after I returned from Vienna. Kelsee Jackson designed the excellent *PowerPoint* presentation I used to announce the results of my research at the RootsTech Conference in Salt Lake City in February 2016.

A great number of archivists in Germany responded to our letters and emails with a variety of answers. Many of those experts were key players in the process of identifying and copying census regulations and name lists. Many of them became our hosts when Jeanne and I accepted invitations to visit their archives and study the documents ourselves. It was a surprise to several of them when we found extensive census lists in their collections—further evidence that this kind of record is not commonly used in genealogical research in Germany.

Leland Meitzler of Family Roots Publishing recognized early on that this book could make a major contribution to the literature of the German-American family history research community. From our first conversation on this topic to the appearance of the book, his enthusiasm has never flagged. Equally interested in the prospect of a book on this topic was Eckehard Brockhaus, the publisher of my handwriting book in the German language. He believed early on that a German version of this book would be as helpful to German researchers as it would to Americans.

Kayla Swan deserves my gratitude for the excellent design of this book and the attractive front cover; this is the third major work she has designed for me. Lauren Wake produced the back cover and Carly Case gave the text one final careful reading. I am indebted to them all for their fine work.

My partner in this study from start to finish is the same partner who has shared life with me for more than forty years—my wife, Jeanne. Her assistance was invaluable as we traversed Germany for seven weeks in search of archival documents. Her services in cataloging, copying, and archiving the documents we found were indispensable as she endeavored to create order out of chaos. Her willingness to devote substantial family resources to a genealogical topic I believe will be important to many people is inspiring. If Jeanne had a nickel for every time she has heard the word "census" . . .

Roger P. Minert
Provo, Utah
March 2016

Dedicated to my wife Jeanne nee Gardner and our daughters Melanie, Julie, Stephanie, and Cassie. We will appear as a complete family group in the U.S. Federal Census when the 1990 lists are released to the public in 2062.

Old genealogists never die—they just lose their census!

(seen by the author on a bumper sticker in Salt Lake City in 1993)

Introduction

Census Records and the American Family History Researcher

One of the principal record types used by family history researchers in the United States has long been the federal census. Mandated by the Constitution, enumerations have taken place in all states and territories since 1790. With the zero year as the standard date of enumeration, the procedures and record formats for a given census year were used uniformly everywhere. With the exception of the loss of the 1890 records in a tragic 1921 fire, the collection of original pages is virtually complete.

The federal census can be accessed with ease via microfilm and at several internet sites, such that researchers can easily find and study original pages. Indexes produced by individuals, societies, and commercial enterprises enable readers a quick look at ancestral candidates. The quality of those indexes is of course dependent upon the skills of indexers and extractors, but savvy users are aware of such restrictions. The fact that census pages represent a combination of primary and secondary records needs to be considered, but this aspect does not diminish the importance of federal census records as documents supporting the longitudinal study of a particular family. The most recent federal census available to the public was conducted in 1940.

Officially, the federal census was to be conducted for two purposes: the apportionment of seats in the House of Representatives and direct taxation (a practice since discontinued). The content of a standard census page increased every ten years until 2000, but was simplified in 2010. Although some residents may have been offended by the questions asked by enumerators over the years, modern researchers are grateful for the detail and hope it is complete and correct.

Additional census records have been compiled by states and territories, some at unpredictable intervals, but even those years can be determined by a study of reliable websites state by state. Some state census records offer even more exact details than the national enumerations regarding birth dates and places. Those records too are usually available for study in microform and with increasing frequency in websites.[1]

German Census Records and Family History Research

Both novice family history researchers and experts who have seen census records in the United States often inquire about similar records in Germany. It would be easy to assume that every country in areas such as Europe not only made but maintains and even shares such records. Inquiries about German census records traditionally elicit such responses from experts as these: "We know that census records exist for the grand duchies of Mecklenburg-Schwerin and Schleswig-Holstein, but we don't know about other German provinces. They probably conducted censuses as well, but we can't tell you when or how or if such records still exist." One of the most experienced genealogical researchers in Germany, Eike Pies, made this observation in 2015: "I've been doing genealogical and family history research for more than fifty years and have never seen a [German] census record."[2]

The potential value of German census records to genealogists is substantial. Indeed, in areas where church records have been lost or before civil records were instituted in 1876, surviving census records will almost always be the only source of genealogical data on the common man. Where other primary documents exist, census records can serve to confirm what is already known.[3]

If in fact census records produced in the United States (and several other nations) are so important to researchers, it behooves us to determine the status of such records in historic German lands. It is beyond question that German states are the home to some of the finest church records compiled since the early sixteenth century and excellent civil records since the end of the eighteenth century. Would such a culture not also compile records of residents, mandated for whatever purposes, by governmental units? The most recent German publication on the topic was written by Rolf Gehrmann in 2009 and offered this comment: "The history of [German] census records has not yet been written."[4]

The Goals of This Study

It is time for the condition described by Gehrmann to be addressed. If it is to be done correctly, the following questions should be treated:

1. In which German states were censuses conducted?
2. When were the censuses conducted?
3. For what purposes were the censuses conducted?
4. What content did each census include?
5. Do original census sheets exist?
6. Where are original census records stored?
7. Have original census records been copied (microfilmed or digitized)?
8. How can researchers gain access to existing census records?

Before the establishment of the German Empire (sometimes called the Second Empire) in 1871, the term "Germany" referred to many independent states (called in turn kingdoms, grand duchies, duchies, principalities, provinces, or free cities). Each state was free to collect records about its citizenry by whatever schedule or manner desired. Fortunately, as will be discussed below, the compilation of census data following the Napoleonic Wars was not totally arbitrary. Important trends in census methods and content have been identified and can be presented as answers to all of the above questions.

However, despite the fact that a united Germany existed from 1871 until 1918 (the end of the First World War), the traditional (and in some cases intensely individual) identity of each of the Empire's thirty-eight states is reflected in the censuses conducted there. In general, the nature of German census records is vastly different from records compiled in the United States under the same title.

Notes

[1] The Family History Library in Salt Lake City, Utah has probably the largest collection of state census records. Its catalog is available for study at *www.familysearch.org*.

[2] Eike Pies interview with Roger P. Minert on August 12, 2015 in Wuppertal, Germany.

[3] Civil records (government vital records) were instituted in the areas under French military occupation from 1798 to 1815. Prussia introduced civil registration on October 1, 1874 and the same system was mandated for all of the German Empire beginning on January 1, 1876.

[4] Rolf Gehrmann, "German Census-Taking Before 1871." (Rostock, Germany: Max-Planck-Institut für demografische Forschung, 2009), 4.

1 A History of Census Records in the German States

The Census in German History from the Napoleonic Wars (1815) to German Unification (1871)

The wars waged by and against French Emperor Napoleon Bonaparte from 1798 to 1815 involved the invasion and conquest of many German states. All of them independent and far smaller than France, those states were totally incapable of fending off the invader who subdued even the kingdom of Preußen at the eastern borders of the German-language territory. Napoleon exerted not only military but also political influence over the occupied territories, founding the kingdoms of Württemberg, Hannover, and Westfalen. On the other hand, he put an end to the Holy Roman Empire of German Nations, which action led to the self-demotion of its emperor Franz II (an Austrian Hapsburg) to Franz I of Austria and also to the de facto separation of Austria from Germany.

With the defeat of Napoleon and the ejection of French governors from German territories, the liberated states sent representatives to Vienna, Austria for what became known as the Congress of Vienna. That conclave in 1815 resulted in the re-drawing of many borders across the German-language territory of central Europe. Excluding Luxembourg, Switzerland, and Austria, there were forty German states in 1816. That number eventually increased to forty-two, then decreased to thirty-eight over the next fifty-five years.[1] With most other territories in Europe already existing in the form of kingdoms or empires, several German states longed for a union that would allow protection against invaders, as well as make them an economic force to be reckoned with. This pan-Germanic thinking led to the formation of several inter-state organizations.

The first census enumerations in German states were conducted in 1816 simply to allow the ruler to know precisely the size of his state. Indeed, some states, counties, and even cities had conducted census campaigns as early as the seventeenth century (often under titles other than "census"). Rolf Gehrmann provided this reason for those early censuses:

> The growing interest of the early modern state, and especially of enlightened absolutist rulers in demographic measure as measure of the wealth of the state, led to a total count of the population. ... these counts were considered part of the yearly balance sheet of the state... The principle of yearly counting was maintained for some time after 1815.[2]

In several German states, counts were done in 1816 and repeated annually via a rather simple method: using the numbers from the previous year, officials determined how many persons had been born or had died by the end of the current calendar year and the numbers were adjusted accordingly. The data regarding births and deaths were taken from the records of the local churches. In only very rare instances were the names of residents recorded in those early enumerations.[3]

The first union of German states was the Germanic Confederation established at the conclusion of the Congress of Vienna. Henderson's description of the Confederation is illuminating:

> The Confederation was a *Staatenbund* and not a *Bundesstaat*—that is to say, it was a union of sovereign States in which unanimity was essential before joint action could be taken and it was a not a federation of States in which the members gave up some of their sovereign rights to the central power."[4]

The Confederation featured a parliament, but it was not a true legislative body and the men convening in Frankfurt am Main were more like ambassadors than representatives wielding the power of the vote. There was initially no discussion of unification, because such a development would have necessitated concessions by some if not all of the rulers (mostly monarchs) whose states belonged to the Confederation.

The initial challenge encountered by the German states in the early days of the Confederation was one that the body had no power to address: customs. Merchants transporting goods on intra- and interstate routes were plagued by a myriad of rules, regulations, and fees that made life miserable for merchants and consumers alike. Some products crossed borders as many as ten times and the final prices to consumers rose to prohibitive levels. Of course, conditions were ideal for smugglers and states incurred high costs in policing their borders. The various solutions to the customs question eventually gave rise to the compilation of census records in Germany in the third decade of the nineteenth century.

The first attempt at coordinating customs regulations and revenues came from the largest member

of the Confederation—the kingdom of Preußen. However, Prussian action in this regard was perceived to be political as well as economic. According to Hahn,

> …the process of unification in matters of customs was more than economic from the very beginning. Although the states involved in the establishment of customs unions were generally pursuing particularistic more than nationalistic aims, the customs unions dealt with the great political questions of the time—especially the matter of national unity and constitutional rights.[5]

The eastern provinces of Preußen enacted a customs union in 1818 and the kingdom's western provinces did likewise a year later. The two regions united in this effort in 1821, but no other states were interested in joining the movement under Prussian leadership—with the exception of the tiny Sachsen duchy of Schwarzburg-Sondershausen that found itself surrounded to seventy percent by Preußen; she joined in 1819 as a matter of self-preservation. The next

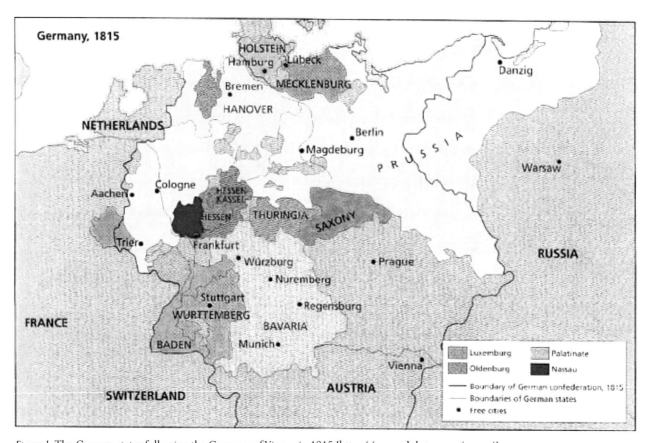

Figure 1. The German states following the Congress of Vienna in 1815 [http://www.dukatz.com/maps/]

state to align itself with the Preußen customs union was the county of Anhalt-Bernburg in 1826.

The grand duchy of Hesse (with the capital city of Darmstadt) was the first state to see benefits in joining the Prussian customs union and entered into negotiations in the late 1820s. In response to this development, two other states formed their own union in January 1828: Bayern and Württemberg; they shared many miles of borders and their treaty took effect on July 1, 1828.[6] The Prusso-Hessian treaty was concluded just three weeks later and the era of competing German customs unions had begun.

It was precisely this movement that can be given credit for the expansion of German census records. On a strictly local level, census enumerations had taken place in several German-language territories of Europe well before 1800, but the records were compiled at various times, for different reasons, under numerous titles, and by different methods. Countless towns, cities, counties, districts, and states recorded the names of some or all residents under titles such as *Volkszählung* [census], *Bürgerbuch* [registry of citizens]; *Haushaltungslisten* [lists of heads of household], *Hauslisten* [lists of residents], *Einwohnerregister* [lists of residents], *Bevölkerungslisten* [lists of residents], *Untertanenverzeichnisse* [lists of subjects], *Wählerlisten* [lists of voters], *Konskriptionslisten* [military registry], *Seelenregister* [lists of parish members], and several others. Population figures and statistics are available in some form or another for several German states before 1815.[7]

In order for the officials of any customs union to distribute proportionately among the member states the fees collected at border stations, a census had to be conducted at regular intervals to establish the precise number of residents in each state. Thus the first systematic census enumerations in most German states were instituted to fulfill the requirements of a customs union. Only then could a coherent picture of German census records emerge—generally and specifically. Gehrmann concluded that the basis for the first German census enumerations of the nineteenth century was not demographic but economic.[8] As evidence of this assertion, throughout the twentieth century, census compilations often included the numbers of dwellings, livestock, and even fruit trees.

Figure 2. This 1720 census listed all heads of households with counts of residents by gender. [Stadtarchiv Heide, Schleswig-Holstein]

Many of the central and northern German states formed their own customs union in December 1828. However, Henderson suggests that they did so more in an effort to check the expansion of the two existing unions than to actually regulate interstate commerce.[9] The states included in the *Mitteldeutscher Handelsverein* [Central German Commercial Union] were Hannover, Sachsen (kingdom), Hessen-Kassel, Nassau, Brunswick, Oldenburg, Frankfurt am Main, Bremen, and seven of the eight Saxon duchies (often referred to as Thüringen [Thuringia]). Those states agreed to not join any other union before 1834, but some of the smaller states in that organization began to defect as early as 1832.[10]

Thus by the 1830s, many of the states in the German Confederation were not only collecting census data annually for local purposes, but also reporting the statistics to their respective unions every second or third year. Those census records were kept solely for the purpose of the distribution of customs revenues and had nothing to do with such issues as parliamentary representation, military conscription, or taxation.[11] Due to the fact that some states employed different procedures, Michel concluded that such census records enjoyed only varying degrees of reliability.[12]

The Expansion of Customs Unions—and Census Records

Despite the fear on the part of some smaller German states that any expanding customs union that included Preußen would lead to greater political power on the part of the largest state in the German lands, many more states joined the movement.[13] This resulted in the establishment on January 1, 1834 of a customs union called by one word without modifiers: the *Zollverein* [Customs Union]. The treaty establishing the *Zollverein* had been signed in 1833 and mandated that the agreement be extended after eight years.[14] The *Zollverein* combined the two existing unions (Preußen/Hessen-Darmstadt and Bayern/Württemberg) with the kingdom of Sachsen, Kurhessen, and fifteen other small states, yielding a population of some 23.5 million.[15] The member states were to enjoy the status of equal partners.

The foundational document stating the aims of the *Zollverein* and the regulations for census enumerations among the member states was published in 1834 and again in 1845.[16] The opening paragraph justifies a census:

> The member states have agreed that in order to ensure that the customs revenues collected by the member states (after the deduction of expenses, rebates, and discounts) are properly distributed, the population of each state is to be determined every three years. The procedure of the census should be identical in all states so that the distribution of revenues can be done equitably. The census is to be taken in December of every third year in every state.[17]

The original document mandated that a census be conducted every third year on December 1.[18] (The 1845 revised version moved the target date to December 3.) Cities with more than 30,000 inhabitants would be allowed as much as three days to complete the process. If the date fell on a Sunday or a holiday, the next working day would be the target date. Other provisions stipulated that "every individual" be counted; exceptions were carefully defined. Many foreigners qualified as local residents and were to be included.

According to Hahn, the *Zollverein* "was not the product of one great foundational document, but rather a complex network of intertwined bilateral and multilateral treaties emerging from 1819 to 1833 with one common goal: a customs and commerce system with no internal fees and uniform external fees."[19] Nevertheless, several other German states refused to ally themselves with the *Zollverein* for a variety of reasons—the primary reason being a perceived net loss in revenue. Just four months after the founding of the *Zollverein*, Hannover and Braunschweig formed their own competing entity and called it the *Steuerverein* [Tax Union]. It began its function the next year and a census mandated on May 1, 1834 was to provide the population baseline.[20] The *Steuerverein* was soon expanded to include the northern states of Oldenburg (1836) and Schaumburg-Lippe (1838). During the 1830s, the other member states of the short-lived *Mitteldeutscher Handelsverein* joined the *Zollverein*. Most of the German states had taken sides by the end of that decade.

By 1840, only a few states were still resisting membership in either the *Zollverein* or the *Steuerverein*—principally Baden, Mecklenburg-Schwerin, Mecklenburg-Strelitz, Schleswig-Holstein, and the free historic Hanseatic port cities. However, the concept of a customs union proved to be advantageous and one by one most of the hold-outs acquiesced. During those years, the balance of economic

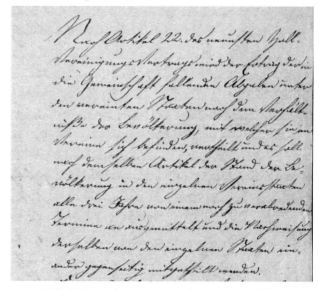

Figure 3. The Württemberg Ministry of Finance issued this statement in early 1834: "Member states of the Zollverein must conduct a census every three years." [Hauptstaatsarchiv Stuttgart E146 33380]

power was shifting toward Preußen. Several members of the *Steuerverein* bolted to the *Zollverein* and by 1854 the former ceased to exist.[21]

The *Zollverein* treaty was extended in 1841, 1853, and 1865 and census records supporting the provisions of the treaty were compiled every three years in all member states beginning in 1834. Schleswig-Holstein joined the group in 1866 and by then all but the cities of Hamburg and Bremen and the two Mecklenburg duchies were on board. In 1867, the union's conference that was opened by King Wilhelm I of Preußen produced a new treaty. The handwriting on the wall was visible to most Germans: the *Zollverein* could soon be replaced by a Germany founded primarily on political principals and only secondarily for commercial purposes.

Although the distribution of customs revenues was accomplished based on recent population figures, census lists were introduced in 1840 because prior data had been primarily statistical and somewhat doubtful (having often been taken from police or tax registers). However, states were still free to collect even more information than required by either of the surviving customs unions.[22]

The innovation of 1840 was crucial, resulting in the appearance of individuals' names on lists compiled throughout much of Germany. The individuals listed were usually the home owners or heads of households, the remaining inhabitants being represented simply by numbers of persons in gender and age categories.

The *Zollverein* did not mandate enumeration procedures until 1843 with this regulation: "A true counting of each person living in each house is to take place…" Enumerators were no longer allowed to simply use previously-collected listings of residents compiled for other purposes, such as residential registration or church *Seelenregister*.[23] The month of December was chosen by the member states as the best time for the collection of census data, believing that most people would be home in that season.

Gehrmann stated that listings of inhabitants by name were rare in the early census years and concluded that "…1846 must be established as the year of reference, and not 1834…"[24] However, many of the records identified in the current study were produced in census enumerations before 1846 and do indeed show individual names of adults and even children (see examples below). By 1858, the *Zollverein* (then representing nearly all of the German states) mandated the use of comprehensive lists and this new standard would be maintained henceforth.

Precisely how much revenue was collected each year at border customs stations in those days is not a critical consideration in this discussion, but what was paid out is found in documents collected in the current investigation. For example, instructions circulated to towns within the grand duchy of Saxe-Weimar-Eisenach in 1858 and 1861 directed officials to remind heads of households that the *Zollverein* would allot 2 *Thaler* for each person correctly documented.[25] It can be assumed that there was not a state in Germany that could afford to undercount its population.

By 1864, the regulations stipulated that the names of all persons in all states be recorded on forms designed for that content.[26] That requirement was meant to provide for the counting of each person and simultaneously to prevent the counting of any person more than once. It is interesting to note that many German states had already introduced that content in their census records.[27]

Michel elucidated the evolution of German census records in two eras—the first being 1816 to 1867. The lack of uniformity in census methodology described above makes his scheme appear logical. Another study traced the development through three phases over the same fifty-one years—the initial one being from 1816 to 1834.[28] That last year was chosen due to the founding of the *Zollverein*. Their second phase lasted from 1834 to 1852 when the *Steuerverein* broke down and the *Zollverein* emerged as the great customs power. The third phase lasted from 1852 to 1867 when the first all-German census was enumerated. Both studies portrayed the introduction of the every-name lists in 1840 (in Preußen) and 1843 (in the entire *Zollverein*) as a critical innovation in the content of census records.

Figure 4. Most of the northern German states were hesitant to join the *Zollverein.* [http://www.paedagogik.net/wochenthemen/bismarck/zollverein.html]

Census Records by State from 1816 to 1864

Documents exhibited in this book adequately illustrate the conclusion that German states were free to mandate and carry out census campaigns whenever needed until or unless they joined one of the customs unions mentioned above. Even if they belonged to an organization such as the *Zollverein*, they were free to collect more than the required data and to design their own enumeration pages. Kraus summarized this condition: "The methods used to collect the population data varied constantly, not only from year to year within a state, but also from state to state."[29] A review of the table showing the extensive variation of contents of census enumerations in the duchy of Sachsen-Altenburg, e.g., supports that statement (see Chapter 28). At the opposite end of the spectrum is the principality of Schaumburg-Lippe: identical content items were used there for five consecutive census campaigns from 1839 through 1852, then a new set of items was recorded identically in four more enumerations from 1855 through 1864 (see Chapter 34). For details on each of the thirty-eight states of the German Empire, see Chapters 5–42.

The Regional Character of German Census Records

The census data compiled in accordance with the statutes of the various German customs unions from 1818 to 1864 represent the third most important source of genealogical data for all Germans (following church records and civil records).[30] During that time period, each census was mandated and enumerated by the province, reflecting the tradition of particularism—the primacy of the state over the nation. Even as late as 1916, instructions for the conduct of the census were issued by government entities in the capital cities of several states—not in the imperial offices in Berlin. For example, users of census records will note that the 1890 census was carried out by officials of the duchy of Anhalt for its citizens. The data belonged to the duchy and were simply shared with the empire. The content of the Anhalt census pages conformed to the requirements of the empire, but the format and layout of those pages was determined locally. In many respects, the census records of the thirty-eight states of the German Empire (1871-1918) are similar, but each retains its local flavor.

When comparing the data among the states, one must consider the different instructions given the enumerators before 1867, even when based on the regulations of the *Zollverein*. Those regulations allowed the member states a great deal of autonomy in determining their respective methodologies for the collection of data that were not well delineated by the *Zollverein*.

Gehrmann was correct regarding the census history he hoped would appear some day: "...a comprehensive history can only be written with the help of archival sources."[31] He also stated that "only the primary resources" can resolve questions regarding census methodology in Germany before 1867.[32] The details presented in this book were compiled through an examination of the holdings of hundreds of provincial, regional, county, and city archives in modern Germany, France, and Poland. It would be close to impossible to fill all of the gaps in the tables presented in the following chapters, but determined researchers will likely make the attempt to do so.

Researchers in the United States and several other nations where every-name census records were compiled in the nineteenth century may wonder whether it is reasonable to expect to find such records in Germany. Gehrmann wrote, "every census of this order before 1840 must be considered exceptional. Such exceptions exist, but they are rare."[33] With the help of archivists in Germany, many such rare documents have been found and are shown in the provincial chapters. It is safe to assume that other similar documents can be found in the thousands of government archives in Germany as well as in other countries where former German territory is located—such as France and Poland.

Figure 5. As late as 1910, the grand duchy of Baden executed the national census under its own title. The forms used made no mention of the imperial government or the Statistical Office in Berlin to which the results were submitted. [Stadtarchiv Konstanz S II 12676]

Notes

[1] For example, the states of Hesse-Kassel, Nassau, and the free city of Frankfurt am Main merged to form the Prussian province of Hessen-Nassau in 1866. Henderson provides excellent detail regarding such changes in *The Zollverein,* 3.

[2] Gehrmann, Rolf. "German Census-Taking Before 1871." (Rostock, Germany: Max-Planck-Institut für demografische Forschung, 2009), 6.

[3] When more formal census campaigns were mandated, the practice of simply adjusting the numbers of the previous calendar year using birth and death data was done separately as a mathematical tradition.

[4] W. O. Henderson, *The Zollverein* (London: Frank Cass, 1959), 10.

[5] Hans-Werner Hahn, *Geschichte des Deutschen Zollvereins* (Göttingen: Vandenhoeck und Ruprecht, 1984), 5. All translations from German by Roger P. Minert.

[6] Henderson, *The Zollverein,* 41.

[7] For statistical census years for all German states since 1816, see Antje Kraus, *Quellen zur Bevölkerungsstatistik Deutschlands 1815–1871* (Boppard am Rhein, Germany: Harald Boldt, 1980).

[8] Gehrmann, "German Census-Taking," 6.

[9] Henderson, *The Zollverein,* 57–61.

[10] Henderson, *The Zollverein,* 68–69, 83.

[11] There were no representative assemblies constituted by population within the German Confederation.

[12] Harald Michel, "Volkszählungen in Deutschland: Die Erfassung des Bevölkerungsstandes von 1816 bis 1933," in *Jahrbuch für Wirtschaftsgeschichte* 1985/II, (Berlin: DeGruyter), 80.

[13] Most German monarchs of the era were ready and willing to exclude Austria from the pan-German political movement. The total resolution of the Austrian question did not come until the short but decisive 1866 war in which the Prussian army easily routed the Austrians in Bohemia (Königgrätz).

[14] Hahn, *Geschichte des Deutschen Zollvereins,* 102.

[15] Hahn, *Geschichte des Deutschen Zollvereins,* 76.

[16] Centralbüreau des Zollvereins, "Grundsätze über die Bevölkerungs-Aufnahme in den Zollvereinsstaaten nach den Vereinbarungen vom 31. Januar 1834 und vom 23.

Oktober 1845," 1 (Berlin: Centralbüreau des *Zollvereins*, 1845).

17 Centralbüreau des *Zollvereins*, "Grundsätze über die Bevölkerungs-Aufnahme in den Zollvereinsstaaten," 1.

18 A copy of the original document issued in 1837 indicated that the date of the campaign was chosen because it was likely that the greatest portion of the population would be at home rather than during some other season of the year.

19 Hahn, *Geschichte des Deutschen Zollvereins*, 79.

20 On March 12, 1836, the kingdom of Hannover issued a proclamation regarding the new census required by the *Steuerverein* (*Gesetz-Sammlung für das Königreich Hannover, Jahrgang 1836*). The text of the *Zollverein* regulations can be found under the title "Hauptprotokoll der Vollzugskommission in München vom 14.02.1834, Artikel 22."

21 Henderson, *The Zollverein*, 214–215.

22 Gehrmann, "German Census-Taking," 12.

23 Kraus, *Quellen*, 16.

24 Gehrmann, "German Census-Taking," 16.

25 The author of the instructions was a Mr. Haberfeld, grand-ducal director of the second administrative district. The document bears the date October 28, 1861.

26 Kraus, *Quellen*, 16.

27 Gehrmann, "German Census-Taking," 14.

28 Statistisches Bureau Berlin, "Die Volkszahl der Deutschen Staaten nach den Zählungen seit 1816," in *Monatshefte zur Statistik des Deutschen Reichs für das Jahr 1879* [2], *Die Statistik des Deutschen Reichs*, Vol. 37/2; urn:nbn:de:zbw-drsa_3721 (Berlin: Verlag des Königlich Preussischen Statistischen Bureaus, 1879).

29 Kraus, *Quellen*, 3.

30 Genealogies of royal and noble families trace descendants back with reliability to the 12th century in some cases, but those families represent less than one percent of the Germanic population.

31 Gehrmann, "German Census-Taking," 4.

32 Gehrmann, "German Census-Taking," 4.

33 Gehrmann, "German Census-Taking," 15.

2 The Census of 1867: The Great Transition

The census of 1867 was for all practical purposes the first national census. Almost all of the German states belonged to either the *Zollverein* or the North German Confederation or both and were thus required to participate. Each organization had been established primarily for economic purposes and required a periodic census of its members, but the methods and content were still not entirely uniform between the two organizations: the *Zollverein* counted only the local residents while the Confederation counted any person present in a given locality during the night before the target date as well as residents who were absent that night.

Among the thousands of documents collected during the compilation of this book, only one was found that emanated from the office of the "Chancellor of the North German Confederation" in Berlin.[1] Otto von Bismarck represented the *Bundesrat* [representative council] of that organization when he issued a decree on October 9, 1867, that a census be performed among the member states on December 3 of that year. The decree indicated that the census was important for two primary reasons: the funding of a common military force and the sharing of costs supporting the Confederation. The distribution of customs duties was thus no longer the prime motivation for a census campaign.

Bismarck's text reads,

> ...considering the fact that the *Zollverein* has scheduled its next census for the end of this year anyway, and that all of its member states are to participate, the Royal Government of Preußen has prepared forms and instructions for a census and presented them to the *Bundesrat* with the recommendation that they be used throughout the Confederation.[2]

That same Bismarck was Prussian prime minister. Whether he was attempting to extend his sphere of influence beyond Preußen or was genuinely offering to save other German states the effort needed to produce the census literature cannot be determined here. Whatever his intention may have been, he stressed the requirement that a line be devoted to each and every individual to include first and last names, gender, age, occupation or status, and citizenship. At the same time, locals away from home for certain purposes were specifically to be excluded from the count.

Gehrmann emphasized the national nature of the campaign that year: "The 1867 census has to be considered the first in the history of the Reich. Not only did all states participate, but the population counted was also ... the effective (*faktische* or *ortsanwesende*) population."[3] Michel stated that the 1867 enumeration represented the "development of the modern German census" and set the standard for subsequent census enumerations.[4]

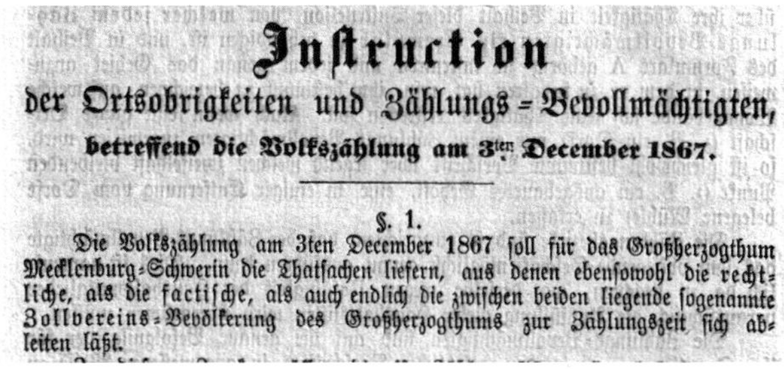
Instruction

der Ortsobrigkeiten und Zählungs-Bevollmächtigten,

betreffend die Volkszählung am 3ten December 1867.

§. 1.

Die Volkszählung am 3ten December 1867 soll für das Großherzogthum Mecklenburg-Schwerin die Thatsachen liefern, aus denen ebensowohl die rechtliche, als die factische, als auch endlich die zwischen beiden liegende sogenannte Zollvereins-Bevölkerung des Großherzogthums zur Zählungszeit sich ableiten läßt.

Figure 1. The 1867 instructions issued by the government of Mecklenburg-Schwerin indicated that the first purpose of the census was to satisfy local statistical needs, the second to conform with *Zollverein* standards. [Stadtarchiv Wismar 4063]

The prime vehicle of the 1867 census was the *Haushaltungsliste* [household list] that was to be filled out by each head of household. Officials responsible for specific households in well-defined *Zählbezirken* [enumeration districts consisting of perhaps fifty households] distributed the sheets beginning November 30 and collected them on December 3 or (at the latest) the next day.[5] Specific details were required for each person, and foreigners were asked about their citizenship status. Gehrmann wrote that the population count that year was more reliable (not the number of consumers but the number of residents); the population total actually decreased, but by less than one percent of the expected totals (based on the 1864 enumeration).[6]

From the instructions given to town officials and individual enumerators, it is clear that all of the German states were veterans of previous census campaigns. The self-identity of each state is reflected in the fact that the census instructions were issued not by the *Zollverein* or the Confederation, but by the government of the state (usually the respective ministry of the interior). The instructions issued by most states indicated that the census was conducted in accordance with the statutes of one of those interstate unions. The Prussian version of the instructions listed that reason as the second of two, the primary justification being

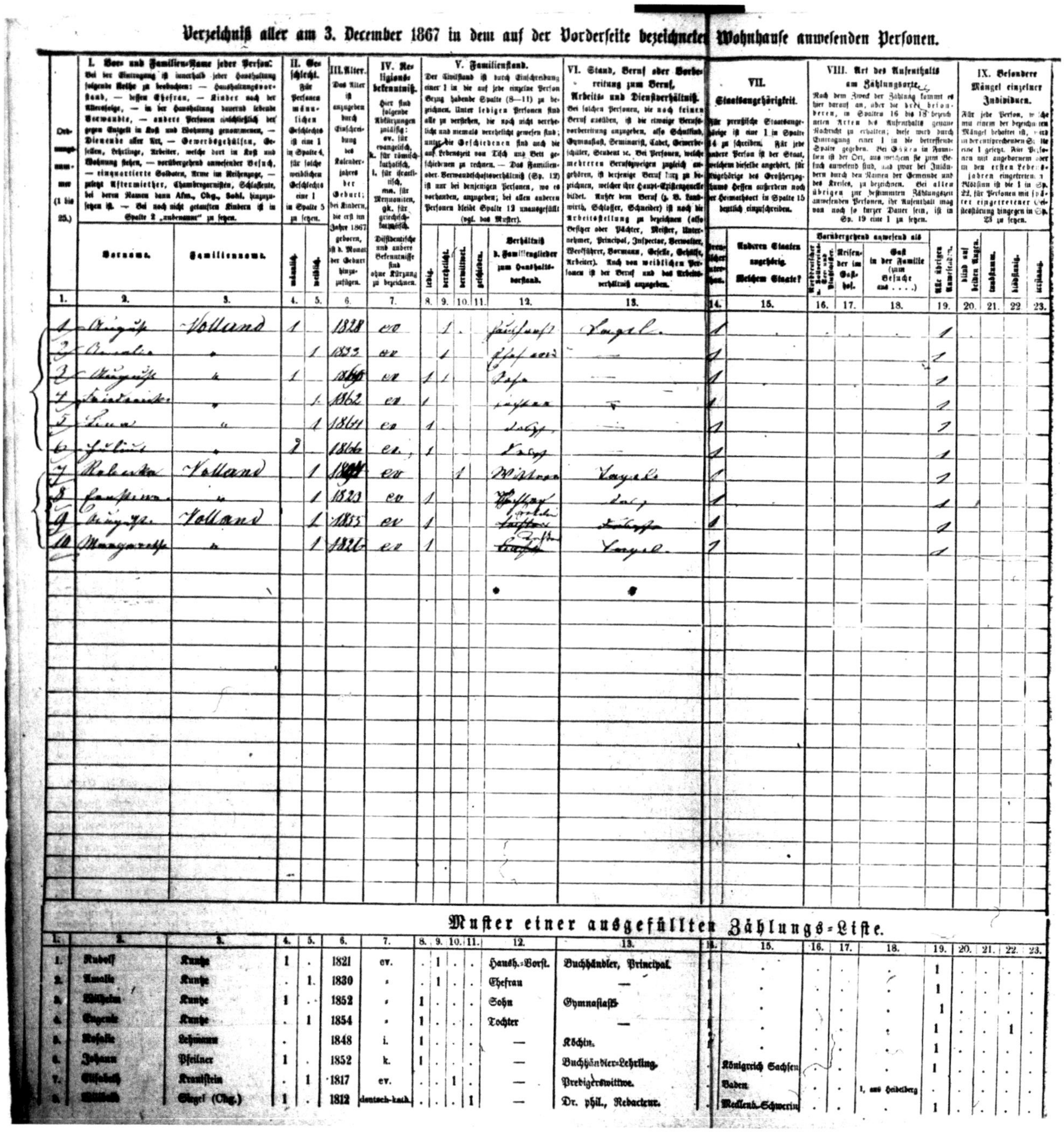

Figure 2. The Prussian version of the 1867 census (used in all thirteen Prussian provinces) had verbose instructions on both sides of the paper as well as a sample family at the bottom. This is the inside view (pages 2 and 3); the paper was folded between columns 13 and 14. [Gebesee, Sachsen-Provinz; Kreisarchiv Erfurt]

to provide important statistical information for the Prussian government in Berlin.

As stated in the instructions for the 1867 census, officials were to count the persons from the name lists, to enter the numbers onto statistical reports for enumerations districts, to transfer those totals to community statistical reports, and from there to county and provincial statistical reports. Officials at each level were instructed to monitor lists for completeness and correctness.

However the texts of the instructions to local officials and enumerators were worded, the current investigation determined that individual household pages were printed identically in many of the states.[7] Others had almost identical content but differed in appearance.

The instructions for the Prussian version of the 1867 census (by column) are more extensive than used in any German state prior to that year. Primary headings are designated by Roman numerals and secondary headings by Arabic numerals as follows:

I. First and last name of each person; persons in each household should be entered in this order: head of household, his wife, children in order of age; other relatives who are permanent residents in this household; other persons including those under hire with room and board; servants of all kinds; occupational helpers such as apprentices and journeymen with room and board; temporary visitors; quartered soldiers of the army; finally any sub-lessees [*Aftermiether*] and other persons who merely sleep there [*Chambergarnisten, Schlafleute*] should be designated as *Afm, Chg, Schl*; the term "unknown" is to be entered in column 2 for children not yet baptized.

II. Gender: for male persons enter a 1 in column 4, for female persons enter a 1 in column 5.

III. Age: enter the calendar year of the person's birth; if the child was born in 1867, enter the month of birth.

IV. Religion: the following abbreviations may be used in this column: *ev.* for Protestant, *k.* for Roman Catholic; *i.* for Jewish (Israelite); *mn.* for Mennonites; *gk.* for Greek Orthodox; dissidents and other church names are to be written out.

V. Marital status: this status is shown by writing a 1 in the appropriate column (8–11) for each person; single persons are those who are not currently married and have never been married; persons living in separation for life are to be counted as divorced; the designation of the relation of each person to the head of household is only to be recorded where such a relationship exists; for all other persons an entry is to be made in column 12 (see sample list).

VI. Occupation: status, occupation, or occupation in training, employment, and servitude. For persons without current employment, the status of their training is to be indicated, such as pupil, prep-student, cadet, trainee, or university student. For persons to whom more than one kind of status applies, the principal activity should be indicated; along with the occupation (such as farmer, mechanic, or tailor), the employment is to be shown (such as owner, lessee, master, entrepreneur, principal, inspector, administrator, superintendent, foreman, journeyman, apprentice, laborer); the same kind of information is to be shown for females.

VII. Citizenship: Enter a 1 in column 14 for Prussian citizens. For other persons, the state of which they are citizens is to be listed. For persons from the grand duchy of Hessen, the town is also to be listed in column 15.

VIII. Manner of residence: it is the purpose of this census to determine the manner of residence for each person as indicated in columns 16 through 18. Enter a 1 in the appropriate column. The town of residence should be shown for each guest (for persons from this state, enter both the town and the county. For all other persons (regardless of the brevity of their stay), enter a 1 in column 19.

IX. Special deficiencies: Enter a 1 in the appropriate column for any person dealing with that condition. For any person born with insanity or who became insane in the first few years of life, enter a 1 in column 22. Enter a 1 in column 23 for any person who became insane later in life.

Secondary column headings were as follows:

1. consecutive number of inhabitant
2. given name
3. surname
4. masculine
5. feminine
6. age
7. religion
8. single
9. married
10. widowed
11. divorced
12. relationship of household members to the head of household
14. citizens of Prussia
15. citizens of other states (which states?)
16. maritime persons working for the North German Confederation or the *Zollverein*
17. travelers in inns [hotels, etc.]
18. guests in the household (coming from where?)
19. all other persons present in the household
20. blind in both eyes
21. deaf-mute
22. idiot
23. insane

The Hessen version of the 1867 census features much shorter column headings. The most significant difference is the inclusion of the birth place in column 6 (a feature that is most valuable to family history researchers). Shown below is a page recorded in the town of Rödgen near Gießen. The exterior of the sheet (pages 1 and 4 effectively) has lengthy instructions, while the interior pages (2 and 3) feature personal data for every individual to be recorded in columns 1–10 and 11–23 respectively.

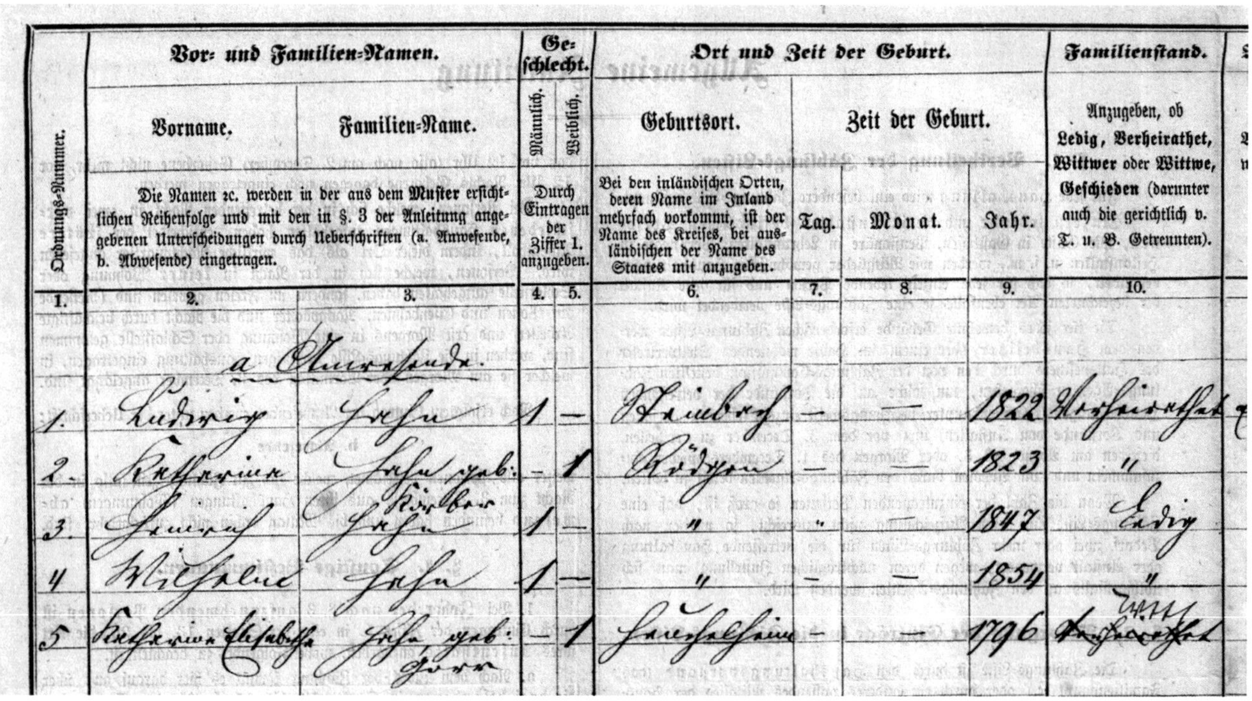

Figure 3. The left-hand page of the Hessen version of the 1867 census [Rödgen, Hessen; Stadtarchiv Gießen, 4 RÖ 103]

Religion.	Stand oder Beruf.	Art des Aufenthalts.								Ansässigkeitsort.	Staatsangehörigkeit (Heimathsort).	Anmerkungen.
Bei Christen wird auch die Confession angegeben.	Hauptbeschäftigung (voran, sodann) mit Erwerb verbundene Nebenbeschäftigungen, Arbeits- und Dienstverhältniß, auch Verwandtschaftsverhältniß zum Haushaltungsvorstand.	Durch Eintragen der Ziffer 1. anzugeben (vergl. Anleitg. §. 4, Ziff. 1., sowie auch §. 2, Abs. 2.)								Als Ansässigkeitsort ist bei Personen, welche sich selbstständig ernähren und eine eigene Haushaltung führen, der Ort ihrer dauernden Niederlassung zum Betriebe ihres Geschäfts &c., bei unselbstständigen Personen der Ort, woselbst ihre Familie ansässig ist oder doch zuletzt ansässig war, anzusehen.	Für jede Person ist der Staat, welchem dieselbe angehört, für Angehörige des Großherzogthums Hessen der Heimathsort (bei mehrfach vorkommenden Ortsnamen unter Angabe des Kreises) deutlich einzuschreiben.	Vergl. Anleitung §. 4, Ziffer 1. a., 1. b. und 2., sowie das Muster.
		Vorübergehend anwesend als			Die übrigen Anwesenden	Nicht über 1 Jahr Abwesende			Alle übrigen Abwesenden			
		Norddeutscher u. Bahreiner-Seeund Flußschiffer.	Reisender im Gasthof.	Gast in der Familie.		als See- oder Flußschiffer.	auf Land- oder Seereisen.	auf Besuch außerhalb des Orts.				
11.	12.	13.	14.	15.	16.	17.	18.	19.	20.	21.	22.	23.
franzöfisch	Bezirksbrennerhof u. Landwirth	—	—	—	1	—	—	—	—	Rödgen	Rödgen	
"	Ehefrau				1	—	—	—	—	"	"	
"	Sohn				1	—	—	—	—	"	"	
"	"				1	—	—	—	—	"	"	
"	Mutter	—	—	—	1	—	—	—	—	"	"	

Figure 4. The right-hand page of the Hessen version of the 1867 census [Rödgen, Hessen; Stadtarchiv Gießen, 4 RÖ 103]

The Bavarian version of the 1867 census differed vastly from the forms used in other states. For example, the age was stated generally in columns 5–8 in two categories of each gender: "under 14 years" or "over 14 years." A wide variety of religious classifications appeared: "Catholic, Protestant, Reformed, Greek Orthodox, Mennonite, Anabaptist, Irwingian, German Catholic, Friend of Light, Jewish, or other non-Christians."

In general it can be stated that any researcher studying ancestors or other persons of interest in Germany would do well to search for them in the 1867 census. However, if the location is not known to at least the county level, this search is not practicable.[8]

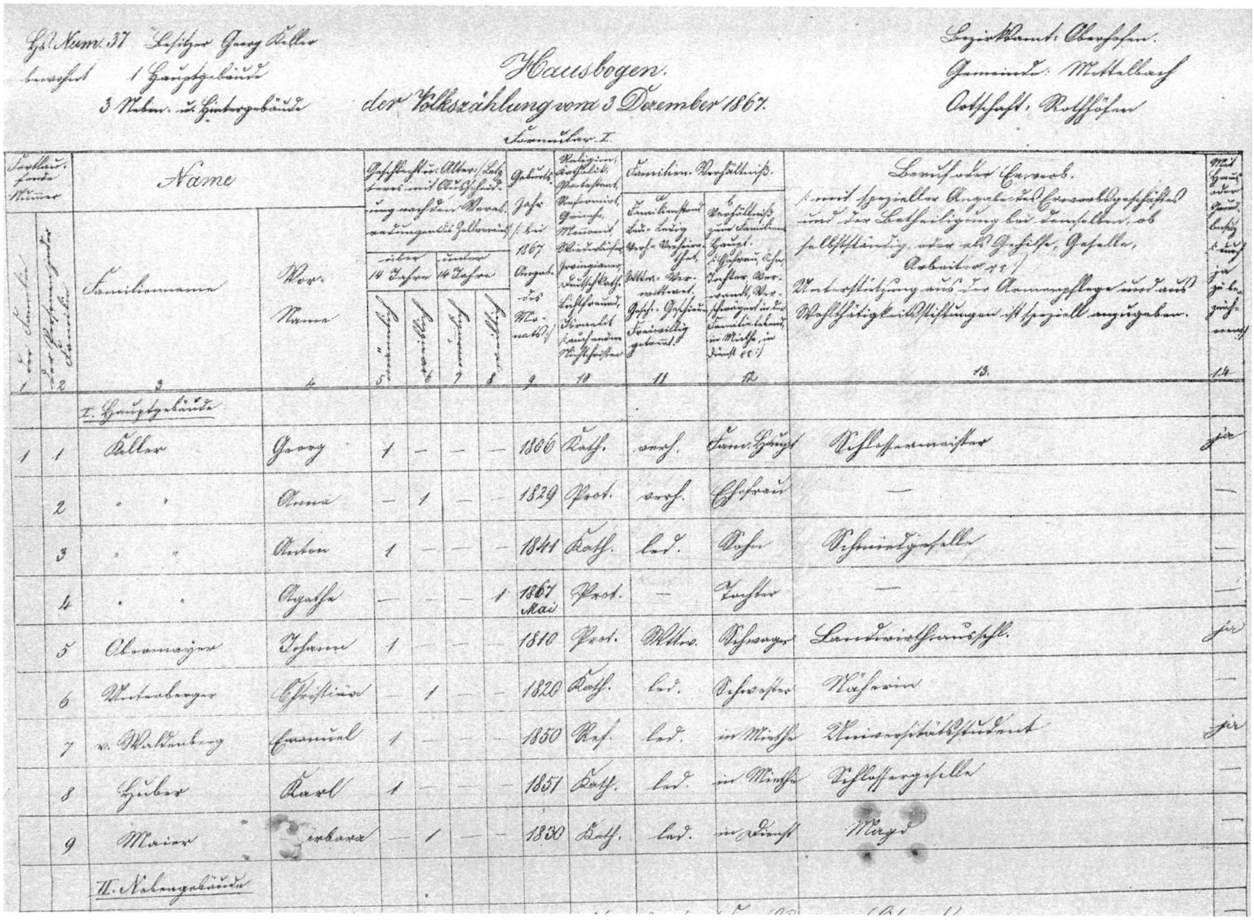
Hausbogen der Volkszählung vom 3 Dezember 1867.

Name

Figure 5. This census form used hand-written column headings that were lithographed. [Mindelheim, Bayern, https://familysearch.org/search/image/index#uri=https%3A%2F%2Ffamilysearch.org%2Frecapi%2Fsord%2Fwaypoint%2FMCDY-BWL%3A242635301%3Fcc%3D1941345]

Notes

1. Otto von Bismarck, Proclamation October 9, 1867 from the Bundesrat of the North German Confederation (Niedersächsisches Landesarchiv Bückeburg Dep 9C Nr 637).

2. Otto von Bismarck, "Proclamation." Nordeutscher Bund. October 9, 1867.

3. A person had to be physically present to be counted. Gehrmann, Rolf. "German Census-Taking Before 1871." (Rostock, Germany: Max-Planck-Institut für demografische Forschung, 2009), 15.

4. Michel, "Volkszählungen," 84.

5. In all census instructions beginning in 1867, local officials were told that if December 3 fell on a Sunday or a holiday, the campaign was to begin the next day. However, the data collected were to reflect the population status as of December 3.

6. Gehrmann, "German Census-Taking," 15.

7. Even the dates of the announcements of the upcoming census campaigns differed from state to state—as if each state were deciding independently whether to participate. For example, the grand ducal office in Baden issued the announcement on September 19, the royal Prussian office on October 12, the interior ministry of Sachsen-Weimar-Eisenach on October 23, the interior ministry of Sachsen-Meiningen on October 25, and the Royal Bavarian office not until November 21.

8. Fortunately, Gehrmann was quite incorrect in assuming that the original family pages of the 1867 census were all destroyed. He concluded, "... it is impossible to find original census lists after 1864—only in exceptional cases were copies or compilations from the individual forms made for local purposes." As will be shown below, literally thousands of those pages survive. See Gehrmann 16.

3 Census Records during the German Empire 1871–1918

The German Empire that came to life in the Palace of Versailles near Paris on January 18, 1871 meant the end of the *Zollverein* and the North German Confederation, but the tradition of census enumerations continued. The Franco-Prussian War of 1870–71 had interfered with the census that was scheduled for December 3, 1870, but the process was continued exactly one year later. Beginning in 1875, a national census was conducted in December in five-year intervals. The First World War caused another interruption in the schedule, but a census was enumerated in 1916. With the collapse of the German Empire in November 1918, the history of German census records entered a new and unpredictable phase.

The basic premise of the imperial census was the establishment and maintenance of common standards, instructions, documents, and procedures in all of the thirty-eight states. The process of producing such a census would require several attempts and in many ways mirrors the slow evolution that took place among the states in the five decades before 1871.

The census campaigns conducted under the German empire had very similar processes. Enumeration districts composed of no more than fifty households were to be established and volunteer officials (where possible) recruited for the campaign. The owner or supervisor of each building was to see that the records for each household were complete and correct before the forms were collected by the agent. The imperial government was allowed to vary the information collected from census year to census year.[1] States wishing to collect data beyond what was required were allowed to do so using individual *Zählkarten* [enumeration cards]. This led to an enormous amount of documentation, as will be shown below.

From the *Haushaltungsliste,* only the number of persons was transferred to a *Controlliste* that featured a line for each head of household by name and thus represented the population of a *Zählbezirk* [enumeration district]. The numbers (without names) were next transferred to the *Ortsliste* [town summary page] that included a line for each *Zählbezirk* and thereby established the population of the town. County and provincial officials moved those numbers to further pages on each higher geopolitical level. Final totals were submitted to the Imperial Bureau of Statistics in Berlin and publications issuing from that office included only statistics.

The founding of the empire required a new constitution with two bodies of legislature: the *Reichstag* and the *Bundestag*. It was in the latter body that decisions regarding census enumerations were made. The first such ruling was issued in the summer of 1871 and stipulated that the initial national enumeration was to take place on December 1 of that year.

This first nation-wide census featured a great deal of supporting and instructional literature, including a message meant to inspire cooperation (assuming a patriotic spirit throughout the new empire). Under the title "The Census of the German Empire on December 1, 1871 and the Support Desired from the Press and the Churches," it began with these words:

> During the last days of November of this year, thousands upon thousands of volunteer letter carriers will knock at the doors of their fellow citizens and deliver to them census forms in open envelopes. Those forms are meant for the recording of the names of the people who dwell there. These cards and papers are the tolls needed for the census that will be conducted throughout the empire on December 1—from the Memel River [northeast] to the Mosel by Metz [southwest] and from Königsau [by Denmark] to Lake Constance [south by Switzerland]—an area of more than 10,000 square kilometers [sic]. Every family in Prussia [not Germany!] will receive such an envelope and every head of

household is asked to record on a small card his own name and the name of each person in his household, their gender, age, occupation, education, religion, etc. The cards are to be returned on December 1 or 2 to the man who brought them. There will be approximately 120,000 such men out and about on those days in Preußen alone—a veritable army, well organized, consisting of men of all status and occupations, from the highest to the lowest, all of them convinced that they are participating in a grand patriotic work. And so it is. A census is undoubtedly one of the best ways for a nation to get to know itself....[2]

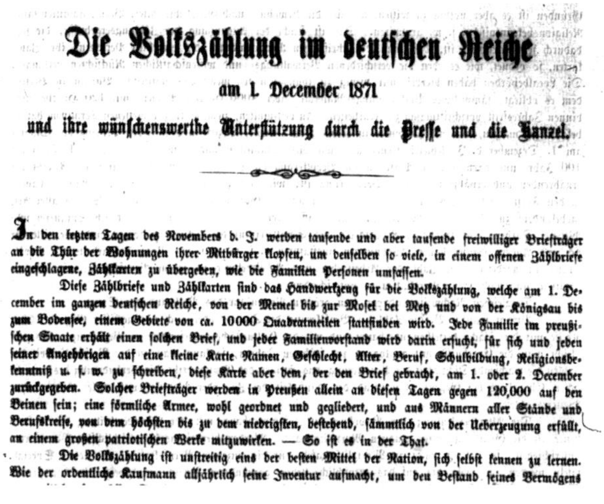

Die Volkszählung im deutschen Reiche

am 1. December 1871

und ihre wünschenswerthe Unterstützung durch die Presse und die Kanzel.

In den letzten Tagen des Novembers d. J. werden tausende und aber tausende freiwilliger Briefträger an die Thür der Wohnungen ihrer Mitbürger klopfen, um denselben so viele, in einem offenen Zählbriefe eingeschlagene, Zählkarten zu übergeben, wie die Familien Personen umfassen.

Diese Zählbriefe und Zählkarten sind das Handwerkzeug für die Volkszählung, welche am 1. December im ganzen deutschen Reiche, von der Memel bis zur Mosel bei Metz und von der Königsau bis zum Bodensee, einem Gebiete von ca. 10000 Quadratmeilen stattfinden wird. Jede Familie im preußischen Staate erhält einen solchen Brief, und jeder Familienvorstand wird darin ersucht, für sich und jeden seiner Angehörigen auf eine kleine Karte Namen, Geschlecht, Alter, Beruf, Schulbildung, Religionsbekenntniß u. s. w. zu schreiben, diese Karte aber dem, der den Brief gebracht, am 1. oder 2. December zurückgegeben. Solcher Briefträger werden in Preußen allein an diesen Tagen gegen 120,000 auf den Beinen sein; eine förmliche Armee, wohl geordnet und gegliedert, und aus Männern aller Stände und Berufskreise, von dem höchsten bis zu dem niedrigsten, bestehend, sämmtlich von der Ueberzeugung erfüllt, an einem großen patriotischen Werke mitzuwirken. — So ist es in der That.

Die Volkszählung ist unstreitig eins der besten Mittel der Nation, sich selbst kennen zu lernen. Wie der ordentliche Kaufmann alljährlich seine Inventur aufmacht, um den Bestand seines Vermögens

Figure 1. The first of four pages of the patriotic essay introducing the national census in 1871. The document was written by Dr. Ernst Engel of the Royal Statistical Office in Berlin.

This four-page essay reviewed the statistics compiled for Preußen since 1820 (to show the growth of the kingdom) and mentioned the importance of the census to determine military strength ("to defend our country, ... our numbers will convince our neighbors to keep peace with us"). The writer indicated that the census would involve papers weighing 4,000 *Zentner* [about 200 tons] and that it would take 120 assistant civil servants to compile the data in the Berlin office over perhaps one year's time. The census would help determine how old or young the people are; how many persons work to support how many others; the ages of married people and the duration of their marriages and "perhaps help us find a way to prevent the trend of celibacy among young men and women." The census would facilitate predictions regarding production and consumption of resources and the gross national product; those numbers could be used to help states make adjustments in occupational distribution, etc., etc. "All in all it is clear that a good census can be one of the most useful and valuable resources of the government."[3]

The author, Ernst Engel (1821–1896), was well-known in the science of statistics; he insisted that the English press and churches had supported their national census well, but complained that they only did the counting every ten years ("not often enough"). "Nobody can tell precisely what has changed in a country until a new census is taken."[4] His final statements were meant to tug at the heartstrings of the reader:

> ...everything grows from census to census, the number of people, houses, trains, ships and all of that shows that we are moving forward. The census measures this. Let us see to it that the census is done as well as possible and may God grant that the next census shows the greatness and the prosperity of the Vaterland. The English press supported the census on April 3, 1871. Let us approach the census with confidence and trust in God... Thus we hope that our press and our churches will offer similar support so that by Easter next year at the latest the results of the first general German census of December 1, 1871 can be announced to the German people. That will be a testimony that Germany deserves a high position among the nations, not just because of its power and the brilliance of its weapons, but because of the ingenuity, ambition, and virtue of its citizens.[5]

Ernst Engel was the head of the Royal [not Imperial!] Statistical Bureau in Berlin.[6] This statement was probably not circulated among all of the states in Germany, but rather only in the thirteen Prussian provinces and a few other states. According to Puttkammer and Mühlbrecht, the instructions and forms emanating from Berlin in 1871 were used only by Preußen, Lauenburg (a district in Schleswig-Holstein), Braunschweig, Waldeck, and Hamburg.

The full set of documents sent to those few states from the national *Innenministerium* [Interior Ministry] in Berlin for the census campaign of 1871 included these elements (identified by alphabetical characters as follows):

A. *Zählkarte*: the card to be filled out for each individual
B. Example of a *Zählkarte* filled out
C. Lists of persons present on December 1
D. General instructions
E. Instructions for the town authorities: these included the procurement of the forms to be distributed, filled out, and collected; the selection/assignment and training of enumerators, and the transfer of data to the next higher government office.
F. Instructions for the enumerators: these included the responsibility to be very familiar with all forms to be used; to see that all forms were filled out correctly or to fill them out himself; to treat any adult living alone in a home as a head of household; to treat e.g. the director of a hospital or a prison as a head of household; and to transfer the names and numbers from the *Zählkarte* to columns 1–3 of the *Controlliste*.
G. *Controlliste* (sample); the name of each head of household was to be transferred from the household list to a line on this form, along with only the total number of members of the household by gender and number. (States not using the *Zählkarte* transferred the numbers from the *Haushaltsvorstandsliste* to the *Controlliste*.)
H. Statistical summary: from the *Controlliste* the total numbers of persons (by gender and number but not by name) were transferred to this list that represented the entire enumeration district. The resulting numbers were transferred to yet another form (*Ortsliste*) that included totals for the town or the city.

Census Forms Used in the German Empire from 1871 to 1916

The five forms shown below constitute the literature printed for national census campaigns throughout the life of the German Empire. During those ten enumerations, individual states continued to print these pages under their own governmental titles and included a few items not required by national standards.

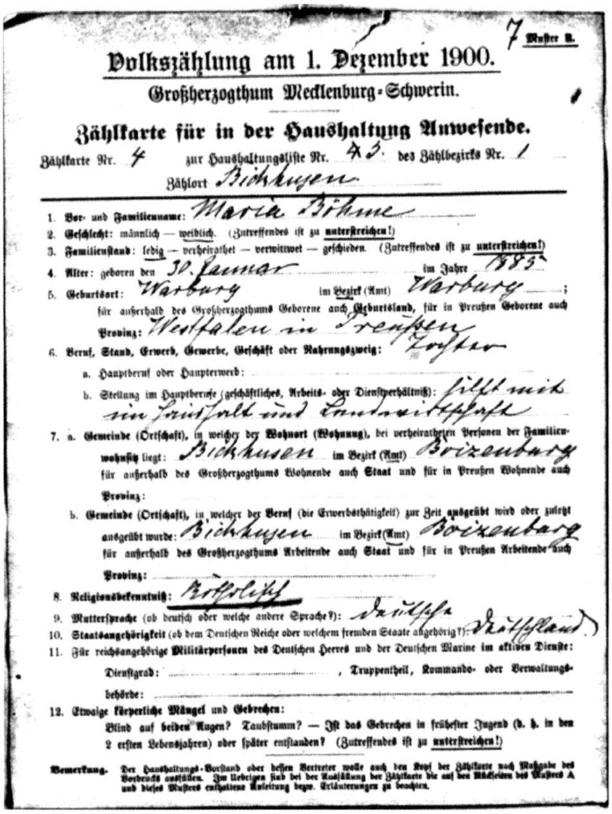
7 Muster B.

Volkszählung am 1. Dezember 1900.

Großherzogthum Mecklenburg-Schwerin.

Zählkarte für in der Haushaltung Anwesende.

Zählkarte Nr. 4 zur Haushaltungsliste Nr. 45. des Zählbezirks Nr. 1

Zählort Bickhusen

1. Vor- und Familienname: Maria Böhme
2. Geschlecht: männlich — weiblich. (Zutreffendes ist zu unterstreichen!)
3. Familienstand: ledig — verheirathet — verwittwet — geschieden. (Zutreffendes ist zu unterstreichen!)
4. Alter: geboren den 30. Januar im Jahre 1885
5. Geburtsort: Warburg im Bezirk (Amt) Warburg; für außerhalb des Großherzogthums Geborene auch Geburtsland, für in Preußen Geborene auch Provinz: Westfalen in Preußen
6. Beruf, Stand, Erwerb, Gewerbe, Geschäft oder Nahrungszweig: Tochter
   a. Hauptberuf oder Haupterwerb:
   b. Stellung im Hauptberufe (geschäftliches, Arbeits- oder Dienstverhältniß): hilft mit in Haushalt und Landwirtschaft
7. a. Gemeinde (Ortschaft), in welcher der Wohnort (Wohnung), bei verheiratheten Personen der Familienwohnsitz liegt: Bickhusen im Bezirk (Amt) Boizenburg; für außerhalb des Großherzogthums Wohnende auch Staat und für in Preußen Wohnende auch Provinz:
   b. Gemeinde (Ortschaft), in welcher der Beruf (die Erwerbsthätigkeit) zur Zeit ausgeübt wird oder zuletzt ausgeübt wurde: Bickhusen im Bezirk (Amt) Boizenburg; für außerhalb des Großherzogthums Arbeitende auch Staat und für in Preußen Arbeitende auch Provinz:
8. Religionsbekenntniß: katholisch
9. Muttersprache (ob deutsch oder welche andere Sprache?): deutsche
10. Staatsangehörigkeit (ob dem Deutschen Reiche oder welchem fremden Staate angehörig?): Deutschland
11. Für reichsangehörige Militärpersonen des Deutschen Heeres und der Deutschen Marine im aktiven Dienste: Dienstgrad: , Truppentheil, Kommando- oder Verwaltungsbehörde:
12. Etwaige körperliche Mängel und Gebrechen: Blind auf beiden Augen? Taubstumm? — Ist das Gebrechen in frühester Jugend (d. h. in den 2 ersten Lebensjahren) oder später entstanden? (Zutreffendes ist zu unterstreichen!)

Bemerkung. Der Haushaltungs-Vorstand oder dessen Vertreter wolle auch den Kopf der Zählkarte nach Maßgabe des Vordrucks ausfüllen. Im Uebrigen sind bei der Ausfüllung der Zählkarte die auf den Rückseiten des Musters A und dieses Musters enthaltene Anleitung bezw. Erläuterungen zu beachten.

Figure 2. A rarity: an individual *Zählkarte* from a town in Mecklenburg-Schwerin. Most of these pages were destroyed after the information was transferred as numbers to the household list. [https://familysearch.org/ark:/61903/1:1:MVY1-FDP]

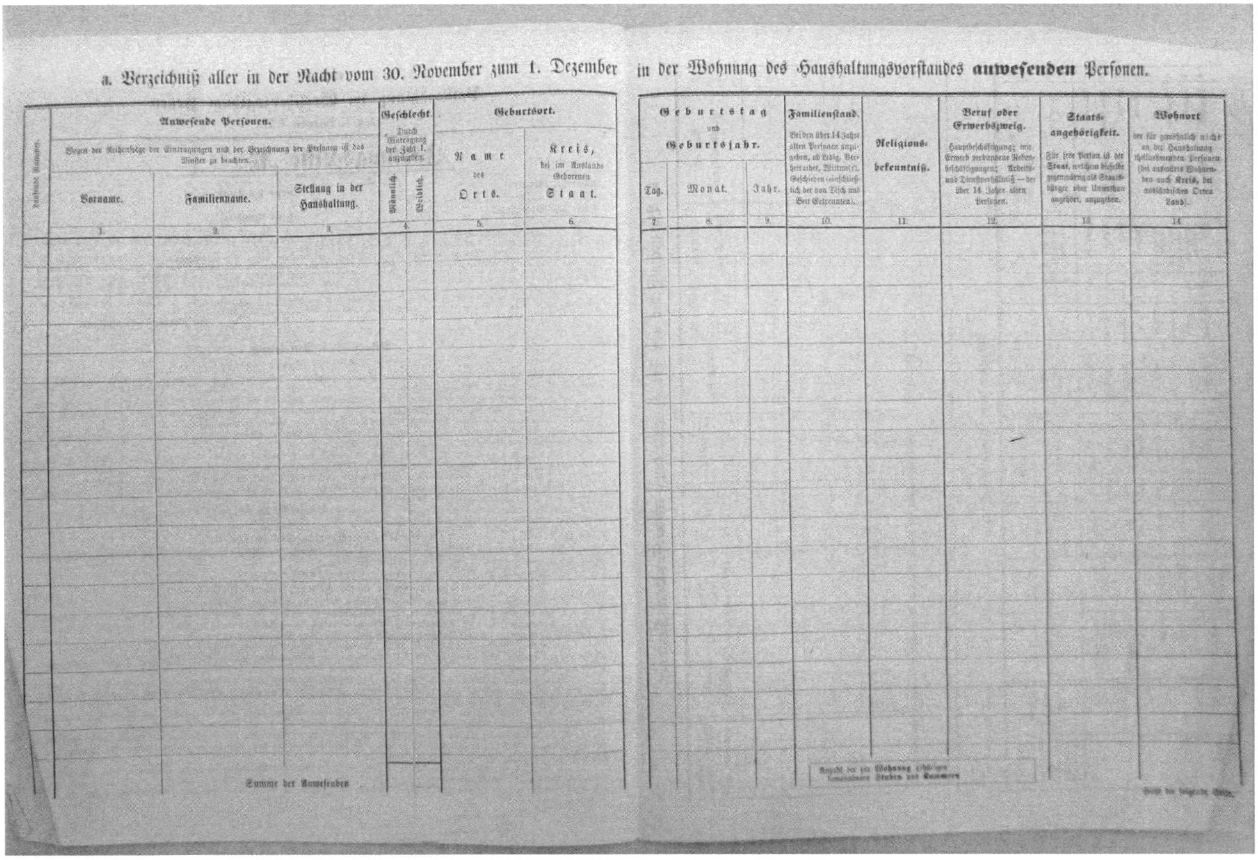

Figure 3. This *Haushaltungsliste* was used in some states instead of the *Zählkarte*.

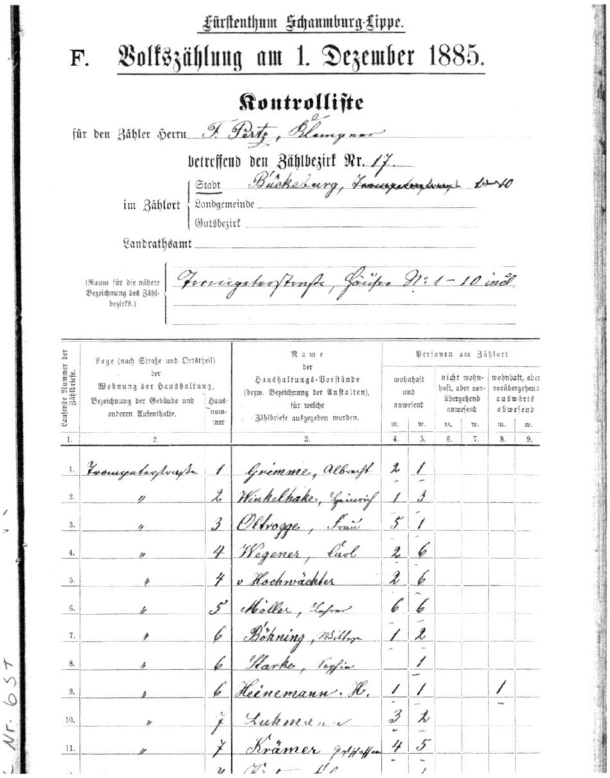

Figure 4. This 1885 *Controlliste* shows the counts of persons in each household; the data were taken from the *Haushaltsvorstandslisten*. [Bückeburg, Schaumburg-Lippe; Niedersächsisches Landesarchiv Bückeburg Dep 9C Nr 637]

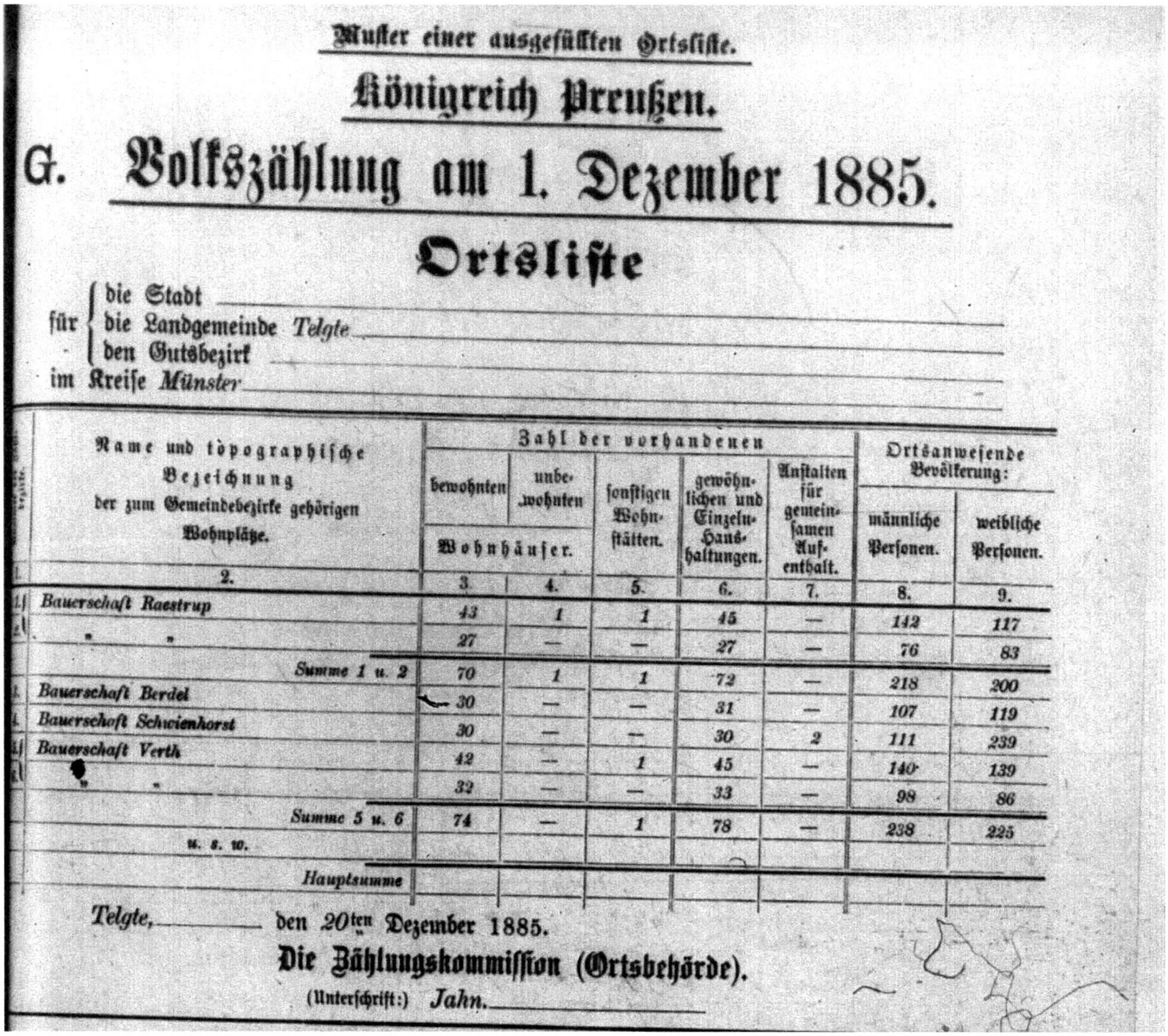

Muster einer ausgefüllten Ortsliste.

Königreich Preußen.

G. Volkszählung am 1. Dezember 1885.

Ortsliste

für { die Stadt / die Landgemeinde *Telgte* / den Gutsbezirk }
im Kreise *Münster*

	Name und topographische Bezeichnung der zum Gemeindebezirke gehörigen Wohnplätze.	Zahl der vorhandenen					Ortsanwesende Bevölkerung:	
		bewohnten Wohnhäuser.	unbewohnten Wohnhäuser.	sonstigen Wohnstätten.	gewöhnlichen und Einzeln-Haushaltungen.	Anstalten für gemeinsamen Aufenthalt.	männliche Personen.	weibliche Personen.
1.	2.	3.	4.	5.	6.	7.	8.	9.
1	*Bauerschaft Raestrup*	*43*	*1*	*1*	*45*	—	*142*	*117*
2	" "	*27*	—	—	*27*	—	*76*	*83*
	Summe 1 u. 2	*70*	*1*	*1*	*72*	—	*218*	*200*
3	*Bauerschaft Berdel*	*30*	—	—	*31*	—	*107*	*119*
4	*Bauerschaft Schwienhorst*	*30*	—	—	*30*	*2*	*111*	*239*
5	*Bauerschaft Verth*	*42*	—	*1*	*45*	—	*140*	*139*
6	" "	*32*	—	—	*33*	—	*98*	*86*
	Summe 5 u. 6	*74*	—	*1*	*78*	—	*238*	*225*
	u. s. w.							
	Hauptsumme							

Telgte, den *20ten* Dezember 1885.

Die Zählungskommission (Ortsbehörde).

(Unterschrift:) *Jahn.*

Figure 5. Names were reduced to numbers when the data from the *Controllisten* were moved to the *Ortsliste* (town summary).

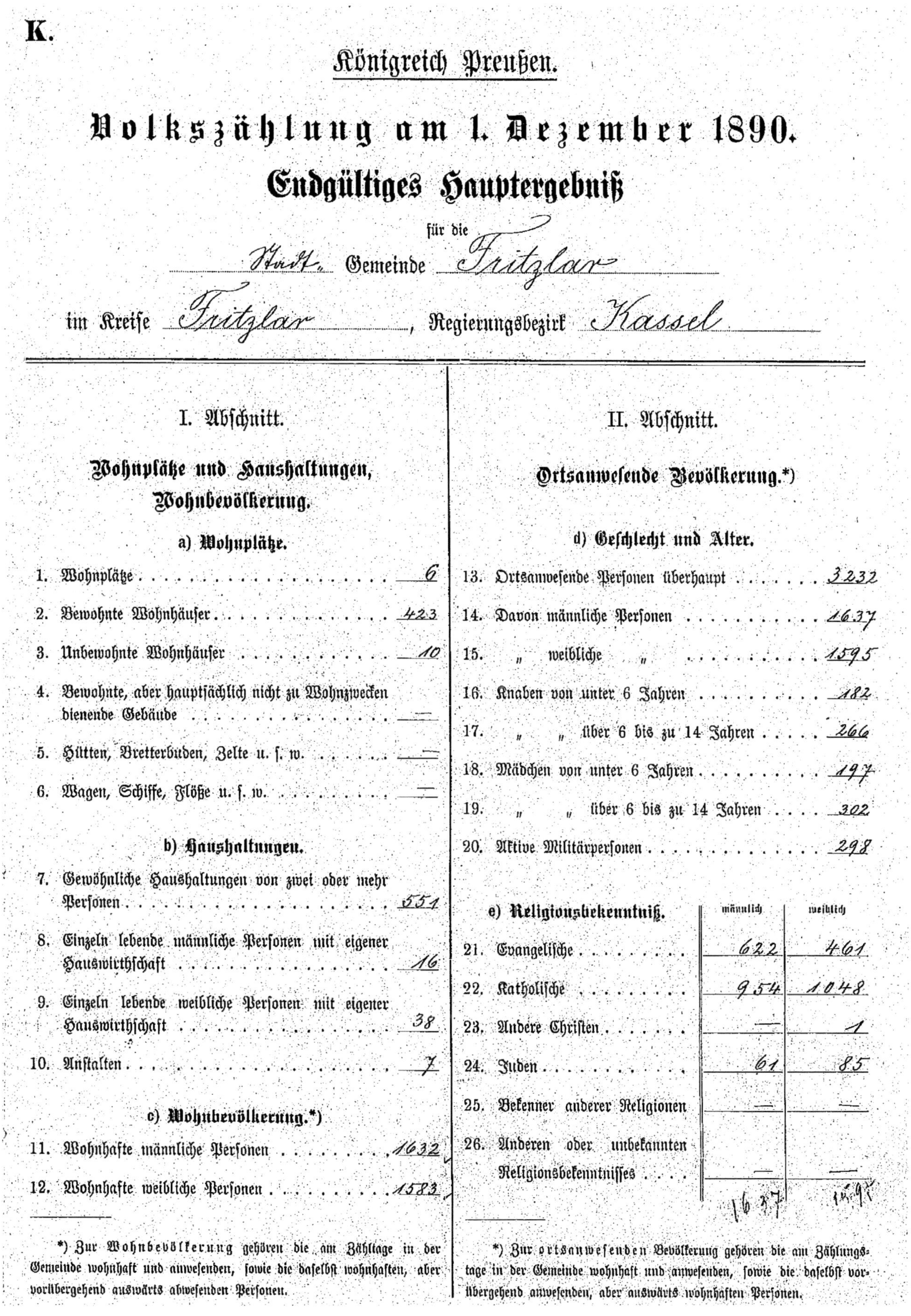

K.

Königreich Preußen.

Volkszählung am 1. Dezember 1890.

Endgültiges Hauptergebniß

für die

Stadt. Gemeinde _Fritzlar_

im Kreise _Fritzlar_, Regierungsbezirk _Kassel_

I. Abschnitt.

Wohnplätze und Haushaltungen, Wohnbevölkerung.

a) Wohnplätze.

1. Wohnplätze 6
2. Bewohnte Wohnhäuser 423
3. Unbewohnte Wohnhäuser 10
4. Bewohnte, aber hauptsächlich nicht zu Wohnzwecken dienende Gebäude . . . . . —
5. Hütten, Bretterbuden, Zelte u. s. w. . . . —
6. Wagen, Schiffe, Flöße u. s. w. . . . . —

b) Haushaltungen.

7. Gewöhnliche Haushaltungen von zwei oder mehr Personen 551
8. Einzeln lebende männliche Personen mit eigener Hauswirthschaft 16
9. Einzeln lebende weibliche Personen mit eigener Hauswirthschaft 38
10. Anstalten 7

c) Wohnbevölkerung.*)

11. Wohnhafte männliche Personen 1632
12. Wohnhafte weibliche Personen 1583

II. Abschnitt.

Ortsanwesende Bevölkerung.*)

d) Geschlecht und Alter.

13. Ortsanwesende Personen überhaupt 3232
14. Davon männliche Personen 1637
15. „ weibliche „ 1595
16. Knaben von unter 6 Jahren 182
17. „ „ über 6 bis zu 14 Jahren 266
18. Mädchen von unter 6 Jahren 197
19. „ „ über 6 bis zu 14 Jahren 302
20. Aktive Militärpersonen 298

e) Religionsbekenntniß.

	männlich	weiblich
21. Evangelische	622	461
22. Katholische	954	1048
23. Andere Christen	—	1
24. Juden	61	85
25. Bekenner anderer Religionen . .	—	—
26. Anderen oder unbekannten Religionsbekenntnisses . . .	—	—
	1637	1595

---

*) Zur Wohnbevölkerung gehören die am Zähltage in der Gemeinde wohnhaft und anwesenden, sowie die daselbst wohnhaften, aber vorübergehend auswärts abwesenden Personen.

*) Zur ortsanwesenden Bevölkerung gehören die am Zählungstage in der Gemeinde wohnhaft und anwesenden, sowie die daselbst vorübergehend anwesenden, aber auswärts wohnhaften Personen.

Figure 6. Taken from the _Ortslisten_, these are the final totals for the city of Fritzlar after the census of 1890. [Stadtarchiv Fritzlar]

According to Michel, the data sought in all states for all individuals under the first national census were as follows:[7]

1. relation to head of household
2. gender
3. birth place
4. birth year
5. marital status
6. religion
7. occupation or employment
8. citizenship
9. place of residence (if not permanently here)
10. persons absent from this household on December 1

The national directives for 1871 allowed the states to gather additional information if desired, but restricted that additional information to the following: precise birth date, native language, level of education, handicaps, and reason for being at the current location (if not a permanent resident).

Because many of the states were still attempting to act as independent entities not yet subsumed by the empire, the regulations for the census sent to local authorities in many states did not cite the Statistical Bureau in Berlin as the origin. For example, a communique from the grand duchy of Baden dated September 30, 1871 indicated that "the grand duke had decided" that his state would participate in the census mandated by the national government. The government of Sachsen-Meiningen in Hildburghausen issued a similar statement on November 12. Cards for individuals were not used in Baden; a page issued to each head of household facilitated the recording of the same data included on the Prussian *Zählkarte*.

Only the five German states named above used the individual *Zählkarte* in 1871, while all others employed a *Haushaltungsliste* [a page showing all persons in a given household]. Thus somewhat different instructions were issued to towns and enumerators under that system. Nevertheless, the same basic data was collected for individuals throughout Germany.

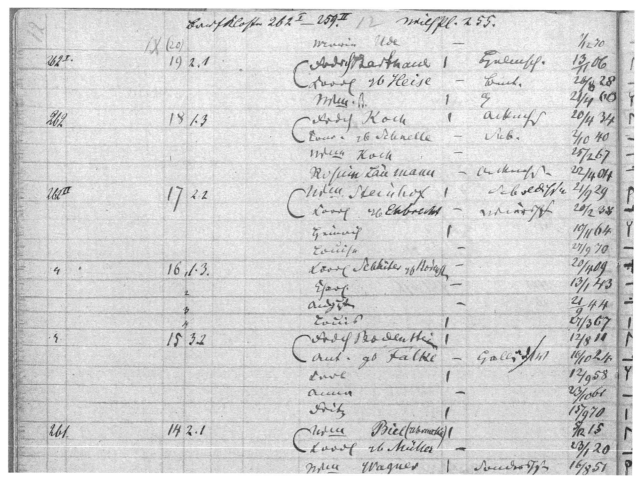

Figure 7. Original lists of residents from the 1871 census were not often preserved, but they do exist. This one is a left-hand page from the town of Gandersheim, Braunschweig. [Niedersächsisches Landesarchiv Wolfenbüttel 254 N, Nr. 1]

1875 German Empire Census

The analysis of the 1871 census was apparently complicated by misunderstandings regarding two major issues: birth place and occupation. The instructions for enumerators of the 1875 census featured very detailed interpretations of those aspects of each person's status. A question was added regarding the status of men on active or reserve status in the military. The following are the topics of the questions included on the *Zählkarte* for 1875:

1. first and last name
2. gender
3. birth date
4. marital status
5. religion
6. citizenship
7. place of residence (if not here: town, county, state)
8. for military personnel: command post and unit
9. occupation
10. principal employment
11. secondary occupation
12. secondary employment
13. does this person employ more than five persons?
14. details of business that employs more than five persons

As in 1871, the census campaign of 1875 was still not carried out uniformly in all states of the empire. Preußen, Lauenburg, Hessen, both Mecklenburgs, Oldenburg, Braunschweig, Waldeck, Schaumburg-Lippe, Lippe, Bremen, Hamburg, and Elsaß-Lothringen used the individual *Zählkarte*, while the rest still employed the *Haushaltungsliste*. Again, the instructions and the forms designed for the census usually were printed over the signature of the minister of the interior of the state from its capital city, not from the Statistical Bureau in Berlin.

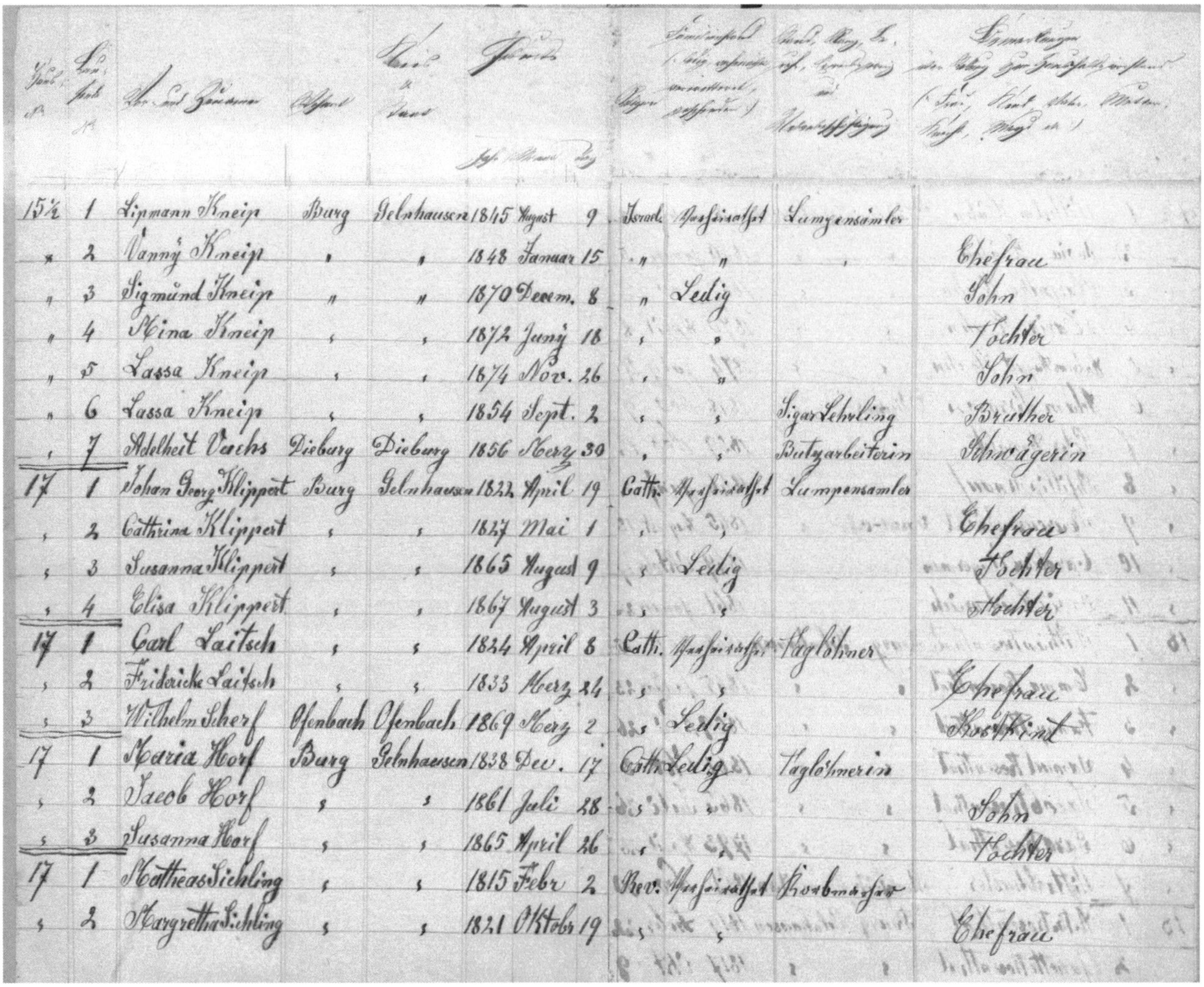

15½	1	Lipmann Kneip	Burg	Gelnhausen	1845 August 9	Israel.		Lumpensammler	
"	2	Vanny Kneip	"	"	1848 Januar 15	"	"		Ehefrau
"	3	Sigmund Kneip	"	"	1870 Decem. 8	"	Ledig		Sohn
"	4	Mina Kneip	"	"	1872 Juny 18	"	"		Tochter
"	5	Lassa Kneip	"	"	1874 Nov. 26	"	"		Sohn
"	6	Lassa Kneip	"	"	1854 Sept. 2	"	"	Zigarlehrling	Bruder
"	7	Adelheit Oechs	Dieburg	Dieburg	1856 Merz 30	"	"	Butzarbeiterin	Schwägerin
17	1	Johan Georg Klippert	Burg	Gelnhausen	1822 April 19	Cath.		Lumpensamler	
"	2	Cathrina Klippert	"	"	1827 Mai 1	"			Ehefrau
"	3	Susanna Klippert	"	"	1865 August 9	"	Ledig		Tochter
"	4	Elisa Klippert	"	"	1867 August 3	"			Tochter
17	1	Carl Laitsch	"	"	1824 April 8	Cath.		Taglöhner	
"	2	Fridaicke Laitsch	"	"	1833 Merz 24	"	"		Ehefrau
"	3	Wilhelm Scherf	Offenbach	Offenbach	1869 Merz 2	"	Ledig		Kostkind
17	1	Maria Horf	Burg	Gelnhausen	1838 Dec. 17	Cath.	Ledig	Taglöhnerin	
"	2	Jacob Horf	"	"	1861 Juli 28	"			Sohn
"	3	Susanna Horf	"	"	1865 April 26	"			Tochter
17	1	Mattheas Sichling	"	"	1815 Febr 2	Ref.		Korbmacher	
"	2	Margretha Sichling	"	"	1821 Oktober 19	"	"		Ehefrau

Figure 8. A page from the 1875 census of Burg, Hessen-Nassau [Stadtarchiv Gelnhausen]

1880 German Empire Census

The following are the topics of the questions included in the census for 1880:

1. first and last name
2. gender
3. birth date
4. birth place; state of birth if not Preußen
5. permanent residence if not here; county of residence if not in this state
6. place of residence if absent from here
7. citizenship if not Preußen
8. religion
9. marital status
10. relationship to head of household
    a. how are you related?
    b. are you employed by head of household?
    c. do you only sleep in this household?
11. handicaps
12. occupation, profession, or office
13. are you self-employed?
14. are you employed by another?

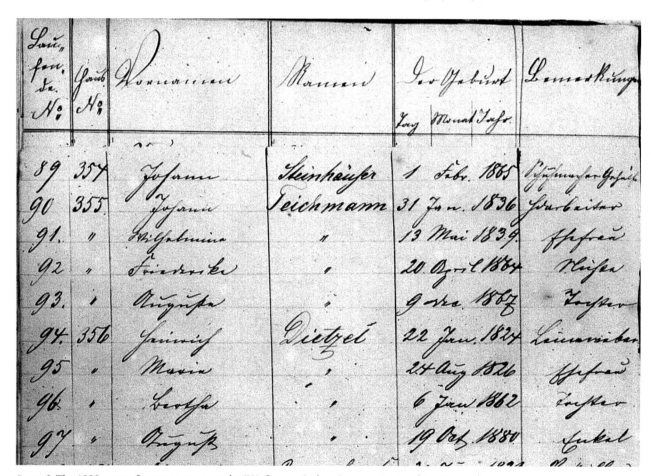

Figure 9. The 1880 census form was quite simple. [Weißensee, Sachen-Provinz; Kreisarchiv Sömmerda]

1885 German Empire Census

The following are the topics of the questions included
in the census for 1885:

1. first and last name
2. gender
3. birth date
4. marital status
5. birth place
6. religion
7. occupation
8. citizenship
9. military personnel: assignment and unit
10. place of residence if not permanently here
11. place of residence if temporarily absent from this household
12. comments

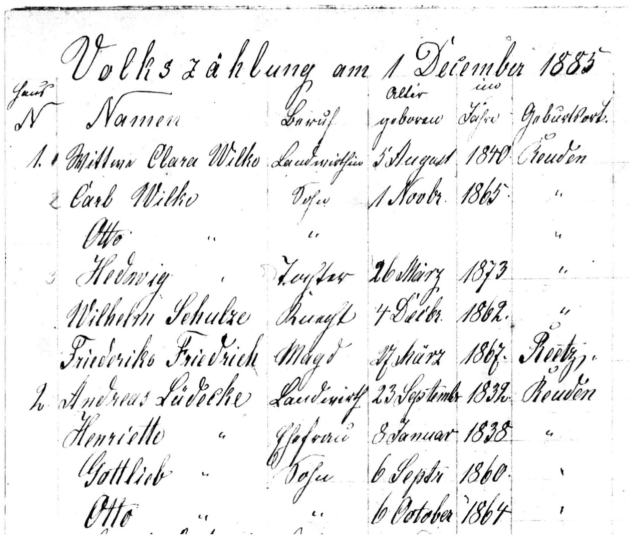

Figure 10. The 1885 census form was still handwritten in many areas. [Reuden, Anhalt; Kreisarchiv Zerbst]

1890 German Empire Census

The following are the topics of the questions included
in the census for 1890:

1. first and last name
2. relationship to head of household
3. gender
4. age (birth date or age in years)
5. marital status
6. occupation and specialty
7. birth place (town and county)

8. if on active military duty (status and unit)
9. religion
10. citizenship
11. native language
12. persons temporarily here (permanent place of residence and county)

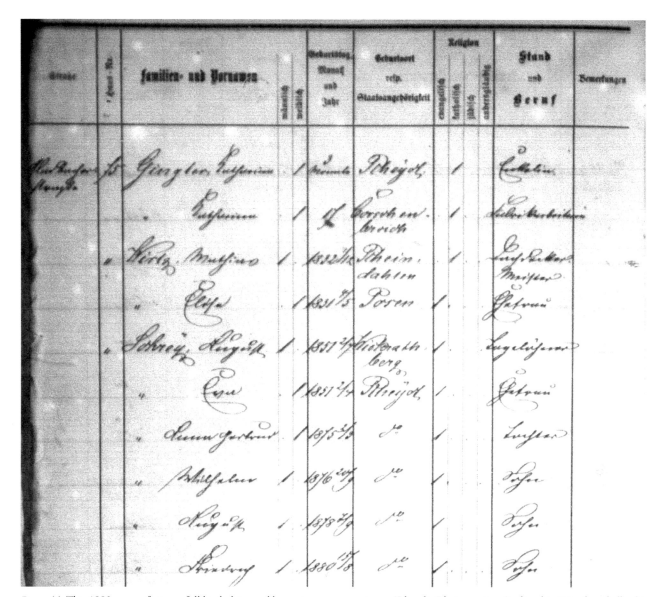

Figure 11. This 1890 census features full birth dates and home towns or provinces. [Rheydt, Rheinprovinz; Stadtarchiv Mönchengladbach]

1895 German Empire Census

The following are the topics of the questions included
in the census for 1895:

1. first and last name
2. gender
3. age (birth date or age in years)
4. marital status
5. religion
6. citizenship

7. occupation and specialty
8. employment and duration thereof
9. if on active military duty (status and unit)
10. if male 39–45: member of militia and if trained
11. handicaps

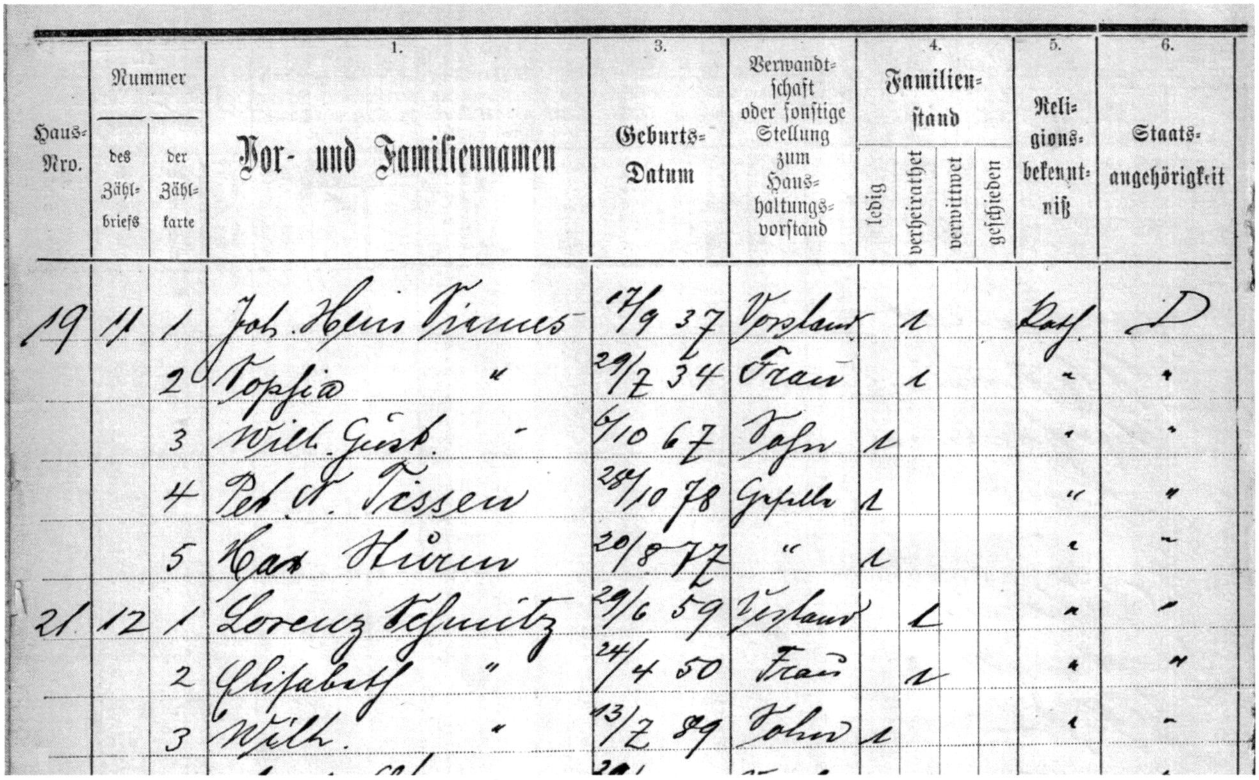

Haus-Nro.	Nummer des Zähl-briefs	Nummer der Zähl-karte	Vor- und Familiennamen	Geburts-Datum	Verwandt-schaft oder sonstige Stellung zum Haushaltungs-vorstand	Familienstand ledig	Familienstand verheirathet	Familienstand verwittwet	Familienstand geschieden	Religions-bekenntniß	Staats-angehörigkeit
19	11	1	Joh. Hein Timmes	17/9 37	Vorstand	1				kath.	D
		2	Sophia "	29/7 34	Frau	1				"	"
		3	Will. Gink	5/10 67	Sohn	1				"	"
		4	Pet. H. Tessen	28/10 78	Geselle	1				"	"
		5	Kas. Hünen	20/8 77	"	1				"	"
21	12	1	Lorenz Schmitz	29/6 59	Vorstand		1			"	"
		2	Elisabeth "	24/4 50	Frau		1			"	"
		3	Will. "	13/2 89	Sohn	1					

Figure 12. 1895 census from Lobberich, Rheinprovinz [Stadtarchiv Kempen GALobberich101.2]

1900 German Empire Census

The following are the topics of the questions included in the census for 1900:

1. first name
2. last name
3. status or occupation
4. day of birth
5. month of birth
6. year of birth
7. religion
8. town of birth
9. county of birth
10. country of birth
11. citizenship
12. comments

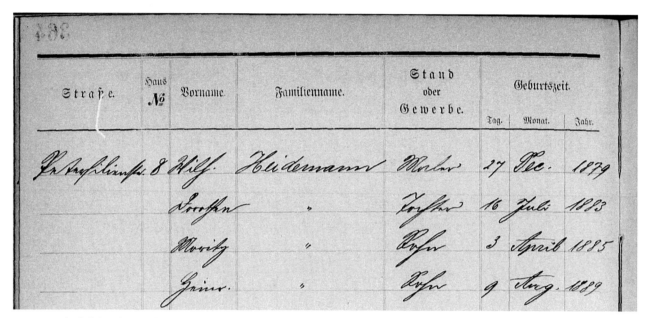

Figure 13. The left-hand page of the 1900 census [Minden, Westfalen; Stadtarchiv Minden]

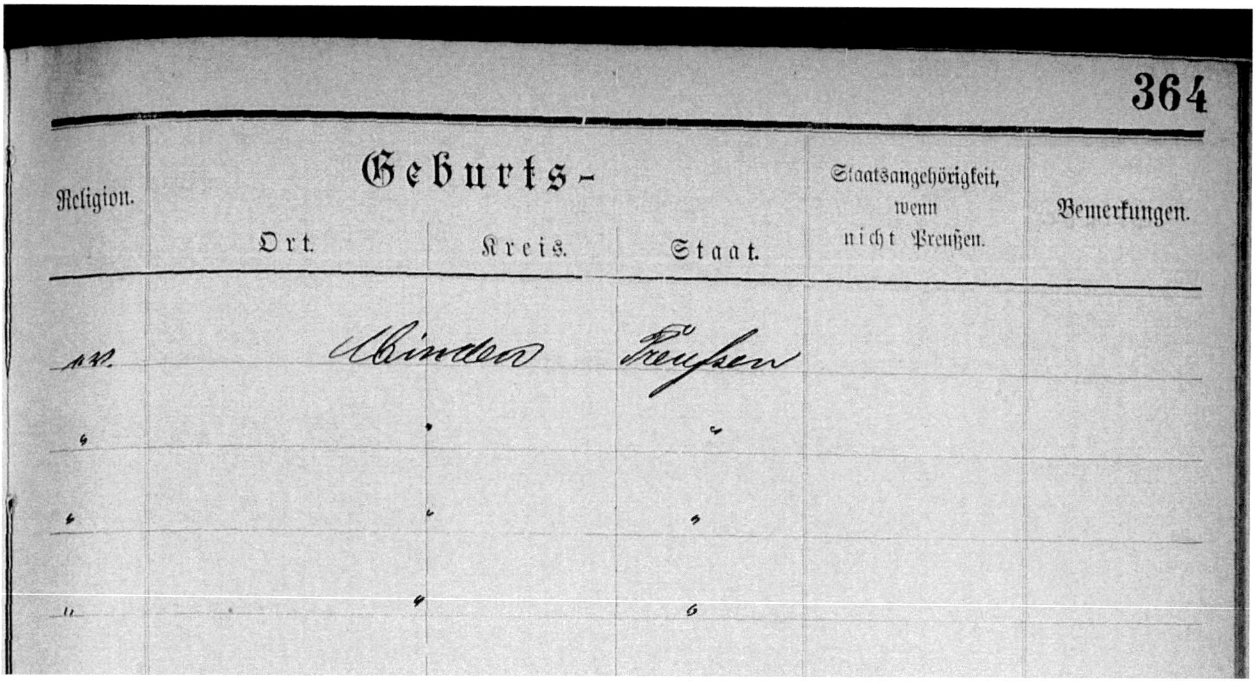

Figure 14. The right-hand page of the 1900 census has the town, county, and province of birth. [Minden, Westfalen; Stadtarchiv Minden]

1905 German Empire Census

The following are the topics of the questions included
in the census for 1905:

1. first name
2. last name
3. relationship to head of household
4. marital status
5. male
6. female
7. day of birth
8. month of birth
9. year of birth
10. principal occupation
11. position in employment
12. religion
13. citizenship
14. whether active military

15–17 for men 39 to 45 years of age

15. army training
16. navy training
17. no training

Seite 2.										

	Namen der anwesenden Personen. (Siehe Anleitung Ziff. 3.) Bei den Einträgen ist folgende Reihenfolge zu beobachten: Haushaltungsvorstand, Ehefrau, Kinder, sonstige Anverwandte, häusliche und gewerbliche Dienstboten, Gewerbsgehilfen, sonstige Wohnungsgenossen, Schlafleute und vorübergehend Anwesende.		Verwandtschaftliche oder sonstige Stellung zum Haushaltungsvorstand. Beispiele sonstiger Stellung: Dienstbote für häusliche oder gewerbliche Verrichtungen, Gewerbsgehilfe oder Lehrling, Mieter ohne eigene Wirtschaft, Kost- und Schlafgänger, Pensionär, Pflegling, Logiergast.	Familienstand. Anzugeben ob ledig (d. h. weder verheiratet noch verheiratet gewesen), verheiratet, Witwe (r), geschieden.	Geschlecht (durch 1 zu bezeichnen.)		Geburtstag und Geburtsjahr.			Hauptberuf (Hauptberuf (Hauptwerb) (Siehe Anleitung Ziff. 4.)
Laufende Nummer.	Vorname. 1.	Familienname. 2.	3.	4.	männlich. 5.	weiblich. 6.	Tag. 7.	Monat. 8.	Jahr. 9.	10.
1.	Friedrich	Haubold	Haushaltungsvorstand	verheiratet	1		26.	April	1840	Leineweberei
2.	Berta	„	Ehefrau	verheiratet		1	7.	Juni	1844	
3.	Hugo	„	Sohn	ledig	1		5.	Januar	1865	Tuchweberei
4.	Anna	„	Tochter	ledig		1	30.	Dezember	1875	
5.	August	„	Bruder	geschieden	1		2.	August	1862	Schlosserei
6.	Marie	Schwabe	Dienstbote	ledig		1	15.	März	1876	Dienstmädchen für
7.	Albert	Zingler	Geselle	ledig	1		3.	Februar	1865	Leineweberei
8.	Abraham	Stiebel	Gast auf Besuch	Witwer	1		6.	Juni	1842	Handel mit Wolle
9.	Robert	Köhler	Einquartiert	ledig	1		8.	Mai	1884	Militärdienst
			Summe der Anwesenden		6	3				

1.	Karl Günther	zg. Fürst von Sch. Sondershausen	Haushaltungsvorstand	verheir.	1		7.	August	1830	Regent
2.	Marie	zg. Fürstin von Sch. u. Sondershausen, Prinzessin zu Sachsen	Ehefrau	„		1	28.	Juni	1845	
3.	Elisabeth	von Stein		ledig		1	23.	Sept.	1867	Hofdame
4.	Auguste	Cämmerer		Witwe		1	16.	Febr.	1837	Kastellanin
5.	Frieda	Kißler		ledig		1	27.	Dez.	1864	Kammerzofe
6.	Bertha	Dreier		„		1	14.	Febr.	1880	Hofdame...
7.	Margarethe	Kindervater		„		1	18.	Oktbr.	1884	Hausmädchen
8.	Zilla	Hellmund	Verwandtschaft...	„		1	6.	Oktbr.	1882	
9.	Else	Kestermann	zu	„		1	30.	Juni	1887	
10.	Antonia	Fischer	1 und 2	„		1	14.	Juli	1880	Hilfsköchin

Figure 15. The 1905 census has both instructions and sample entries. [Staatsarchiv Thüringen, Schwarzburg-Rudolstadt, Hofmarschallamt Sondershausen 0820, left-hand page]

Hauptberuf (Haupterwerb) und Stellung im Hauptberuf.		Religions-bekenntnis. Abkürzungen: E. für Angehörige der evangelisch-lutherischen Landeskirche des Fürstentums (Siehe Anleitung Ziff. 6). K. für römisch-katholisch. I. für israelitisch. Andere Bekenntnisse sind ohne Kürzung einzutragen.	Staats-angehörigkeit (ob reichsangehörig oder welchem fremden Staate angehörig). Für Angehörige deutscher Staaten ist „D.", für jede andere Person ist der Staat, welchem dieselbe gegenwärtig als Staatsbürger oder Untertan angehört, anzugeben. (Siehe Anleitung Ziff. 7.)	Ob im aktiven Dienste des deutschen Heeres oder der deutschen Marine stehend. Für alle im aktiven Dienste stehenden reichsangehörigen Militärpersonen des Heeres und der Marine, mit Einschluß der Militärbeamten und -Ärzte und der auf bestimmte Zeit Beurlaubten, ist außer dem Worte „aktiv" der Truppenteil, die Kommandobehörde u. s. w. anzugeben. (Siehe Anleitung Ziff. 8.)	Ob militärisch ausgebildet oder ob nicht militärisch ausgebildet. Für reichsangehörige, landsturmpflichtige Männer im 39. bis zum vollendeten 45. Lebensjahre (aus der Geburtszeit vom 1. Dezember 1860 bis 31. Dezember 1866 einschließlich). (Siehe Anleitung Ziff. 9.) durch Eintragung einer 1 zu bezeichnen.		
Beruf (Haupterwerb). (Siehe Anleitung Ziff. 4)	Stellung im Hauptberuf (Haupterwerb). (Siehe Anleitung Ziff. 5.)				Militärisch ausgebildet im Heere.	in d. Marine.	Nicht militärisch ausgebildet.
10.	11.	12.	13.	14.	15.	16.	17.
	selbständig	E.	D				
		E.	D				
	Fabrikarbeiter	E.	D		1		
		E.	D				
	Geselle	E.	D			1	
	häusliche Arbeiten	K.	D				
	Geselle	E.	D				1
	Hausierer	I.	Österreich				
	Musketier	Herrnhuter	D	aktiv, 96. Regiment			
		E.	D				
		E.	D				
		E.	D				
		E.	D				
		E.	D				
		E.	D				
		E.	D				
		E.	D				
		E.	D				

Figure 16. The abbreviations are E. (Evangelisch) and D. (Deutschland). [Staatsarchiv Thüringen, Schwarzburg-Rudolstadt, Hofmarschallamt Sondershausen 0820, right-hand page]

1910 German Empire Census

The following are the topics of the questions included
in the census for 1910:

1. relation to head of household
2. gender
3. marital status
4. birth date
5. occupation and employment
6. whether on active military duty
7. religion
8. citizenship

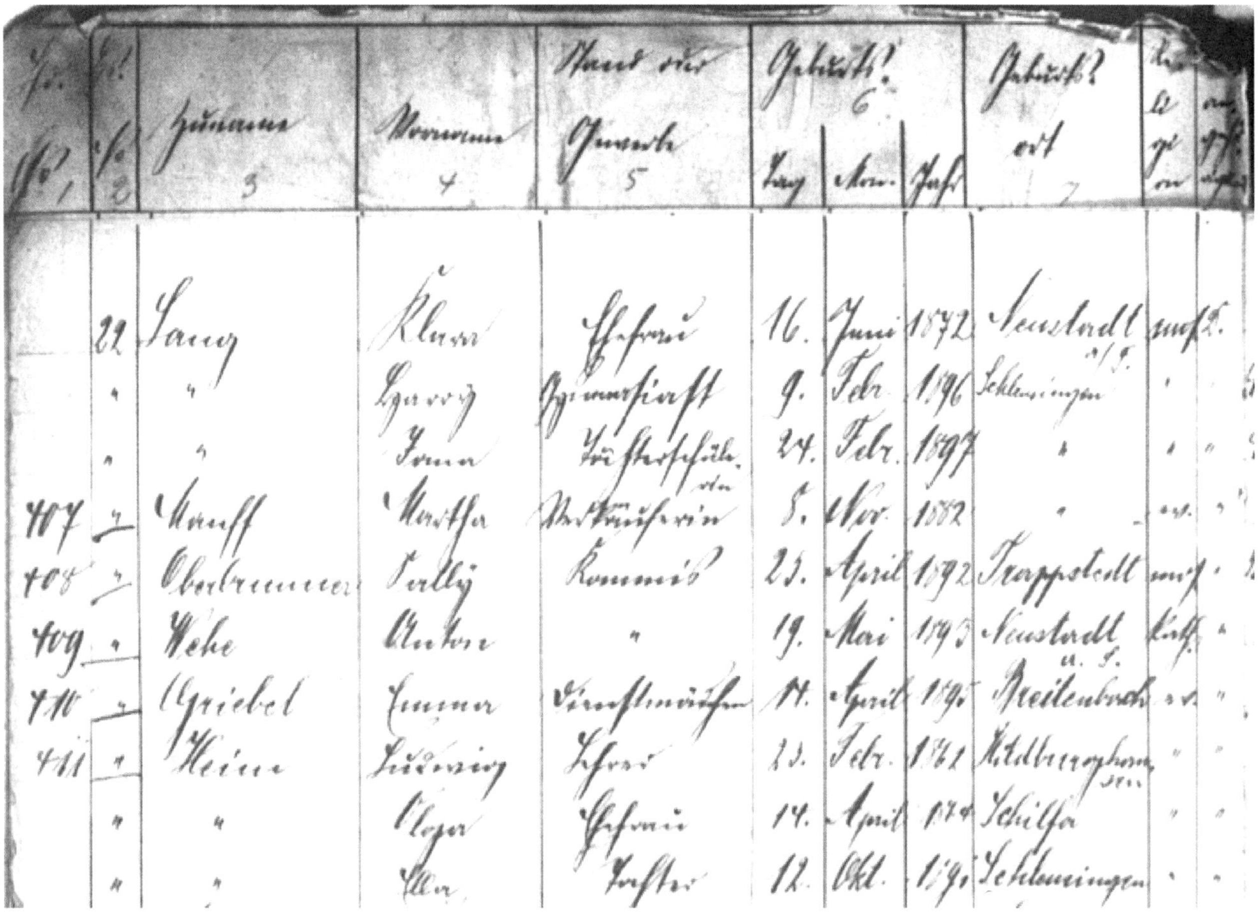

Figure 17. A common way to save paper and writing in a census book: only the last page of this 1910 census book has the column headings. [Schleusingen, Sachsen-Meiningen; Kreisarchiv Hildburghausen]

1916 German Empire Census

The following are the topics of the questions included in the census for 1916:

1. given name
2. surname
3. status or relationship to head of household
4. gender
5. birth date
6. marital status
7. citizenship
8. employment
9. employer or employee on July 31, 1914
10. type of business at place of employment on July 31, 1914
11. current occupation
12. current position at place of employment
13. current type of business at place of employment
14. if born before December 1, 1899 active military status
15. if born before December 1, 1899 reserve military status
16. status if military invalid
17. status if prisoner of war

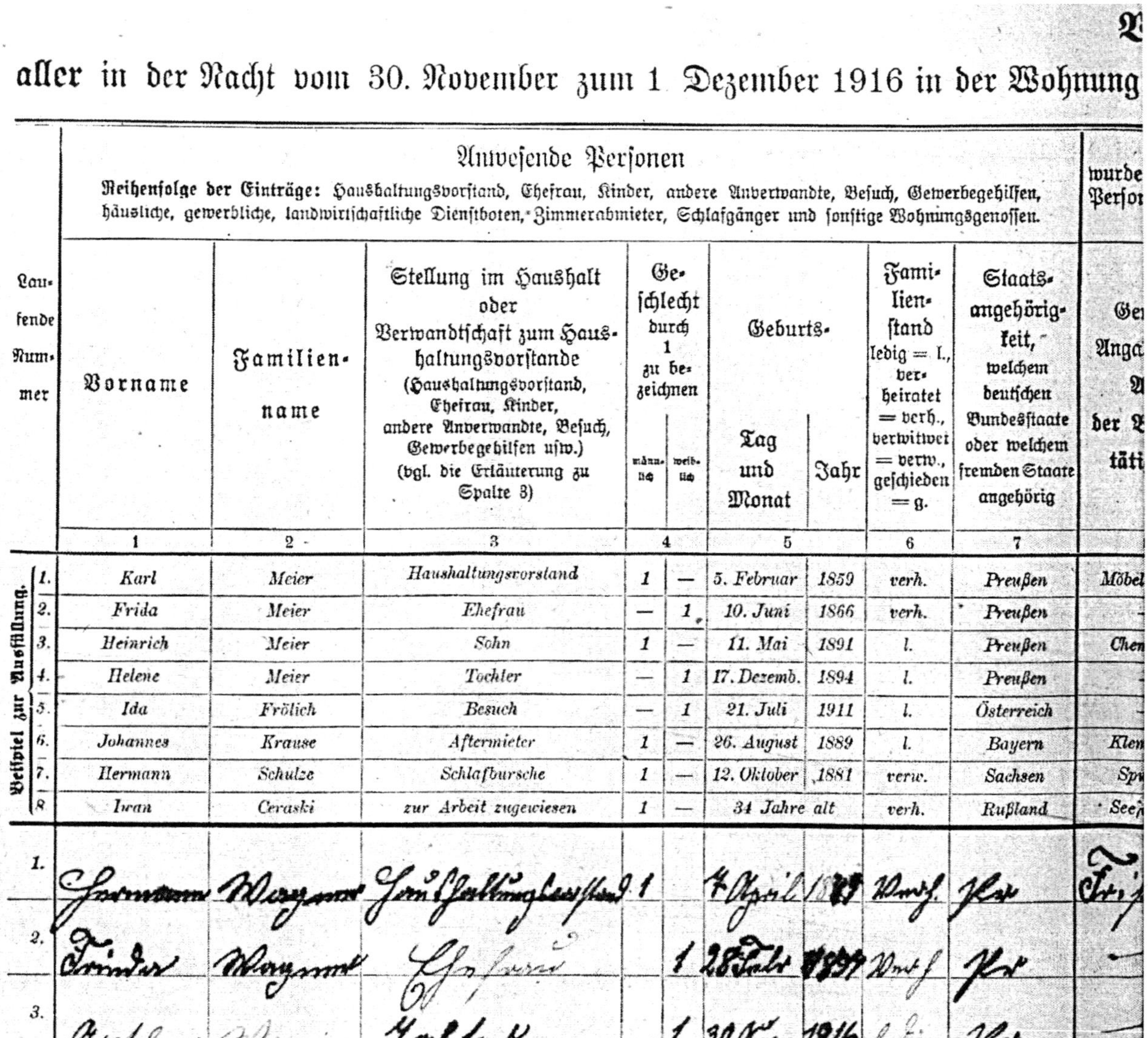

aller in der Nacht vom 30. November zum 1. Dezember 1916 in der Wohnung

Anwesende Personen

Reihenfolge der Einträge: Haushaltungsvorstand, Ehefrau, Kinder, andere Anverwandte, Besuch, Gewerbegehilfen, häusliche, gewerbliche, landwirtschaftliche Dienstboten, Zimmerabmieter, Schlafgänger und sonstige Wohnungsgenossen.

Laufende Nummer	Vorname	Familienname	Stellung im Haushalt oder Verwandtschaft zum Haushaltungsvorstande (Haushaltungsvorstand, Ehefrau, Kinder, andere Anverwandte, Besuch, Gewerbegehilfen usw.) (vgl. die Erläuterung zu Spalte 3)	Geschlecht durch 1 zu bezeichnen: männlich	weiblich	Geburts- Tag und Monat	Jahr	Familienstand ledig = l., verheiratet = verh., verwitwet = verw., geschieden = g.	Staatsangehörigkeit, welchem deutschen Bundesstaate oder welchem fremden Staate angehörig	wurde Person Ge… Anga… der … täti…
	1	2	3	4		5		6	7	
Beispiel zur Ausfüllung. 1.	Karl	Meier	Haushaltungsvorstand	1	—	5. Februar	1859	verh.	Preußen	Möbel
2.	Frida	Meier	Ehefrau	—	1	10. Juni	1866	verh.	Preußen	–
3.	Heinrich	Meier	Sohn	1	—	11. Mai	1891	l.	Preußen	Chem
4.	Helene	Meier	Tochter	—	1	17. Dezemb.	1894	l.	Preußen	–
5.	Ida	Frölich	Besuch	—	1	21. Juli	1911	l.	Österreich	–
6.	Johannes	Krause	Aftermieter	1	—	26. August	1889	l.	Bayern	Klem
7.	Hermann	Schulze	Schlafbursche	1	—	12. Oktober	1881	verw.	Sachsen	Spi
8.	Iwan	Ceraski	zur Arbeit zugewiesen	1	—	34 Jahre alt		verh.	Rußland	Seef
1.	Hermann	Wagner	Haushaltungsvorstand	1		4 April	18[illegible]	verh.	Pr.	[illegible]
2.	Frieda	Wagner	Ehefrau		1	28 Juli	18[illegible]	verh.	Pr.	–
3.	[illegible]	[illegible]	Tochter		1	30 Aug	1916	ledig	Pr.	

Figure 18. The left-hand page of the 1916 census used in Sachsen-Provinz

...cher Beruf ...palte 1 u. 2 eingetragenen ...Kriege (31. Juli 1914) ...sgeübt?		Welches ist ihre **gegenwärtige** Berufstätigkeit?			Für alle reichsdeutschen männlichen Personen, die **vor dem 1. Dezember 1899** geboren sind, ist das gegenwärtige Militärverhältnis anzugeben, und zwar:		Für reichs-deutsche Kriegs-be-schädigte ist anzu-geben, ob sie Militär-pension oder Militär-rente aus Anlaß des gegen-wärtigen Krieges erhalten (ja oder nein)	Falls sich unter den in Spalte 1 u. 2 eingetragenen Personen Kriegs-gefangene (Militär- oder Zivil-gefangene) befinden, sind sie in dieser Spalte mit „Milgef." oder mit „Zivgef." zu bezeichnen
...tellung ...Beruf, ...	Art des Betriebs, in welchem der Beruf aus-geübt wurde. (Für Beamte und Militärpersonen anzugeben Behörde, Truppenteil usw.)	Genaue Angabe der Art der Berufs-tätigkeit	Stellung im Beruf, ob: selbständig, Inhaber, Meister, Haus-gewerbetreibender, Angestellter, Werkmeister, Geselle, Lehrling, Arbeiter, Heim-arbeiter usw (Für Beamte und Militärpersonen Titel, Dienstgrad usw.)	Art des Betriebs, in welchem der Beruf ausgeübt wird. (Für Beamte und Militärpersonen anzugeben Behörde, Truppenteil usw.) Wenn zur Zeit ohne Erwerbstätigkeit, ist hier einzutragen „außer Stellung", „erwerbslos", „arbeitslos" o. dgl.	für die im aktiven Dienst stehenden, ob: kv. (kriegsverwendungs-fähig). gv. (garnison-verwendungsfähig). zgv. (zeitig garnison-verwendungsfähig). av. (arbeitsverwendungs-fähig). zav. (zeitig arbeits-verwendungsfähig). Falls auf Heimats- oder Arbeitsurlaub Befindliche darunter sind, ist dies in dieser Spalte anzugeben	für die nicht im aktiven Dienste stehenden, ob: kv. (kriegsverwendungs-fähig). gv. (garnison-verwendungstätig). zgv. (zeitig garnison-verwendungstätig). av. (arbeits-verwendungstätig). zav. (zeitig arbeits-verwendungstätig). d.u. (dauernd untauglich). z.u. (zeitig untauglich). n.g. (noch nicht aus-gemustert). n.l. (nicht mehr land-sturmpflichtig). Falls aus dem Heeres-dienst zur Arbeit Ent-lassene (Reklamierte) darunter sind, ist dies in dieser Spalte anzugeben		
9	10	11	12	13	14	15	16	17
...nhaber	Möbelfabrik	Modelltischler	Werkmeister	Kraftwagenfabrik		n. l.	—	
—	—	—	—	—	—	—	—	
...gestellter	Farbenfabrik	Soldat	Vizewachtmeister	27. Feld-Art.-Reg.	kv.Heimatsurlaub		—	
		Mäntelnäherin	Heimarbeiterin	für das Kriegsbekleidungsamt	—	—	—	
...Geselle	städt. Elektrizitätswerk	—	—	—	—	d. u.	ja	
...Arbeiter	Strumpfwaren-fabrik	Dreher	Arbeiter	Munitionsfabrik	—	zgv., reklamiert	—	
		Landarbeiter			—	—	—	Milgef.
(signature)	*(signature)*	*(signature)*	*(signature)*		—	*(signature)*	—	

Figure 19. The right-hand page of the 1916 census used in Sachsen-Provinz

Notes

[1] For impressive details regarding the additional census data collected by states, see "Die Volkszahl der Deutschen Staaten nach den Zählungen seit 1816," 6, 7.

[2] Ernst Engel, "Die Volkszählung im Deutschen Reiche am 1. Dezember [1871] und ihre wünschenwerthe Unterstützung durch die Presse und die Kanzel."

[3] Engel, "Die Volkszählung im Deutschen Reiche."

[4] Engel, "Die Volkszählung im Deutschen Reiche."

[5] Engel, "Die Volkszählung im Deutschen Reiche."

[6] In 1875, Engel's name appeared on a similar appeal with the appearance of the new census instructions and supporting literature.

[7] Michel, Harald. "Volkszählungen in Deutschland: Die Erfassung des Bevölkerungsstandes von 1816 bis 1933." *Jahrbuch für Wirtschaftsgeschichte* 1985/II. Berlin: DeGruyter, 89.

4 Census Records in the German States from 1816 to 1864

As described above, the history of census records in the German states from the Congress in Vienna in 1815 to the first national census campaign in 1867 is quite complex. The individual needs of the states were not always addressed in the requirements of organizations to which they belonged. In an attempt to show specific instructions and census forms for each of the thirty-eight states that joined together to establish the German Empire in 1871, an extensive campaign was conducted that resulted in more than one thousand letters and emails, complemented by dozens of visits by the author in city, county, and state archives in Germany. Documents were sought in connection with each of the census years identified by recent books on the topic. In some states, the desired documents were found for nearly every census year from 1816 through 1864, but in others states few if any documents could be found. The collection would be more extensive if every city archivist could be contacted and would respond, but that is not a reasonable expectation.[1]

Each state chapter in this book has six main components: location, census history, census instructions by year, census content by year, suggestions on how to gain access to surviving census records, and representative census images. In some cases, the boundaries of the state during the nineteenth century are quite different from today and comments are provided regarding the ramifications for research in those areas.

In studying the descriptions of census records presented below for each of the states (before the first "national" census campaign that was carried out in 1867) as well as in the tables, researchers should keep the following in mind:

1. the head of household was not always the owner of the dwelling,
2. the head of household might have been an unmarried person living independently,
3. the age used in all records found in this study to distinguish an adult was fourteen years (the age at which public schooling ended, formal apprenticeship or employment began, and the child was confirmed in church—if Christian),
4. the term *Bedienstete*, though usually referring to male servants, could refer to both male and female servants and laborers,
5. pre-printed pages featured either the German *Fraktur* alphabet or the modern Antigua font.

Instructions were issued every census year for every state, but many of those have yet to be located; many indicate simply that the procedures used in the previous census year be repeated. Specific instructions will not be mentioned in provincial chapters unless they differ from previous years. In the tables, the symbol X indicates that the information was required.

The states are presented in this book in alphabetical order by their German names, with English equivalents in brackets.

Many census forms have been found as attachments to the instructions, suggesting to provincial officials how the forms could be printed or lithographed locally or ordered from the provincial capital to fulfill local enumeration needs.

No attempt has been made in this book to collect or represent the numbers of inhabitants counted anywhere at any time. Those numbers are of far less importance to family historians and genealogists than the names of inhabitants, their biographical data, or their location when the record was compiled.[2] On the other hand, most if not all of the statistics collected from the pages on which names were recorded found their way into official publications. That fact emphasizes the value of the census campaigns to the respective governments.

The initial goal for this book was the location and procurement of a typical census page for each state in each enumeration year, but it soon became clear that such an ambitious goal could not be reached given the temporal restrictions of this study. Thousands of pages were indeed found, but in some cases it was determined that more than one style of enumeration page was used in the same province the same year. Thus it is possible that the only image found for a given year is one used by the minority of towns or enumerators in that province; nevertheless, the content of each page should be very similar each year.

The quality of the images shown in this book is not always excellent. Researchers who have worked with microfilms or digitized copies of handwritten documents from nineteenth-century Germany will not be surprised that some documents are too dark, too light, out of focus, or suffer from the fact that the original page has or had flaws.

Many images chosen for display have been cropped for purposes of economy. For example, there is no particular reason to show all twenty-fives names on a page when the first ten will serve as samples of format and content. In the case of support literature, it was considered sufficient to show the introduction rather than all pages of a given document.

The use of German place names can cause serious confusion among family history researchers. It was decided for this book that the acquaintance with the German names is important product knowledge, thus the heading for a chapter will feature the German name first (for example):

Braunschweig [Brunswick]

and all subsequent references to that duchy will appear as Braunschweig (no italics). Likewise, if that duchy is mentioned in other chapters, only the German name will be used. In cases where the spelling is the same in both languages (such as Brandenburg or Posen), there should be no confusion.

See Appendix D for a list of all German state names in both languages.

Notes

1 Nearly one-half of the German archivists who responded indicated that they had some census records in their collections.

2 See Kraus for excellent collections of population numbers for all states and all years.

5 Anhalt

I. Location

The duchy of Anhalt in central Germany was surrounded by the Prussian provinces of Sachsen, Hannover, and Brandenburg. The entire territory is part of the modern German state of Sachsen-Anhalt. The historic capital was Dessau.

II. Census Enumerations in Anhalt

Census data were collected in Anhalt only for local purposes in 1818, 1827, 1830, and 1833. The duchy joined the *Zollverein* in 1834 and a census was conducted there every three years from 1834 through 1864.[1] In 1867, Anhalt took part in what was essentially the first national German census. Under the German Empire, census enumerations took place in Anhalt in 1871, every five years from 1875 to 1910, and finally in 1916.[2]

III. Specific Instructions to Town Officials and Enumerators

Of all of the regulations for census enumerations in Anhalt, the following are considered to be particularly important:

> 1834: count foreigners; don't count persons living there temporarily or active military personnel

> 1837: conduct the census on December 20; send both the lists and the report to the state government within two weeks

> 1846: observe new rules: write the name of every individual by going house to house; do not use lists previously compiled for other purposes; the list may be filled out by the head of household; include absent persons

and those living here for a short time but do not include travelers in inns or family guests

> 1849: organize residents in seven classes (according to real estate owned) as well as into occupation categories

IV. Content of Census Records in Anhalt from 1818 to 1864

	1818	1827	1830	1833	1834	1837	1840	1843	1846	1849	1852	1855	1858	1861	1864
Missing or incomplete image					X				X					X	X
Only head of household is named	X	X	X	X	X	X	X	X							
Total persons in household	X	X	X	X	X	X	X	X	X	X	X	X	X		
Name of owner of dwelling	X	X													
Total persons in dwelling	X														
Every person is named									X	X	X	X	X		
Men	X	X	X	X	X	X	X	X							
Women	X	X	X	X	X	X	X	X							
Children			X	X											
Children under 14		X			X		X								
Servants		X	X	X											
Journeymen			X	X											
Apprentices			X	X											
Widows			X												
Parent(s)-in-law					X										
Other relatives					X										
Single males					X										
Single females					X										
Civilians					X	X	X	X							
Military personnel					X	X	X	X							
Males under 14						X		X							
Females under 14						X		X							
Occupations										X	X	X	X	X	
Age										X	X	X	X		
Religion										X	X	X	X		
Handwritten document	X	X	X	X	X	X	X	X	X						
Printed column headings										X	X	X	X		

V. Accessibility of Census Records in Anhalt

The principal source of existing census records is the Landesarchiv Sachsen-Anhalt located at Heidestraße 21 in Dessau-Roßlau (postal code 06842). The website is www.landesarchiv.sachsen-anhalt.de. Researchers may direct inquiries to the archive of any city or town [Stadtarchiv] in historic Anhalt. (See Appendix A for suggestions on how to write the inquiry.) Census records of several Anhalt towns have been microfilmed by the Family History Library and can be located there via a catalog search under the name of the town. As of this writing, no digital images of census records in this duchy are known to be accessible on the Internet.

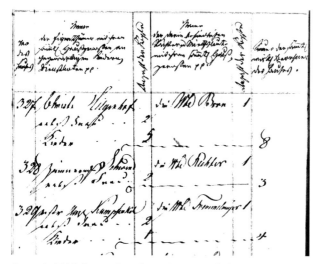

Figure 1. 1818 Census Page from Coswig, Anhalt

Column headings: consecutive number of the house; name of the owner with his family members and children, servants, etc.; total number of those residents; names of lessees or renters and their households; total number of those persons; total number of residents in the dwelling [Stadtarchiv Coswig]

Nro			
194.	Richter		
	Stage		
	Fiering		
	Rickman Wilh:		
195.	Wendler		
	Daute		
	Kaufmann		
	Winklers		a.
196.	Machetanz		
	Zabel		
	Kramer		
	Wolf		
197.	Rosenthal		

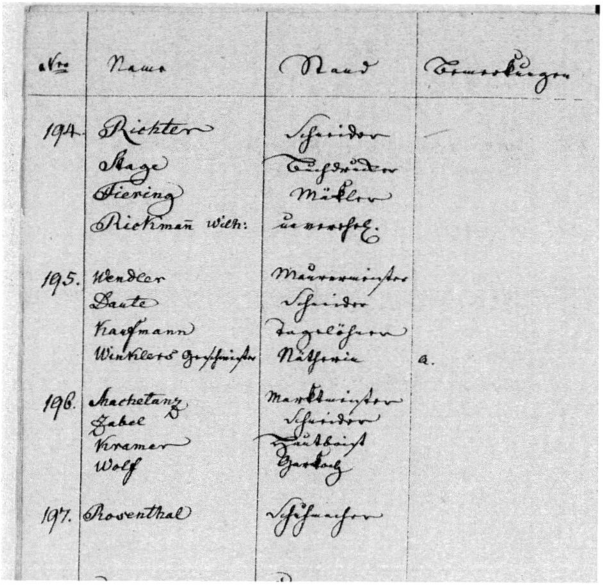

Figure 2. 1834 Census Page from Köthen, Anhalt

Column headings: consecutive number of houses; name; status; comments [Stadtarchiv Köthen]

No. des Hauses.	Vor- u. Familien-Namen der sämmtlichen Bewohner eines jeden Hauses oder jeder Besitzung. (Unter fortlaufender Nummer anzugeben.)	Stand und Gewerbe.	Lebensjahr, worin jeder Einzelne sich befindet.	Religion.	Zahl der Bewohner eines jeden Hauses.	Bemerkungen.
20						
21.						

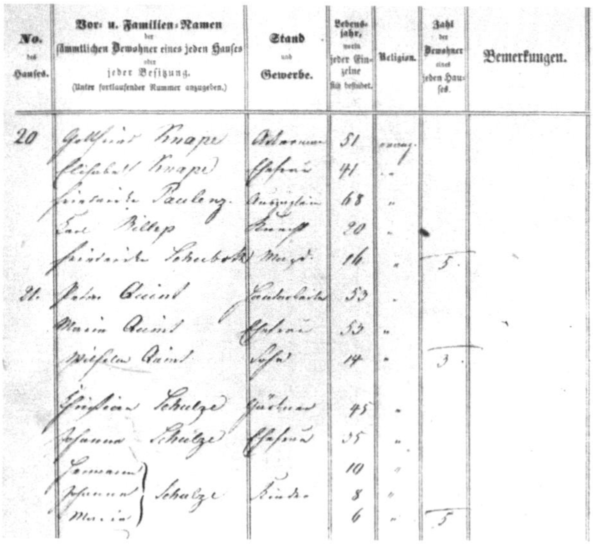

Figure 3. 1855 Census Page from Coswig, Anhalt

Column headings: consecutive number of the house; first and last names of all persons residing in each house or each apartment; status or occupation; age in years; religion; total number of residents in each house; comments [Stadtarchiv Coswig]

Bezeichnung der Gebäude: Angabe der Lage nach Straße etc.	Haus-№ bezw. andere Bezeichnung der Baulichkeit	Namen der Haushaltungsvorstände, für welche die Zählbriefe abgegeben wurden	an oder	Laufende № der Zählbriefe	In der Haushaltung wohnhaft und anwesend	nicht wohnhaft, aber in derselben vorübergehend anwesend	wohnhaft, aber aus derselben vorübergehend abwesend	Bemerkungen.
1	2	3		4	5 6	7 8	9 10	

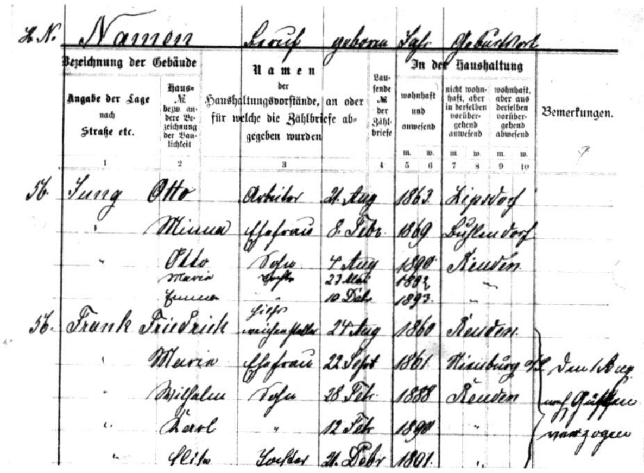

Figure 4. 1890 Census Page from Reuden, Anhalt

Column headings (handwritten titles replace printed titles): name of each resident; status or occupation; birth date; birth place; comments; dwelling [Kreisarchiv Zerbst; FHL microfilm 1569835]

Notes

[1] Beginning in 1841, annual population figures were calculated in non-census years using this formula: the population count from the previous year plus the number of children born, minus the number of persons who died. The information was usually provided by the keepers of church records. Antje Kraus, *Quellen zur Bevölkerungsstatistik Deutschlands 1815–1871*, Band 1 (Boppard, Germany: 1980), 272.

[2] Kraus, *Quellen,* 19, 271–276.

6 Baden

I. Location

The grand duchy of Baden in southwestern Germany was bordered on the west across the Rhine by the French (and later German) province of Elsaß-Lothringen, on the north by the grand duchy of Hessen, on the east by the kingdom of Württemberg, and on the south by Switzerland. The capital city was Karlsruhe.

II. Census Enumerations in Baden

The first known census campaigns in Baden after the Napoleonic wars occurred annually from 1816 until 1822; they were head counts only.[1] The first census involving the names of heads of households was apparently done in 1823 and repeated almost annually through 1830. A law enacted in 1832 required enumerations in 1833, 1836, 1839, and 1845, but another law regulating grand ducal customs operations required additional enumerations in 1834, 1837, 1840, and 1843.

Baden remained aloof of the customs unions forming elsewhere among the German states in order to more fully enjoy the advantages of dealing with France, Switzerland, and the Rhine River traffic. The government of the grand duchy continued to pursue its own census data collection every three years from 1846 to 1864. In 1867, the population of Baden was counted as part of a campaign carried out all over the German Confederation and among *Zollverein* states. Under the German Empire, enumerations were done in 1871, every five years from 1875 to 1910, and finally in 1916.

III. Specific Instructions to Town Officials and Enumerators

The following regulations governed the conduct of census enumerations in Baden:

1833: local government officials are to carry out the work; begin in October; report results to the county office

1846: each enumerator is to sign the paper indicating that the data is complete and correct; the results will affect the distribution of customs duties

1852: pay close attention to the numbers of emigrants and immigrants since the last census; enter in columns 12, 13, and 14 the number of persons born, married, and died since the census of 1849; (other instructions are given for several of the 21 total categories)

1864: if local authorities need assistance in carrying out the census, they should appoint only persons who know the local populace well, such as pastors, teachers, medical doctors, et al.; an agent should not be assigned so many dwellings that he cannot visit them all on December 3; forms are to be distributed to heads of households on November 30 or December 1; adults living alone and supporting themselves are to be counted as heads of households; military personnel will be counted by military authorities; should anyone object to the census based on a belief that his taxes will be affected by the information collected, the agent is to assure him that such is not the case; this census must produce the best possible results so that the grand duchy of Baden does not lag behind other German states in this regard

IV. Content of Census Records in Baden from 1823 to 1864

	1823	1825	1828	1831	1834	1837	1840	1843	1846	1849	1852	1855	1858	1861	1864
No images available		X		X			X	X							
Name of head of household	X		X						X	X	X	X	X	X	
Lutheran (by gender)	X		X		X	X									
Catholic (by gender)	X		X		X	X									
Reformed (by gender)	X		X												
Mennonite (by gender)	X		X		X	X									
Jewish (by gender)	X		X		X	X									
Total males	X		X												
Total females	X		X												
Total residents	X		X		X	X			X	X	X	X	X	X	
Name of every person					X	X									X
Local employees (by gender)					X	X			X	X	X	X	X	X	
Foreign employees (by gender)					X	X			X	X	X	X	X	X	
Religion									X	X	X	X	X	X	X
Persons over 14 years									X	X	X	X	X	X	
Persons under 14 years									X	X	X	X	X	X	
Gender									X	X	X	X	X	X	X
Marital status															X
Year of birth															X
Occupation															X
Citizenship															X
Birthplace															X
Disabilities															X
Local residents (by gender)															X
Guests (by gender)															X
Locals away from home															X
Handwritten	X		X		X	X			X	X	X	X	X		
Pre-printed pages														X	X

V. Accessibility of Census Records in Baden

As of this writing, no census records of Baden communities are found on microfilm in the Family History Library, nor can they be found as digital images in websites, but researchers should look for such media now and then. The best method is still an inquiry to the archive of a town or a county where the person under investigation is believed to have lived. (See Appendix A for suggestions for writing such an inquiry.)

VI. Selected Images of Baden Census Records

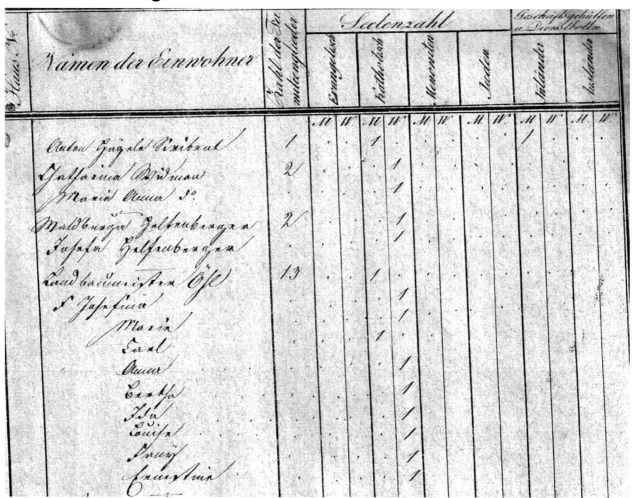

Figure 1. 1833 Census Page from Konstanz, Baden

Column headings: dwelling number; name of each resident; number of persons in each family; Lutheran males; Lutheran females; Catholic males; Catholic females; Mennonite males; Mennonite females; Jewish males; Jewish females; local male laborers; local female laborers; foreign male laborers; foreign female laborers [Stadtarchiv Konstanz S II 7804]

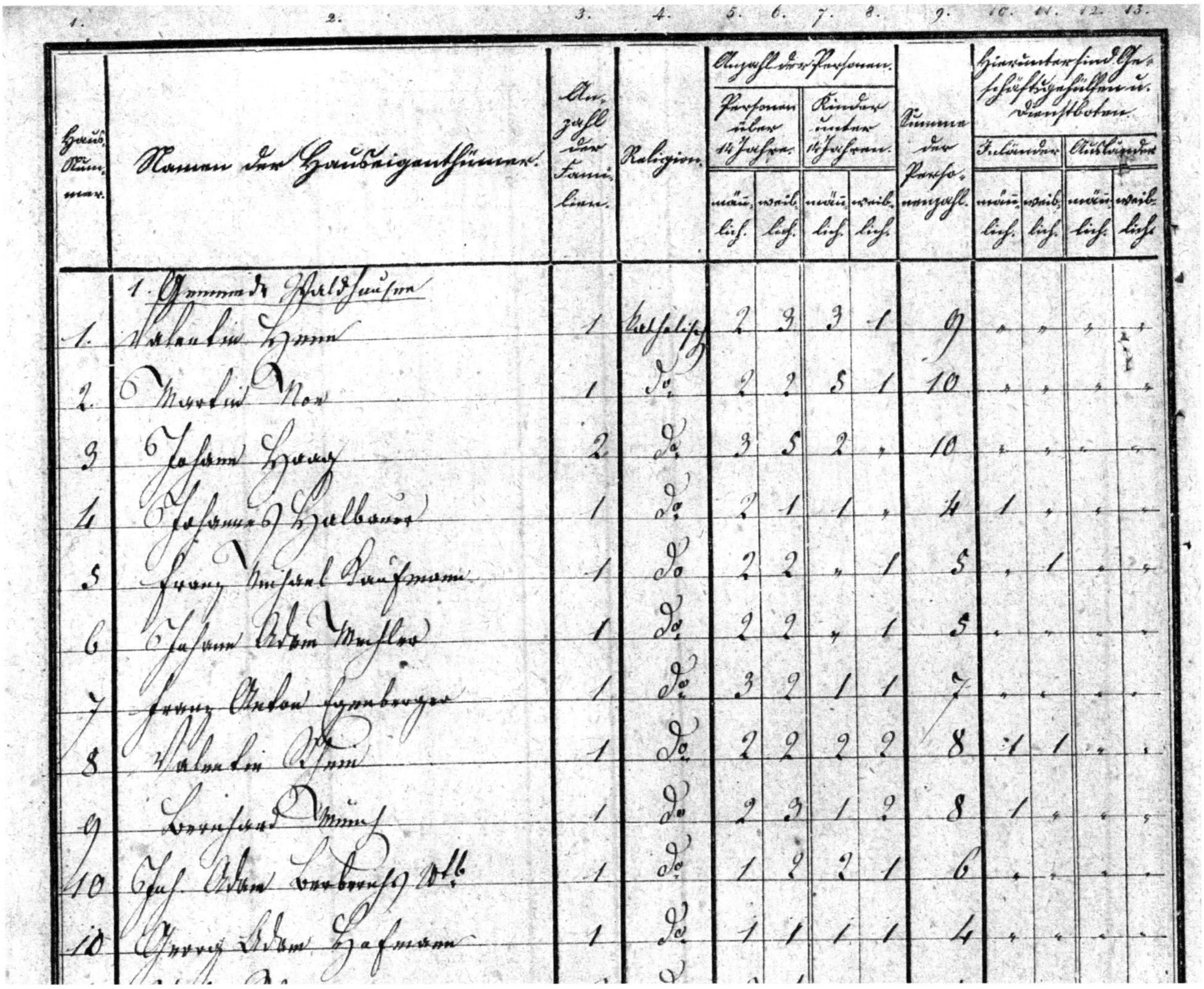

1.	2.	3.	4.	5.	6.	7.	8.	9.	10.	11.	12.	13.

Haus Num. mer.	Namen der Hauseigenthümer.	Anzahl der Familien.	Religion.	Anzahl der Personen				Summe der Personen zugleich	Hierunter sind beschäftigte u. Dienstboten			
				Personen über 14 Jahren		Kinder unter 14 Jahren			Inländer		Ausländer	
				männlich	weiblich	männlich	weiblich		männlich	weiblich	männlich	weiblich
	1. Gemeinde Waldhausen											
1.	Valentin Zimm	1	katholisch	2	3	3	1	9	,	,	,	,
2.	Martin Nox	1	do.	2	2	5	1	10	,	,	,	,
3.	Johann Heinz	2	do.	3	5	2	,	10	,	,	,	,
4.	Johannes Halbans	1	do.	2	1	1	,	4	1	,	,	,
5.	Franz Michael Kaufmann	1	do.	2	2	,	1	5	,	1	,	,
6.	Johann Adam Müller	1	do.	2	2	,	1	5	,	,	,	,
7.	Franz Anton Leinberger	1	do.	3	2	1	1	7	,	,	,	,
8.	Valentin Zimm	1	do.	2	2	2	2	8	1	1	,	,
9.	Leonhard Zimm	1	do.	2	3	1	2	8	1	,	,	,
10.	Joh. Adam Lambrecht ?	1	do.	1	2	2	1	6	,	,	,	,
10.	Franz Adam Lachmann	1	do.	1	1	1	1	4	,	,	,	,
			do.									

Figure 2. 1846 Census Page from Waldhausen, Baden

Column headings: house number; full name of resident; number of families; religion; males over 14; females over 14; males under 14; females under 14; total residents; local male employees; local female employees; foreign male employees; foreign female employees [Stadtarchiv Buchen]

Lfd.Nr.	Vergl. Anleitung 8. **Namen** aller zur Haushaltung gehörenden, auch der kürzer oder länger abwesenden, sowie der in der Wohnung der Haushaltung sich aufhaltenden Personen, und zwar in folgender Reihenfolge: 1. Haushaltungsvorstand, Familienhaupt; — 2. die Frau; — 3. die Kinder, sofern sie nicht eine selbstständige Haushaltung gegründet haben; — 4. Verwandte, Verschwägerte, Pflegekinder und sonstige, in die Familie aufgenommene Personen; — 5. die Dienstboten und 6. die Geschäfts- und Gewerbsgehilfen (Verwalter, Commis, Aufseher, Gesellen, Lehrlinge 2c.), welche in der Haushaltung Kost und Wohnung oder Wohnung allein haben; — 7. gegen Vergütung in Kost und Wohnung Genommene; — 8. Personen, welche von dem Haushaltungsvorstande in dessen Wohnung ein oder mehrere einzelne Zimmer oder eine Schlafstelle in Miethe genommen haben; — 9. Gäste und sonst vorübergehend Anwesende.	Ob abwesend? durch Eintragung einer 1 zu bezeichnen.	**Religion.** Durch Anfangsbuchstaben oder Anfangssilbe zu bezeichnen: **E.**vangelisch (lutherisch, reformirt unirt) **K.**atholisch, **M.**ennonitisch, **D.**eutsch-katholisch, **Gr.**iechisch, **Bapt.**istisch 2c. **J.**sraelitisch.		**Geburts= jahr.**	**Familien- stand.** Durch Anfangsbuchstaben zu bezeichnen: **L.**edig, **V.**erheira-thet, **W.**ittwe(r) **G.**eschieden.	**Stand und Beruf.** 1. Angabe des Nahrungs- und Erwerbszweiges, der Berufsbeschäftigung, des Titels 2c. Hat eine Person mehrere Nahrungszweige 2c., so ist der hauptsächlichste voranzustellen (z. B. Rentner, Gutsbesitzer und Major a. D. 2c.). 2. Wo aus dieser Angabe nicht hervorgeht, ob der Beruf, das Gewerbe 2c., selbstständig (auf eigene Rechnung) oder in einem Dienst- und Abhängigkeitsverhältnisse geübt wird, ist dies durch einen Zusatz aufzuklären (ob Gut- oder Hofbesitzer, Pächter, Prinzipal, Meister; ob ... Geschäfts- oder Werkführer, Commis, Geselle, Lehrling, Fabrikarbeiter, Ackerknecht 2c., in Dienst, in Condition), z. B. Landwirth, Pächter; Schlosser, Meister; Schreiner, Lehrling; Gärtner, in Diensten. 3. Bei Frauen und Mädchen, welche eine besondere Erwerbsthätigkeit üben, ist diese anzugeben (Lehrerin, Näherin, Fabrikarbeiterin 2c.).
	Vorname. / **Familienname.**		**Männ-lich.**	**Weib-lich.**			
	1.	2.	3.		4.	5.	6.
1	Wilhelm Sterk		K		1834	V	Fuhrgrüßfabrikant
2	Marie Sterk geb. Schütted			K	1839	V	
3	Josepha Wensler geb. Oberreg			K	1809	W	Rent.
4	Louise Göggel			K	1848	L	Ladnyimgsfr
5	Mathilde Graus			K	1842	L	Köchin
6	Anton Braun		K		1825	L	Knecht
7	Simphorean Lehman		K		1837	L	Müllemorfer
8	Theodor Heitz		E		1835	L	Färbermeister
9							

Figure 3. 1864 Census Page from Konstanz, Baden (left-hand page)

Column headings: 1 given name and surname; 2 whether present; 3 religion and gender; 4 year of birth; 5 marital status; 6 occupation or employment [Stadtarchiv Konstanz S II 8350]

Heimath.	Geburtsort oder =land.	Bemerkungen. Vergl. Anleitung 9.	Nach dem 3. Dezbr. 1850 geboren (d. h. unter 14 Jahren), durch 1 zu bezeichnen.	Durch die Zählungsbeamten auszufüllen durch eine 1 in der betr. Spalte.							Ord. Nr.
1. Für die dem Groß-herzogthum Angehöri-gen ist **Baden** zu schrei-ben. 2. Für Ausländer ist das **Land**, dem sie an-gehören, zu schreiben.	1. Für die am Orte der Zählung Gebore-nen ist **hier** zu schrei-ben. 2. Für die an einem andern Orte des Groß-herzogthums Gebore-nen ist **Baden** zu schrei-ben. 3. Für die im Aus-lande Geborenen ist das **Land** der Geburt zu schreiben.	In dieser Spalte ist anzugeben: 1. ob eine Person sich als **Gast** in der Fa-milie aufhält oder im Gasthause **eingekehrt** ist. Ist sie ein wandernder Geselle oder Gewerbs-gehilfe, so ist dies ausdrücklich anzuführen; 2. für die **Abwesenden** a. das **Land** des gegenwärtigen Aufenthalts. Befindet sich der Abwesende im Großherzog-thume, so ist **Baden**, wenn in einer anderen Haushaltung am Zählungsorte selbst (als Dienst-bote, Zögling, Militär, Kranker &c.) **hier** zu schreiben; b. der **Zweck** der Abwesenheit (Reise, Geschäfte, Besuch, Gewerbsbetrieb im Umherzie-hen, Unterricht, Militärdienst, im Krankenhaus, als Geselle, Fabrikarbeiter, Dienstbote, in Con-dition &c.; c. die **Dauer** der bisherigen Abwe-senheit, falls dieselbe mehr als ein Jahr beträgt; 3. ob eine Person **blind** oder **taubstumm** ist, mit Angabe seit welchem Lebensjahr.		**Anwesende.**		**Abwesende.**					
				Anwe-sende mit Aus-schluß der Gäste.	Gäste mit Aus-schluß der wandern-den Gesel-len &c.	auf Reisen mit Ein-schluß zum Gewerbs-betrieb Um-herziehen-ber	sonstig Ab-wesende.				
				Männlich.	Weiblich.	Männlich.	Weiblich.	Männlich.	Weiblich.	Männlich.	Weiblich.	
7.	8.	9.	10.	11.		12.		13.		14.		
Baden	[illegible]			1								1
Baden	hier				1							2
A	his				1							3
[illegible]	[illegible]				1							4
Baden	Baden				1							5
Baden	Baden			1								6
Baden	Baden	[illegible]		1				✗				7
Schweitz	Schweitz			1								8
												9

Figure 4. 1864 Census Page from Konstanz, Baden (right-hand page)

Column headings: 7 citizenship; 8 birthplace (town if local, state if foreign); 9 guests temporarily here; 10 whether born after December 3, 1850; 11 local residents (by gender); 12 temporary guests (by gender); 13 locals away from home (by gender); 14 others away from home (by gender); consecutive number [Stadtarchiv Konstanz S II 8350]

Bezeichnung der Gebäude.		Namen der Haushaltungs-vorstände, an oder für welche die Haushaltungslisten abgegeben wurden	Laufende Nr. der Haushaltungslisten	Zahl der darin eingetragenen anwesenden Personen:			Darunter sind		Bemerkungen.
Nach der Lage: Straße, Platz usw. oder Dorf, Weiler, Zinken, Hof, einzelnes Haus usw.	Haus-Nr.			Männliche	Weibliche	Zus.	aktive Militärpersonen (Sp. 14 der Haushaltungsliste)	Kriegsgefangene (Sp. 18/9 der Haushaltungsliste)	(Hier sind Angaben über ausfallende Haus-Nummern, nicht bewohnte Gebäude oder unbebaute Grundstücke, über Gasthäuser, sowie über die Art der im Zählbezirk vorkommenden Anstalten usw. zu machen.)
1	2	3	4	5	6	7	8	9	10
		Übertrag	17	26	40	66		1	
Altstädtervorstadt	161	Zimmermann J.	18	1	1	2			
"	474	Andreas Schmidle	19	2	2	4			
"	165	Gern ... lt	20	1	1	2			
"	476	Burk Elisab.	21	.	2	2			
"	155	Wittmer Wilh.	22	.	1	1			
"	155	" Ludw.	23	3	2	5			
"	476	Burck Wilh.	24	5	2	7	.		
"	156	Lang Heinrich	25	1	1	2			
"	149	Spinner H.	26	2	3	5			
"	149	Schmidt Dietrich	27	1	1	2			

Figure 5. 1916 Control List from Eppingen, Baden

Column headings: 1 street; 2 house number; 3 name of head of household; 4 consecutive number of household; 5 male residents; 6 female residents; 7 total residents; 8 active military personnel; 9 prisoners of war; 10 comments [Stadtarchiv Eppingen A 2418]

Notes

[1] Antje Kraus, *Quellen zur Bevölkerungsstatistik Deutschlands 1815-1871*, Band 1 (Boppard, Germany: Harald Boldt, 1980), 19, 39-44.

7 Bayern [Bavaria]

I. Location

The kingdom of Bayern in southern Germany was bordered on the west by Württemberg, on the north by the province of Hessen-Nassau, several of the Saxon duchies (Thüringen), and Sachsen (Königreich), and on the east and south by the Austrian Empire. The modern state of Bayern is only slightly smaller in size after the loss of the district of the Palatinate (west of the Rhine River). The capital city is and has long been Munich.

II. Census Enumerations in Bayern

The first known census data were collected in Bayern in 1825. In 1828 Bayern joined with Württemberg in a customs union and census enumerations took place in 1830 and 1833.[1] The kingdom joined the *Zollverein* on March 2, 1833 and a census was conducted there every three years from 1834 through 1864.[2] Bayern joined with all other German states in the census campaign of 1867. Under the German Empire, census enumerations took place in Bayern in 1871, every five years from 1875 to 1910, and finally in 1916.

III. Specific Instructions to Town Officials and Enumerators

From 1810 to 1824, annual census enumerations (head counts only) took place in Bayern; the local police office was responsible for the data collection. By reducing the frequency to every third year as of 1825, the government hoped to simplify the process and simultaneously improve the accuracy of the data.[3] Subsequent instructions were based on the requirements of the customs unions. Here are some of the major changes in directions given for record-keeping over the next four decades:

1828: follow the guidelines of 1808; count home owners, those living in dwellings owned by the community, and those renting; use the form provided; complete the work in the next eight weeks

1830: we don't need to repeat the instructions of 1819, 1825, and 1826; select educated men as enumerators

1832: finish by September 30

1834: we are doing a census as stipulated in the *Zollverein* ruling of March 22, 1833 (Article 22); begin on December 1 and finish in December; we can't skip the 1834 census even though we did one in 1833; study first the errors made in 1833; count active military personnel and foreigners but not visitors; local police offices will direct the campaign

1837: don't count travelers; count locals temporarily absent from their homes; count foreigners who have been here for more than one year; don't count active military personnel and their families and servants

1843: count workers from elsewhere; don't use existing lists of residents, but start from scratch; count foreigners even if they haven't been here for a full year

1846: start on December 3 and finish within three days; members of households may fill out papers; enumerators should check the lists for completeness and correctness; count locals working away from home but not journeymen and apprentices

1849: don't sit at home to fill out forms; go personally from house to house; don't begin before December 3; don't record the names of all persons counted

1852: start on December 6; big cities may take two to three days; check for accuracy if numbers differ greatly from results three years ago; definition of "family" [head of household] can include property owners who are not married; employed servants living in the master's home are not heads of households even if married; you don't have to use the lithographed forms sent you by the county; you may use lined paper

1855: start on December 3

1864: distribute forms to families on December 2; names of all family members are to be recorded; heads of households need not be married; retired persons living with children are not heads of households

IV. Content of Census Records in Bayern from 1818 to 1864

	1818	1819	1825	1828	1830	1833	1834	1837	1840	1843	1846	1849	1852	1855	1858	1861	1864
No image available																	X
Only head of household named	X	X	X	X	X	X	X	X	X	X	X	X	X	X	X	X	
Total persons in household	X	X	X	X	X	X		X	X	X	X	X	X	X	X	X	
Occupations	X	X	X	X	X	X		X	X	X	X	X	X	X	X	X	
Religion	X																X
Property	X	X															
Comments		X				X				X	X	X					
Men			X	X	X		X			X	X	X	X	X	X	X	
Women			X	X	X		X			X	X	X	X	X	X	X	
Males under 14			X	X	X	X	X	X		X	X	X	X	X	X	X	
Females under 14			X	X	X	X	X	X		X	X	X	X	X	X	X	
Servants			X	X	X	X		X									
Journeymen			X	X	X												
Maids			X	X	X	X		X									
Total persons in dwelling			X			X	X	X		X	X	X	X	X	X	X	
Military personnel			X														
Officials, clergy			X		X												
Doing business			X		X												
Catholic			X		X												
Lutheran			X		X												
Reformed			X		X												
Jewish			X		X												
Other			X		X												
Owns the home				X	X			X									
In employer's home				X	X												
Rents home				X	X												
Name of owner of dwelling						X											
Recent arrivals						X											
Birth place								X									
Birth date								X									
Widowed													X				
Name of every person																	X
Status of every person																	X
Various versions				X	X												
Handwritten document	X	X	X	X	X	X	X	X	X	X	X	X	X	X	X		

V. Accessibility of Census Records in Bayern

Due to the extreme size of this kingdom (with some 35,000 towns) there is no one or even principal source of existing census records. A recent inquiry to the *Bayerisches Hauptstaatsarchiv* in Munich elicited this response: "We have nothing but statistics from the census campaigns before 1918."[4] A regional *Staatsarchiv* is found in each of eight major Bayern cities. Staff members in those archives may have little to offer and will likely direct you to study the archive's catalog (which can be done in the Internet). If you know the town or even the county in historic Bayern where the persons in question lived, it is best to contact the archive there. (See Appendix A for instructions on how to write the inquiry.) Keep in mind that the Pfalz [Palatinate] district is now included in the state of Rheinland-Pfalz. Bayern census records in the collection of the Family History Library are quite rare, but a periodic search in that catalog by town is a good tactic and takes little time. Digital copies of Bavarian census records are not yet common, but this condition is expected to improve.

Figure 1. 1830 Census Page from Mindelheim, Bayern

    Column headings [left-hand page only]: house number; first and last name of resident; number of households in the dwelling; total number of civilians (men, women; children by gender; number of servants (men, craftsmen, women); total persons in the household [http://wiki-de.genealogy.net/Mindelheim/Archivalien_des_Stadtarchivs_Mindelheim]

VI. Selected Census Images in Bayern

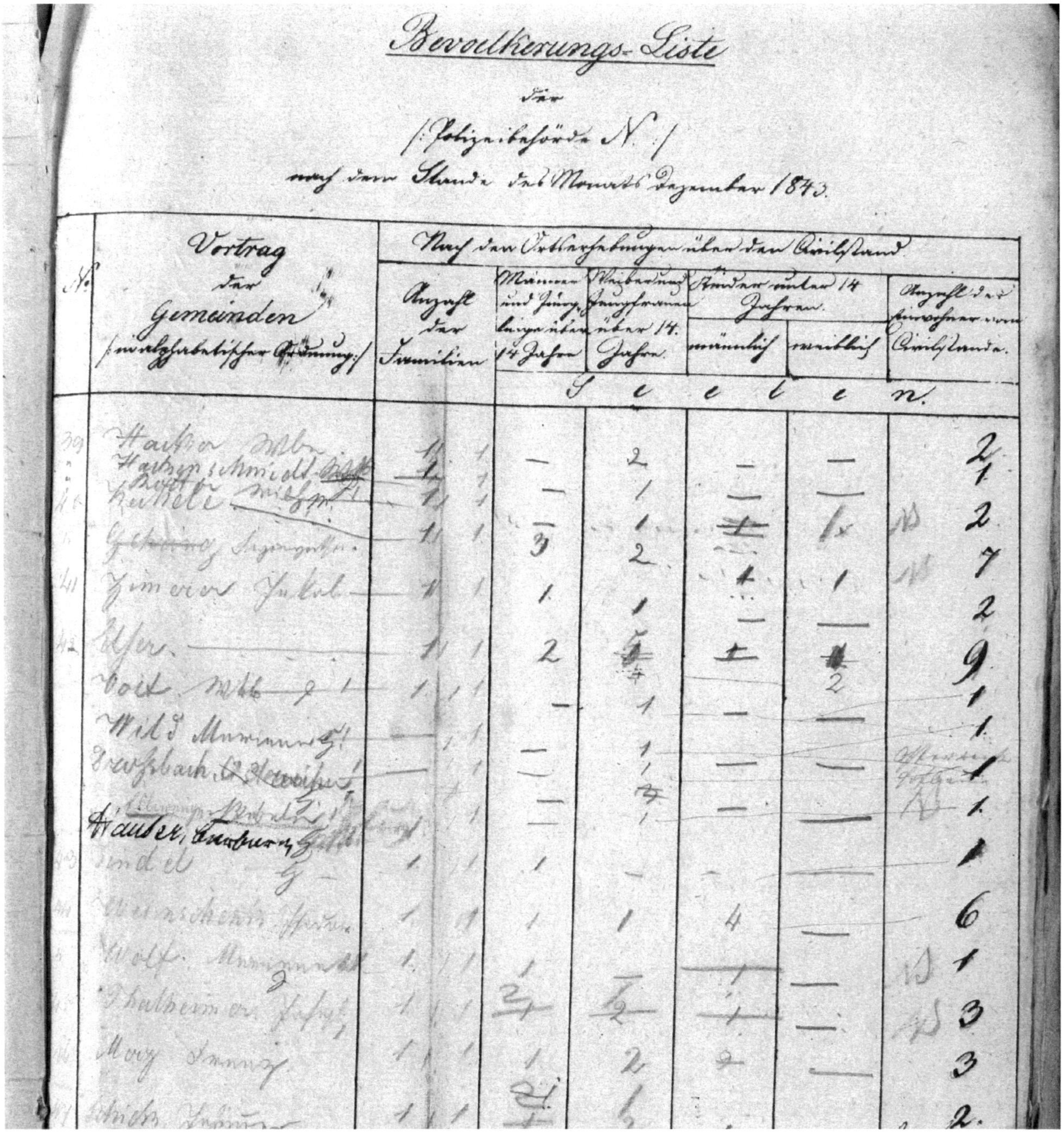
Bevölkerungs-Liste
der
Polizeibehörde N. I
nach dem Stande des Monats Dezember 1843.

Figure 2. 1843 Census Page from Dinkelsbühl, Bayern

Column headings: dwelling owner; number of households; civilian population (males over 14, females over 14; males under 14; females under 14); total civilian residents [https://familysearch.org/search/catalog/1475971?availability=Family%20History%20Library]

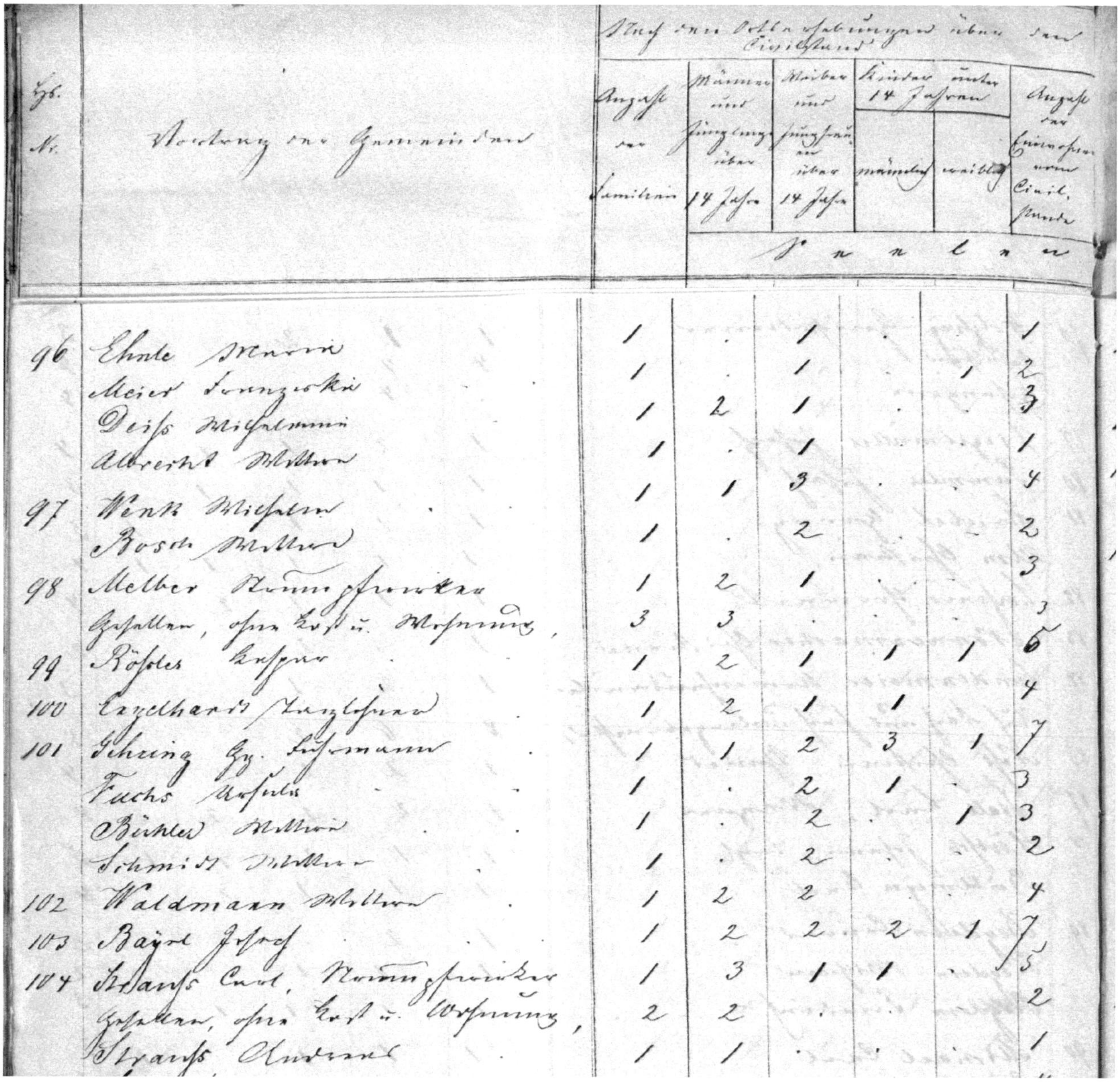

Figure 3. 1861 Census Page from Dinkelsbühl, Bayern

Column headings: dwelling number; head of household; civilian population (males over 14, females over 14; males under 14; females under 14); total civilian residents [https://familysearch.org/search/catalog/1475971?availability=Family%20History%20Library]

Notes

[1] Antje Kraus, *Quellen zur Bevölkerungsstatistik Deutschlands 1815–1871*, Band 1 (Boppard am Rhein, Germany: Harald Boldt, 1980), 21, 63–80.

[2] Otto Klingelhöffer, "Der Zollverein im Jahr 1865" in *Zeitschrift für die gesamte Staatswissenschaft*, v. 19 (1863), 96.

[3] Harald Michel, "Volkszählungen in Deutschland: Die Erfassung des Bevölkerungsstandes von 1816 bis 1933," in *Jahrbuch fürWirtschaftsgeschichte* 1985:II (Bochum, Germany: Ruhr-Universität, 1985), 85.

[4] Annelie Hopfenmüller letter to Roger P. Minert on January 20, 2015.

8 Brandenburg

I. Location

The geographical and political core of Preußen [Prussia], the province of Brandenburg was surrounded on the west by the provinces of Sachsen and Hannover, on the north by Mecklenburg and Pommern, on the east by Westpreußen and Posen, and on the south by Schlesien. The capital was Berlin.

II. Census Enumerations in Brandenburg

As one of the seven eastern provinces of the kingdom of Preußen, Brandenburg was included in a Prussian customs union in 1818. All Prussian provinces were to produce and submit to the statistical bureau in Berlin annual statistical tables from 1817 to 1822. The schedule was then altered to require such data only every three years, but no set of strict standards guided the enumerations. City officials were to carry out the work.[1] Although the campaigns of the 1820s were designed to produce only statistics, the records of several years featured the names of heads of households.

Brandenburg was automatically accepted into the Prusso-Hessian Customs Union that was founded in February 1828. Census enumerations followed triennially and the schedule continued without interruption even after the establishment of the *Zollverein* [Customs Union] on January 1, 1834. Under the strong influence of Preußen, the *Zollverein* required census records every three years for three full decades and the quality of those records steadily improved.

A national census was enumerated in 1867 in conjunction with the North German Confederation. Under the German Empire, enumerations were done in Brandenburg in 1871, every five years from 1875 to 1910, and finally in 1916.[2]

III. Specific Instructions to Town Officials and Enumerators

For many census years (especially under the *Zollverein*), instructions for enumerators in Prussian provinces were repeated in identical text. Instructions for the years 1822 through 1852 have not been identified in Brandenburg locations, but would have been similar if not identical to those provided officials in other provinces of Preußen. Significant new and revised instructions for Brandenburg census campaigns are summarized as follows:

> 1855: do not count active military personnel; if the form is not filled out on December 3, the data should reflect the residents' status as of that date; persons who do not cooperate will be fined

> 1858: local officials are to announce the upcoming census in the newspaper

> 1861: do not count persons in inns or those visiting families; count persons in hospitals and prisons, etc.; for persons living in one location and working in another, count them where they are on the night of December 2-3; for persons owning more than one dwelling, count them where they are on December 2-3

> 1864: do not count persons who have been absent from their home town for more than one year; officials who do not carry out the census according to instructions are to be fined; an enumeration district should not include more than 600 people; non-government persons assigned to assist in the campaign may be paid a maximum of one *Thaler*

IV. Content of Census Records in Brandenburg from 1822 to 1864

	1822	1825	1828	1831	1834	1837	1840	1843	1846	1849	1852	1855	1858	1861	1864
No images available	X	X	X	X				X							
Name of head of household					X	X									
Males under 14					X	X									
Females under 14					X	X									
Males 15–60					X										
Females 15–60					X										
Males over 60					X										
Females over 60					X										
Total residents					X	X	X		X	X	X	X	X	X	X
Males 14–16					X										
Females 14–16					X										
Married males					X	X									
Married females					X	X									
Persons 21–25					X	X									
Persons 26–32					X	X									
Persons 33–39					X	X									
Lutherans					X	X									X
Catholics					X	X									X
Other Christians					X										X
Jewish (citizens?)					X	X	X		X	X	X	X	X	X	X
Persons 0–5 (by gender)						X									
Persons 6–7 (by gender)						X									
Persons 8–14 (by gender)						X									
Persons 15–16 (by gender)						X									
Males 17–20						X									
Males 40–45						X									
Males 46–60						X									
Males over 60						X									
Females 17–45						X									
Females 45–60						X									
Females over 60						X									
Total females over 14						X									
Total males						X									
Total females						X									
Reformed Lutherans						X									
Mennonites						X									
Name of every resident							X		X	X	X	X	X	X	X
Status or occupation							X		X	X	X	X	X	X	X
Age at last birthday							X		X	X	X	X	X	X	
Comments							X		X	X	X	X	X	X	X
Year of birth															X
Greek Orthodox															X
Dissidents															X
Handwritten					X	X									
Pre-printed pages							X	X	X	X	X	X	X	X	X

V. Accessibility of Census Records in Brandenburg

The major regional archives for the former Prussian province of Brandenburg have few documents relating to census enumerations there.[3] Researchers should direct their inquiries to the archives of towns and counties, where excellent census records have been found in a few instances. (See Appendix A for suggestions about communicating with archivists.) For those parts of Brandenburg that are now in Poland, the matter is somewhat more complex but not altogether hopeless; local Polish archives have maintained documents created when the populace consisted only of Germans (pre-1946). Brandenburg census records on microfilm in the Family History Library are rare, but a study of the catalog now and then may turn up new holdings. As of this writing, no Brandenburg census records are known to be available in digital form on the Internet.

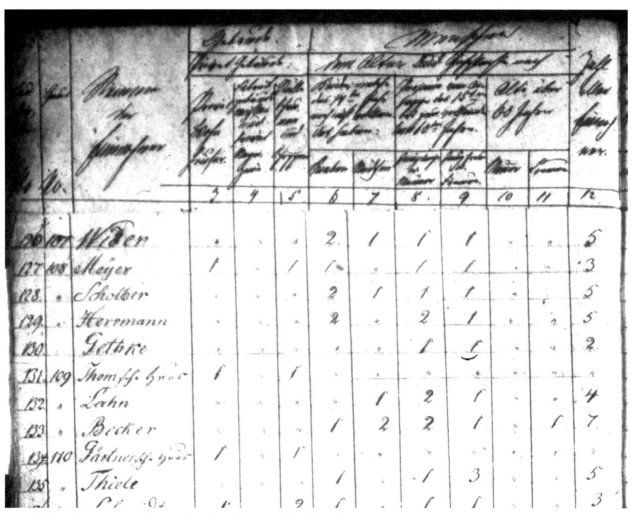

Figure 1. 1834 Census Page for Eberswalde, Brandenburg (left-hand page)

Column headings: name of head of household; private home; factory; barns and stalls; males under 14; females under 14; males 15–60; females 15–60; males over 60; females over 60; total residents [Magistrat Eberswalde]

VI. Selected Images of Brandenburg Census Records

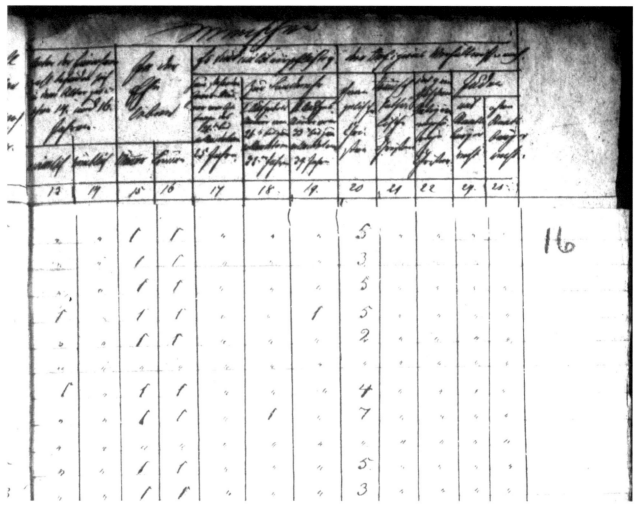

Figure 2. 1834 Census Page for Eberswalde, Brandenburg (right-hand page)

Column headings: males 14–16; females 14–16; married males; married females; males 21–25; males 26–32; males 33–39; Lutherans; Catholics; other Christians; Jewish with citizenship; Jewish without citizenship [Magistrat Eberswalde]

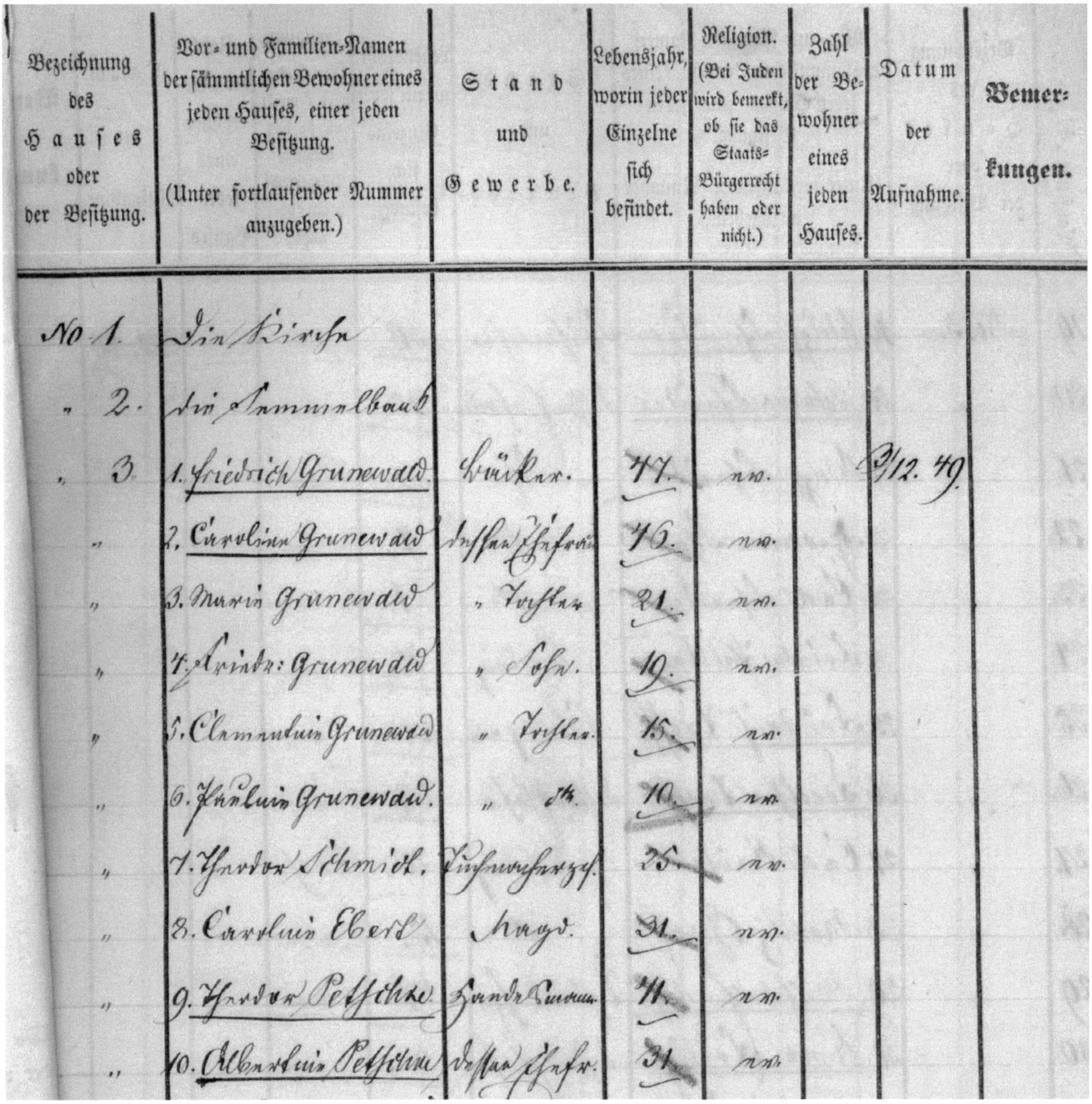

Bezeichnung des Hauses oder der Besitzung.	Vor- und Familien-Namen der sämmtlichen Bewohner eines jeden Hauses, einer jeden Besitzung. (Unter fortlaufender Nummer anzugeben.)	Stand und Gewerbe.	Lebensjahr, worin jeder Einzelne sich befindet.	Religion. (Bei Juden wird bemerkt, ob sie das Staats-Bürgerrecht haben oder nicht.)	Zahl der Be-wohner eines jeden Hauses.	Datum der Aufnahme.	Bemer-kungen.
No 1.	Die Kirche						
„ 2.	die Communalbau?						
„ 3.	1. Friedrich Grunewald	Drücker.	47.	nn.		3/12. 49	
„	2. Caroline Grunewald	dessen Ehefrau	46.	nn.			
„	3. Marie Grunewald	„ Tochter	21.	nn.			
„	4. Heinr: Grunewald	„ Sohn.	19.	nn.			
„	5. Clementine Grunewald	„ Tochter.	15.	nn.			
„	6. Pauline Grunewald.	„ dt.	10.	nn.			
„	7. Theodor Schmidt.	Schuhmacherg.	25.	nn.			
„	8. Caroline Ebert	Magd.	31.	nn.			
„	9. Theodor Petschke	Handr.Linien..	41.	nn.			
„	10. Albertine Petschke	dessen Ehefr.	31.	nn.			

Figure 3. 1849 Census Page for Forst, Brandenburg

Column headings: description of dwelling; first and last name of each resident; status or occupation; age at last birthday; religion (citizenship status if Jewish); total residents; date of entry; comments [Stadtarchiv Forst]

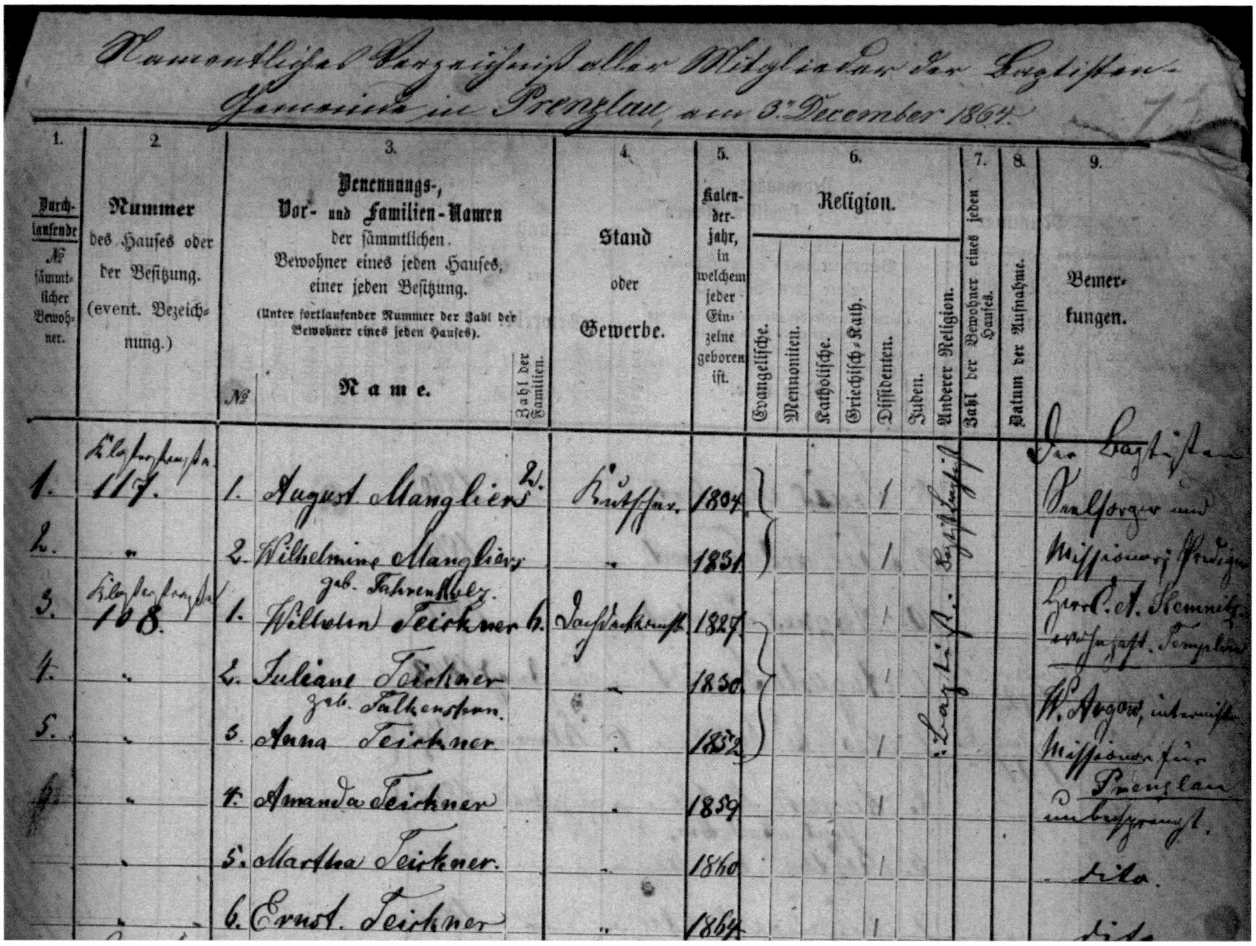

Figure 4. 1864 Census Page for Prenzlau, Brandenburg

Column headings: description of dwelling; first and last name of each person; status or occupation; birth year; Lutherans; Mennonites; Catholics; Greek Orthodox; dissidents; Jewish; other Christians; total residents; date of entry; comments [Stadtarchiv Prenzlau]

Notes

[1] Harald Michel, "Volkszählungen in Deutschland: Die Erfassung des Bevölkerungsstandes von 1816 bis 1933," in *Jahrbuch für Wirtschaftsgeschichte* 1985:II (Bochum, Germany: Ruhr-Universität, 1985), 85.

[2] Antje Kraus, *Quellen zur Bevölkerungsstatistik Deutschlands 1815–1871*, Band 1 (Boppard, Germany: Harald Boldt, 1980), 25–26, 201–206.

[3] Communications with the Landesarchiv Brandenburg in Potsdam and the Geheimes Staatsarchiv Preußischer Kulturbesitz in Berlin confirm this generalization.

9 Braunschweig [Brunswick]

I. Location

The duchy of Braunschweig consisted of several separate territories spread across northern Germany. Those parcels of land were surrounded on the west by the principality of Lippe (Detmold) and three Prussian provinces: Westfalen and Hannover to the north and Sachsen to the east and south. The duchy and its capital city bear the same name.

II. Census Enumerations in Braunschweig

The first known Braunschweig census enumerations that included the names of individuals took place in 1822 and 1828. During that decade, annual population counts were done based on the practice of adding to the total of the previous year the number of children born, then subtracting the number of persons who died.[1] As part of the effort to slow the growth of the Prusso-Hessian Customs Union, Braunschweig joined with several northern and central states to establish the *Mitteldeutscher Handelsverein* [Central German Commerce Union] in 1828. After that organization declined in the early 1830s, Braunschweig joined with Hannover to form the *Steuerverein* [Tax Union] in 1834 and compiled census records as directed.[2]

The *Steuerverein* expanded to include Oldenburg and Schaumburg-Lippe by 1838, but was never strong enough to compete with the *Zollverein* [Customs Union]. The two groups merged in 1854 and Braunschweig cooperated with the new association by conducting census enumerations every three years until 1864.[3]

Another census was enumerated in Braunschweig in 1867 in conjunction with the North German Confederation, which resulted in a census for all of Germany. Under the German Empire, enumerations were done there in 1871, thereafter every five years from 1875 to 1910, and finally in 1916.

III. Specific Instructions to Town Officials and Enumerators

The instructions provided for the census were based on the fact that the duchy had just joined with Hannover in the *Steuerverein* and that the procedures needed to produce a more precise count of the population. Significant changes in regulations over the years are as follows:

1834: the results of the current year need to be compared to the last census and major differences explained; final numbers must be submitted to the county office by January 2, 1835

1836: use the form provided to print enough pages to meet your local needs

1843: it is critical that the new revised forms be used; they must be printed soon so that the census can be conducted this month [December]; do not count military personnel

1849: the target date is December 3 and the campaign must be concluded by December 5

1852: count all foreigners; do not count visitors in inns or local homes; count locals living elsewhere; count persons who own more than one home in the location of their winter residence

1864: if local authorities allow poor quality work to be done, the county will have revisions and corrections made and the costs will be charged to the town

IV. Content of Census Records in Braunschweig from 1822 to 1864

The census pages used in 1822 and 1828 probably required more details than any other pages used in Germany at the time. The pre-printed forms used from 1843 to 1849 were identical.

	1822	1828	1830	1834	1836	1839	1843	1846	1849	1852	1855	1858	1861	1864
No images available			X	X	X	X				X			X	X
Name of dwelling owner	X													
Name of head of household	X													
Status or occupation	X	X					X	X	X		X	X		
Married males	X													
Married females	X	X												
Unmarried males	X	X												
Unmarried females	X	X												
Persons under 14	X													
Persons 14–20	X													
Persons 20–30	X													
Persons 30–40	X													
Persons 40–50	X													
Persons 50–60	X													
Persons 60–70	X													
Persons 70–80	X													
Persons 80–90	X													
Persons 90–100	X													
Age in years	X										X	X		
Name of each resident		X					X	X	X		X	X		
Miners		X												
Unrelated boys under 14		X												
Unrelated boys over 14		X												
Sons (over and under 14)		X												
Daughters (over, under 14)		X												
Apprentices and journeymen		X												
Other employees (three categories)		X												
Old and infirm (by gender)		X												
Total residents		X					X	X	X					
Description or address of dwelling							X	X	X			X		
Age at last birthday							X	X	X					
Persons over, under 14 (by gender)							X	X	X			X		
Religion							X	X	X		X	X		
Birth place											X	X		
Comments							X	X	X		X	X		
If supported by the church											X	X		
Type of dwelling (3 categories)											X			
Gender											X			
Citizenship status											X	X		
Handwritten	X	X												
Pre-printed pages							X	X	X		X	X		

V. Accessibility of Census Records in Braunschweig

Although it is not common to find state archives with substantial collections of census documents, the Niedersächsisches Landesarchiv in Wolfenbüttel has such records from several towns. The website with the catalog for that archive is https://www.arcinsys. niedersachsen.de/arcinsys/start.action?oldNodeid=.

Nevertheless, the more promising option for researchers is an inquiry to an archive in a town or a county (see Appendix A for suggestions on writing such an inquiry). As of this writing, no digital images of Braunschweig census records are known to be available on the Internet. The Family History Library has no microfilms of census records from this duchy, but a periodic search by town name might yield modern acquisitions.

VI. Selected Images of Braunschweig Census Records

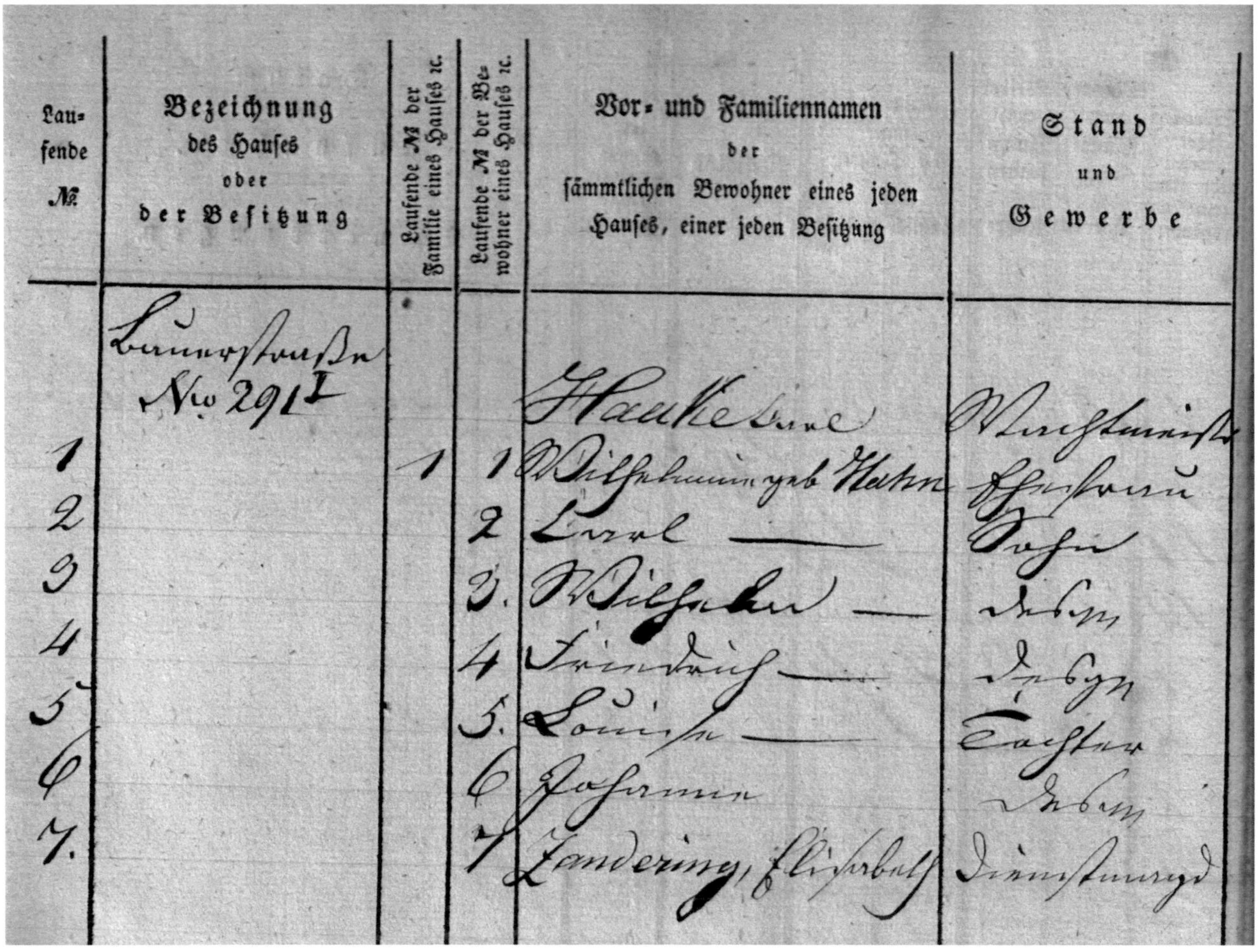

Figure 1. 1843 Census Page from Helmstedt, Braunschweig (left-hand page)

Column headings: description of address of the dwelling; number of the household in that dwelling; number of person in that household; first and last name of each inhabitant; status or occupation [Stadtarchiv Helmstedt]

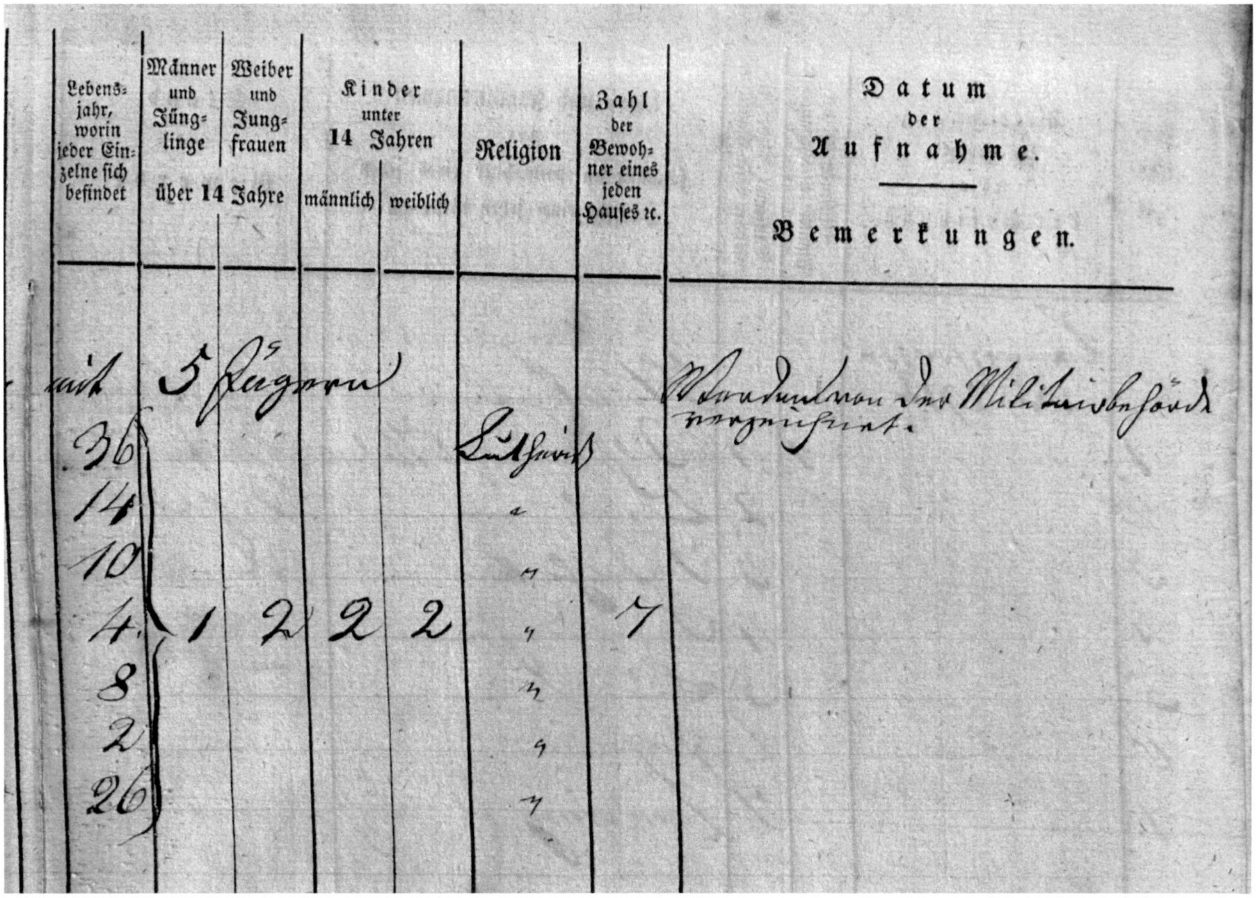

Lebens= jahr, worin jeder Ein= zelne sich befindet	Männer und Jüng= linge über 14 Jahre	Weiber und Jung= frauen	Kinder unter 14 Jahren männlich	weiblich	Religion	Zahl der Bewoh= ner eines jeden Hauses ꝛc.	Datum der Aufnahme. ___ Bemerkungen.
seit 5 Heyern							*[handwritten note]*
36					Lutherisch		
14					ꞏ		
10					ꞏ		
4	1	2	2	2	ꞏ	7	
8					ꞏ		
2					ꞏ		
26					ꞏ		

Figure 2. 1843 Census Page from Helmstedt, Braunschweig (right-hand page)

Column headings: age at last birthday; males over 14; females over 14; males under 14; females under 14; religion; total residents in household; comments [Stadtarchiv Helmstedt]

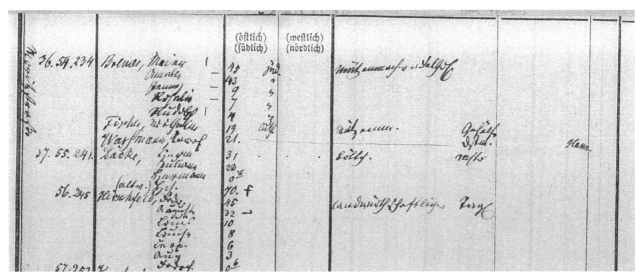

Figure 3. 1864 Census Page from Gandersheim, Braunschweig

   Column headings: dwelling number, household number; full name of resident; age; status [Niedersächsisches Landesarchiv Wolfenbüttel, WO 254 N, Nr. 16 (1852–1875)]

Notes

[1] Antje Kraus, *Quellen zur Bevölkerungsstatistik Deutschlands 1815–1871*, Band 1 (Boppard, Germany: 1980), 19.

[2] W. O. Henderson, *The Zollverein* (London: Frank Cass, 1959), 214–215.

[3] Antje Kraus, *Quellen*, 43–48.

10 Bremen (Hansestadt Bremen)

I. Location

The Hanseatic (free) city of Bremen is located at the mouth of the Weser River near the North Sea. Its only land neighbor in the nineteenth century was the kingdom of Hannover. Two dozen smaller towns were included within the borders of the city of Bremen, including the port of Bremerhaven at the mouth of the Weser River.

II. Census Enumerations in Bremen

The first census of record was enumerated there in 1823.[1] From 1828 on, the city's leadership rejected several invitations to participate in a customs union (due to their fine trade agreements with importers from foreign lands).[2] Nevertheless, census enumerations with names were carried out there and in the towns within its jurisdiction, the first of which can be dated 1828.[3] The next was in 1833, then every three years until 1867, when every German state was involved in what could be called the first national census. Under the new German Empire, enumerations were done in Bremen in 1871, every five years from 1875 to 1910, and finally in 1916.

Unfortunately, no census records compiled in the free city of Bremen before 1871 have survived.[4] The same can be stated for all census records that resulted from enumerations conducted under the national system from 1871 through 1916. However, the city archive in Bremerhaven (a part of Bremen since 1827) has census records for at least four towns before 1916.[5]

III. Specific Instructions to Town Officials and Enumerators

As of this writing, no official regulations have been located.

IV. Content of Census Records in Bremen from 1828 to 1864

The catalog of the Stadtarchiv Bremerhaven shows census records for the following years in towns belonging to the state of Bremen:

	1828	1833	1836	1839	1842	1845
no images available	X	X	X	X	X	X

	1848	1852	1855	1861	1864
no images available	X	X	X	X	X

V. Accessibility of Census Records in Bremen

As indicated above, the only known source of existing census records is the city archive in Bremerhaven.

VI. Selected Images of Bremen Census Records

No census images from the free city of Bremen have been obtained as of this writing.

Notes

1   Antje Kraus, *Quellen zur Bevölkerungsstatistik Deutschlands 1815–1871*, Band 1 (Boppard, Germany: 1980), 27, 249–254.

2   W. O. Henderson, *The Zollverein* (London: Frank Cass, 1959), 159, 188.

3   Daniela Stammer letter to Roger P. Minert on October 15, 2015. Kraus found population totals as early as 1812. Population statistics were calculated in non-census years using this formula: the total population of the previous year plus the number of children born minus the number of persons who died. The information was likely provided by the civil registry offices [*Standesamt*].

4   Bettina Schleier letter to Roger P. Minert on January 16, 2015.

5   Daniela Stammer letter to Roger P. Minert on October 15, 2015.

11 Elsaß-Lothringen [Alsace-Lorraine]¹

I. Location

The twin provinces of Elsaß and Lothringen were ceded to the French Empire as of 1815 and remained there until the Franco-Prussian War of 1870–71 when they were acquired by the victorious Germans (who proclaimed their new empire in the Palace of Versailles near Paris in January 1871). Bordered by France on the west, its northern neighbors were the grand duchy of Luxembourg, the Prussian Rheinprovinz, and Bayern (the Palatinate). Across the Rhine to the east was the grand duchy of Baden and to the south Switzerland.

II. Census Enumerations in Elsaß-Lothringen

Under the French government, census data were collected in the Lower Elsaß (*Bas-Rhin* with its capital in Strasbourg) as early as 1801 and every five years thereafter until 1866.² Even in regions where the residents were entirely German (ethnically and linguistically), the language of the census forms was French.

In the Upper Elsaß regions (*Haut-Rhin* with its capital in Colmar) and *Merthe-et-Moselle* (Lothringen with its capital in Nancy), enumerations began in 1836 and continued as in the Lower Elsaß. Under the German Empire following the Franco-Prussian War, census data were collected in the provinces in 1871, with instructions and census pages provided in both German and French. The census continued every five years from 1875 to 1910 and the last one was enumerated in 1916. At the conclusion of the First World War, Elsaß-Lothringen again became a part of France.

III. Specific Instructions to Town Officials and Enumerators

No official instruction pages for the census enumerations from 1836 to 1866 have been found, but the uniformity of the enumeration pages allows the assumption that the procedures for all but one of those years were the same. Indeed, identical page formats were used in each year except 1851. In that year, three additional important details of importance were requested of the residents in Elsaß-Lothringen: nationality, religion, and handicap status. Those details were not collected again before the province was incorporated into the German Empire in 1871.

IV. Content of Census Records in Elsaß-Lothringen from 1818 to 1864

	1836	1841	1846	1851	1856	1861	1866
Names of all persons in the household	X	X	X	X	X	X	X
Occupation	X	X	X	X	X	X	X
Familial status	X	X	X	X	X	X	X
Gender	X	X	X	X	X	X	X
Age in years	X	X	X	X	X	X	X
Comments	X	X	X	X	X	X	X
Nationality				X			
Catholic				X			
Calvinist (Reformed Lutheran)				X			.
Lutheran				X			
Jewish				X			
Other religions				X			
Disabilities				X			
French language	X	X	X	X	X	X	X
Pre-printed forms	X	X	X	X	X	X	X

V. Accessibility of Census Records in Elsaß-Lothringen

The great majority of census records in Elsaß-Lothringen have survived the passage of time and all are available for study. The archive for the Unterelsaß [Bas-Rhin] region is in Strassbourg (Conseil Départemental du Bas-Rhin with website http://new.archives.bas-rhin.fr); all census records in that collection can be viewed as digital images. For the Oberelsaß [Haut-Rhin] region, the archive is in Colmar (Archives départementales http://www.archives.haut-rhin.fr/Detail_Archives_Anciennes.aspx?id=44); census records there are not yet available online. Lothringen census records can be located in Nancy (Conseil Départemental d Meurthe-et-Moselle with website http://www.archives.meurthe-et-moselle.fr/fr/aide-a-la-recherche/etudier-le-patrimoine-local/population.html). Some of the census records in those archives can be copied for private research purposes. Currently there are no census records from Elsaß-Lothringen on microfilm in the Family History Library.

VI. Selected Census Images in Elsaß-Lothringen

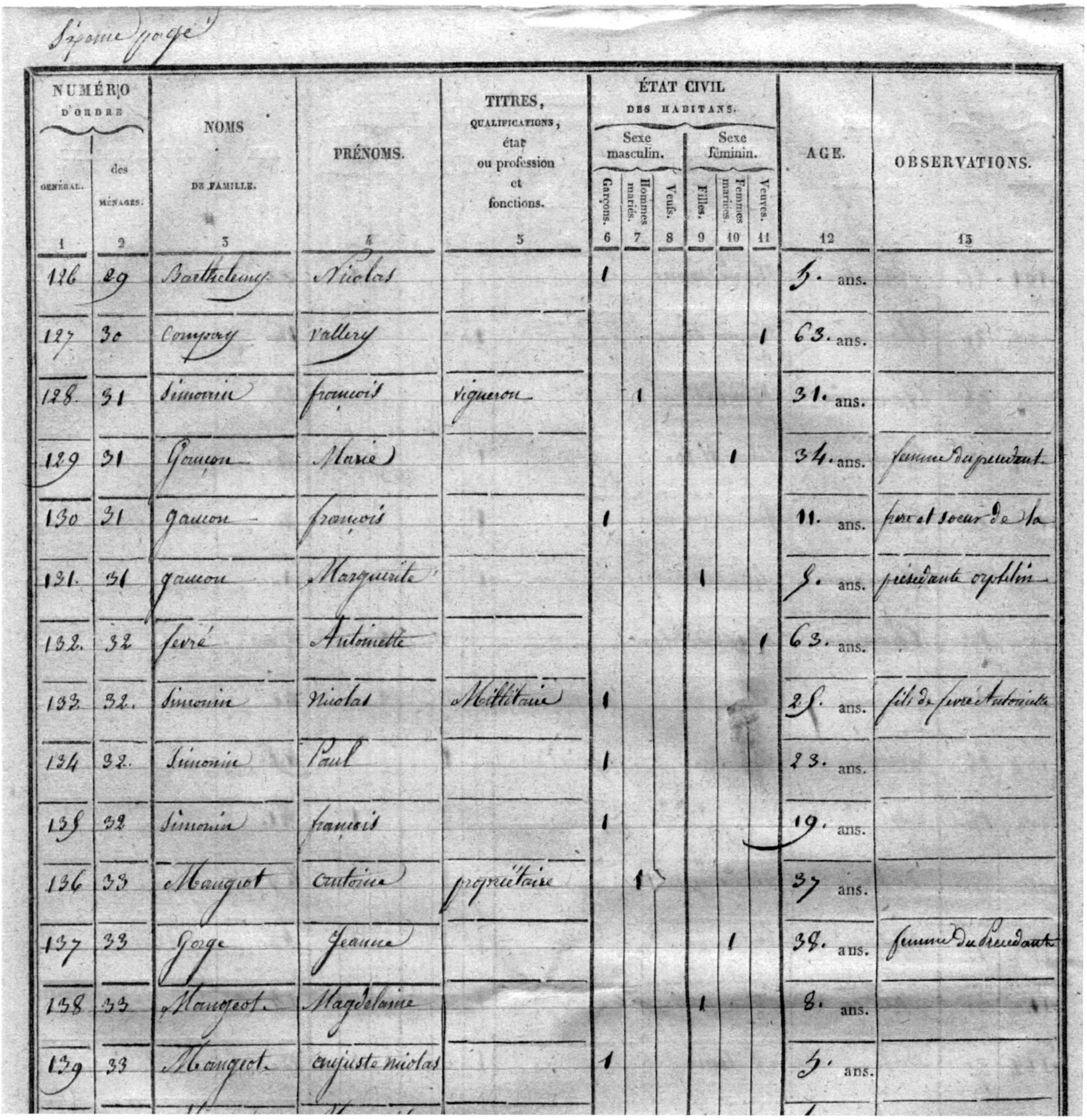

Septième page

NUMÉRO D'ORDRE		NOMS	PRÉNOMS.	TITRES, QUALIFICATIONS, état ou profession et fonctions.	ÉTAT CIVIL DES HABITANS.						AGE.	OBSERVATIONS.
					Sexe masculin.			Sexe féminin.				
GÉNÉRAL.	des MÉNAGES.	DE FAMILLE.			Garçons.	Hommes mariés.	Veufs.	Filles.	Femmes mariées.	Veuves.		
1	2	3	4	5	6	7	8	9	10	11	12	13
126	29	Barthelemy	Nicolas		1						5. ans.	
127	30	Compary	Vallery							1	63. ans.	
128	31	Simonin	françois	vigneron		1					31. ans.	
129	31	Gauçon	Marie						1		34. ans.	femme du précédent
130	31	gauçon	françois		1						11. ans.	frere et soeur de la
131.	31	gauçon	Marguerite						1		8. ans.	précédente orphelin
132.	32	fevré	Antoinette							1	63. ans.	
133	32.	Simonin	Nicolas	Militaire	1						25. ans.	fils de fevré Antoinette
134	32.	Simonin	Paul		1						23. ans.	
135	32	Simonin	françois		1						19. ans.	
136	33	Mangeot	antoine	propriétaire		1					37 ans.	
137	33	gorge	Jeanne						1		39. ans.	femme du précédent
138	33	Mangeot.	Magdelaine						1		8. ans.	
139	33	Mangeot.	aujuste nicolas		1						5. ans.	

Figure 1. 1836 Census Page from Autreville, Elsaß-Lothringen

Column headings [French]: consecutive number of persons; dwelling number; surname; given name; status or occupation; number of civilians: males (unmarried, married, widowers), females (unmarried, married, widows); age in years; comments [Conseil Départemental de Meurthe-et-Moselle]

DÉSIGNATION		NUMÉROS PAR QUARTIER, VILLAGE, hameau ou rue.			NOMS DE FAMILLE.	PRÉNOMS.	PROFESSIONS.	ÉTAT CIVIL DES HABITANTS.						AGE.	NATIONALITÉ.		
des quartiers, ou hameaux.	Des rues.	des maisons.	des ménages.	des individus.				Garçons.	Hommes mariés.	Veufs.	Filles.	Femmes mariées.	Veuves.		Français d'origine.	Naturalisé français.	Etrangers.
1.	2.	3.	4.	5.	6.	7.	8.	9.	10.	11.	12.	13.	14.	15.	16.	17.	18.
				690	Baillet	Marie Louise	leur fille sans profes.	"	"	"	1	"	"	6	1	"	"
				691	Baillet	Marie Céline	leur fille id	"	"	"	1	"	"	8	1	"	"
				692	Baillet	Jules	leur fils id	1	"	"	"	"	"	3	1	"	"
				693	Parmentel	Nicolas	Builiet	"	1	"	"	"	"	61	1	"	"
		1	2	694	Dasse	Barbe	sa femme id	"	"	"	"	1	"	60	1	"	"
				695	Parmentel	Thomas	leur fils id	1	"	"	"	"	"	20	1	"	"
Observé 696 pour 561 bis																	
	Rue de la forge	1	1	1	Baroche	Augustin Père	Rentier	"	1	"	"	"	"	74	1	"	"
1			2	2	Baroche	Jn Nicolas	Propriétaire	"	1	"	"	"	"	38	1	"	"
				3	Lemoine	Marie	sa femme sans profes.	"	"	"	"	1	"	37	1	"	"
				4	Baroche	Marie Elisabet	leur fille id	"	"	"	1	"	"	2	1	"	"
				5	Baroche	Augustin	Charpentier	"	1	"	"	"	"	48	1	"	"
		2	3	6	Bidierjean	Marie Thérèse	sa femme sans profes.	"	"	"	"	1	"	45	1	"	"
				7	Baroche	Augustine	leur fille id	"	"	"	1	"	"	9	1	"	"
			4	8	Baroche	Jn Bt	Propriétaire	"	1	"	"	"	"	41	1	"	"
		3		9	Rolle	Marie Barbe	sa femme sans profession	"	"	"	"	1	"	33	1	"	"
				10	Baroche	Marie	leur fille id	"	"	"	1	"	"	9	1	"	"

Figure 2. 1851 Census Page from Azerailles, Elsaß-Lothringen (left-hand page)

Column headings: 1 name of the section of town; 2 street name; 3 dwelling number; 4 family number; 5 person's number; 6 surname; 7 given name; 8 status or occupation; 9–14 civilian residents; 9 unmarried males; 10 married males; 11 widowers; 12 unmarried females; 13 married females; 14 widows; 15 age in years; 16 native French; 17 naturalized French; 18 foreigners [Conseil Départemental de Meurthe-et-Moselle]

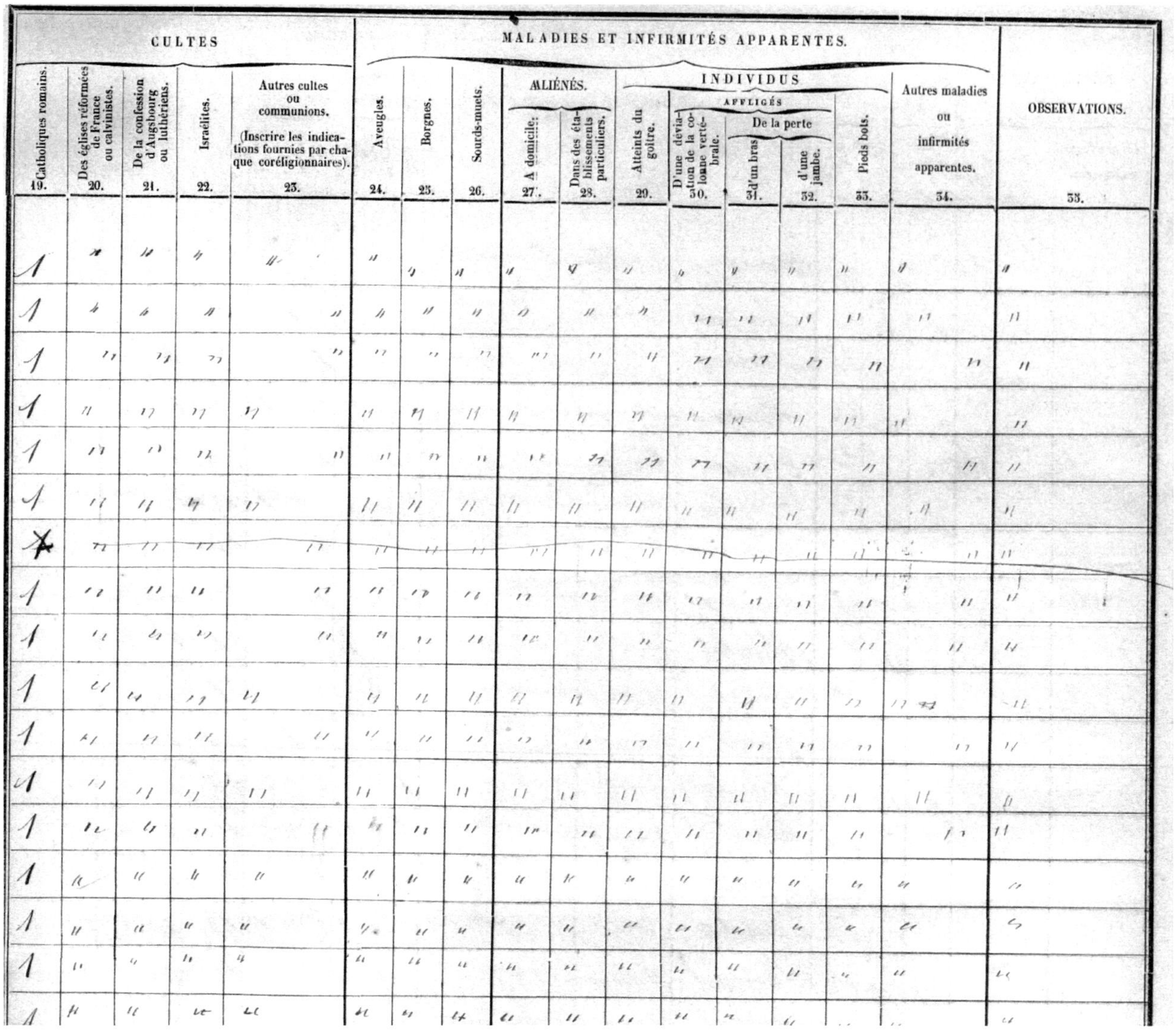

Figure 3. 1851 Census Page from Azerailles, Elsaß-Lothringen (right-hand page)

Column headings: 19 Catholics; 20 French Reformed (Calvinists); 21 Lutherans; 22 Jewish; 23 Other religions (enter name); 24–34 illnesses and other apparent infirmities; 24–25 blind; 26 deaf and dumb; 27 confined at home; 28 institutionalized; 29 goitre; 30 deviation of the spinal column; 31 lost an arm; 32 lost a leg; 33 club feet; 34 other apparent illnesses or infirmities [Conseil Départemental de Meurthe-et-Moselle]

Notes

[1] The author expresses his appreciation to Madeleine Calcaterra of Sarralbe, France for her assistance with French-language communications and French-German tranlations.

[2] Antje Kraus, *Quellen zur Bevölkerungsstatistik Deutschlands 1815–1871*, Band 1 (Boppard, Germany: 1980), 30, 333–335.

12 Hamburg (Hansestadt Hamburg)

I. Location

The Hanseatic (free) city of Hamburg is located at the mouth of the Elbe River near the North Sea. Schleswig-Holstein was the only neighboring state to the north and east in the nineteenth century, and the kingdom of Hannover the only neighbor to the south and west.

II. Census Enumerations in Hamburg

The first census of record was enumerated in the city of Hamburg in 1823. From 1828 on, the city's leadership rejected several invitations to participate in a customs union (due to their fine trade agreements with importers from foreign lands). City census enumerations are known to have taken place for internal purposes in 1851, 1857, and 1862.[1] In 1867, the city was included in the North German Confederation census campaign. Under the German Empire, enumerations were done in Hamburg in 1871, thereafter every five years from 1875 to 1910, and finally in 1916.

III. Accessibility of Census Records in Hamburg

Unfortunately, local experts report that no census instructions or enumerations compiled in this city before 1871 have survived.[2] Nevertheless, the population statistics that resulted from census campaigns conducted in Hamburg exist for many census years and in great detail.[3]

Notes

[1] Kristin Kalisch email to Roger P. Minert on February 6, 2015.

[2] Andrea Bentschneider email to Roger P. Minert on February 27, 2015.

[3] Antje Kraus, *Quellen zur Bevölkerungsstatistik Deutschlands 1815–1871*, Band 1 (Boppard, Germany: Harald Boldt, 1980), 261–265.

13 Hannover [Hanover]

I. Location

The kingdom of Hannover lay in northwestern Germany—surrounded to the west by the Netherlands and the grand duchy of Oldenburg, on the north by the grand duchies of Schleswig-Holstein and the North Sea, on the east by the grand duchy of Mecklenburg-Schwerin and the Prussian provinces of Brandenburg and Sachsen. Neighbors to the south were the principality of Lippe (Detmold) and the Prussian province of Westfalen. The kingdom became a Prussian province in 1866. The capital city of the province was likewise called Hannover.

II. Census Enumerations in Hannover

The first census enumerated in Hannover in the post-Napoleonic era took place in 1816 and was an independent campaign of the kingdom; only numbers were collected. In an effort to slow the growth of the Prusso-Hessian Customs Union, Hannover united with several northern and central states to establish the *Mitteldeutscher Handelsverein* [Central German Commerce Union] in 1828. After that organization declined in the early 1830s, Hannover joined with Braunschweig to form the *Steuerverein* [Tax Union] in 1835 and the compilation of census records followed appropriately.[1]

The *Steuerverein* expanded by 1838 to include Oldenburg and Schaumburg-Lippe, but was never strong enough to compete with the *Zollverein* [Customs Union] that was led by Preußen. The two groups merged in 1851–52 and Hannover cooperated with the *Zollverein* by conducting census enumerations every three years until 1864.[2] Another census was enumerated in 1867 in conjunction with the North German Confederation and the *Zollverein*. Under the German Empire, enumerations were done there in 1871, thereafter every five years from 1875 to 1910, and finally in 1916.[3]

III. Specific Instructions to Town Officials and Enumerators

In general, the instructions given to local governments and enumerators in the kingdom of Hannover were more detailed than in most other states. Both the instructions and the *Urlisten* [lists] were printed beginning in 1830. It is interesting to note that in most versions of the instructions, the reader is reminded that the "kingdom would participate in the census" based on a "royal [Hannoverian] decision" to support the campaign that was mandated by the *Steuerverein* or the *Zollverein*. Important innovations among the instructions are shown below:

> 1816: use the format provided; count all males and females over and under 16 years of age; bailiffs should do the counting; submit the reports within eight days; count the hearths (any home with a fireplace); count military veterans

> 1820: count inhabitants in every town; classify each town by size; count people by numbers only; count officials and clergy in different categories; submit reports by Easter next year [1821]

> 1833: distribute the forms provided beginning June 20; do the count on July 1; go to every house; count every person with his/her age, religion, and marital status; record the name of every head of household; count persons temporarily absent and foreigners working here; don't count journeymen or apprentices away from home or students and visitors here; count deaf, mute, and blind persons; count by age groups, gender, and religion (in five categories); count people in hospitals and prisons

1836: the *Steuerverein* member states agreed on 1 May 1834 to do this census; follow instructions of 1833 more carefully to avoid problems encountered that year; supervisors are to compare the results of 1833 and 1836 to find mistakes

1842: *Urlisten* are to be collected from heads of households, not from children or servants; any persons attempting to avoid participation in the census can be fined

1852: begin and finish on December 3; don't count military personnel, family guests, or people staying in inns; list every individual on the *Urlisten*; don't use any list previously compiled; the enumerator is to fill out every list; if many mistakes are found, the process must be repeated and the person who made the mistakes will be required to pay for the revision; the *Urlisten* are to be carefully preserved; government officials and teachers should be asked to help if the enumerators are overly burdened; some people were left out of the 1848 census, so be careful to list everybody

1858: enumerators should only allow the head of household to fill out the list if he has the proper qualifications [abilities] to ensure correctness

1861: use caution in enlisting help to fill out the lists; on age designations, round up or down to the full year

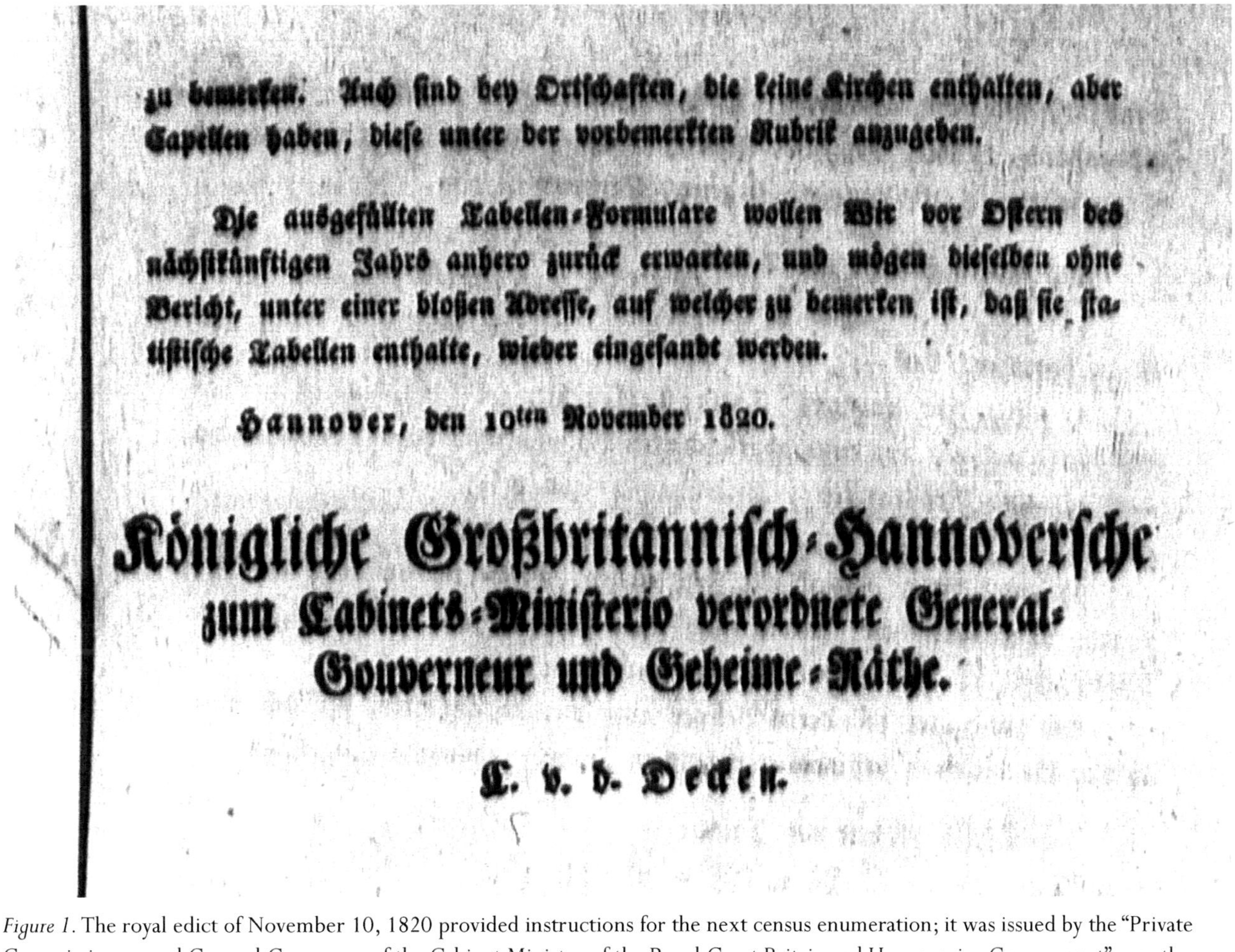
zu bemerken. Auch sind bey Ortschaften, die keine Kirchen enthalten, aber Capellen haben, diese unter der vorbemerkten Rubrik anzugeben.

Die ausgefüllten Tabellen-Formulare wollen Wir vor Ostern des nächstkünftigen Jahrs anhero zurück erwarten, und mögen dieselben ohne Bericht, unter einer bloßen Adresse, auf welcher zu bemerken ist, daß sie statistische Tabellen enthalte, wieder eingesandt werden.

Hannover, den 10ten November 1820.

Königliche Großbritannisch-Hannoversche zum Cabinets-Ministerio verordnete General-Gouverneur und Geheime-Räthe.

C. v. d. Decken.

Figure 1. The royal edict of November 10, 1820 provided instructions for the next census enumeration; it was issued by the "Private Commissioners and General Governors of the Cabinet Ministry of the Royal Great Britain and Hannoverian Government" over the signature of C. v. h. Decken. [Stadtarchiv Duderstadt]

IV. Content of Census Records in Hannover from 1816 to 1864

In 1830, pre-printed forms were introduced that required very specific details on each person on facing pages. Few changes in content occurred after that. The Hannover census of 1852 is considered to be one of the most valuable in Germany; not only did the royal government mandate that year that every person's name be recorded, but the regulations provided that the *Urlisten* be preserved for possible reference at a later date. It is not known precisely how many of the *Urlisten* survive today, but the 1852 census is valued by family history researchers in Germany and elsewhere. The same requirement to preserve the *Urlisten* is found in the instructions for 1858, 1861, and 1864.

	1816	1821	1829	1830	1833	1836	1839	1842	1845	1848	1852	1855	1858	1861	1864
Only head of household is named	X		X	X	X	X	X	X	X	X					
Total persons in household	X	X	X	X	X	X	X	X	X	X	X	X	X	X	X
Comments	X														
Males over 16	X														
Females over 16	X														
Males under 16	X														
Females under 16	X														
Name of home owner		X													
Occupation			X								X	X	X	X	X
Total males				X	X	X	X	X	X	X	X	X	X	X	X
Males married				X	X	X	X	X	X	X	X	X	X	X	X
Total females				X	X	X	X	X	X	X	X	X	X	X	X
Females married				X	X	X	X	X	X	X	X	X	X	X	X
Lutheran				X	X	X	X	X	X	X	X	X	X	X	X
Reformed				X	X	X	X	X	X	X	X	X	X	X	X
Catholic				X	X	X	X	X	X	X	X	X	X	X	X
Mennonite				X	X	X	X	X	X	X					
Jewish				X	X	X	X	X	X	X	X	X	X	X	X
Age by groups and gender					X	X	X	X	X	X	X	X	X	X	X
Widows					X	X	X	X	X	X	X	X	X	X	X
Widowers					X	X	X	X	X	X	X	X	X	X	X
Married persons					X	X	X	X	X	X	X	X	X	X	X
Other Christians											X	X	X	X	X
Age											X	X	X	X	X
Relationship to head of household											X	X	X	X	X
Every person is named											X	X	X	X	X
Handwritten document	X	X	X												
Printed column headings				X	X	X	X	X	X	X	X	X	X	X	X
Different versions											X	X	X	X	X

V. Accessibility of Census Records in Hannover

All of the territory of the old kingdom and province of Hannover is included in the modern state of Lower Saxony [*Niedersachsen*] that has a large and impressive archival system consisting of seven regional archives in major cities. The archives [*Landesarchive*] in Aurich, Hannover, Osnabrück, and Stade contain documents from towns and counties in nineteenth-century Hannover.

It will be most efficient for researchers to write to the archive in a town or a county where ancestors are known or believed to have lived (see suggestions in Appendix A for writing an efficient inquiry).

Hannover census records in the collection of the Family History Library are not common, but a search in that catalog by town is a good tactic and takes little time. Some digital images of census records can probably be found on the Internet.

A genuine rarity among census records exists in this territory: an index to the records of the 1852 census is partially complete and can be accessed through the website: hist.de/publishers-list.htm (last updated in 2010). Publications include indexes for several hundred communities.

VI. Selected Census Images in Hannover

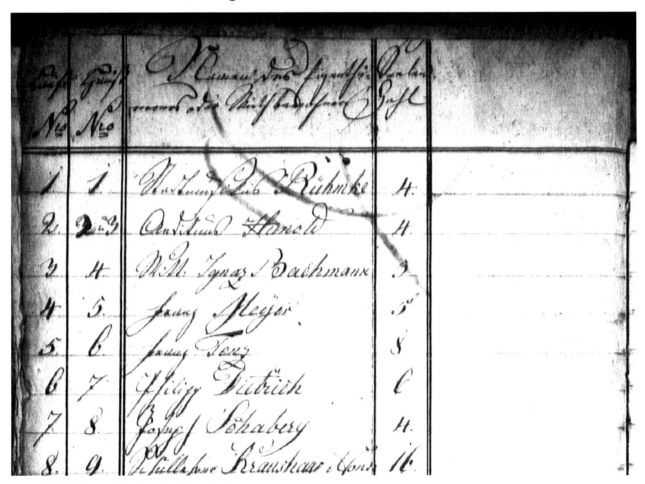

Figure 2. 1821 Census Page from Duderstadt, Hannover

Column headings: consecutive number of dwelling; number of household; name of owner; total number of residents in household [Stadtarchiv Duderstadt]

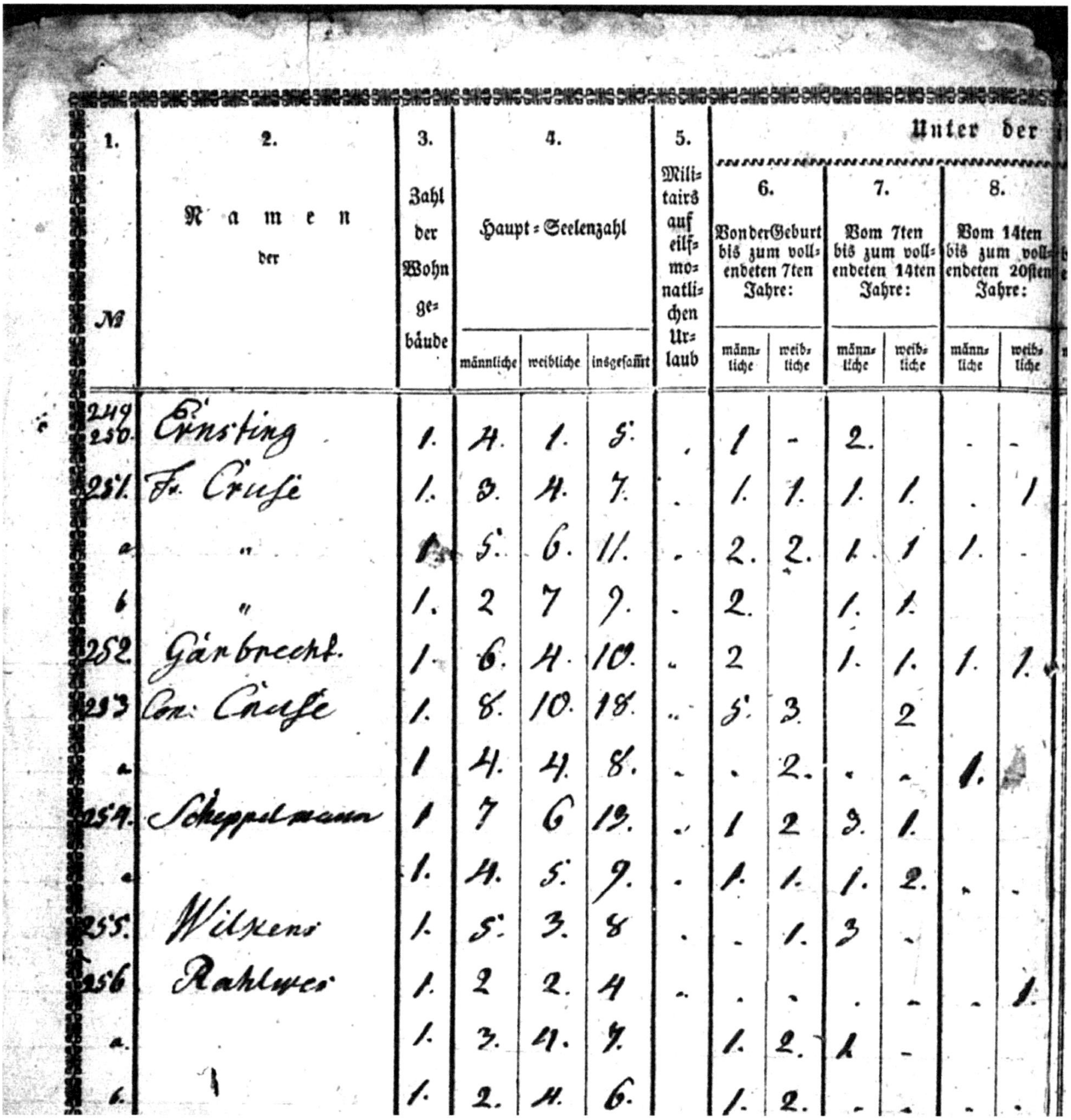

1.	2. Namen der	3. Zahl der Wohngebäude	4. Haupt = Seelenzahl			5. Militairs auf eilfmonatlichen Urlaub	Unter der					
№							6. Von der Geburt bis zum vollendeten 7ten Jahre:		7. Vom 7ten bis zum vollendeten 14ten Jahre:		8. Vom 14ten bis zum vollendeten 20sten Jahre:	
			männliche	weibliche	insgesamt		männliche	weibliche	männliche	weibliche	männliche	weibliche
249 250	Ernsting	1.	4.	1.	5.	.	1	-	2.		-	-
251	Fr. Cruse	1.	3.	4.	7.	.	1.	1.	1.	1		1
a	"		5.	6.	11.	-	2.	2.	1	1	1.	
b	"	1.	2	7	9.	-	2.		1.	1		
252	Gärbrecht	1.	6.	4.	10.	-	2		1.	1.	1.	1.
253	Con: Cruse	1.	8.	10.	18.	-	5.	3.		2		
a		1	4.	4.	8.	-	.	2.	.	-	1.	
254	Scheppelmann	1	7	6	13.	-	1	2	3.	1.		
a		1.	4.	5.	9.	-	1.	1.	1.	2.	-	
255	Wilxens	1.	5.	3.	8			1.	3	-		
256	Rahlwes	1.	2	2.	4	-	.	.	.		-	1.
a		1.	3.	4.	7.		1.	2.	1	-		
b		1.	2.	4.	6.		1.	2.				

Figure 3. 1833 Census Page from Nienburg, Hannover (left-hand page)

Column headings: 1 number of household; 2 name of head of household; 3 number of dwellings; 4 total number of persons (male, female, total); 5 number of military personnel on leave for eleven months; 6–16 detail on persons in column 4: 6 age from birth to 7 years (male, female); 7 from 7 to 14 years (male, female); 8 from 14 to 20 years (male, female) [Stadtarchiv Nienburg]

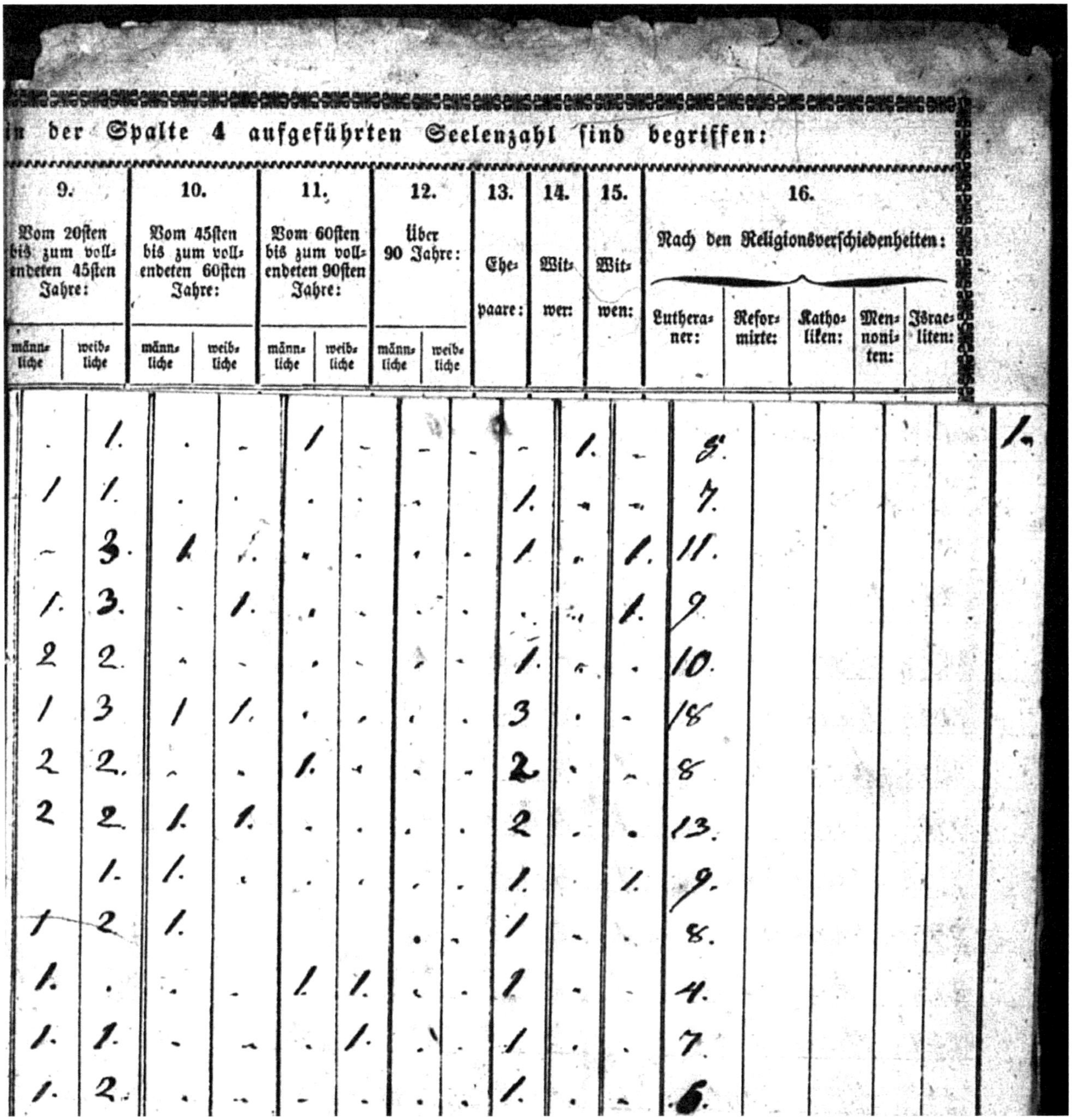

9. Vom 20sten bis zum vollendeten 45sten Jahre:		10. Vom 45sten bis zum vollendeten 60sten Jahre:		11. Vom 60sten bis zum vollendeten 90sten Jahre:		12. über 90 Jahre:		13. Ehepaare:	14. Witwer:	15. Witwen:	16. Nach den Religionsverschiedenheiten:				
männliche	weibliche	männliche	weibliche	männliche	weibliche	männliche	weibliche				Lutheraner:	Reformirte:	Katholiken:	Mennoniten:	Israeliten:
.	1.	.	–	1	–		–	–	1.	–	8.				1
1	1.	.			–	.	.	1.	–	–	7.				
–	3.	1	.	.	.	.	.	1	.	1.	11.				
1.	3.	–	1.	.	.	.	.	1	.	1.	9.				
2	2.	.	.	.	.	.	.	1.	.	.	10.				
1	3	1	1.	.	.	.	.	3	.	–	18				
2	2.	.	.	1.	.	.	–	2	.	–	8				
2	2.	1.	1.	.	.	.	.	2	.	.	13.				
.	1.	1.	.	.	.	.	.	1.	.	1.	9.				
1	2	1.	.	.	.	.	.	1	.	–	8.				
1.	.	.	–	1	1.	.	–	1	.	–	4.				
1.	1.	–	–	.	1.	.	.	1	.	–	7.				
1.	2	.	–	–	.	.	.	1.	.	.	6.				

Figure 4. 1833 Census Page from Nienburg, Hannover (right-hand page)

Column headings: 9 from 20 to 45 years (male, female); 10 from 45 to 60 years (male, female); 11 from 60 to 90 years (male, female); 12 over 90 years (male, female); 13 married persons; 14 widowers; 15 widows; 16 religion (Lutheran, Reformed Lutheran, Catholic, Mennonite, Jewish) [Stadtarchiv Nienburg]

Haus=No.	Zahl der Wohnhäuser.	Vor= und Familiennamen der sämmtlichen Bewohner eines jeden Hauses oder einer jeden Besitzung, unter fortlaufender Numerirung der zu einer jeden Haushaltung gehörenden Personen.	Standes=, Berufs= und Erwerbs=Verhältnisse. Bezeichnung derselben:	N. der Classe.	Lebensjahr, worin Jeder sich befindet.	Anzahl der Einw.		verheirathete				nach Religions=Verschiedenheiten				
						männlich.	weiblich.	männlich.	weiblich.	Wittwer.	Wittwen.	Lutheraner.	Reformirte.	Katholiken.	sonst. christl. Sect.	Israeliten.
		6 Louis Hillebrecht	Sohn der No 2.		3.	1						1				
		1 Robert Körber	Friseur		49.	1		1				1				
		2 Marie Körber	dessen Ehefrau		47.		1		1			1				
		3 Carl „	d. Sohn, Weißbinderlehrling		15.	1						1				
		4 Anna „	deren Tochter		9.		1					1				
		5 Sophie „	dsbgl.		2.		1					1				
31.	1.	1 Friedrich Hübeler	Kürschnermstr.		53.	1				1		1				
		2 Minna Hübeler	dessen Tochter		21.		1					1				
		1 Conrad Weygand	Zimmermstr.		64.	1				1		1				
		2 Carl Weygand	d. Sohn, Zimmergesell		34.	1		1				1				
		3 Christine „	dessen Ehefrau		26.		1		1			1				
		4 Victor „	deren Sohn		2.	1						1				
		5 Louise Hesse	Dienstmagd		18.		1							1		

Figure 5. 1864 Census Page from Göttingen, Hannover

Column headings: house number; number of households; given name and surname; status and occupation; class number; age on next birthday; number of persons (male and female); married persons (male and female, widowers, widows); religion (Lutherans, Reformed Lutherans, Catholics, other Christian sects; Jewish) [Magistrat der Stadt Göttingen]

Notes

[1] W. O. Henderson, *The Zollverein* (London: Frank Cass, 1959), 214–215.

[2] Otto Klingelhöffer, "Der *Zollverein* im Jahr 1865" in *Zeitschrift für die gesamte Staatswissenschaft*, v. 19 (1863), 96.

[3] Antje Kraus, *Quellen zur Bevölkerungsstatistik Deutschlands 1815–1871*, Band 1 (Boppard, Germany: Harald Boldt, 1980), 24, 117–122.

14 Hessen [Hesse]

I. Location

The grand duchy of Hessen (with capital city of Darmstadt) was located in southwestern Germany—surrounded on the west by the Prussian Rheinprovinz, on the north by the Prussian province of Hessen-Nassau, on the east by the kingdom of Bayern, and on the south by Baden and the Palatinate (a district of Bayern).

II. Census Enumerations in Hessen

Hessen joined with Preußen to form the second customs union on February 14, 1828, but census records were collected as early as 1816 (generally by pastors and only with head counts). Those two major states were joined by many others in the founding of the *Zollverein* [Customs Union] on January 1, 1834.[1] Census enumerations were then conducted every three years until 1864. In 1867, the member states of the *Zollverein* joined in a census campaign that included the North German Confederation as well.[2] Under the German Empire, enumerations were done in Hessen in 1871, every five years from 1875 to 1910, and finally in 1916.[3]

III. Specific Instructions to Town Officials and Enumerators

The instructions circulated in Hessen in 1818 stipulated that the counting was to be done in order to determine the numbers of residents by religions. The mayor of each town was to see that all persons were to be counted, with the exception of persons on active military duty and persons only passing through town. The requested data were to be collected within ten days.

For several decades, census forms in Hessen remained remarkably consistent in design and content. Few deviations from the norm have been identified, but some variations in column headings and text have been found. Major changes in procedures or new data to be collected over the years are as follows:

1820: record the names of all persons, the relation of each to the head of household, the age in years and the birthplace

1825: begin after Easter and finish within one month; go from house to house, including mills, etc.; count in categories by age (above and below fourteen years); count all apprentices, journeymen, and domestic servants as well as deaf and mute persons

1834: start on December 1 and finish by December 20

1837: you may start Table II [page 2] before December 1; submit your results in duplicate

1840: make special lists with those persons of high age, such as 90 or 100 years

1846: begin on December 3 and finish on that day, with the exception of large cities where the work may take three days if necessary; every resident is to be counted, including laborers in inns, students, persons in hospitals and prisons, etc.; count residents who are temporarily away at work, but not local apprentices or journeymen living elsewhere; don't count military personnel or families but do count persons who work for them but don't live in their homes

1861: the names of all persons are to be recorded by the head of household according to printed instructions provided to him; the distribution and collection of the forms is to be done by persons selected by the local census committee; the owners or supervisors of inns, hospitals, prisons, etc. are to do the data collection for the inhabitants of their respective institutions

VI. Content of Census Records in Hessen from 1818 to 1864

	1818	1820	1822	1825	1828	1831	1834	1837	1840	1843	1846	1849	1852	1855	1858	1861	1864
Image missing																X	
Total persons	X					X	X	X	X	X	X	X	X	X	X		
Relationship to head of household		X	X	X	X	X	X		X								X
Name of every person		X	X	X	X	X	X		X							X	X
Age in years		X	X	X	X	X	X	X	X	X							
Birth place		X	X	X	X	X	X	X	X	X		X					X
Occupation		X	X	X	X	X	X	X	X	X	X	X	X	X	X		X
Religion				X	X	X	X	X	X	X	X	X	X	X	X		X
Disability				X	X	X	X										
Only head of household named						X	X	X	X	X	X	X	X	X	X		
Gender						X	X	X	X	X	X	X	X	X	X		X
Persons under 14						X	X	X	X	X	X	X	X	X	X		
Persons over 14						X	X	X	X	X	X	X	X	X	X		
Lutheran						X	X	X	X	X	X	X	X	X	X		X
Catholic						X	X	X	X	X	X	X	X	X	X		X
Jewish						X	X		X	X	X	X			X		
Local laborers						X		X	X	X	X	X	X	X			
Foreign laborers						X		X	X	X	X	X	X	X			
Year of birth								X									X
Comments								X				X		X			X
Other Christians								X	X	X	X						
Reformed Lutheran									X	X	X	X					
Other religions						X	X		X			X					
Persons absent																	X
Property owners																	X
Family status																	X
Variant forms used						X	X	X	X	X	X	X					
Pre-printed forms															X	X	X

V. Accessibility of Census Records in Hessen

Because the regional archives in what was once the grand duchy of Hessen are not known to have census documents in their collections, the best thing for researchers to do is write to the archive of the town or the county where the person in question is believed or known to have lived. (See Appendix A for instructions on how to write the inquiry.) Some census records might be found on microfilm in the Family History Library (*FamilySearch.org*). Currently no census records from Hessen are known to be in digital form on the Internet.

VI. Selected Census Images from Hessen

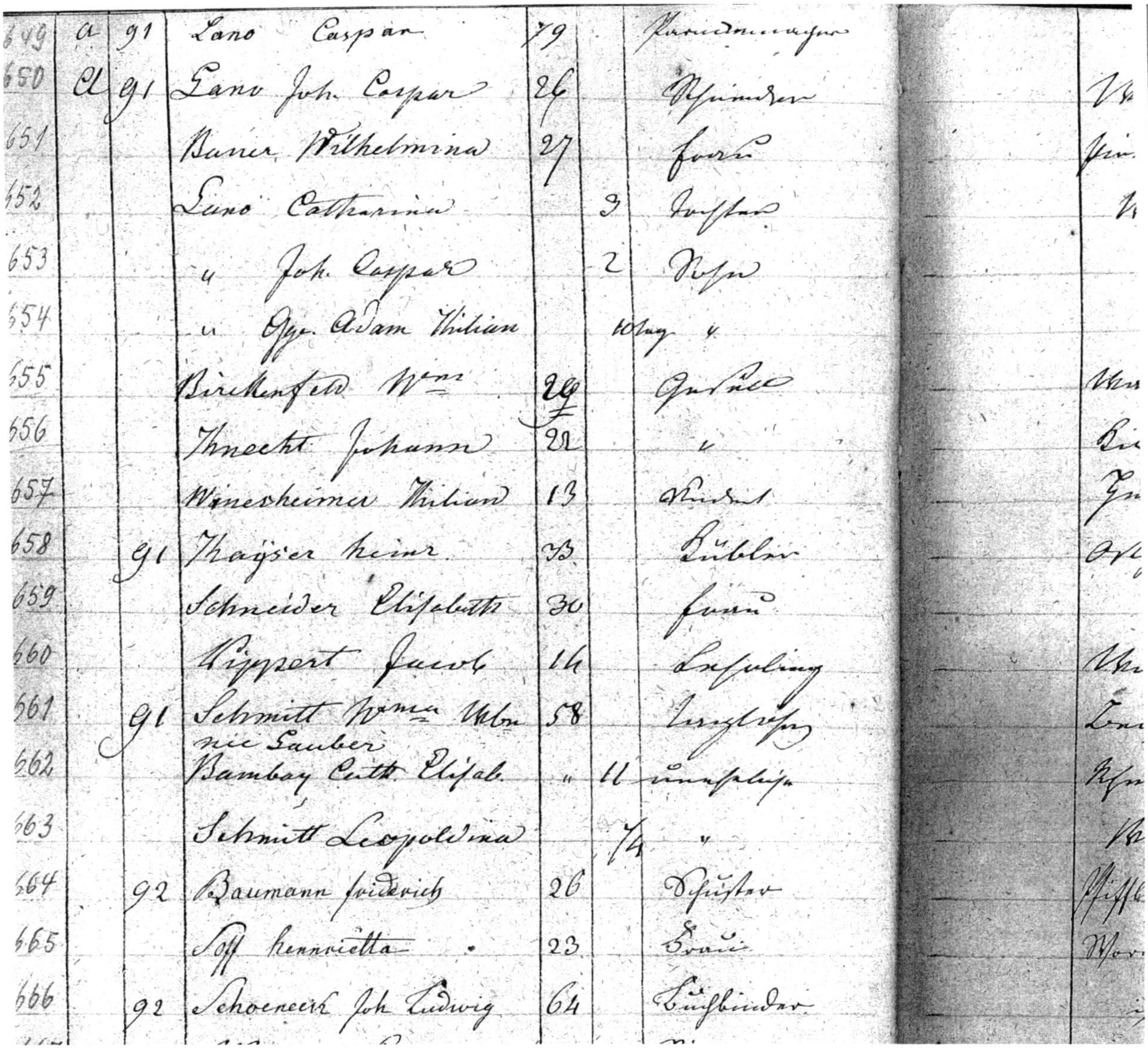

Figure 1. 1820 Census Page from Worms, Hessen (left-hand page)

Column headings: consecutive number of persons; number of household; name of each individual; age if over fourteen years; age if under fourteen years; status or occupation [the right-hand page lists birth place and statistical categories; column headings appear only on the first page of the book] [Stadtarchiv Worms 5:21]

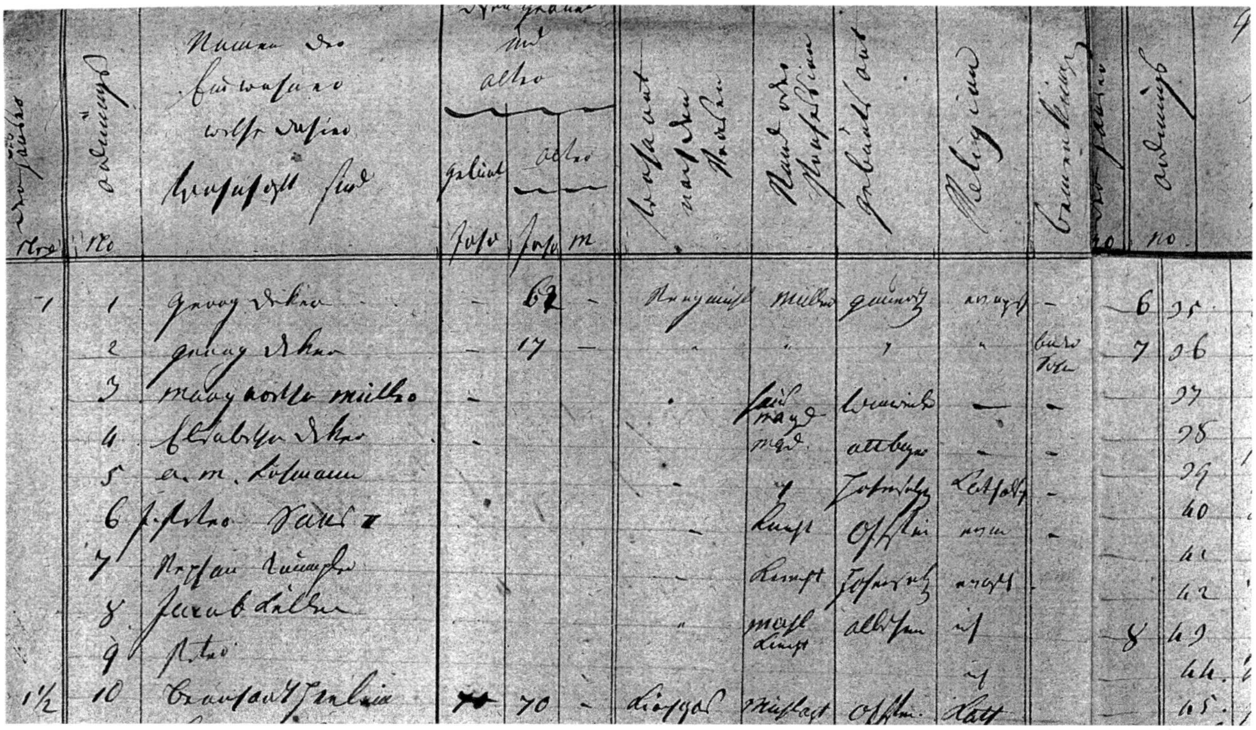

Figure 2. 1837 Census Page from Offstein, Hessen

Column headings: number of dwelling; number of household; head of household; birth year, age in years, age in months, name of street, status or occupation; birth place; religion; comments [Stadtarchiv Worms 240:93]

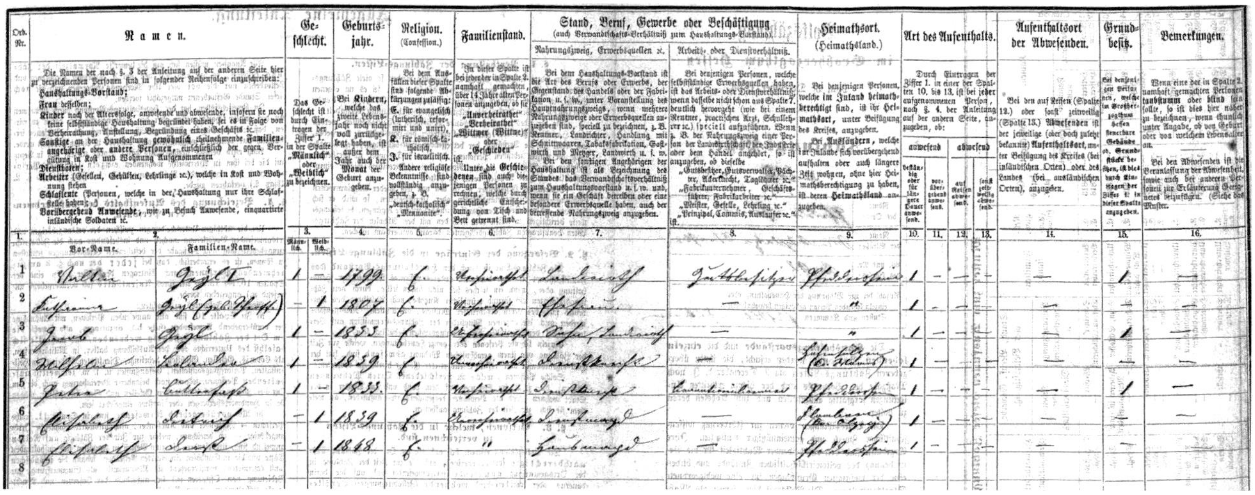

Figure 3. 1864 Census Page from Herrnsheim, Hessen

Column headings: 1 consecutive number of persons; 2 given name and surname; 3 gender; 4 birth year; 5 religion; 6 marital status; 7 primary source of income; 8 employment; 9 home town; 10 if long-time resident; 11 if present temporarily; 12 absent traveling; 13 absent under other circumstances; 14 residence of absent persons, including county and country; 15 property ownership; 16 comments [the reverse of this page has instructions; one page per household] [Stadtarchiv Worms 40:387]

Notes

[1] Otto Klingelhöffer, "Der *Zollverein* im Jahr 1865," in *Zeitschrift für die gesamte Staatswissenschaft*, v. 19 (1863), 96.

[2] Beginning in 1841, population statistics were also collected in every non-census year by means of this formula: total number of persons from the year before plus the number of persons born minus the number of persons who died (the numbers being taken from local church records). See Antje Kraus, *Quellen zur Bevölkerungsstatistik Deutschlands 1815–1871*, Band 1 (Boppard, Germany: Harald Boldt, 1980), 59.

[3] Kraus, *Quellen*, 20–21, 57–62.

15 Hessen-Nassau [Hesse-Nassau]

I. Location

The province of Hessen-Nassau was situated in western central Germany—bordered on the west by the Prussian Rheinprovinz and on the north by the Prussian province of Westfalen and the principality of Waldeck. Neighboring states to the east were Prussian Sachsen and several of the Saxon duchies. The grand duchy of Hessen (Darmstadt) and the kingdom of Bayern lay to the south. The northern exclave of Hessen (Darmstadt) was totally surrounded by Hessen-Nassau. In 1816 this territory featured the independent states of Hessen-Kassel and Nassau, as well as the free city of Frankfurt am Main. The historical capital of Hessen-Nassau was Kassel.

II. Census Enumerations in Hessen-Nassau

Census records were compiled in one or more of the three states (Hessen-Kassel, Nassau, Frankfurt) in 1818, 1821, and 1827. All three joined the fledgling *Mitteldeutscher Handelsverein* [Central German Commerce Union] in 1828 as part of the effort to slow the growth of the Prusso-Hessian Customs Union. After the former organization collapsed in the early 1830s, the three states were added to the expanding *Zollverein* [Customs Union] (the last being Frankfurt am Main in January 1836).[1] Another census enumeration took place in 1832, after which the states observed the *Zollverein*'s three-year census schedule from 1834 to 1864.[2]

By 1866, the three states had merged to become the Prussian province of Hessen-Nassau and another census was enumerated in 1867 in conjunction with the North German Confederation. Under the German Empire, enumerations were done there in 1871, thereafter every five years from 1875 to 1910, and finally in 1916.

III. Specific Instructions to Town Officials and Enumerators

The following directives represent innovations or revisions from previous census campaigns:

1840: work as quickly as possible without risking errors; count all persons present except for foreigners not here for at least one year; don't count active military personnel or their dependents

1855: use the enclosed pre-printed form; do not miss even one person, because that will reduce the funding received by this office; record any disabilities the residents have; indicate the marital status of males over 22 years of age and females over 18 as well as any person married under the legal age; count local workers temporarily away from home; indicate the home town of any foreigner

1858: finish the census by the second day (with the exception of the city of Kassel); do not use any other source, such as residential registration lists; the household lists may be handed out a day or two before the target date; military personnel will be counted separately by military administration; persons owning more than one dwelling are to be counted where they live in the winter; under "comments" indicate why a local person living elsewhere is not counted; single persons supporting themselves are to be counted as heads of households

IV. Content of Census Records in Hessen-Nassau from 1818 to 1864

	1818	1824	1827	1832	1834	1837	1840	1843	1846	1849	1852	1855	1858	1861	1864
No images available	X							X	X	X	X	X			
Name of head of household		X	X	X	X	X	X								
Gender		X													
Males under 14		X		X	X	X	X						X	X	X
Females under 15		X		X	X	X	X						X	X	X
Journeymen			X												
Male laborers			X												
Female laborers			X												
Males under 7			X												
Males 8–14			X												
Males 15–70			X												
Females under 7			X												
Females 8–14			X												
Females 15–70			X												
Males 15–60				X	X	X	X								
Females 15–60				X	X	X	X								
Males over 60				X	X	X	X								
Females over 60				X	X	X	X								
Total residents		X	X	X	X	X	X								
First and last name of each resident													X	X	X
Marital status		X											X	X	X
Disabilities													X	X	X
Status and occupation													X	X	X
Age at next birthday													X	X	X
Religion			X										X	X	X
Males over 14													X	X	X
Females over 14													X	X	X
Origin of foreigners															X
Number of families in dwelling													X	X	X
Handwritten pages				X	X	X	X								
Pre-printed pages													X	X	X

V. Accessibility of Census Records in Hessen-Nassau

As of this writing, no census records of this province have been located in the collection of the Family History Library, but periodic inspections of the catalog are a good idea. If the town or the county of the person in question is known, inquiries can be directed to the archives in or near those locations. (See Appendix A for suggestions about writing efficient letters and emails.) Currently, there are no known digital images of Hessen-Nassau census documents on the Internet.

VI. Selected Images of Hessen-Nassau Census Records

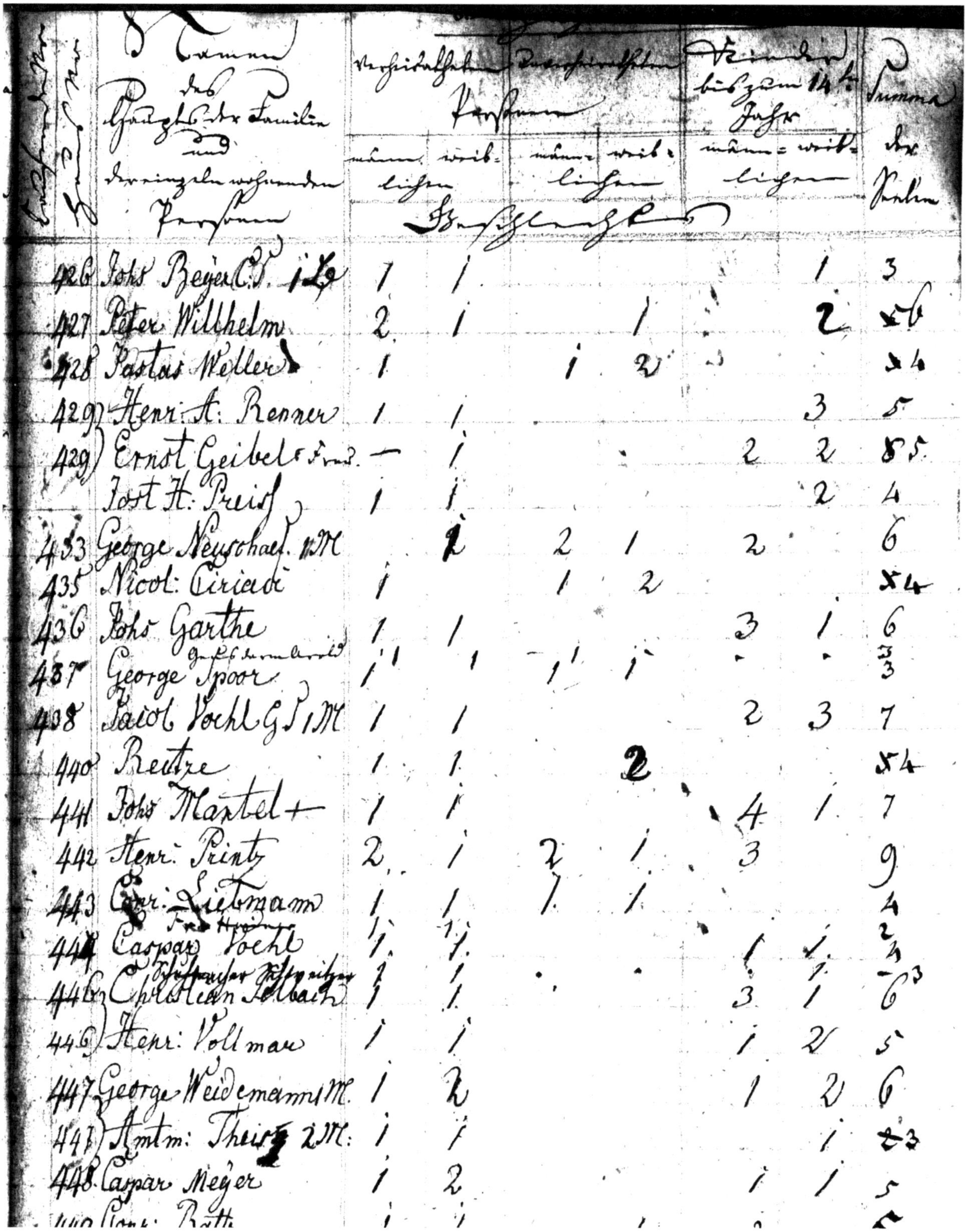

Figure 1. 1824 Census Page from Frankenberg, Hessen-Nassau

Column headings: consecutive entry number; house number; head of household; married males; married females; unmarried males; unmarried females; males under 14; females under 14; total inhabitants [Stadtarchiv Frankenberg/Eder Nr. 4]

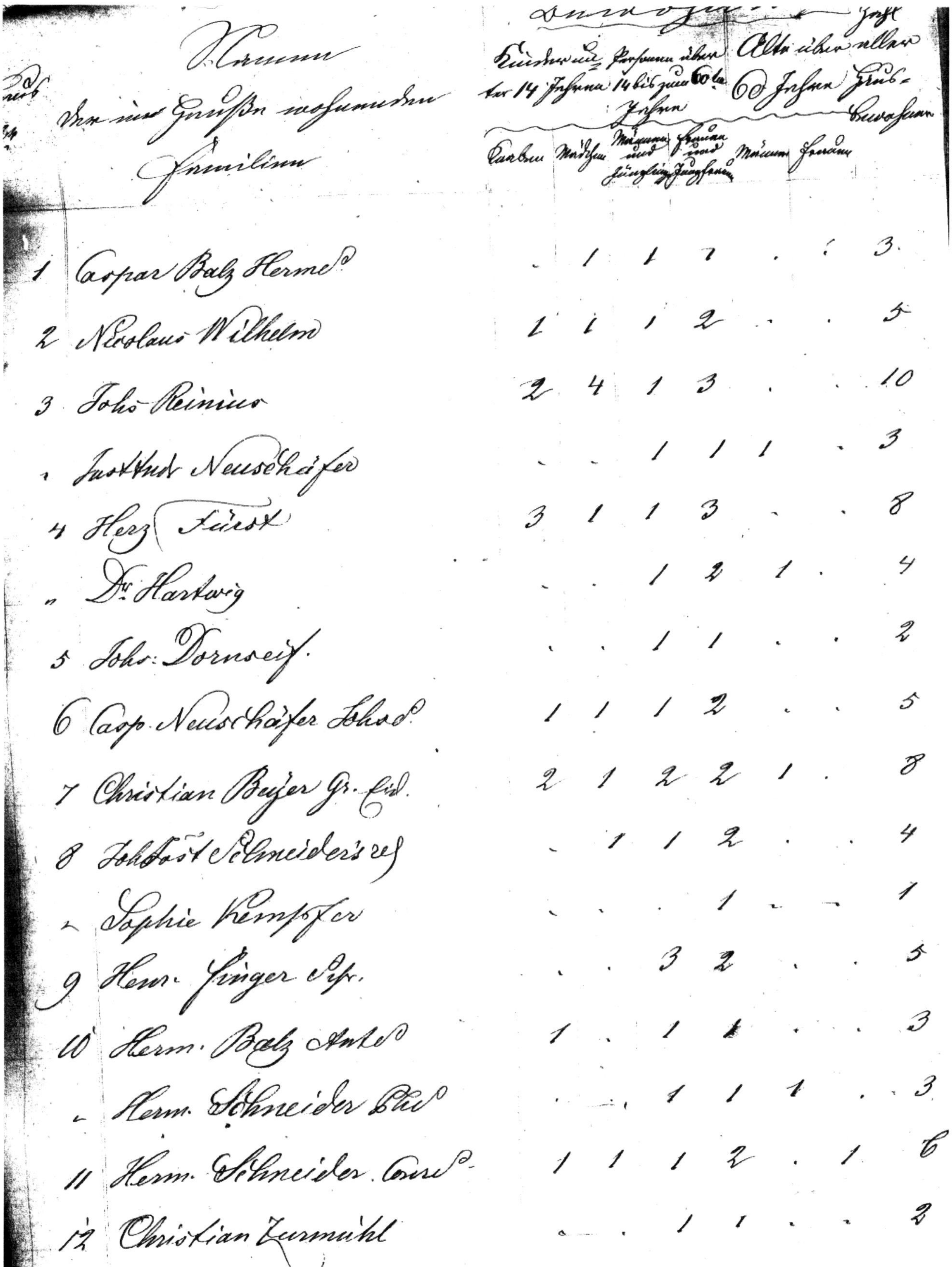

Figure 2. 1840 Census Page from Frankenberg, Hessen-Nassau

House no.	Head of household	Males under 15	Females under 15	Males 15–60	Females 15–60	Males over 60	Females over 60	Total inhabitants
1	Caspar Balz Hermes		1	1	2			3
2	Nicolaus Wilhelm	1	1	1	2			5
3	Johs Reinius	2	4	1	3			10
	Just And. Neuschäfer			1	1	1		3
4	Herz Fürst	3	1	1	3			8
„	Dr. Hartwig			1	2	1		4
5	Johs. Dornseif			1	1			2
6	Casp. Neuschäfer Johs	1	1	1	2			5
7	Christian Beyer Gr. Fd.	2	1	2	2	1		8
8	Joh.Just Schneider's rel		1	1	2			4
„	Sophie Kempfer				1			1
9	Henr. Finger Schr.			3	2			5
10	Herm. Balz Ante	1		1	1			3
„	Herm. Schneider Phil			1	1	1		3
11	Herm. Schneider Conr.	1	1	1	2		1	6
12	Christian Zurmühl			1	1			2

Column headings: house number; head of household; males under 15; females under 15; males 15–60; females 15–60; males over 60; females over 60; total inhabitants [Stadtarchiv Frankenberg/Eder Nr. 4]

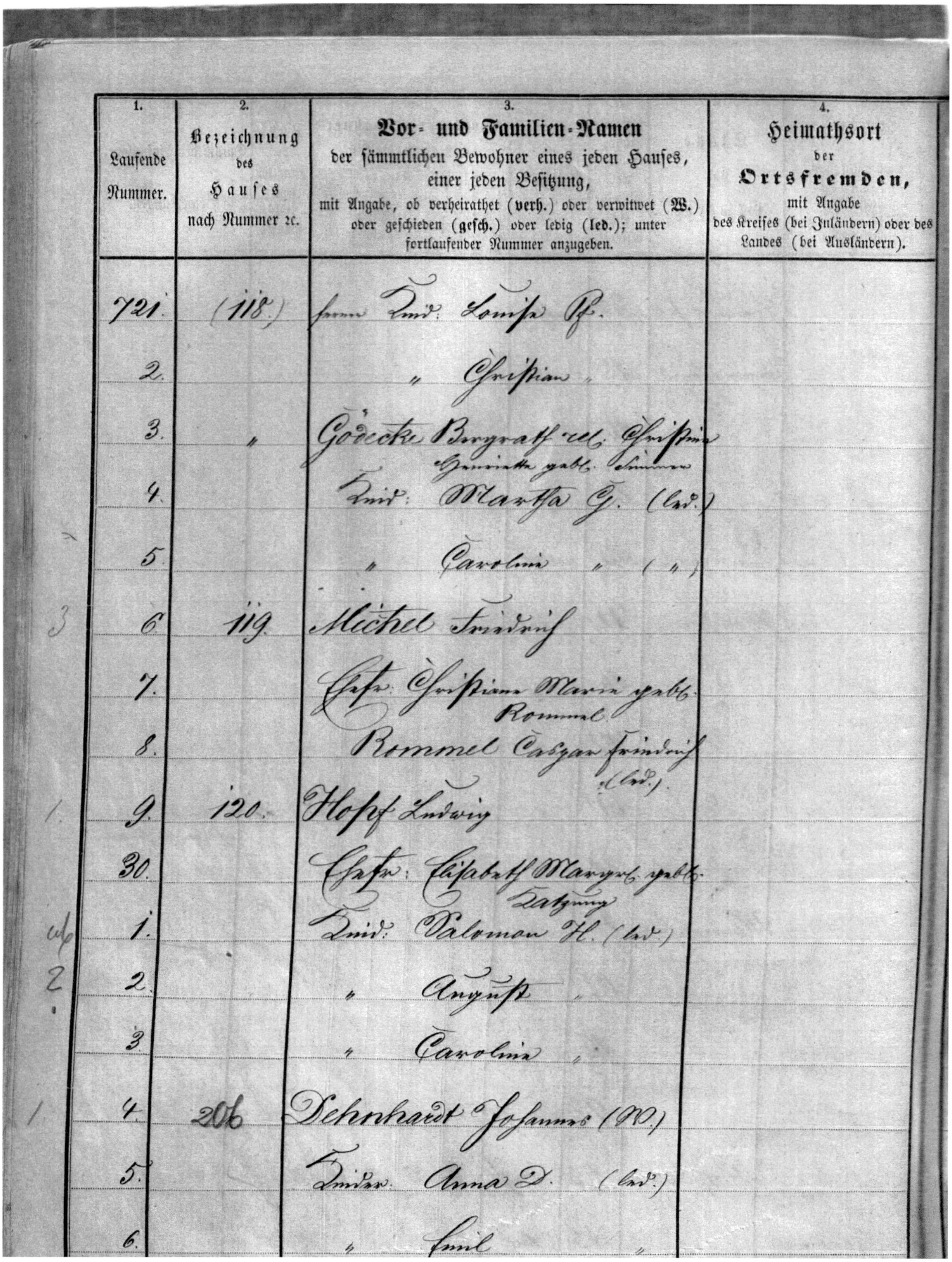

1. Laufende Nummer.	2. Bezeichnung des Hauses nach Nummer ꝛc.	3. Vor- und Familien-Namen der sämmtlichen Bewohner eines jeden Hauses, einer jeden Besitzung, mit Angabe, ob verheirathet (verh.) oder verwittwet (W.) oder geschieden (gesch.) oder ledig (led.); unter fortlaufender Nummer anzugeben.	4. Heimathsort der Ortsfremden, mit Angabe des Kreises (bei Inländern) oder des Landes (bei Ausländern).
721	(118.)	_Frau Wwe. Louise Pf._	
2.	"	_Christian_	
3.	"	_Gödecke Burgraff el. Christine geb._	
4.		_Kind. Martha G. (led.)_	
5.		" _Caroline_ "	
6.	119	_Michel Friedrich_	
7.		_Ehefr. Christiane Marie geb. Rommel_	
8.		_Rommel Caspar Friedrich (led.)_	
9.	120.	_Hopf Ludwig_	
30.		_Ehefr. Elisabeth Margret geb._	
1.		_Kind. Saloman H. (led.)_	
2.		" _August_	
3.		" _Caroline_	
4.	206	_Dehnhardt Johannes (W.)_	
5.		_Kinder Anna D. (led.)_	
6.		" _Emil_	

Figure 3. 1864 Census Page from Schmalkalden, Hessen-Nassau (left-hand page)

Column headings: consecutive number of persons; house number; name of each resident and marital status; home town of foreigners (with county if from Hessen-Nassau, with country if elsewhere) [Stadtarchiv Schmalkalden C III/9a Nr. 9]

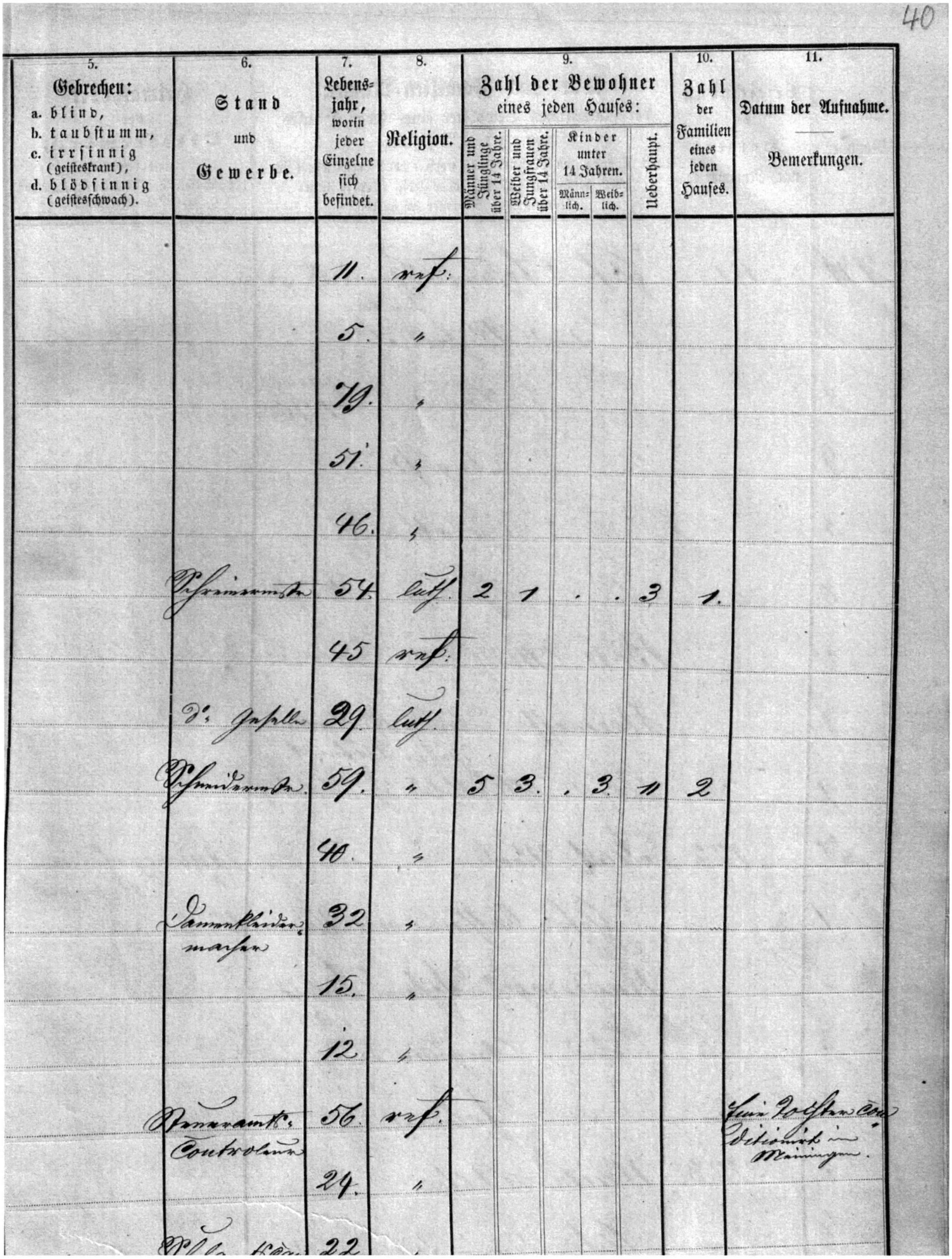

5. Gebrechen: a. blind, b. taubstumm, c. irrsinnig (geisteskrant), d. blödsinnig (geistesschwach).	6. Stand und Gewerbe.	7. Lebens= jahr, worin jeder Einzelne sich befindet.	8. Religion.	9. Zahl der Bewohner eines jeden Hauses:					10. Zahl der Familien eines jeden Hauses.	11. Datum der Aufnahme. ——— Bemerkungen.
				Männer und Jünglinge über 14 Jahre.	Weiber und Jungfrauen über 14 Jahre.	Kinder unter 14 Jahren.		Ueberhaupt.		
						Männ=lich.	Weib=lich.			
		11.	ref:							
		5.	„							
		79.	„							
		51.	„							
		46.	„							
	Schriunwiter	54.	luth	2	1	.	.	3	1	
		45.	ref.							
	D: Gesellen	29.	luth							
	Schmidrmeister	59.	„	5	3.	.	3	11	2	
		40.	„							
	Damenkleider macher	32	„							
		15.	„							
		12	„							
	Renteramts Controleur	56.	ref.							Zur Volksten tion Diecomiet in Meiningen.
		24.	„							
	Wd. Frau	22.								

Figure 4. 1864 Census Page from Schmalkalden, Hessen-Nassau (right-hand page)

Column headings: disabilities; status and occupation; age at next birthday; religion; males over 14; females over 14; males under 14; females under 14; number of families in dwelling; date of entry and comments [Stadtarchiv Schmalkalden C III/9a Nr. 9]

Laufende Nummer der Zählbriefe.	Bezeichnung der Gebäude oder sonstigen Wohnstätten. Angabe der Lage nach Straße und Ortsteil, Wohnplatz. 1.	Haus-nummer oder andere Bezeichnung der Baulichkeit. 2.	Name der Haushaltungsvorstände oder Bezeichnung der Anstalten, für welche Zählbriefe ausgegeben wurden. 3.	Ortsanwesende Personen. männl. 4.	weibl. 5.	Darunter sind reichs-angehörige aktive Militär-personen. 6.	Bemerkungen. 7.	Laufende Nummer der Zählbriefe.	Bezeichnung sonsti... Angabe na... Straße und Wohn... 1
			Vorige Seite . . .	29 34	25 23	—			
15.	Schülstraße	75ᶜ	Urban	1	1	—		40.	Langst
16.	"	76	Meyer Fenis	2	2	—		41.	"
17.	"	77	Görling	3	4	—		42.	"
18.	"	"	Fahney	1	4	—		43.	"
19.	"	78ᶜ	Koh	4	1	—		44.	"
20.	"	79	Wilkening	3	1	—		45.	
21.	"	80	Weber	2	2	—		46.	
22.	"	81	Bante Fr.	2	1	—		47.	
23.	"	"	" Fr. H.	2	1	—		48.	
24.	"	82	Schäfer	1	2	—		49.	
25.	"	83	Groß Frau	2	3	—		50	
26.	"	69½	Korff	4	1	—		51.	
27.	"	"	Ebbeke Wtw.	—	1	—		52.	
28.	Langstraße	84	Hartung	3	3	—		53.	
29.	Schülstraße	84b	Klinge	2	5	—		54.	
30.	Langstraße	85	Grening	3	2	—		55.	
31.	"	"	Kruse	3	2	—		56.	
32.	"	85½	Krüger	2	1	—		57.	
33.	"	"	Brockmann	2	2	—		58.	
34.	"	86	Fallmeier Fr.	2	4	—		59.	
35.	"	"	Reinerke	3	2	—		60.	
36.	"	87	Hürter	4	1	—		61.	

Figure 5. 1905 *Controlliste* Page from Hessisch Oldendorf, Hessen-Nassau

Column headings: street name; house number or name; name of head of household; male residents; female residents; active military personnel; comments [Niedersächsisches Landesarchiv Bückeburg NLA BU Dep 59 Nr 18]

Notes

[1] Otto Klingelhöffer, "Der *Zollverein im Jahr 1865*" in *Zeitschrift für die gesamte Staatswissenschaft*, v. 19 (1863), 96.

[2] Antje Kraus, *Quellen zur Bevölkerungsstatistik Deutschlands 1815–1871*, Band 1 (Boppard, Germany: Harald Boldt, 1980), 24-25, 129–152.

16 Hohenzollern

I. Location

In the nineteenth century, the independent duchies of Hohenzollern-Hechingen and Hohenzollern-Sigmaringen were surrounded almost entirely by the kingdom of Württemberg. They shared only a small border section with the grand duchy of Baden in southwestern Germany. In 1849, Hohenzollern became a province of the far-off kingdom of Preußen (with which it had long shared ancestral connections). The capital city was Sigmaringen.

II. Census Enumerations in Hohenzollern

The first census conducted in the duchies took place in 1816 and was a head count only. The next campaign took place in 1834 after Hohenzollern had joined the new *Zollverein*.[1] The *Zollverein* required that a census be done every three years through 1864.[2] In 1867, the population of Hohenzollern was counted as part of a campaign carried out all over Germany. Under the German Empire, enumerations were done in 1871, every five years from 1875 to 1910, and finally in 1916.

III. Specific Instructions to Town Officials and Enumerators

As of this writing, only the regulations for three census campaigns have been located and are summarized here:

1829: observe the standards set for the 1813 census; record the status or occupation of each person; complete the census by the end of May

1834: record the name of each person with her/his age; count all household members, including servants and employees; count foreigners who have lived here for at least one year

1852: use the same format and content as in 1849; do not record the citizenship status of Jews; engage only agents who are fully qualified to do good work

IV. Content of Census Records in Hohenzollern from 1829 to 1864

	1829	1831	1834	1837	1840	1843	1846	1849	1852	1855	1858	1861	1864
No images available		X		X	X	X	X	X	X	X	X	X	X
Name of head of household	X												
Total male residents	X		X										
Total female residents	X		X										
Persons under 6 (by gender)	X												
Persons 7–14 (by gender)	X												
Persons 15–20 (by gender)	X												
Persons 20–25 (by gender)	X												
Persons 25–40 (by gender)	X												
Persons 40–60 (by gender)	X												
Persons 60–70 (by gender)	X												
Persons 70–80 (by gender)	X												
Persons 80–90 (by gender)	X												
Persons 90–100 (by gender)	X												
Persons over 100 (by gender)	X												
Married persons	X												
Unmarried persons	X												
Widowers	X												
Widows	X												
Divorced persons	X												
Catholics	X												
Lutherans	X												
Jewish	X												
Males away from home	X												
Females away from home	X												
Name of each resident			X										
Status or occupation			X										
Persons under 14 (by gender)			X										
Persons over 14 (by gender)			X										
Age in years			X										
Handwritten forms	X		X										

V. Accessibility of Census Records in Hohenzollern

As of this writing, only one archive has been found that includes even sparse census records in its collection: Staatsarchiv Sigmaringen, a branch of the Landesarchiv Baden-Württemberg system. Nevertheless, researchers may direct inquiries to the archives of any towns in the historic province of Hohenzollern (using reliable gazetteers for that province). (See Appendix A for suggestions about writing efficient inquiries.) Currently the Family History Library has no microfilmed census records for Hohenzollern in its collection and no digitized census images are known to be available on the Internet.

VI. Selected Images of Hohenzollern Census Records

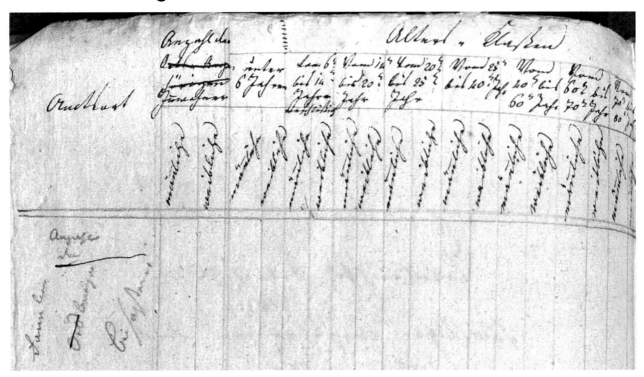

Figure 1. 1829 Census Page from Hohenzollern-Sigmaringen (left-hand page)

Column headings: head of household; total male residents; total female residents; males under 6; females under 6; males 6–14; females 6–14; males 15–20; females 15–20; males 20 to 25; females 20–25; males 25–40; females 25–40; males 40–50; females 40–50; males 50–60; females 50–60; males 60–70; females 60–70; males 70–80; females 70–80 [Staatsarchiv Sigmaringen Ho 86 T 1 Nr. 1515]

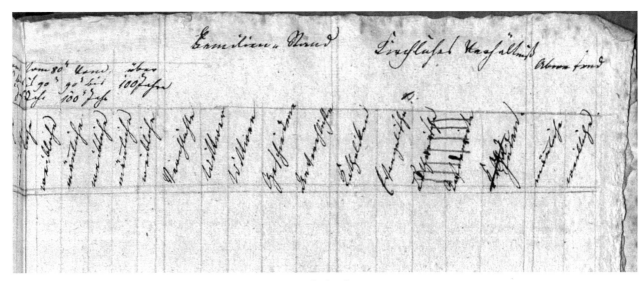

Figure 2. 1829 Census Page from Hohenzollern-Sigmaringen (right-hand page)

Column headings: males 80–90; females 80–90; males 90–100; females 90–100; males over 100; females over 100; married persons; widowers; widows; divorced persons; unmarried persons; Catholics; Lutherans; Jewish; males away from home; females away from home [Staatsarchiv Sigmaringen Ho 86 T 1 Nr. 1515]

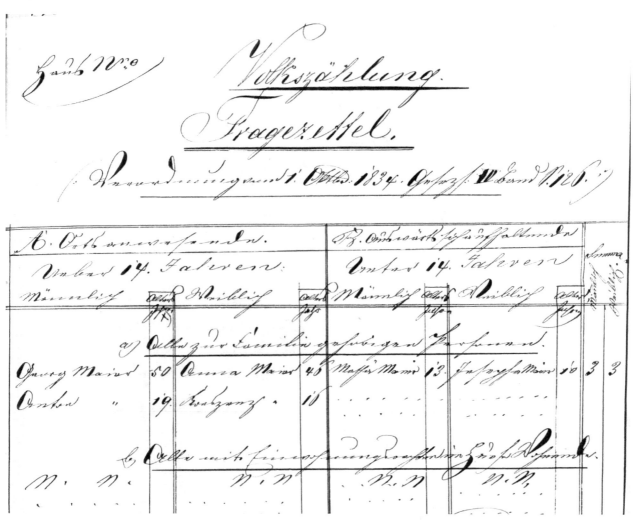

Figure 3. 1834 Census Page from Sigmaringen, Hohenzollern

Column headings: name of each resident; males over 14; females over 14; age; names of persons away from home; total males; total females [Staatsarchiv Sigmaringen Ho 235 T 4-5 Nr. 400]

Notes

[1] Antje Kraus, *Quellen zur Bevölkerungsstatistik Deutschlands 1815–1871*, Band 1 (Boppard, Germany: Harald Boldt, 1980), 219–224.

[2] W. O. Henderson, *The Zollverein* (London: Frank Cass, 1959), 62.

17 Lippe

I. Location

The principality of Lippe lay in northern Germany—surrounded on the west and south by the Prussian province of Westfalen, on the northeast by the kingdom of Hannover, and on the east by the province of Hessen-Nassau and the principality of Pyrmont. Several tiny exclaves were situated to the south. The capital was Detmold and the principality was sometimes called Lippe-Detmold to differentiate it from the principality of Schaumburg-Lippe.

II. Census Enumerations in Lippe

The first census carried out by the principality was dated 1816, but only numbers were collected. Annual counts were conducted for the next six decades, in that the previous year's population total was increased by the current year's total births, then decreased by the current year's total deaths.[1] Lippe resisted the movement that led to the establishment of three customs unions among the German states in 1828 (as well as the *Zollverein* [Customs Union]) and made its own way economically for the next few years. The 1836 census was the first in Lippe to feature the names of persons (heads of households), but the motivation for that census is unclear.

The pressure on Lippe to join the *Zollverein* must have been constant, given the fact that the tiny state was surrounded on three sides by Preußen (the leading power in the *Zollverein*). And so it was that Lippe

Figure 1. On December 14, 1841 the princely government in Detmold instructed local officials to carry out a census in preparation for "the pending annexation of our territory to the *Zollverein*…" [Stadtarchiv Blomberg III/BV 1]

joined in October 1841.[2] The Lippe census of 1852 was conducted based on *Zollverein* guidelines and the triennial pattern was sustained through 1864.[3]

Another census was enumerated in 1867 as a joint effort between the *Zollverein* and the North German Confederation and included all German states. Under the German Empire, enumerations were done in the principality of Lippe in 1871, every five years from 1875 to 1910, and finally in 1916.

III. Specific Instructions to Town Officials and Enumerators

The following instructions for the conduct of the census campaigns over the years are noteworthy:

1828: the census is to be conducted on June 2; the pastors and teachers will carry out the counting; count the number of marriages in the past year and the Jewish residents also but separately

1835: the work is to be carried out by city officials and teachers; count children living in foreign countries but not children living elsewhere within the principality; count local retired military personnel; use the forms provided

1841: the target date is December 31; count foreigners only if they have been here for more than one year; assistants called upon to help the officials will be paid; a census will be taken henceforth every three years

1846: the census is to begin and be concluded on December 3; count the people in hospitals and prisons; count locals working elsewhere except journeymen

1849: a sample finished page is attached to the instructions

IV. Content of Census Records in Lippe from 1828 to 1864

The details required by the census forms in the enumerations of 1835 and 1841 are quite different, but the pre-printed forms used from 1846 through 1864 are apparently identical.

	1828	1835	1841	1843	1846	1849	1852	1855	1858	1861	1864
No images available	X			X		X				X	
Name and status of head of household		X									
Total males		X									
Total females		X									
Total residents		X	X		X		X	X	X		X
Number of sons		X									
Number of daughters		X									
Servants (by gender)		X									
Other relatives (by gender)		X									
Children under 7 (by gender)		X									
Persons age 7–14 (by gender)		X									
Persons age 14–25 (by gender)		X									
Persons age 25–70 (by gender)		X									
Married couples		X									
Widowers		X									
Widows		X									
Livestock (by category)		X			X		X	X	X		X
Comments		X	X								
Description of dwelling			X		X		X	X	X		X
First and last name of each resident			X		X		X	X	X		X
Status or occupation			X		X		X	X	X		X
Age at next birthday			X								
Persons under 14 (by gender)					X		X	X	X		X
Persons over 14 (by gender)					X		X	X	X		X
Total persons in dwelling/on farm etc.					X		X	X	X		X
Pre-printed pages		X	X		X		X	X	X		X

V. Accessibility of Census Records in Lippe

One of three regional archives in the modern German state of Northrhine-Westphalia is located in Demold, the historical capital of Lippe. Some census documents are found there but deal mostly with the statistics that resulted from the enumerations. (http://www.archive.nrw.de/lav/index.php). The best way to find original census lists is to write to the archive of the town of county in question (see Appendix A for instructions on writing the inquiry). As of this writing, there are no digital copies of these records available on the Internet and the Family History Library has only a very few on microfilm in its collection (a search in that catalog now and then might reveal new collection items).

VI. Selected Images of Lippe Census Records

Stadt _Blomberg_   Anzahl aller

Namen der Einwohner	Männer	Frauen	Söhne über 14	Söhne unter Jahr	Töchter	Bei sich habende Verwandte: Geschlechts männlich über 14	unter Jahr	weiblich	Eingeheuerte: Geschlechts männlich über 14	unter Jahr	weiblich	Ladendiener, Schreiber	Laquaien, Kutscher, Vorreuter, Knechte	Gesellen
[handwritten name]		1	1		1									
[handwritten name]	1	1												
[handwritten name]	1	1		1	1									
[handwritten name]	1	1			1									1
[handwritten name]	1	1	1	2	1									
[handwritten name]	1	1			2									1
[handwritten name]	1	1		1	2									1
[handwritten name]	1	1	3		2									
[handwritten name]	1	1	1		2									
[handwritten name]	1	1	1		4									
[handwritten name]									1	1	4			
[handwritten name]	1	1			1									
[handwritten name]	1	1		1	2									
[handwritten name]	1	1	1	2										
[handwritten name]	1	1			3									
[handwritten name]	1	1		2	2									2
[handwritten name]	1	1												
[handwritten name]	1	1	1											
[handwritten name]	1	1												
[handwritten name]	1	1	1		4									

Figure 1. A rare find: 1775 Census Page from Blomberg, Lippe (left-hand page)

Column headings: name of head of household; males; females; sons over 14; sons under 14; other male relatives over 14; other male relatives under 14; female relatives; male employees over 14; male employees under 14; female employees; shop employees and clerks; other employees; journeymen [Stadtarchiv Blomberg III/B V 1]

Perfonen						Art der Handthierung und des Gewerbes	Halten an Vieh						Anmerkungen
Lehr- und Dienst-Jungen		Franzöfinnen und Haushälterinnen.	Köchinnen, Ammen und Mägde	Summe aller Perfonen	darunter find Ausländer		Pferde	Ochfen und Kühe	Rinder und Zuchtkälber	Schaafe	Ziegen	Schweine	
über 14	unter 14 Jahr												
				6	1	*[illegible]*		1					
				4		*[illegible]*		2					
				2		*[illegible]*							
				2	1	*[illegible]*					1		
				3		*[illegible]*	3	2			1	3	
				2		*[illegible]*					1		
				5		*[illegible]*							
				2		*[illegible]*							
				7		*[illegible]*		1	1				
				4		*[illegible]*		2	2	100			*[illegible]*
				3		*[illegible]*							
				4		*[illegible]*							
1				4		*[illegible]*							
1				7		*[illegible]*		1			1		*[illegible]*
				7		*[illegible]*							
				3		*[illegible]*					1		
				2		*[illegible]*		1					*[illegible]*
				3		*[illegible]*							
				4		*[illegible]*					1		*[illegible]*
				3		*[illegible]*							
				1		*[illegible]*		1					
				1		*[illegible]*							

Figure 2. A rare find: 1775 Census Page from Blomberg, Lippe (right-hand page)

Column headings: apprentices over 14; apprentices under 14; domestic servants; cooks, etc.; total residents; total foreigners; occupation; livestock (six categories); comments [Stadtarchiv Blomberg III/BV 1]

98

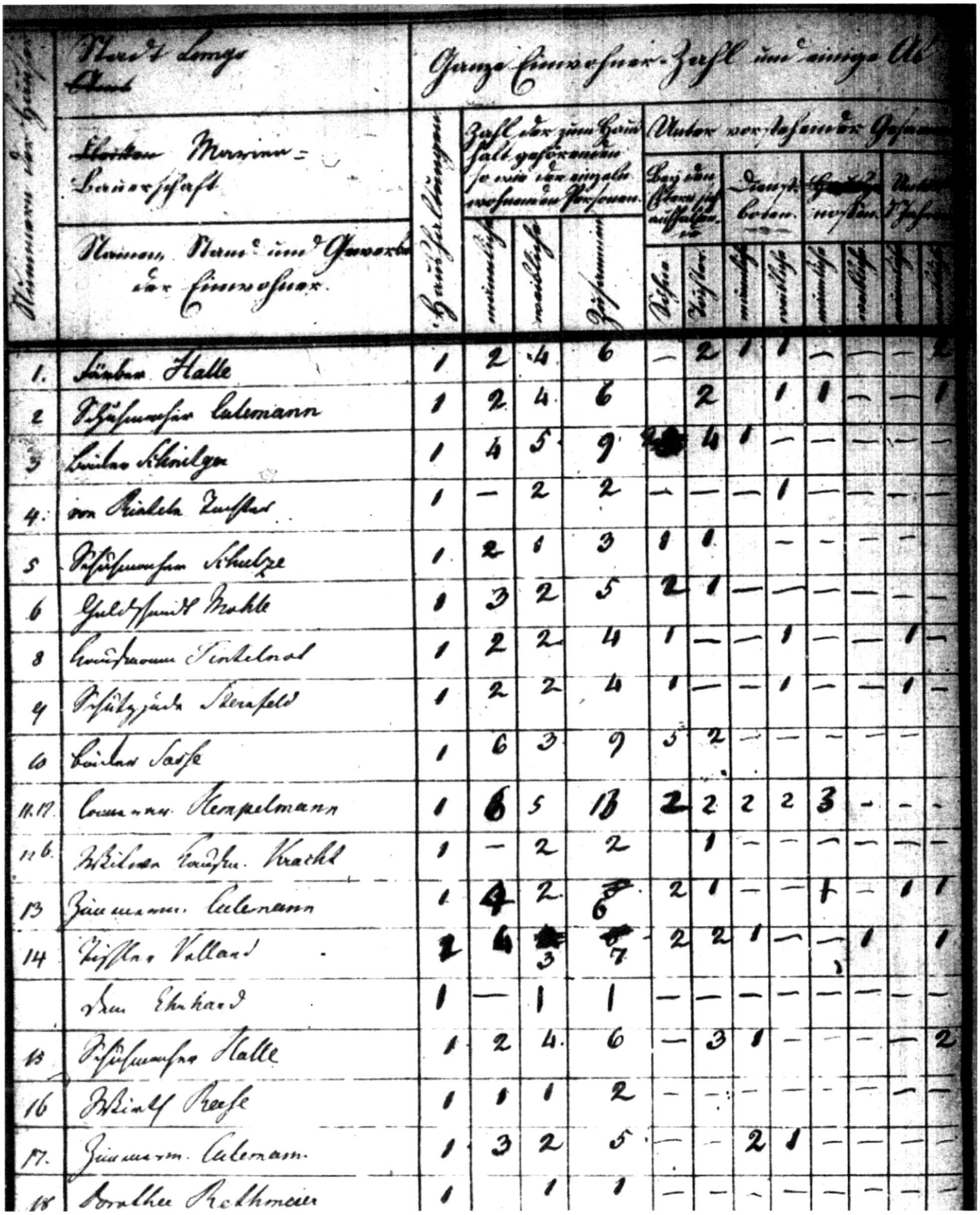

Figure 3. 1835 Census Page from Lemgo, Lippe (left-hand page)

Column headings: consecutive number of dwellings; name of head of household; total males; total females; total residents; total sons; total daughters; servants; other relatives; children under 7 [Stadtarchiv Lemgo]

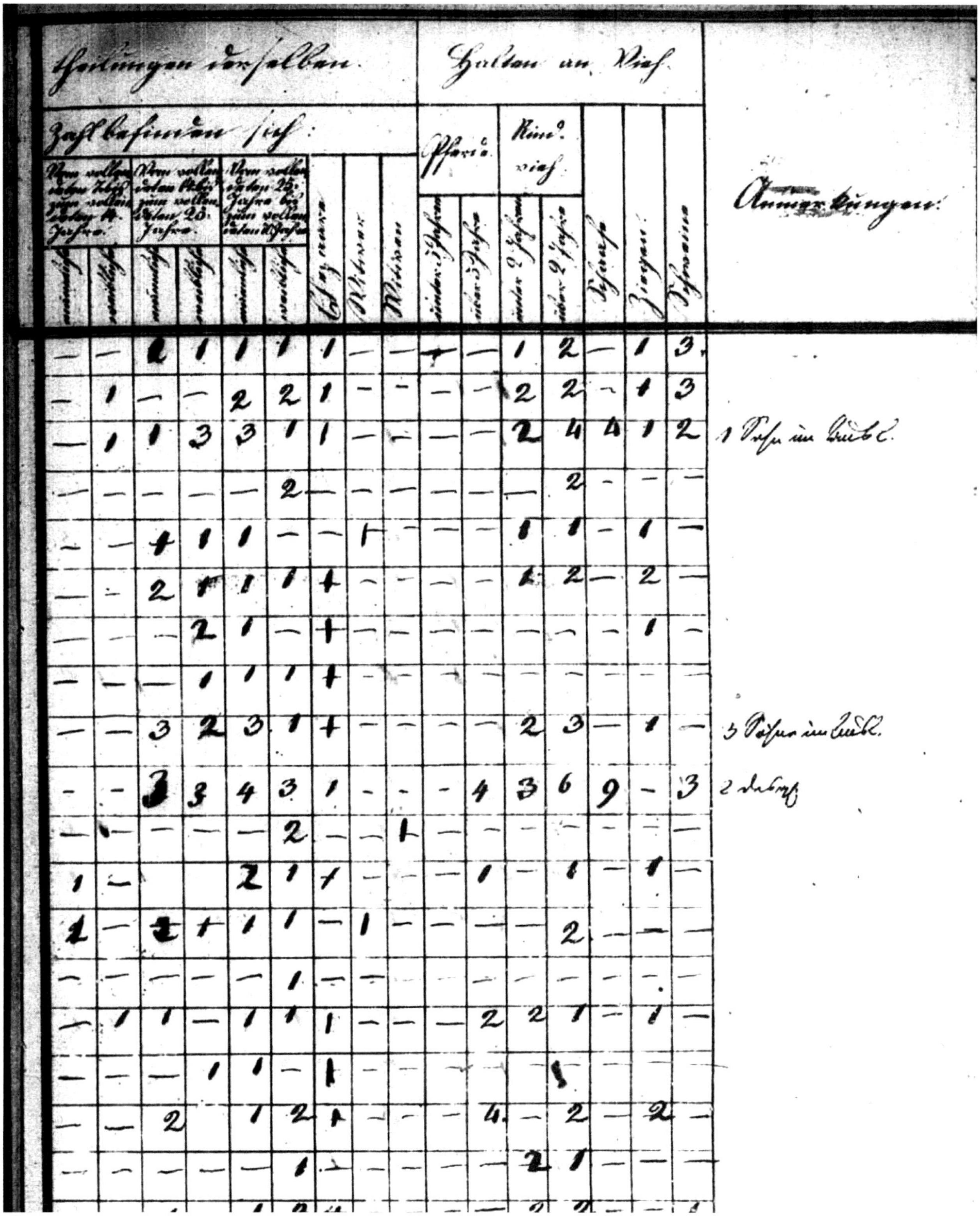

Figure 4. 1835 Census Page from Lemgo, Lippe (right-hand page)

Column headings: males 7–14; females 7–14; males 14–25; females 14–25; males 25–70; females 25–70; couples; widowers; widows; livestock (seven categories) [Stadtarchiv Lemgo]

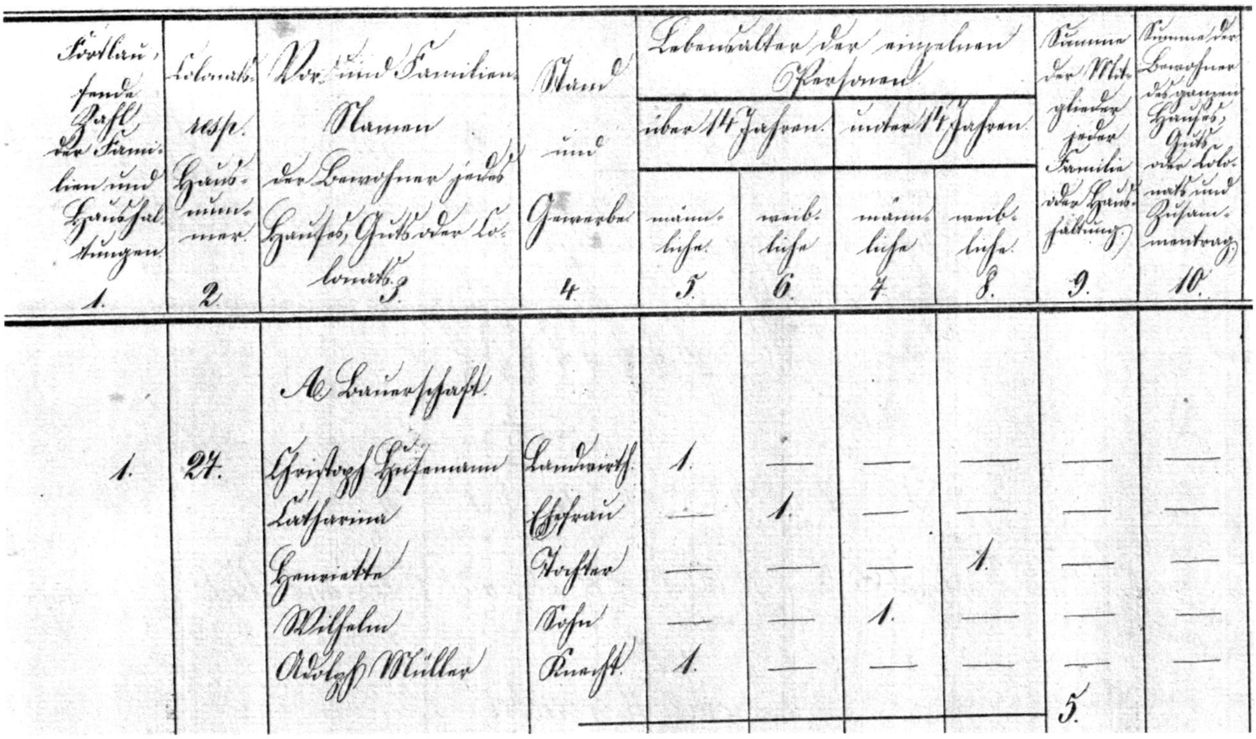

Figure 5. 1852 Census Page from Blomberg, Lippe (left-hand page)

Column headings: consecutive number; dwelling number; name of head of household; status and occupation; males over 14; females over 14; males under 14; females under 14; total family members; total residents [Stadtarchiv Blomberg III/B V 1]

Figure 6. 1852 Census Page from Blomberg, Lippe (right-hand page)

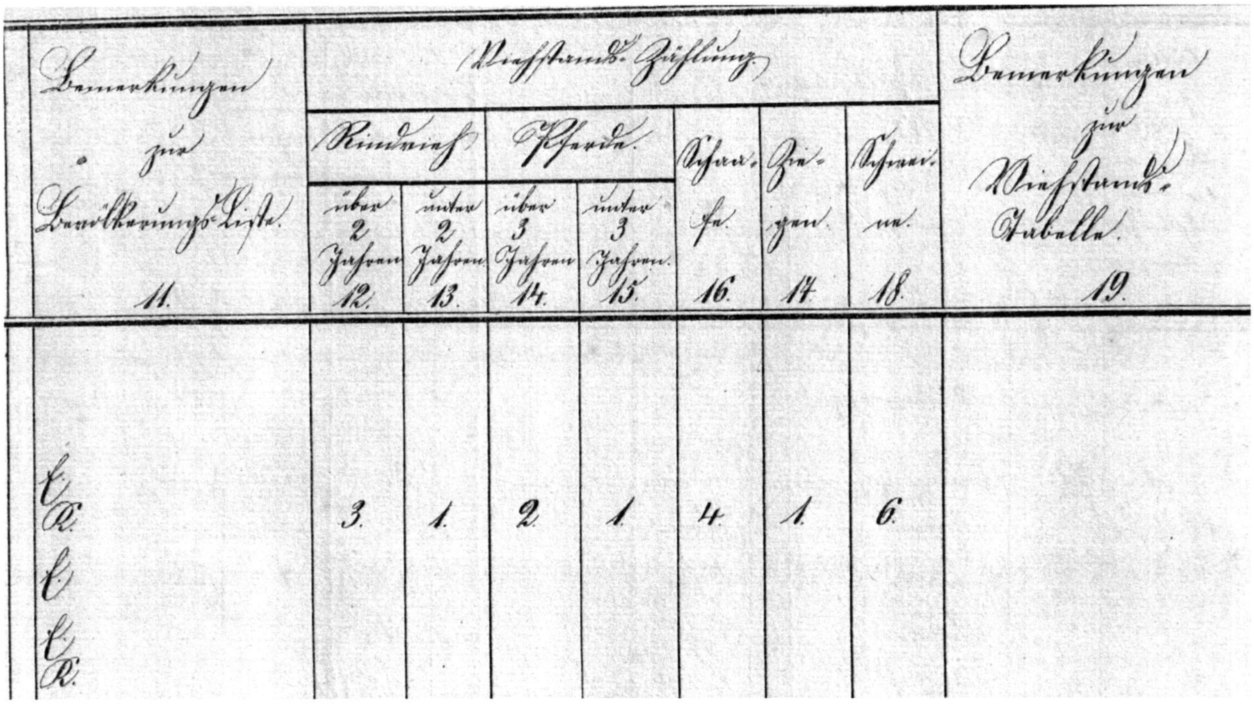

Column headings: notes; livestock (seven classifications); comments on livestock [Stadtarchiv Blomberg III/B V 1]

Notes

[1] Antje Kraus, *Quellen zur Bevölkerungsstatistik Deutschlands 1815–1871*, Band 1 (Boppard, Germany: Harald Boldt, 1980), 26, 231–236.

[2] W. O. Henderson, *The Zollverein* (London: Frank Cass, 1939), 126.

[3] Otto Klingelhöffer, "Der *Zollverein* im Jahr 1865" in *Zeitschrift für die gesamte Staatswissenschaft*, v. 19 (1863), 96.

18 Lübeck (Hansestadt Lübeck) [Luebeck]

I. Location

The free Hanseatic (city) of Lübeck is located at the mouth of the Trave River near the Baltic Sea. Its neighbor states in the early nineteenth century were Schleswig-Holstein to the west and the two Mecklenburg grand duchies (Schwerin and Strelitz) to the east. Several counties directly to the south were added to Lübeck later in the nineteenth century.

II. Census Enumerations in Lübeck

Like its sister Hanseatic cities Bremen and Hamburg, Lübeck declined invitations to join either the *Zollverein* or the *Steuerverein* based on the economic advantages the city enjoyed thanks to its port facilities. It was not until November 1868 that Lübeck finally joined the *Zollverein*.[1] However, for reasons not yet explained, the city had already conducted census enumerations in 1831, 1845, 1851, 1857, and 1862.[2] Those census campaigns at times involved the small communities and rural settlements south of the city.

In 1867, this tiny state joined with all of the German states in what became the first total German census.[3] Under the German Empire, enumerations were done in Lübeck in 1871, every five years from 1875 to 1910, and finally in 1916.

III. Specific Instructions to Town Officials and Enumerators

Only three instances of instructions for the census campaigns in Lübeck have been found and yield the following points of interest:

1845: begin on September 1 and continue without interruption until finished; the data will be collected by members of the guard (in the city) and reservists (in rural areas); count every person, including family members temporarily away from home; count all foreigners except for those here for only a short time; count active military personnel, students, journeymen, sailors, etc.; give the age of each person as of the next birthday; do not count persons born since September 1, but do count persons who died after September 1 and before the enumeration was completed; married persons who are legally or practically separated are to be counted as widows or widowers; in rural areas, retired persons are to be counted as members of whatever family they live with; underline the names of persons who are disabled or insane

1851: begin on September 1 and continue without interruption until finished; for local persons away from here but without permanent residence elsewhere, write "absent" [*abwesend*] under "Comments."

1857: for persons not born in the state of Lübeck, it is sufficient to record the country of birth only; in rural areas where homes have no numbers, a name or description of the dwelling is to be recorded

IV. Content of Census Records in Lübeck from 1831 to 1862

	1831	1845	1851	1857	1862
City residents only	X				
Address of household	X				
Name of head of household only	X				
Occupation	X	X	X	X	X
Number of children	X				
Number of servants	X				
Total persons in household	X				
Comments	X	X	X	X	X
Name of every person		X	X	X	X
Age in years		X	X	X	X
Birth place		X	X	X	X
Status in household		X			
Religion		X	X	X	X
Marital status			X	X	X
Secondary occupation			X	X	X
Property ownership			X	X	
Pre-printed forms	X	X	X	X	X

V. Accessibility of Census Records in Lübeck

Because this was one of the smallest states in Germany before 1916, there are very few places where census records exist, making a search much easier than in larger states. The primary location is the *Archiv der Hansestadt Lübeck* located at Mühlendamm 1–3 in Lübeck (postal code 23552). The address of the website is: archiv.Luebeck.de. A search for the key word *Volkszählung* yields the word *Volkszählungslisten* in red letters. A click on that term provides detail (in German) regarding the census enumerations described above.

Ancestry.com has in its collection digital copies of all census pages from numerous census campaigns in Lübeck (urban and rural). The catalog of the Family History Library currently shows no entries for Lübeck census records during the period in question. Researchers wishing to find census records in towns in rural Lübeck might do well to direct an inquiry to the archive (*Stadtarchiv*) of any town of substantial size; addresses are usually available on the town's website. (See Appendix A for instructions on how to write the inquiry.)

VI. Selected Images of Lübeck Census Records

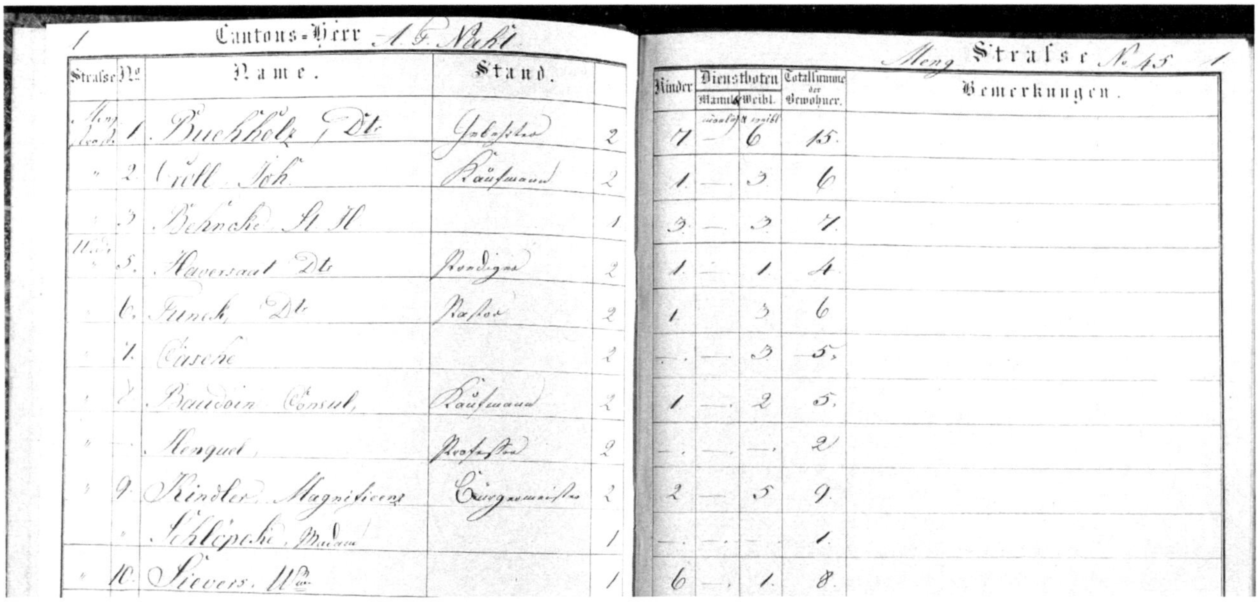

1 Cantons-Herr A. G. Nahl — Meng Strasse No. 45 1

Strasse	No.	Name.	Stand.		Kinder	Dienstboten Männl.	Dienstboten Weibl.	Totalsumme der Bewohner.	Bemerkungen.
Meng Straße	1.	Buchholz J. Dr.	Gelehrter	2	7		6	15.	
"	2.	Crill Joh.	Kaufmann	2	1.	—	3.	6	
"	3.	Behncke H. H.		1	3.	—	3.	7.	
	5.	Haversaat Dr.	Prediger	2	1.		1	4.	
	6.	Funck Dr.	Pastor	2	1		3	6	
	7.	Cusone		2	—	—	3	5.	
	8.	Baudoin Consul	Kaufmann	2	1	—	2	5.	
		Hengael	Professor	2	—	—	—	2	
	9.	Kindler Magnificenz	Bürgermeister	2	2	—	5	9.	
		Schlöpcke, Madame		1	—	—	—	1.	
	10.	Sievers Wwe		1	6	—	1.	8.	

Figure 1. 1831 Census Page from Lübeck

Column headings: street, house number; name; status; number of children; male servants; female servants; total inhabitants; comments [Archiv der Hansestadt Luebeck, Stadt- und Landamt, Volkszählungslisten 1831]

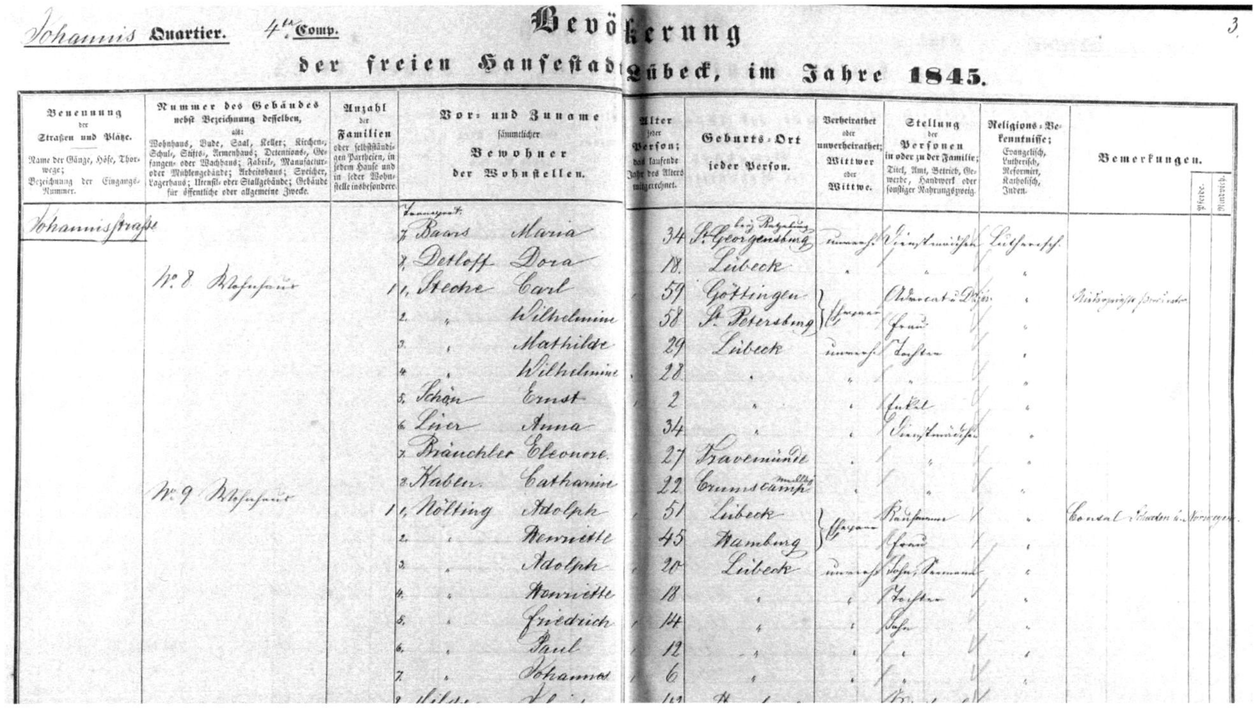

Johannis Quartier. 4te Comp. — 3.

Bevölkerung der freien Hansestadt Lübeck, im Jahre 1845.

Benennung der Straßen und Plätze. Name der Gänge, Höfe, Thorwege; Bezeichnung der Eingangs-Nummer.	Nummer des Gebäudes nebst Bezeichnung desselben, als: Wohnhaus, Bude, Saal, Keller; Kirchen-, Schul-, Stifts-, Armenhaus; Detentions-, Gefangen- oder Wachhaus; Fabrik, Manufactur- oder Mühlengebäude; Arbeitshaus; Speicher, Lagerhaus; Utensil- oder Stallgebäude; Gebäude für öffentliche oder allgemeine Zwecke.	Anzahl der Familien oder selbständigen Partheien, in jedem Hause und in jeder Wohnstelle insbesondere.	Vor- und Zuname sämmtlicher Bewohner der Wohnstellen.		Alter jeder Person; das laufende Jahr des Alters mitgerechnet.	Geburts-Ort jeder Person.	Verheirathet oder unverheirathet; Wittwer oder Wittwe.	Stellung der Personen in oder zu der Familie; Titel, Amt, Betrieb, Gewerbe, Handwerk oder sonstiger Nahrungszweig.	Religions-Bekenntnisse; Evangelisch, Lutherisch, Reformirt, Katholisch, Juden.	Bemerkungen.	Pferde.	Rindvieh.
Johannisstraße			1. Baars	Maria	34	St. Georgensberg	unverh.	Dienstmädchen	Lutherisch			
			2. Detloff	Dora	18.	Lübeck	"	"	"			
	No. 8. Wohnhaus	1	1. Stecher	Carl	59	Göttingen	verh.	Advocat Dr.	"	Rittergutsbesitzer		
			2. "	Wilhelmine	58	St. Petersburg		Frau	"			
			3. "	Mathilde	29	Lübeck	unverh.	Tochter	"			
			4. "	Wilhelmine	28	"	"	"	"			
			5. Schön	Ernst	2	"	"	Enkel	"			
			6. Lüer	Anna	34	"	"	Dienstmädchen	"			
			7. Bräuchler	Eleonore	27	Travemünde	"	"	"			
			8. Kablen	Catharina	22	Crummesse	"	"	"			
	No. 9 Wohnhaus	1	1. Nölting	Adolph	51	Lübeck	verh.	Kaufmann	"	Consul Schweden u. Norwegen		
			2. "	Henriette	45	Hamburg		Frau	"			
			3. "	Adolph	20	Lübeck	unverh.	Sohn, Kaufmann	"			
			4. "	Henriette	18	"	"	Tochter	"			
			5. "	Friedrich	14	"	"	Sohn	"			
			6. "	Paul	12	"	"	"	"			
			7. "	Johannes	6	"	"	"	"			

Figure 2. 1845 Census Page from Lübeck

Column headings: name of street or location; number or other designation of dwelling; number of each family; first and last name of each resident; age at next birthday; birth place of each inhabitant; marital status; status of each member of the household; religion [five specified]; comments (number of horses; number of livestock) [Archiv der Hansestadt Luebeck, Stadt- und Landamt, Volkszählungslisten 1845]

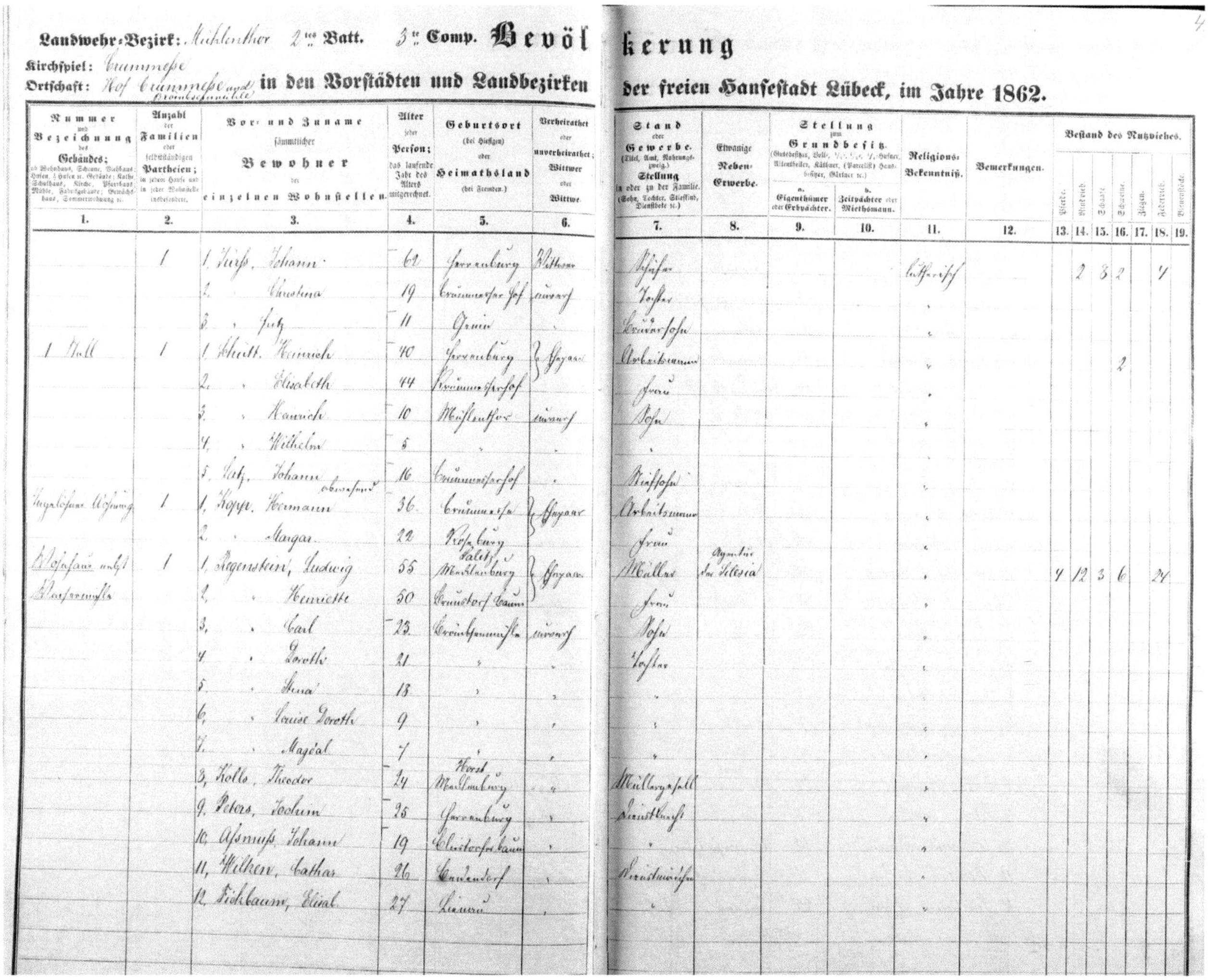

Figure 3. 1862 Census Page from Lübeck

Column headings: name of street or location; number or other designation of dwelling; number of each family; first and last name of each resident; age at next birthday; birth place if local, birth country if foreigner; occupation or position in the household; secondary employment; religion; comments (number of horses; number of livestock) [Archiv der Hansestadt Luebeck, Stadt- und Landamt, Volkszählungslisten 1862]

Notes

[1] W. O. Henderson, *The Zollverein* (London: Frank Cass, 1959), 310.

[2] In 1836, the city began calculating population statistics in all non-census years as well, using this formula: total number of persons in the previous year plus the number of children born minus the number of persons who died. The information was likely provided by the civil registry offices [*Standesamt*]. See Antje Kraus, *Quellen zur Bevölkerungs-, Sozial- und Wirtschaftsstatistik Deutschlands 1815–1871*, Band 1 (Boppard, Germany: Harald Boldt, 1980), 112.

[3] Kraus, *Quellen*, 27, 255–260.

19 Mecklenburg-Schwerin

I. Location

The state of Mecklenburg-Schwerin was raised to a grand duchy as a result of the Congress of Vienna in 1815. Bordered by the Baltic Sea on the northwest, its neighbors in the nineteenth century were Schleswig-Holstein and the kingdom of Hannover on the west, and the Prussian provinces of Pommern on the east and Brandenburg on the south. Sister-state Mecklenburg-Strelitz had land masses on the west and the east as well. The capital city was Schwerin.

II. Census Enumerations in Mecklenburg-Schwerin

The most highly-detailed census known in Germany was conducted throughout Mecklenburg-Schwerin in 1819. The proclamation from Grand Duke Friederich Franz on July 3 of that year stated that "previous censuses have not provided the necessary statistics," thus a more extensive enumeration was scheduled for August.[1] Not only is the 1819 census a rarity in that it lists by name every resident in the grand duchy, but a full birth date is provided, along with the town of birth and the church parish with which the town was affiliated.

In 1826, another edict was issued by the office of the grand duke, stipulating that the population was to be enumerated by November 11 of that year and every successive year in the fall. Each annual census featured the name of every head of household and the forms used featured few revisions or additions from 1826 to 1867. Mecklenburg-Schwerin was the only German state known to have conducted such frequent enumerations with lists of names.

A staunchly independent German state, Mecklenburg-Schwerin avoided alignment with either the *Zollverein* [Customs Union] or the *Steuerverein* [Tax Union], probably due to her vast coastline on the Baltic Sea and the port cities there. It was not until November 1868 that Mecklenburg-Schwerin joined the *Zollverein*.[2]

Figure 1. This 1819 proclamation heralded what would be the finest census record produced in Germany in the nineteenth century [Stadtarchiv Wismar, Ratsakte 4056]

Under the German Empire, enumerations were done in Mecklenburg-Schwerin in 1871, every five years from 1875 to 1910, and finally in 1916.[3] All in all, the grand duchy takes its place as the preeminent location for census records among the German states.

III. Specific Instructions to Town Officials and Enumerators

Regulations for the conduct of the census in Mecklenburg-Schwerin have been located for only two years, but those regulations established a pattern that lasted for more than forty years. Some of the prominent details are as follows:

> 1819: begin the census in August; use the pre-printed form provided; count every person, regardless of age; the local pastor is to review the lists to determine if anyone is missing; the enumerator will sign his name on the finished list; three copies are to be submitted to the office [in Schwerin] by August 25

> 1826: because no census has been taken since 1819, carry out a census by November 11; do another henceforth every year in the fall

IV. Content of Census Records in Mecklenburg-Schwerin from 1819 to 1868

	1819	1826–1827	1828–1829	1830–1838	1839–1850	1851–1856	1857–1867	1868
Gender	X							
First and last name of each person	X							
Birth year and day	X							
Birth place	X							
Church parish of birth place	X							
Status and occupation	X							X
Property owned	X							
How long a resident	X							
Whether single or married	X							
Religion	X							
Comments	X							
Street name		X						
Dwelling		X						
Name of head of household		X	X	X		X	X	X
No. of adult males		X	X			X	X	X
No. of adult females		X	X			X	X	X
Male children not confirmed		X	X					
Female children not confirmed		X	X					
No. of adult military personnel			X	X				
No. of military dependents			X	X				
Name of home owner				X				
No. of adult residents				X				
No. of children not confirmed				X				X
No. of males age 5–14						X		
No. of females 5–14						X		
No. of males under 5 years						X		
No. of females under 5 years						X		
No. of males in school							X	
No. of females in school							X	
No. of males not in school							X	
No. of females not in school							X	
No. of male employees								X
No. of female employees								X
Handwritten column titles		X	X	X	X	X	X	
Pre-printed pages	X							X

V. Accessibility of Census Records in Mecklenburg-Schwerin

For essentially the entire grand duchy, the Family History Library has copies of the 1819 census on microfilm. The same is true for census records of 1867, 1890, and 1900; digital images of those three census enumerations can be viewed through the Family History Library system. The 1819 census was also indexed (by town and by surname) in book form by a team directed by Franz Schubert. Those books can be viewed in the Family History Library and in other libraries and possibly purchased as well. As in other German states, researchers can write to the archive of any Mecklenburg-Schwerin town to inquire regarding census records of any of the other years from 1826 to 1867. (See Appendix A for instructions for writing inquiries.) *Ancestry.com* has images of census records in Mecklenburg-Schwerin for several years.

VI. Selected Images of Mecklenburg-Schwerin Census Records

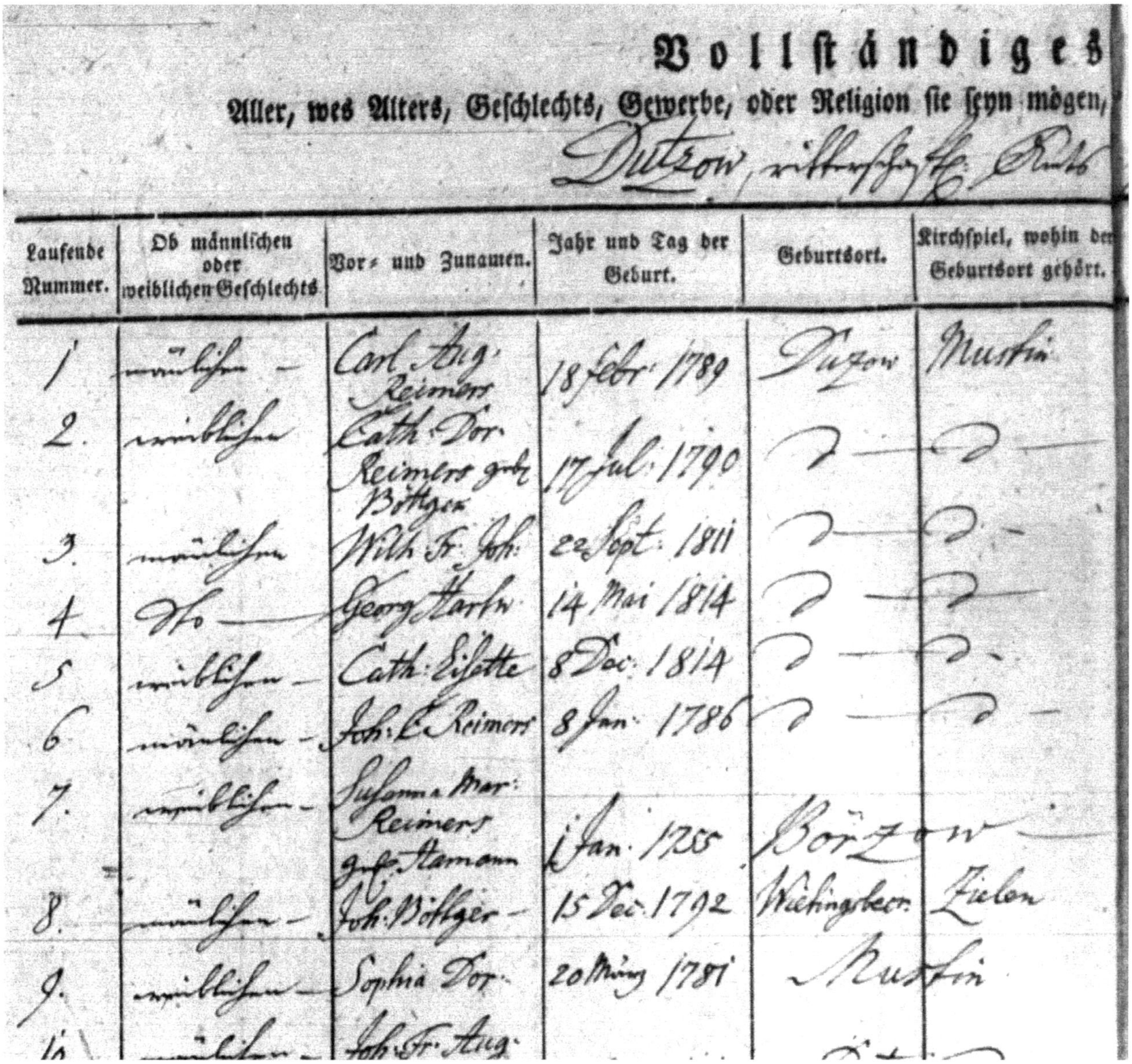

Figure 2. 1819 Census Page from Gadebusch, Mecklenburg-Schwerin (left-hand page)

Column headings: consecutive entry number; gender; first and last name; date of birth; place of birth; parish of birth [FHL microfilm no. 68881]

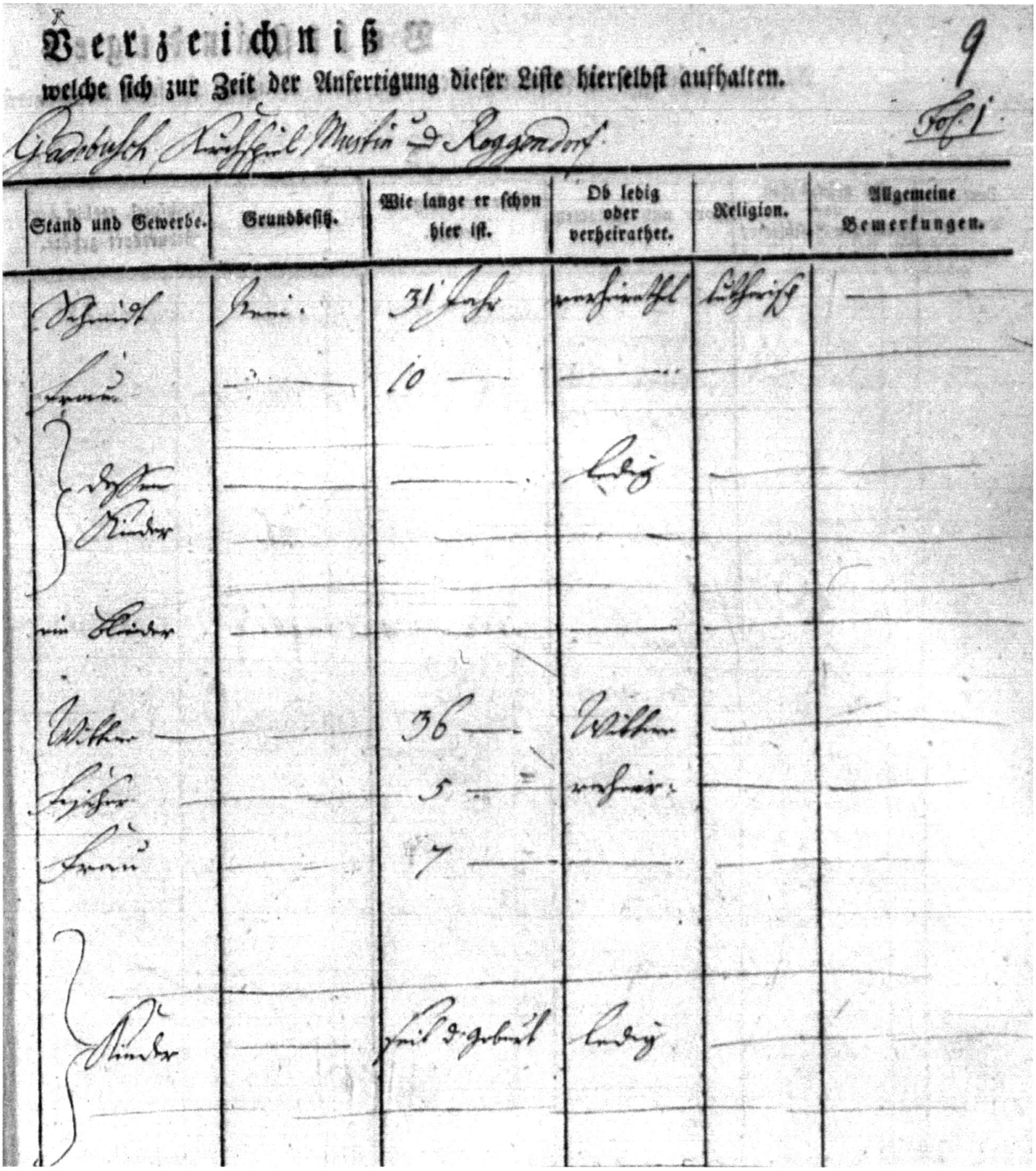

Verzeichniß

welche sich zur Zeit der Anfertigung dieser Liste hierselbst aufhalten.

Gadebusch Kirchspiel Mustin und Roggendorf — 9 — Fol. 1

Stand und Gewerbe.	Grundbesitz.	Wie lange er schon hier ist.	Ob ledig oder verheirathet.	Religion.	Allgemeine Bemerkungen.
Schmidt	Keine	31 Jahre	verheirathet	lutherisch	—
Frau	—	10 —	—	—	—
dessen Kinder	—	—	ledig	—	—
ein Kinder	—	—	—	—	—
Wittwe	—	36 —	Wittwe	—	—
Schäfer	—	5 —	verheir.	—	—
Frau	—	7 —	—	—	—
Kinder	—	seit d. Geburt	ledig	—	—

Figure 3. 1819 Census Page from Gadebusch, Mecklenburg-Schwerin (right-hand page)

Column headings: status or occupation; property ownership; how long a local resident; marital status; religion; comments [Family History Library microfilm 68,881]

Hauseigenthümer	Haushaltervorstand	Erwachsene Personen	Nicht confirmirte Kinder	Auf Militair gehörige Erwachsene Personen	Nicht confirmirte Kinder	Bemerkungen
Schust. Warnow	Inwoh: Mand.	2.				
Wb: Kelpin	Inselben.	4.	4.			
	Inselben.	3.	1.			
	Twed: Reincke	2.				
	Wb: Schlünz	3.				
Hak. Krause	Witt: Ott.	1.				
	Inselben.	3.				
	Kin: Oldenswager	2.				
Zimm: Pfeifer	Fisch: Treptow.	4.	4.			
	Fr: Hass.	4.				
Schum: Lorenz	Haase.	3.				
	Inselben.	5.				
Schust: Reinicke	Schum: Wettrich	2.	2.			
	Inselben.	3.				
	Güsmer	1.				
Roggow.	Inselben.	2.	1.			
	Insch: Mand.	2.	2.			
	Brückmann	2.				
Witt. Pigath	Inselben	1.				
	Rad: Münster	5.				
Witt: Weinrebe	Inselben	8.	2.			
Zimm: Heidtman	Inselben	2.	1.			
	Schust: Hinz	2.				
Schust: Frahm	Inselben.	5.	1.			
Zimm: Probian	Inselben.	2.	1.			
	Kudof: Schröder	—	—	2.	3.	
Knist: Schlüter	Inselben.					

Figure 4. 1835 Census Page from Wismar, Mecklenburg-Schwerin

Column headings: dwelling owner; head of household; number of adults; number of confirmed children; number of adults living on military property; number of unconfirmed children living on military property; comments [Stadtarchiv Wismar, Ratsakte 4057]

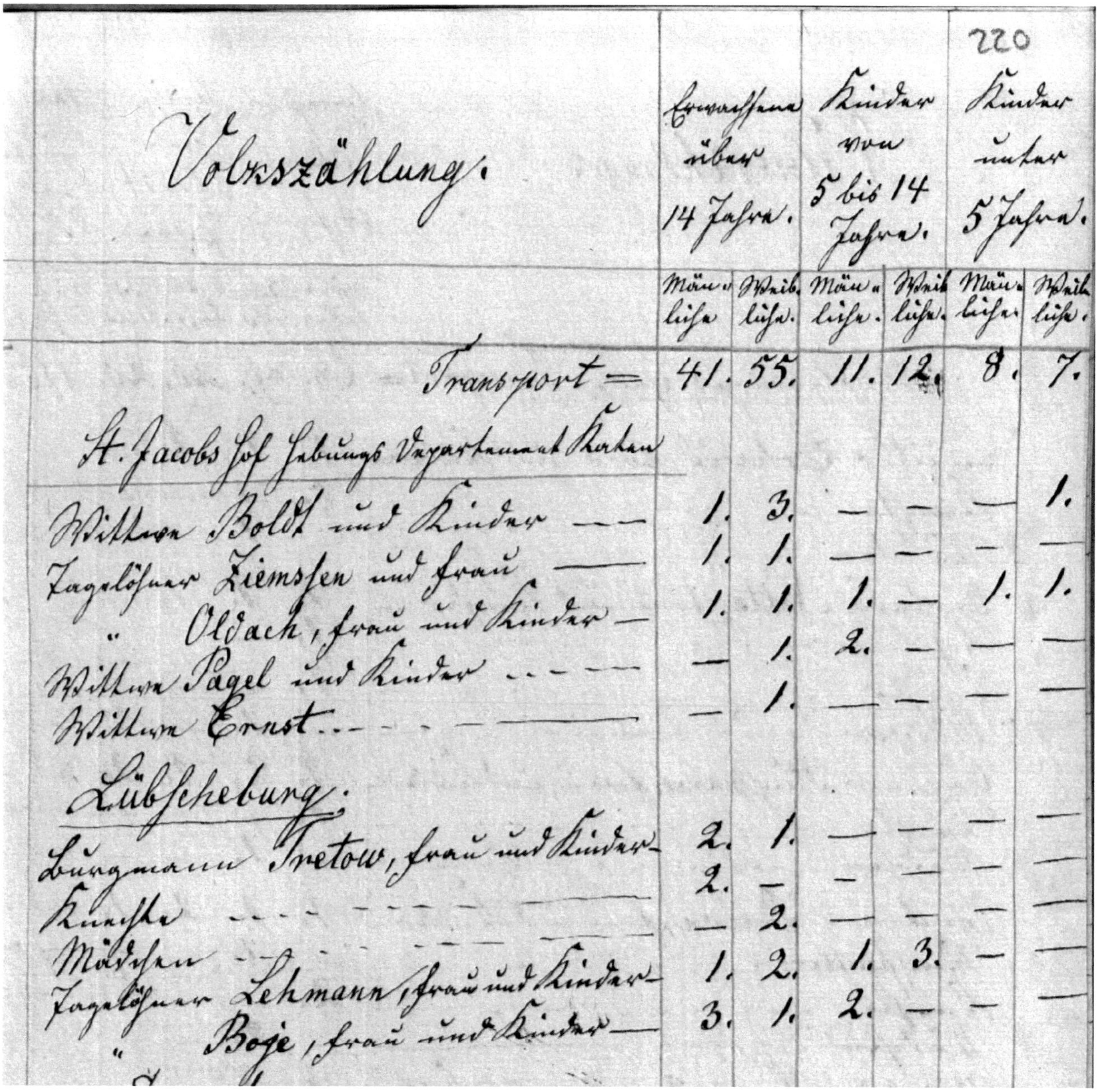

Figure 5. 1851 Census Page from Wismar, Mecklenburg-Schwerin

Column headings: name of head of household; males over 14; females over 14; males 5–14; females 5–14; males under 5; females under 5 [Stadtarchiv Wismar, Ratsakte 4059]

Notes

1. *Großherzoglich Mecklenburg-Schwerinsches officielles Wochenblatt, 1819, Achtzehntes Stück, Sonnabend, den 3ten Julii*, 18.

2. Antje Kraus, *Quellen zur Bevölkerungsstatistik Deutschlands 1815–1871*, Band 1 (Boppard, Germany: Harald Boldt, 1980), 27, 255–260.

3. The author expresses his appreciation to Dr. Niels Joern, director of the city archive in Wismar, for his kind assistance in locating census documents in his collection and making them available for study. As the editor of the *Wismarer Beiträge*, he will include my article "Volkszählungen in Mecklenburg-Schwerin von 1816 bis 1916" in his 2016 issue.

20 Mecklenburg-Strelitz

I. Location

The state of Mecklenburg-Strelitz was raised to the status of grand duchy as a result of the Congress of Vienna in 1815. It consisted of two land masses—a very large one bordering the sister state Mecklenburg-Schwerin on the east and a much smaller one on the opposite side of Mecklenburg-Schwerin. Neighboring states were the Hanseatic city of Lübeck and the dual-duchy of Schleswig-Holstein on the west and the Prussian provinces of Pommern to the east and Brandenburg to the southeast. The capital city was Strelitz, i.e., Neustrelitz.

II. Census Enumerations in Mecklenburg-Strelitz

Staunchly independent German states, Mecklenburg-Strelitz and Mecklenburg-Schwerin both avoided alignment with either the *Zollverein* [Customs Union] or the *Steuerverein* [Tax Union] for decades, probably due to their natural access to the Baltic Sea and the port cities there. (An alliance with the interior German states might actually have led to a decline in import revenues.) It was not until August 1868 that the two grand duchies joined the *Zollverein*.[1]

As a result of its lack of interstate commitments, the government of Mecklenburg-Strelitz was free to conduct census enumerations on her own schedule. That was done only four times before this small state joined the 1867 campaign that involved every one of the thirty-eight German states. Precisely why the two Mecklenburgs participated in the 1867 census is not clear.

Only two census enumerations in this grand duchy can be proved as of this writing: 1848 and 1860. However, population counts were done there annually from 1816 through at least 1871.[2] The formula for the calculation in each successive year

was relatively simple: beginning with the total for the previous year, the number of children born was added and then the number of persons who died was subtracted.

Under the German Empire, enumerations were done in Mecklenburg-Strelitz in 1871, every five years from 1875 to 1910, and finally in 1916.

III. Specific Instructions to Town Officials and Enumerators

Regulations for the conduct of the census have been found for only the year 1860. Here are the most important of the sixteen items circulated among towns and counties:

> Heads of households are all fathers of families and all adults living alone; the names of other members of households are not to be recorded, but are represented by numbers in the appropriate columns; count all persons living and working here, including foreigners and locals working elsewhere; do not count persons traveling through or visiting families

IV. Content of Census Records in Mecklenburg-Strelitz from 1848 to 1866

	1848	1851	1860	1866
No images available		X		X
Name of head of household	X		X	
Status or occupation	X			
Number of citizens	X			
Number of adult males	X			
Number of adult females	X			
Number of male children	X			
Number of female children	X			
Number of male servants	X			
Number of female servants	X			
Total residents	X		X	
Comments	X			
Dwelling address			X	
Total males			X	
Total females			X	
Summary page			X	
Handwritten column headings	X		X	

V. Accessibility of Census Records in Mecklenburg-Strelitz

Original census records for the grand duchy are difficult to locate. None are currently found in the collection of the Family History Library or as digital images on the Internet. The state archive in Schwerin may have some among its holdings.[3] Researchers should direct inquiries to the archives of any towns or counties in the territory as it was constituted before 1918 (gazetteers will provide the names of those towns and the county affiliations). (See Appendix A for suggestions for writing efficient messages in German.) Currently, the Family History Library has no Mecklenburg-Strelitz census documents on microfilm in its collection and none have been found as digital images on the Internet.

VI. Selected Images of Mecklenburg-Strelitz Census Records

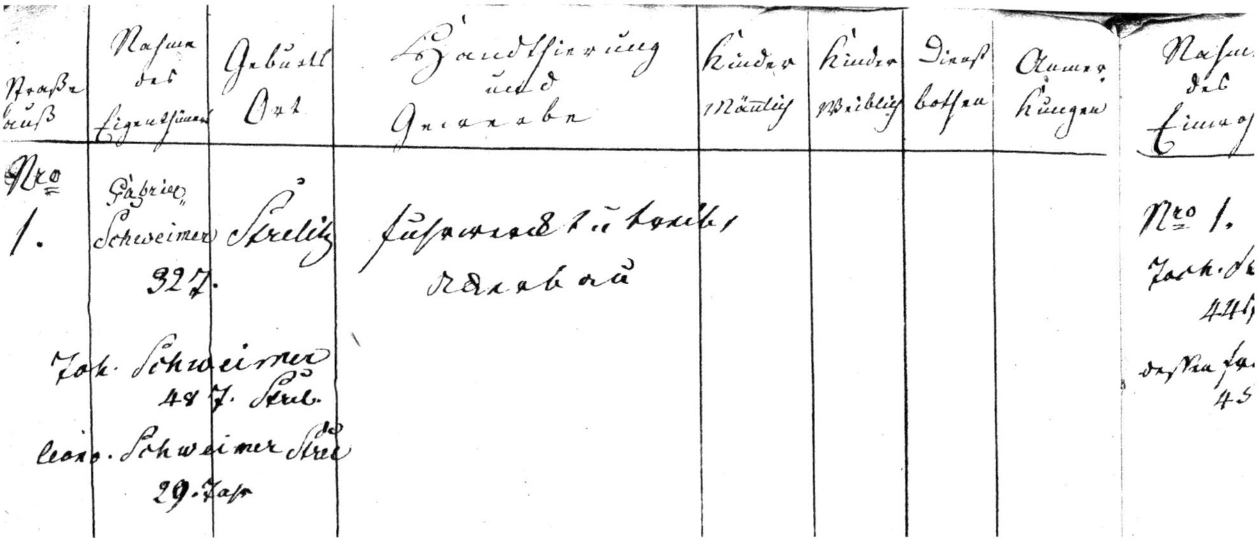

Figure 1. 1795 Census Page from Neustrelitz, Mecklenburg-Strelitz

Column headings: address; name of dwelling owner; birth place; status or occupation; number of male children; number of female children; number of servants/laborers; comments [Stadtarchiv Neustrelitz]

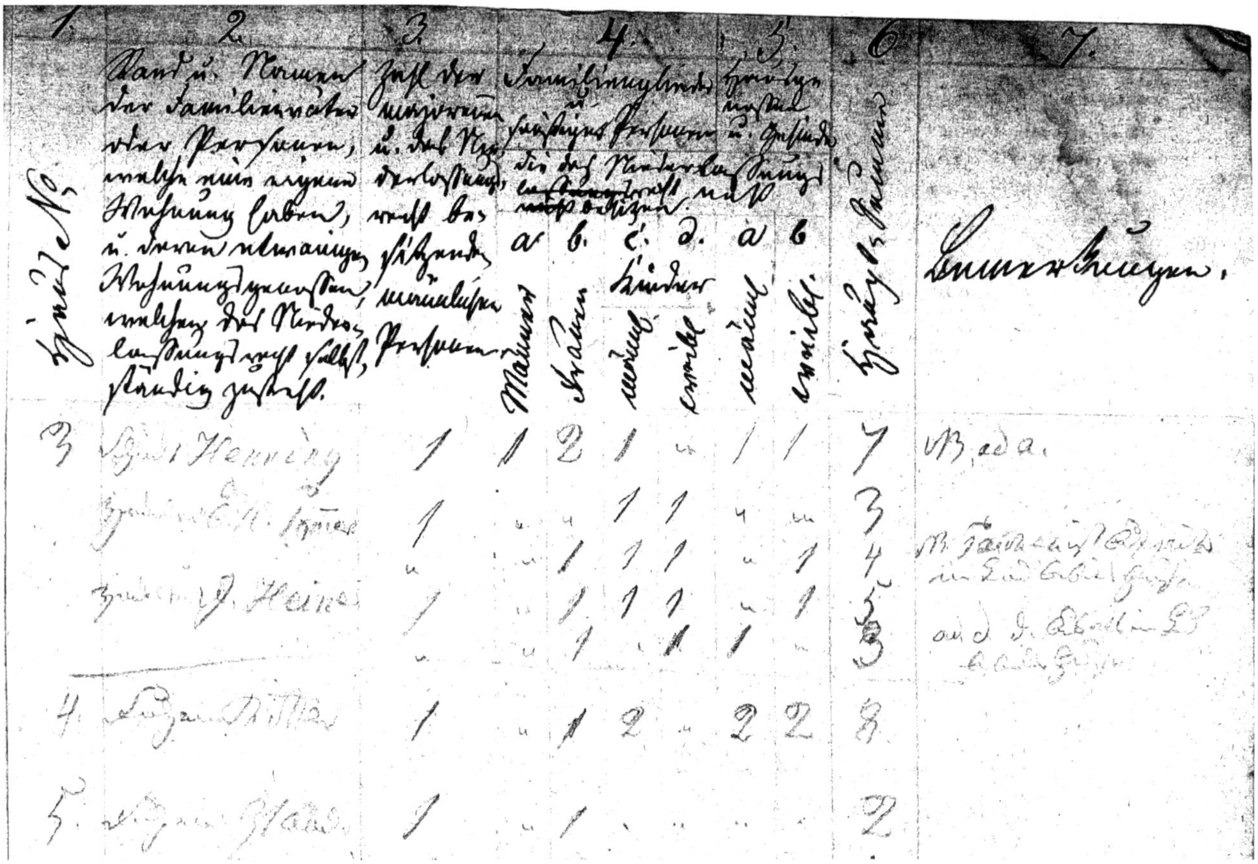

Figure 2. 1848 Census Page from Neustrelitz, Mecklenburg-Strelitz

Column headings: name of head of household with occupation or status; number of persons with citizen status; number of adult males; number of adult females; number of male children; number of female children; number of male servants/laborers; number of female servants; total residents; comments [Stadtarchiv Neustrelitz]

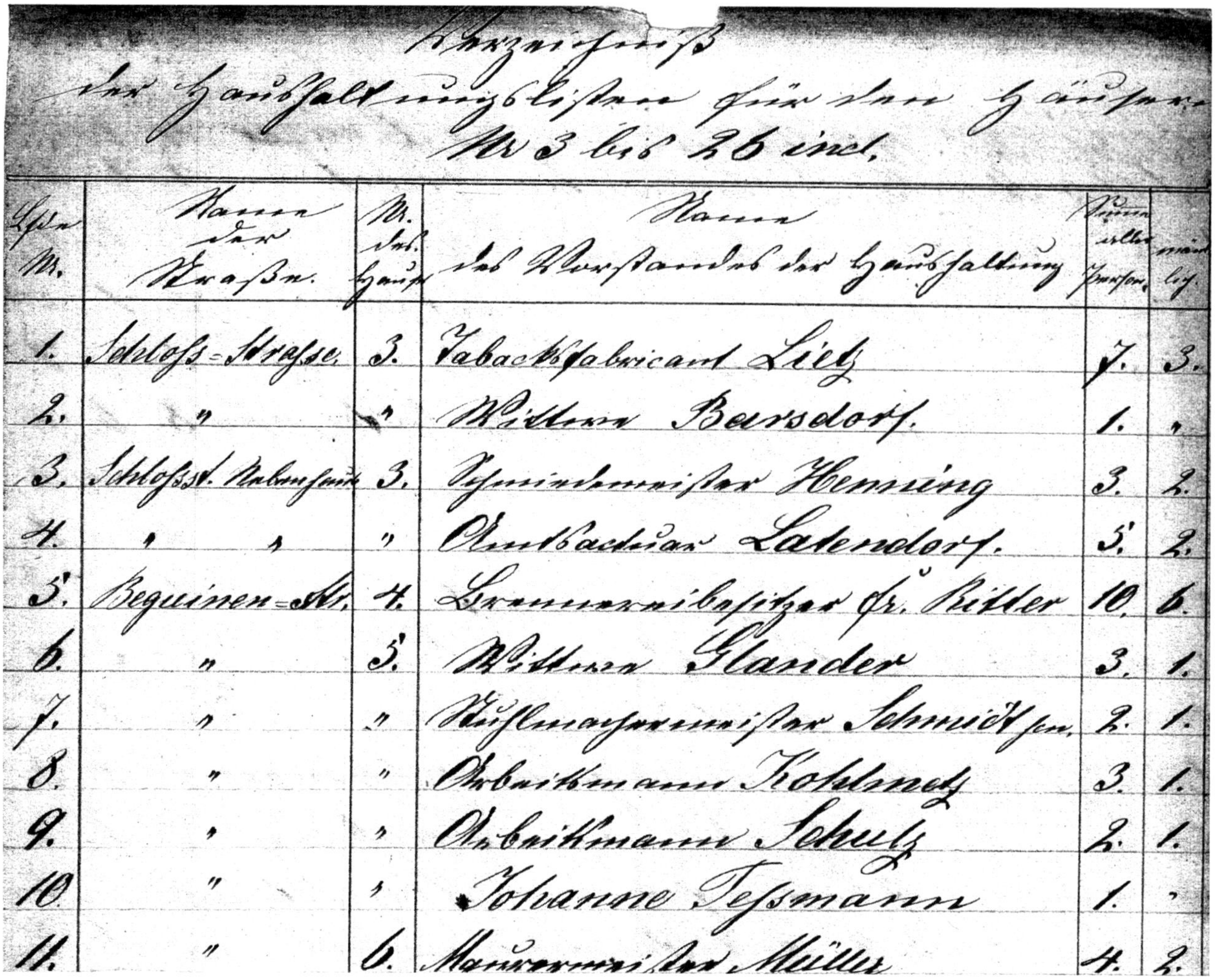

Lfd. Nr.	Name der Straße	Nr. Int. Haus	Name des Vorstandes der Haushaltung	Gesammtzahl aller Personen	männlich
1.	Schloß-Straße	3.	Tabacksfabricant Lietz	7.	3.
2.	"	"	Wittwe Barsdorf.	1.	"
3.	Schloßst. Nebengasse	3.	Schmiedemeister Henning	3.	2.
4.	"	"	Amtsdiener Latendorf.	5.	2.
5.	Beguinen-Str.	4.	Brauereibesitzer Hr. Ritter	10.	6.
6.	"	5.	Wittwe Glander	3.	1.
7.	"	"	Büdnermeister Schmidt jun.	2.	1.
8.	"	"	Arbeitsmann Kohlmetz	3.	1.
9.	"	"	Arbeitsmann Schulz	2.	1.
10.	"	"	Johanne Tessmann	1.	"
11.	"	6.	Maurermeister Müller	4.	2.

Figure 3. 1860 Census Page from Neustrelitz, Mecklenburg-Strelitz

Column headings: name of street; house number; name of head of household; total residents; number of male residents; number of female residents [Stadtarchiv Neustrelitz]

Notes

1. W. O. Henderson, *The Zollverein* (London: Frank Cass, 1939), 310.

2. Antje Kraus, *Quellen zur Bevölkerungsstatistik Deutschlands 1815–1871*, Band 1 (Boppard, Germany: Harald Boldt, 1980), 21, 81–86.

3. Several recent messages from the archive personnel suggest that there may be diverse census documents in the collection there, but the staff could not provide catalog numbers. Researchers may find it profitable to go there or send a qualified representative to look for census documents.

21 Oldenburg

I. Location

The grand duchy of Oldenburg in northern Germany was surrounded on all sides by the kingdom of Hannover—with the exception of its coast along the North Sea. The capital city of the grand duchy was likewise called Oldenburg.

II. Census Enumerations in Oldenburg

The first census enumerated in Oldenburg in the post-Napoleonic era was a head count that took place in 1816 as an independent campaign of the ducal government. It was followed by annual statistical reports and enumerations with the names of individuals in 1821, 1828, and 1835, but not all counties participated in the census.[1] Oldenburg joined the *Steuerverein* [Tax Union] in 1837 and census campaigns were conducted for the purposes of that organization every three years from 1837 through 1852.[2] The *Steuerverein* was discontinued in 1852 and its member states merged with the *Zollverein* [Customs Union] that required a census on a similar three-year schedule.

In 1855, two different censuses were executed—one in July for the *Steuerverein* (the last) and a second in December for the *Zollverein*; it was in 1855 for the first time that all Oldenburg entities were included.[3] The three-year *Zollverein* schedule was maintained through 1864.[4]

The census enumerated in 1867 was done in conjunction with the North German Confederation and the *Zollverein* and included all German states. Under the new German Empire, enumerations were done in Oldenburg in 1871, every five years from 1875 to 1910, and finally in 1916.

III. Specific Instructions to Town Officials and Enumerators

Significant new and revised instructions for Oldenburg census procedures are as follows:

1828: finish the work by April 1; pastors are in charge and teachers may act as assistants; count local military personnel; locals living away from home are to be counted but not foreigners living here

1835: begin and finish the census in January; government employees will carry out the work; count everyone but persons travelling through; count only those foreigners who have been here for at least one year; do not count active military personnel

1840: we are conducting the next census along with Hannover and Braunschweig; begin on July 1

1849: finish the census by November 15

1852: begin the census on July 1

1855: record the names of disabled persons; organize the residents in census districts irrespective of religion; the forms are to be distributed to heads of households on November 28 or 29 and collected from them on December 3

1858: local police officials should do the work; people who own more than one home are to be counted where they spend the winter

IV. Content of Census Records in Oldenburg from 1821 to 1864

Of the seven census years for which records have been found, only the first two are identical in form and content, as shown in this table:

	'21	'28	'35	'37	'40	'43	'46	'49	'52 Jun	'52 Dec	'55	'58	'61	'64
No images available				X			X	X				X	X	X
Name of head of household	X	X			X	X			X					
Number of hearths	X	X												
Number of males	X	X			X	X			X	X				
Number of females	X	X			X	X			X	X				
Total residents	X	X	X		X	X			X					
Number of households			X											
Males over 14			X											
Females over 14			X											
Males under 14			X											
Females under 14			X											
Males 21 this year			X											
Total foreigners			X											
Number of merchants			X											
Persons under 7 (by gender)					X	X			X					
Persons age 8–14 (by gender)					X	X			X					
Persons age 15–25 (by gender)					X									
Persons age 26–45 (by gender)					X									
Persons age 46–60 (by gender)					X	X			X					
Persons age 61–90 (by gender)					X	X			X					
Persons over 90 (by gender)					X				X					
Married persons					X	X			X					
Widowers					X	X			X	X				
Widows					X	X			X	X				
Lutheran					X	X			X	X				
Reformed Lutheran					X	X			X	X				
Catholic					X				X	X				
Mennonite					X				X					
Jewish					X				X	X				
Comments					X				X		X			
Persons age 15–20 (by gender)						X			X					
Persons age 21–45 (by gender)						X			X					
Name of each person in household										X	X			
Status or occupation										X	X			
Age at last birthday										X	X			
Number of males married										X				
Number of females married										X				
Other Christians										X				
Secondary employment if any											X			
Marital status											X			
Mark E if person is living alone											X			
Children attending public school											X			
Children attending private school											X			
Handwritten column headings	X	X	X			X								
Pre-printed pages					X				X	X	X			

V. Accessibility of Census Records in Oldenburg

Although regional archives in Germany generally have few or no census records in their holdings, the Niedersächsisches Landesarchiv in Oldenburg has such records for several towns. The catalog of that archive can be studied at this website: https://www.arcinsys.niedersachsen.de/arcinsys/start.action. Researchers who have a more definite location in mind should send an inquiry to the archive of the closest town or county. (See Appendix A for suggestions on writing an efficient inquiry.) As of this writing, there are no Oldenburg census documents as digital images on the Internet, nor does the Family History Library have microfilmed images of census documents in its collection.

VI. Selected Census Images in Oldenburg

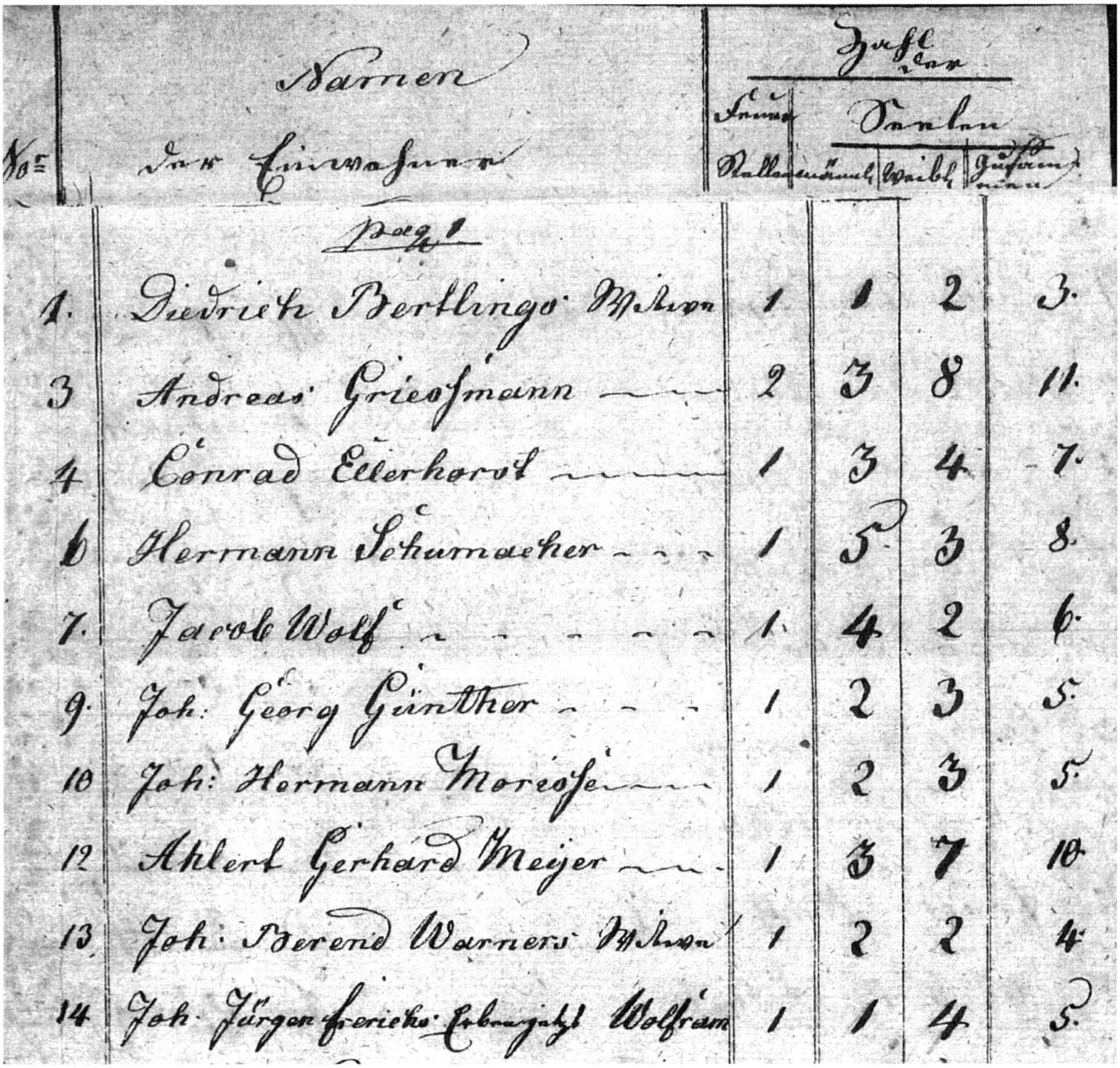

No.	Namen der Einwohner	Feuerstellen	männl.	weibl.	zusammen
1.	Diedrich Bertlings Witwe	1	1	2	3.
3	Andreas Griesmann	2	3	8	11.
4	Conrad Ellerhorst	1	3	4	7.
6	Herrmann Schumacher	1	5	3	8.
7.	Jacob Wolf	1	4	2	6.
9.	Joh: Georg Günther	1	2	3	5.
10	Joh: Hermann Moreiße	1	2	3	5.
12	Ahlert Gerhard Meyer	1	3	7	10.
13	Joh: Berend Warners Witwe	1	2	2	4.
14	Joh: Jürgen Frerichs Erbpächter Wolfram	1	1	4	5.

Figure 1. 1828 Census Page from Wildeshausen, Oldenburg

Column headings: name of head of household; number of hearths; total males; total females; total residents [Niedersächsisches Landesarchiv Oldenburg 76-26, Nr. 91]

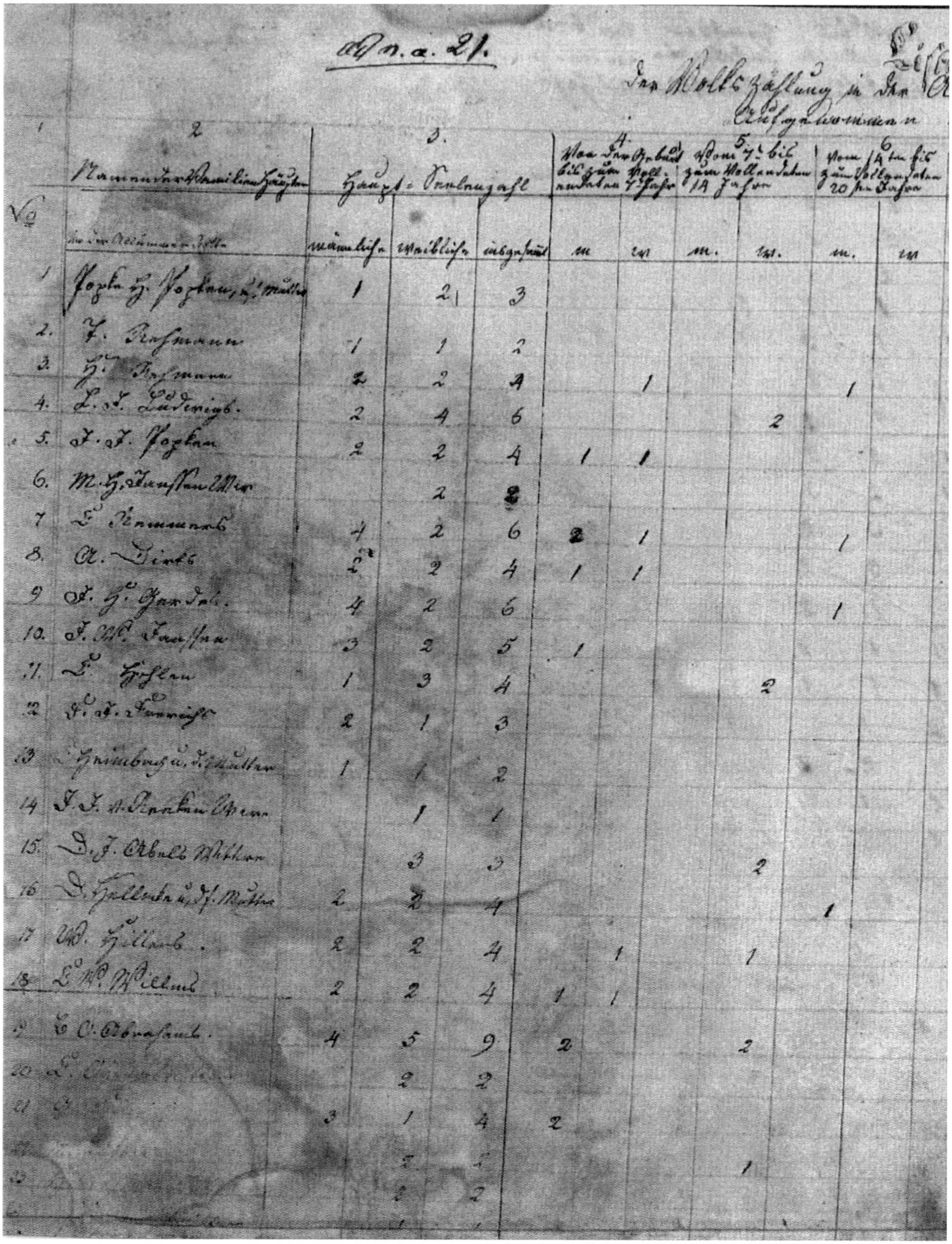

Figure 2. 1843 Census Page from Accum, Oldenburg (left-hand page)

Column headings: name of head of household; total males; total females; total residents; males under 7; females under 7; males 8–14; females 8–14; males 15–20; females 15–20 [Niedersächsisches Landesarchiv Oldenburg 125, Nr. 421]

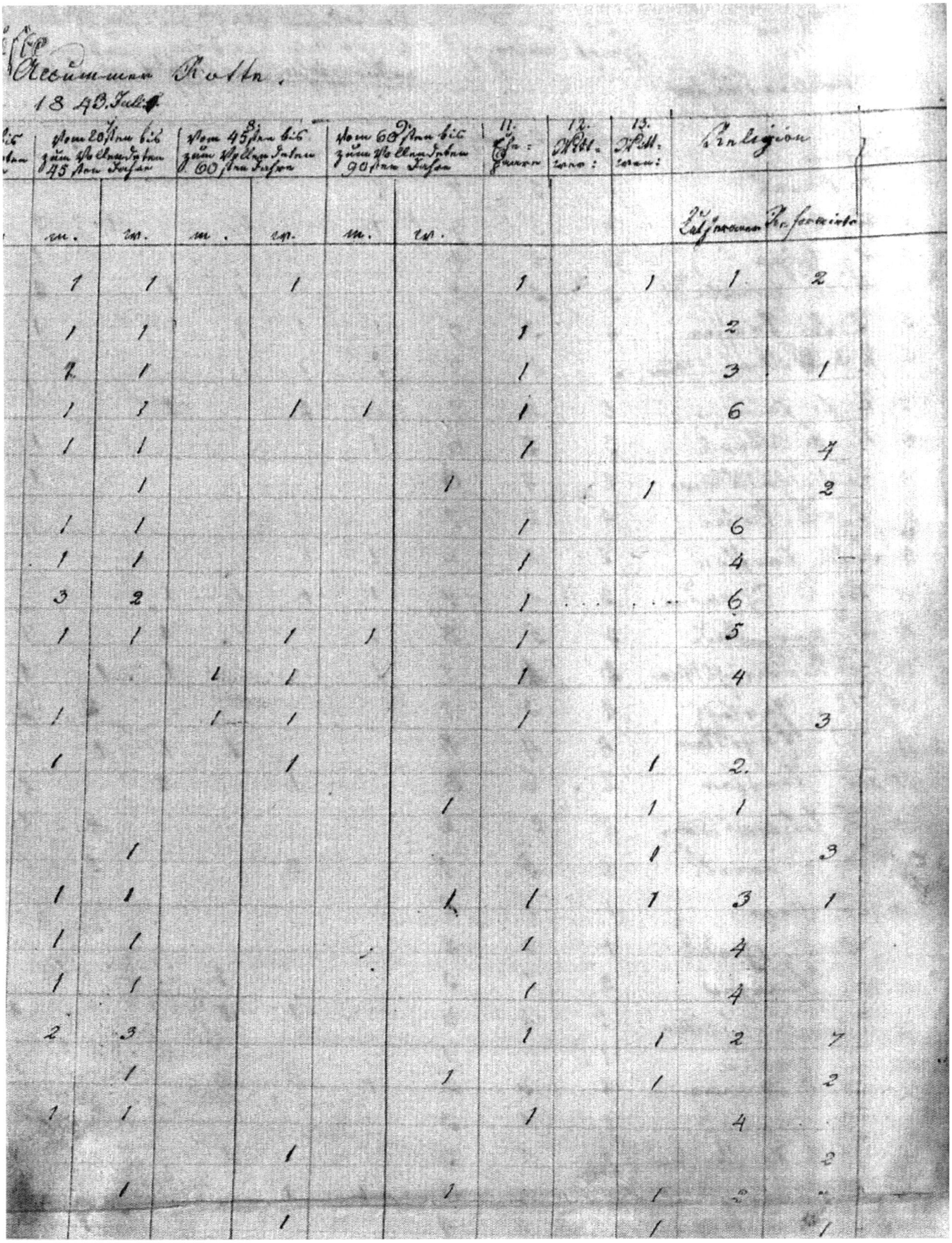

Figure 3. 1843 Census Page from Accum, Oldenburg (right-hand page)

   Column headings: males 21–45; females 21–45; males 46–60; females 46–60; males 61–90; females 61–90; married persons; widowers; widows; Lutherans; Reformed Lutherans [Niedersächsisches Landesarchiv Oldenburg 125, Nr. 421]

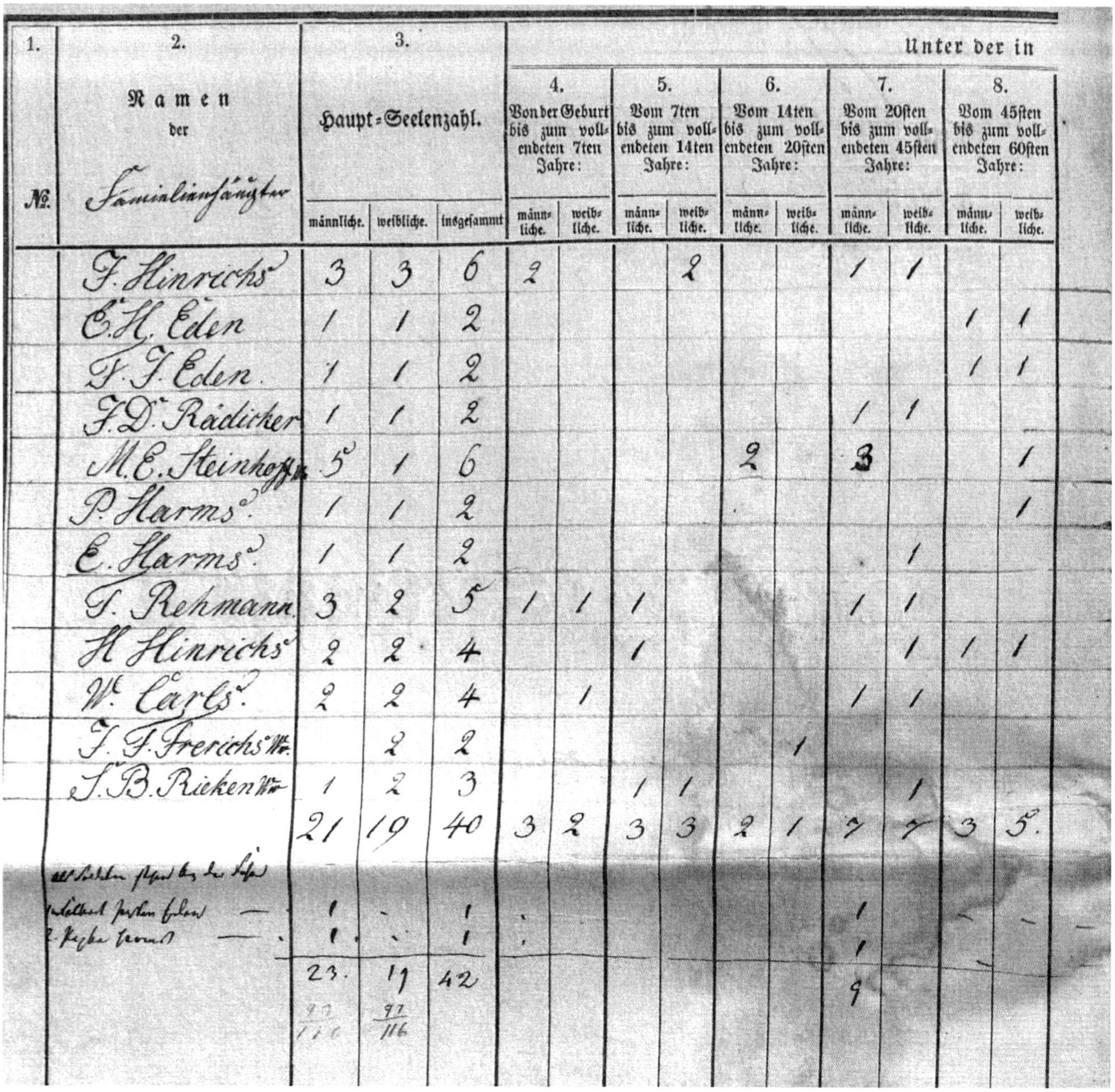

1. No.	2. Namen der Familienhäupter	3. Haupt-Seelenzahl			4. Von der Geburt bis zum vollendeten 7ten Jahre		5. Vom 7ten bis zum vollendeten 14ten Jahre		6. Vom 14ten bis zum vollendeten 20ten Jahre		7. Vom 20sten bis zum vollendeten 45sten Jahre		8. Vom 45sten bis zum vollendeten 60sten Jahre	
		männl.	weibl.	insgesammt	männl.	weibl.	männl.	weibl.	männl.	weibl.	männl.	weibl.	männl.	weibl.
	F. Hinrichs	3	3	6	2			2			1	1		
	C. H. Eden	1	1	2									1	1
	F. I. Eden	1	1	2									1	1
	F. D. Rädicker	1	1	2							1	1		
	M. E. Steinhoff	5	1	6					2		3			1
	P. Harms	1	1	2										1
	E. Harms	1	1	2								1		
	T. Rehmann	3	2	5	1	1	1				1	1		
	H. Hinrichs	2	2	4			1					1	1	1
	W. Carls	2	2	4		1					1	1		
	F. F. Frerichs Wwe.		2	2						1				
	J. B. Rieken Wwe.	1	2	3				1	1		1			
		21	19	40	3	2	3	3	2	1	7	7	3	5
		1		1							1			
		1		1							1			
		23	17	42							9			

Figure 4. 1852 [December] Census Page from Langewerth, Oldenburg (left-hand page)

Column headings: name of head of household; total males; total females; total residents; males and females in age groups: under 7; 7 to under 14; 14 to under 20; 20 to under 45; 45 to under 60 [Niedersächsisches Landesarchiv Oldenburg 125, Nr. 421]

der Spalte 3. aufgeführten Seelenzahl sind begriffen:

9. Vom 60sten bis zum vollendeten 90sten Jahre:		10. Ueber 90 Jahr:		11. Ehepaare:	12. Wittwer:	13. Wittwen:	14. Nach den Religionsverschiedenheiten:					15. Bemerkungen:
männliche.	weibliche.	männliche.	weibliche.				Lutheraner:	Reformirte:	Katholiken:	Mennoniten:	Israeliten:	
				1			6					
				1			2					
				1			2					
				1			2					
						1	3	3				
1				1				2				
1					1		2					
				1			5					
				1			3	1				
1				1	1		4					
	1					1	2					
						1	3					
3	1			8	7	3	29	11				
							1					
							—	1				
							30	12				

Figure 5. 1852 [December] Census Page from Langewerth, Oldenburg (right-hand page)

Column headings: males and females (continue) in age groups: 60 to under 90; over 90; married persons; widows, widowers; Lutherans; Reformed Lutherans; Catholics; Mennonites; Jewish; comments [Niedersächsisches Landesarchiv Oldenburg 125, Nr. 421]

Notes

[1] Antje Kraus, *Quellen zur Bevölkerungsstatistik Deutschlands 1815–1871*, Band 1 (Boppard, Germany: Harald Boldt, 1980), 22.

[2] The history of census campaigns in Oldenburg is especially complicated because various counties belonged to the *Steuerverein* or the *Zollverein* or both at different times. See Puttkamer and Mühlbrecht, "Die Volkszahl der Deutschen Staaten nach den Zählungen von 1816," 14–16.

[3] Ibid.

[4] Kraus, *Quellen*, 93–110. For years in which no formal census was conducted, population statistics were calculated via this formula: total persons from the previous census plus the number of children born minus the number of persons who died. Those numbers were usually provided by those who kept the church records. This practice began in several Oldenburg counties in 1821.

22 Ostpreußen [East Prussia]

I. Location

The Prussian province of Ostpreußen was surrounded on the west by the province of Westpreußen, on the north by the Baltic Sea, and on the south and east by the Russian Empire.[1] The capital city was Königsberg.

II. Census Enumerations in Ostpreußen

The kingdom of Preußen ruled over seven provinces in eastern Germany and two in western Germany shortly after the Congress of Vienna. All Prussian provinces were to produce and submit to the statistical bureau in Berlin annual statistical tables from 1817 to 1822 (head counts). The schedule was then altered to require such data only every three years, but no set of strict standards guided the enumerations. City officials were to carry out the work.[2] Although the campaigns of the 1820s were designed to produce only statistics, the records of several years featured the names of heads of households.

In 1818, Ostpreußen was one of the seven eastern Prussian provinces to be grouped into a customs union. One year later, Westfalen and Rheinprovinz were grouped into a western Prussian customs union. The next predictable step was the inclusion of all nine Prussian provinces in the Prusso-Hessian Customs Union founded in February 1828.

Census enumerations followed triennially and the schedule continued without interruption even after the establishment of the *Zollverein* [Customs Union] on January 1, 1834. Under the strong leadership of Preußen, the *Zollverein* required census records every three years for three full decades and the quality of those records steadily improved.

Another census was enumerated in 1867 in conjunction with the North German Confederation and all German states participated. Under the German Empire, enumerations were done in Ostpreußen in 1871, every five years from 1875 to 1910, and finally in 1916.[3]

III. Specific Instructions to Town Officials and Enumerators

Significant new and revised instructions for Ostpreußen census campaigns have not been located, but the following regulations issued to other Prussian provinces were in effect in Ostpreußen:

1825: if significant differences are found in comparison with the results of 1822, explain the causes of those differences

1840: we are sending you the forms to be used; each page has room for sixty names; police officials should conduct the campaign; do not begin to collect the data before December 1; the work must be completed in towns by December 20 and in cities by December 25, so that the reports can be received in Berlin by December 31; you are allowed to refer to documents previously compiled, such as lists of residents; do not count travelers in inns and active military personnel and their dependents; local residents temporarily away from home are to be counted

1843: refer to the deficiencies in the 1840 census in order to produce more reliable results; count military personnel in reserve status; where the number of enumerators is insufficient, tax officials and retired military officers may be called into service and remunerated appropriately

1846: begin the collection of data on December 3; count all foreigners employed here but not persons traveling through the town; count inmates in prisons and hospitals; persons who own more than one dwelling should be counted where they live in the winter; do not refer to previous lists such as residential registration; in large cities, heads of households may fill out the forms themselves to save enumerator time

1852: the handwriting on the lists must be neat and orderly; should authorities at the next higher level identify mistakes in the local records, the cost of any required corrections shall be charged to the responsible authorities; owners of major estates are to count their respective populations and submit the lists to the local town authorities

1855: persons who refuse to cooperate will be fined

1858: local officials are to announce the upcoming census in the newspaper

1861: for those persons who live in one location and work in another during the week, they are to be counted in the location where they spend the night before the census day; do not count persons in inns or visiting families

1864: do not count persons who have been absent from their home town for more than one year; officials who do not carry out the census according to instructions are to be fined; an enumeration district should not include more than 600 people; non-government persons assigned to assist in the campaign may be paid a maximum of one *Thaler*; count only those foreigners who have lived here for at least one year; record the year of birth rather than the age; children in each family are to be listed in order of their birth

IV. Content of Census Records in Ostpreußen from 1822 to 1864

No images have been found as yet for the Prussian province of Ostpreußen, but the following details have been gathered from Brandenburg, Pommern, and Sachsen and represent what would have been required by the statistical bureau in Berlin for Ostpreußen as well.

	'22	'25	'28	'31	'34	'37	'40	'43	'46	'49	'52	'55	'58	'61	'64
No images available	X	X		X											
Name of each person			X				X	X	X	X	X	X	X	X	X
Name of head of household					X	X									
Married persons (by gender)			X												
Total residents			X		X	X	X	X	X	X	X	X	X	X	X
Age in years			X				X	X	X	X	X	X	X	X	X
Persons under 6 (by gender)			X		X	X									
Persons 7–9 (by gender)			X		X	X									
Persons 10–14 (by gender)			X		X	X									
Persons 15–60 (by gender)			X		X										
Persons over 60 (by gender)			X		X	X									
Lutherans			X		X	X						X	X	X	
Catholics			X		X	X						X	X	X	
Jewish (with citizenship status)					X	X						X	X	X	
Persons 15–16 (by gender)						X									
Males 17–20						X									
Males 21–40						X									
Males 41–60						X									
Males over 60						X									
Females 17–45						X									
Females 46–60						X									
Females over 60						X									
Total females over 14						X									
Total males						X									
Total females						X									
Reformed Lutherans						X									
Mennonites						X									X
Comments			X						X	X	X	X	X	X	X
Status or occupation							X	X	X	X	X	X	X	X	X
Religion							X	X	X	X	X	X			
Blind												X			
Deaf												X			
Greek Orthodox															X
Dissidents															X
Other religions															X
Handwritten column headings			X		X										X
Pre-printed pages						X	X	X	X	X	X	X	X	X	X

V. Accessibility of Census Records in Ostpreußen

The fact that this province was ceded to Poland following World War II complicates the search for original census regulations and lists of inhabitants. As part of this investigation, emails were sent to county and regional archives in what was once the province of Ostpreußen but none of those responded positively regarding census records in their collection.[4] Nevertheless, a letter written in Polish to a government archive (city, county, or regional) found through a search of websites might prove successful. (See Appendix A for suggestions on writing that inquiry in Polish.) As of this writing, no census records are available in the Family History Library on microfilm and no digital images have been located on the Internet.

VI. Selected Images of Ostpreußen Census Records

As of this writing, no images of census records have been found for this province.

Notes

[1] This is a simplified representation. The changes in borders among Prussian provinces in the nineteenth century are legion but not of specific importance here.

[2] Harald Michel, "Volkszählungen in Deutschland: Die Erfassung des Bevölkerungsstandes von 1816 bis 1933," in *Jahrbuch für Wirtschaftsgeschichte* 1985/II, 85.

[3] Antje Kraus, *Quellen zur Bevölkerungsstatistik Deutschlands 1815–1871*, Band 1 (Boppard, Germany: Harald Boldt, 1980), 25–26, 207–212.

[4] The author expresses his appreciation to Magdalena Zajac, a native Polish student at the University of Vienna, who conducted an extensive email campaign with archives in cities that once were in the provinces of Ostpreußen, Posen, Schlesien, and Westpreußen.

23 Pommern [Pomerania]

I. Location

The Prussian province of Pommern bordered the Baltic Sea on the north and was surrounded by the Mecklenburg grand duchies to the west. Other neighboring German states were the Prussian provinces of Brandenburg to the south and Westpreußen to the east. Pommern was divided geographically into *Vorpommern* [Anterior Pomerania], situated west of the Oder River and *Hinterpommern* [Posterior Pomerania], to the east of the Oder. The capital of the province was Stettin.

II. Census Enumerations in Pommern

As one of the seven eastern provinces of the kingdom of Preußen, Pommern was included in a Prussian customs union in 1818. All Prussian provinces were to produce and submit to the statistical bureau in Berlin annual statistical tables from 1817 to 1822 (head counts only). The schedule was then altered to require such data only every three years, but no set of strict standards guided the enumerations. City officials were to carry out the work.[1] Although the campaigns of the 1820s were designed to produce only statistics, the records of several years featured the names of heads of households.

Pommern was automatically accepted into the Prusso-Hessian Customs Union that was founded in February 1828. Census enumerations followed triennially and the schedule continued without interruption even after the establishment of the *Zollverein* [Customs Union] on January 1, 1834. Under the strong leadership of Preußen, the *Zollverein* required census records every three years for three full decades and the quality of those records steadily improved.

Another census was enumerated in 1867 in conjunction with the North German Confederation and all German states participated. Under the German Empire, enumerations were done in Pommern in 1871, every five years from 1875 to 1910, and finally in 1916.[2]

III. Specific Instructions to Town Officials and Enumerators

For many census years (especially under the *Zollverein*), instructions for enumerators in Prussian provinces were repeated in identical text. Significant new and revised instructions for Pommern census campaigns are summarized as follows:

1816: the content of the census has been expanded; use the form provided; submit the results by the first half of January

1819: use the new format with its 33 columns

1825: if significant differences are found in comparison with the results of 1822, explain the cause(s) of those differences

1834: submit the results by January 1

1840: list persons in the same family beginning with the father or the mother, then the children; if more than one family inhabits the same dwelling, list the owner's family first; count every person here on that date except for travelers in inns and active military and their dependents; local residents temporarily away from home are to be counted

1846: count inmates in prisons and hospitals; persons who own more than one dwelling should be counted where they live in the winter

1861: those persons who live in one location and work in another during the week are to be counted in the location where they spend the night before the census day

1864: count only those foreigners who have lived here for at least one year; record the year of birth; children in each family are to be listed in order of their birth

IV. Content of Census Records in Pommern from 1816 to 1864

	'16	'19	'22	'25	'28	'31	'34	'37	'40	'43	'46	'49	'52	'55	'58	'61	'64
No images available		X	X	X		X	X	X	X	X			X	X			X
Name of head of household	X																
Married persons (by gender)	X				X												
Unmarried persons (by gender)	X																
Persons age 0–5 (by gender)	X																
Persons age 6–20 (by gender)	X																
Persons age 21–25 (by gender)	X																
Persons age 26–32 (by gender)	X																
Persons age 33–39 (by gender)	X																
Persons age 40–50 (by gender)	X																
Persons over 50 (by gender)	X																
Births this year (by gender)	X																
Deaths this year (by gender)	X																
Total males	X																
Total females	X																
Total residents	X				X												
Name and status of each person					X												
Age in years					X												
Persons under 6 (by gender)					X												
Persons 7–9 (by gender)					X												
Persons 10–14 (by gender)					X												
Persons 15–60 (by gender)					X												
Persons over 60 (by gender)					X												
Lutherans					X												
Catholics					X												
Comments					X						X	X			X	X	
Name of every resident											X	X			X	X	
Status or occupation											X	X			X	X	
Age at last birthday											X	X			X	X	
Jewish															X	X	
Year of birth																	
Greek Orthodox																	
Dissidents																	
Handwritten column headings	X				X												
Pre-printed pages											X	X			X	X	

V. Accessibility of Census Records in Pommern

The major regional archives for the former Prussian province of Pommern have few documents relating to census enumerations there. Researchers should direct their inquiries to the archives of towns and counties, where excellent census records have been found in a few instances. (See Appendix A for suggestions about communicating with archivists in Germany and Poland.) For those parts of Pommern that are now in Poland, the matter is somewhat more complex but not altogether hopeless; local Polish archives have maintained many documents created when the populace consisted only of Germans (pre-1946). Pommern census records on microfilm in the Family History Library are rare, but a visit to the catalog now and then may turn up new holdings. As of this writing, no Pommern census records are known to be available in digital form on the Internet.

VI. Selected Images of Pommern Census Records

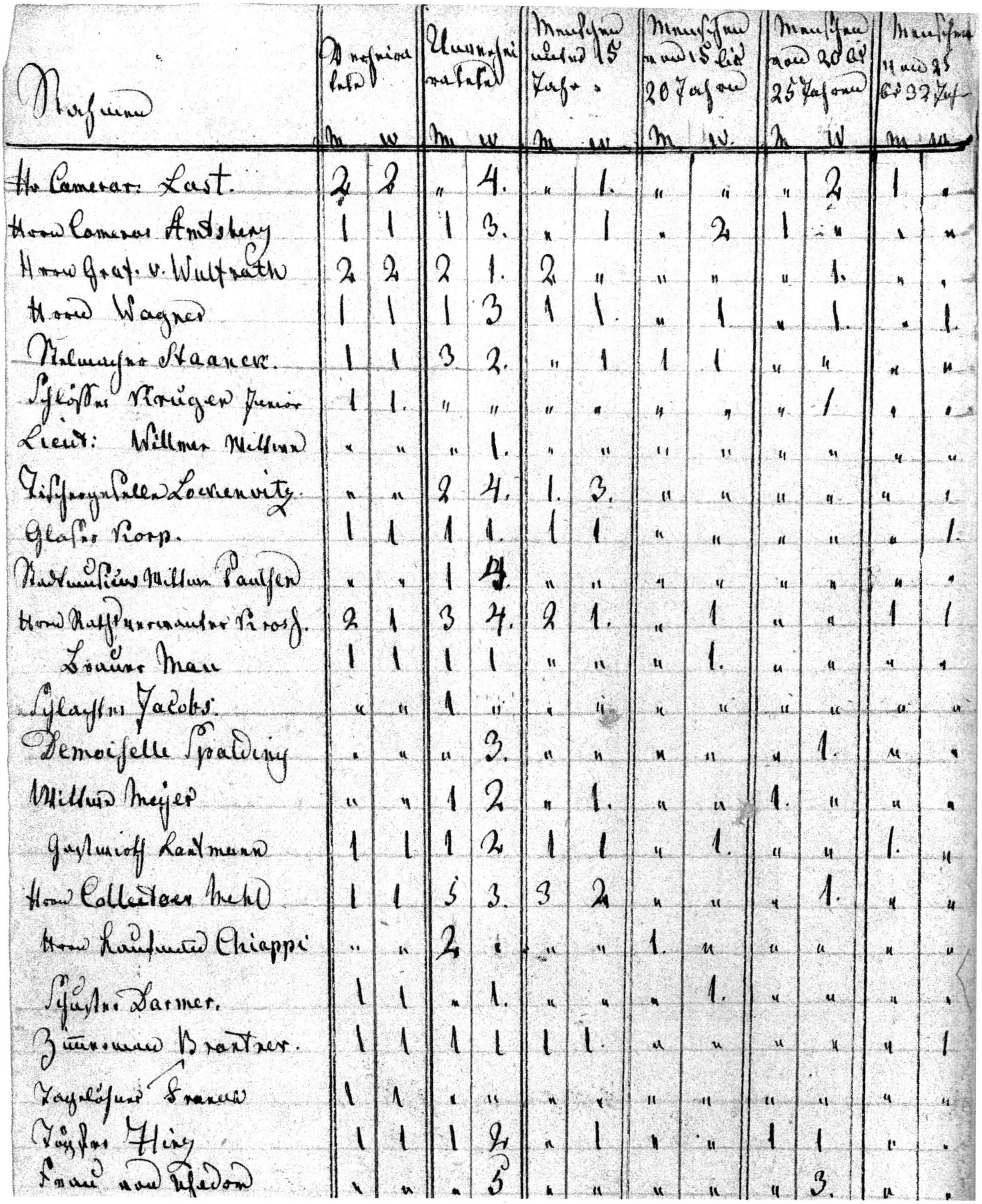

Nahmen	Verheirathete M	W	Unverheirathete M	W	Menschen unter 15 Jahr M	W	Menschen von 15 bis 20 Jahren M	W	Menschen von 20 bis 25 Jahren M	W	Menschen von 25 bis 32 Jahr M	W
Hr Camerar: Last.	2	2	„	4.	„	1.	„	„	„	2	1	„
Herr Camerar Andsberg	1	1	1	3.	„	1	„	2	1	„	„	„
Herr Graf v. Wulfrath	2	2	2	1.	2	„	„	„	„	1.	„	„
Herr Wagner	1	1	1	3	1	1.	„	1	„	1.	„	1.
Malermeister Haaner.	1	1	3	2.	„	1	1	1	„	„	„	„
Schlösser Krüger Junior	1	1.	„	„	„	„	„	„	„	1	„	„
Lieut: Willmer Wittwe	„	„	„	1.	„	„	„	„	„	„	„	„
Tischergesellen Loewenwitz.	„	„	2	4.	1.	3.	„	„	„	„	„	1
Glaser Korp.	1	1	1	1.	1	1	„	„	„	„	„	1.
Rathmännin Wittwe Paulsen	„	„	1	4.	„	„	„	„	„	„	„	„
Herr Rathskammermeister Pirosch.	2	1	3	4.	2	1.	„	1	„	„	1	1
Brauer Man	1	1	1	1	„	„	„	1.	„	„	„	„
Schlachter Jacobs.	„	„	1	„	„	„	„	„	„	„	„	„
Demoiselle Spalding	„	„	„	3.	„	„	„	„	„	1.	„	„
Wittwe Meyer	„	„	1	2	„	1.	„	„	1.	„	„	„
Gastwirth Hartmann	1	1	1	2	1	1	„	1.	„	„	1.	„
Herr Collecteur Kehl	1	1	5	3.	3	2	„	„	„	1.	„	„
Herr Kaufmann Chiappi	„	„	2	„	„	„	1.	„	„	„	„	„
Schuster Darmer.	1	1	„	1.	„	„	„	1.	„	„	„	„
Zimmermann Brantzer.	1	1	1	1	1	1.	„	„	„	„	„	1
Tagelöhner Kramer	1	1	„	„	„	„	„	„	„	„	„	„
Jäger Hinz	1	1	1	2	„	1	„	„	1	1	„	„
Frau von Usedom	„	„	„	5	„	„	„	„	„	3.	„	„

Figure 1. 1816 Census Page for Bergen, Pommern (left-hand page)

Column headings: name of head of household; married males; married females; unmarried males; unmarried females; males under 15; females under 15; males 15–19; females 15–19; males 20–24; females 20–24; males 25–31; females 25–31 [Kreisarchiv Vorpommern-Rügen 353 III 860]

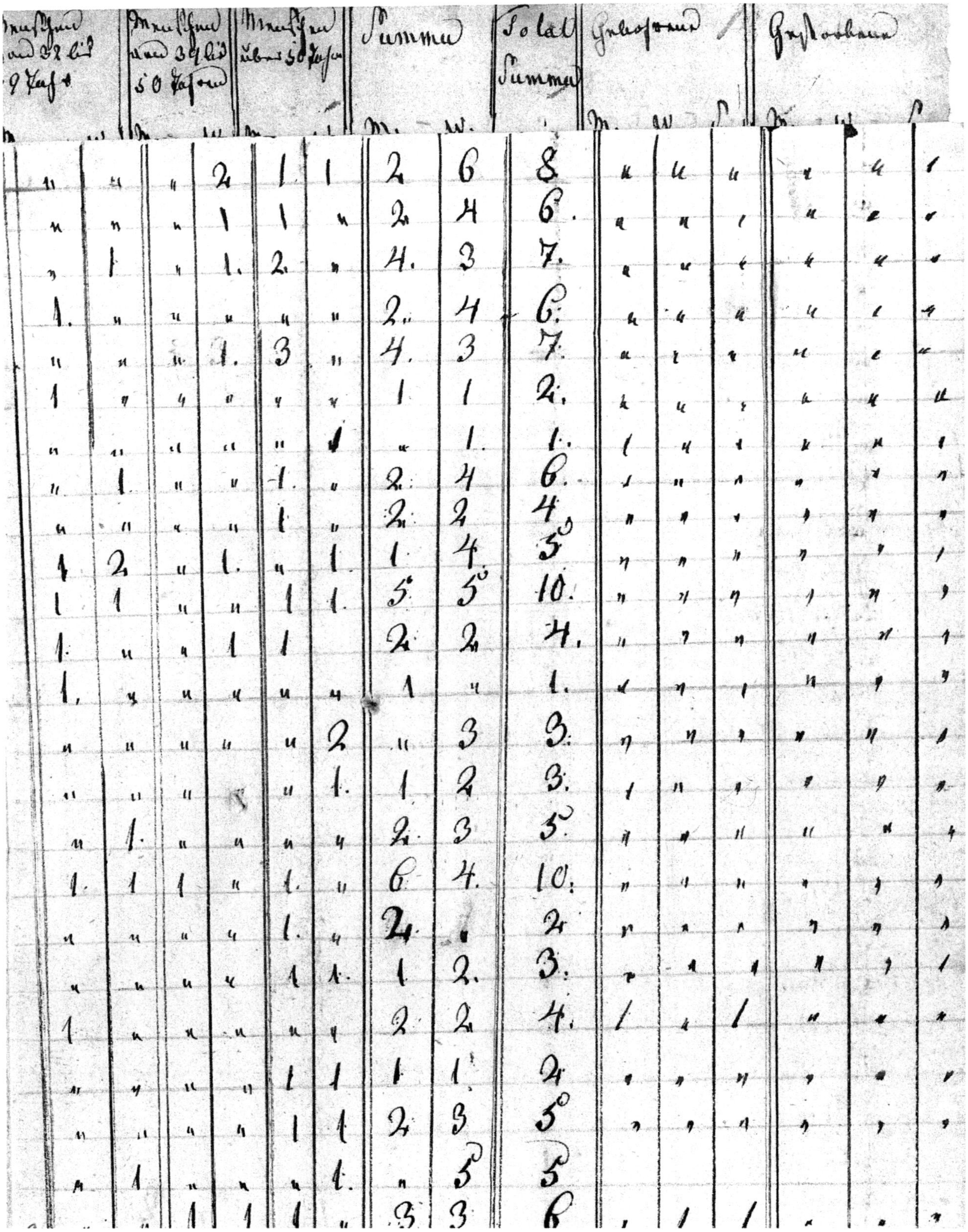

Figure 2. 1816 Census Page for Bergen, Pommern (right-hand page)

Column headings: males 32–38; females 32–38; males 39–49; females 39–49; males over 50; females over 50; total males; total females; total residents; males born this year; females born this year; total births this year; males who died this year; females who died this year; total deaths this year [Kreisarchiv Vorpommern-Rügen 353 III 860]

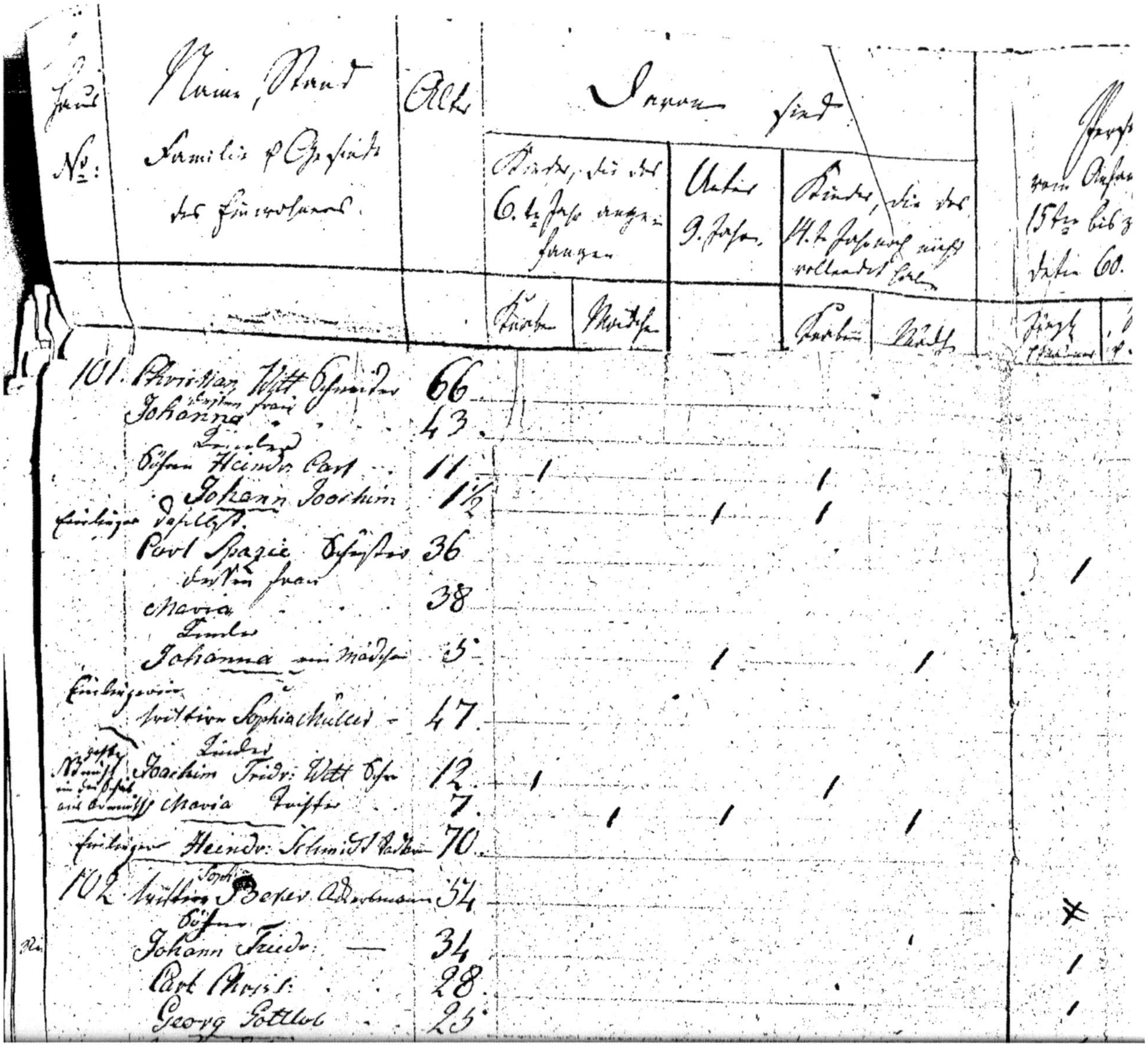

Figure 3. 1828 Census Page for Tribsees, Pommern (left-hand page)

Column headings: name and status of each person; age; males under 6; females under 6; persons 7–9; males under 14; females under 14 [Landesarchiv Greifswald 38b Tribsees Nr 1671]

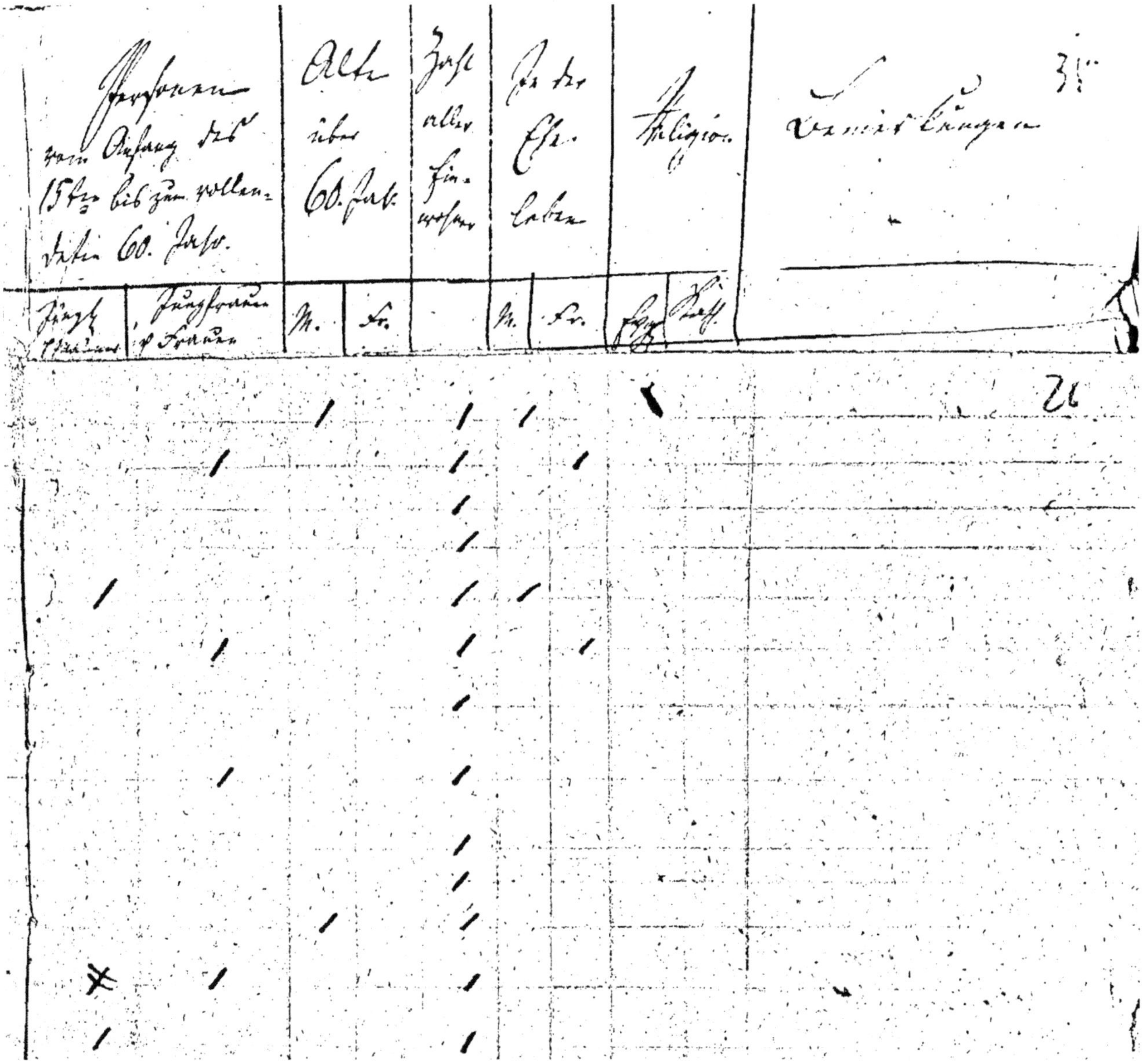

Figure 4. 1828 Census Page for Tribsees, Pommern (right-hand page)

Column headings: males 15–60; females 15–60; males over 60; females over 60; total residents; married males; married females; Lutherans; Catholics; comments [Landesarchiv Greifswald 38b Tribsees Nr 1671]

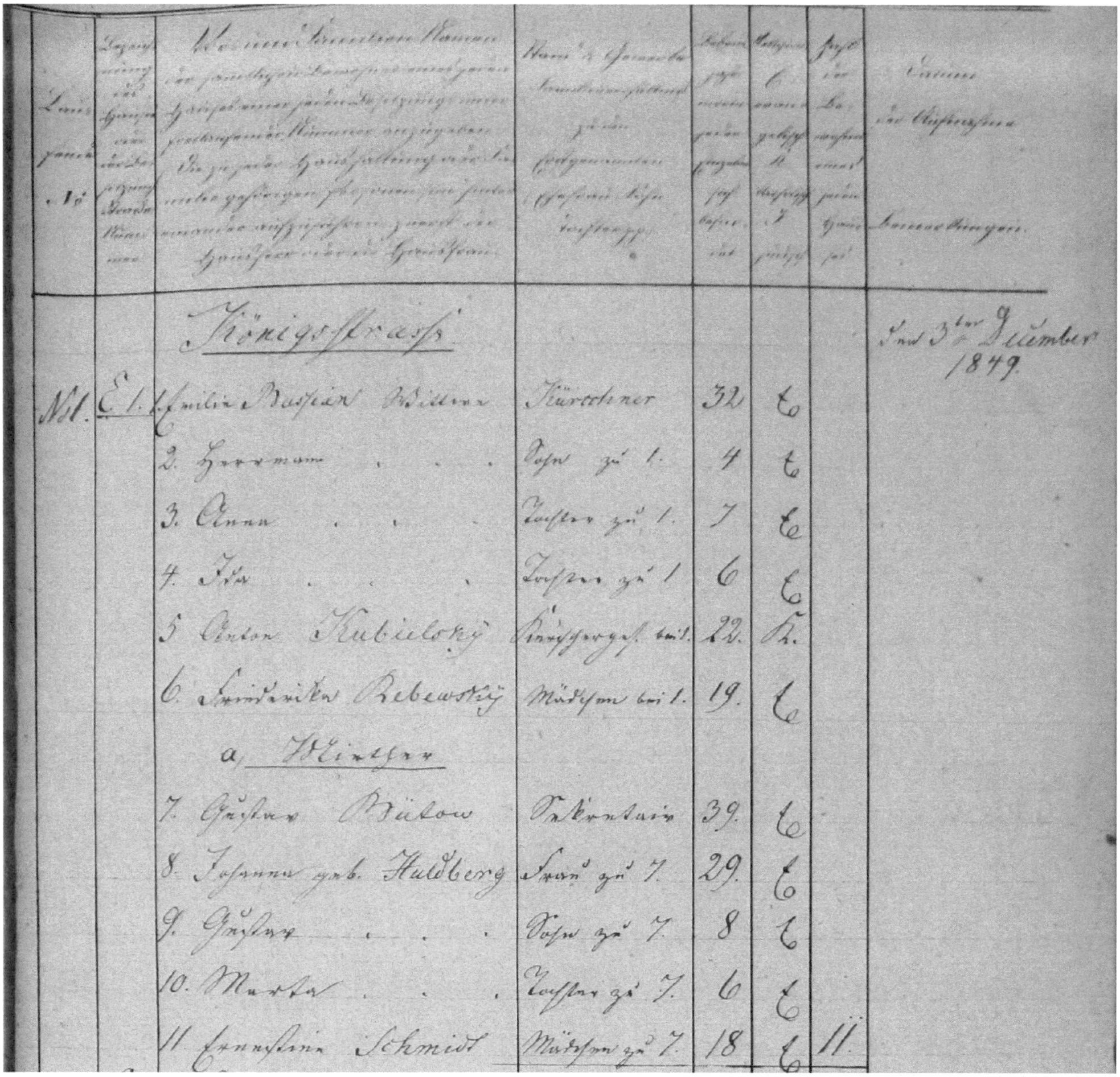

Figure 5. 1849 Census Page for Bergen, Pommern

    Column headings: number or description of dwelling; first and last name of each resident; status or occupation; age at last birthday; religion (Lutheran, Catholic, Jewish); total residents; date of entry and comments [Kreisarchiv Vorpommern-Rügen 353 III 860]

Notes

[1] Harald Michel, "Volkszählungen in Deutschland: Die Erfassung des Bevölkerungsstandes von 1816 bis 1933," in *Jahrbuch für Wirtschaftsgeschichte* 1985/II, 85.

[2] Antje Kraus, *Quellen zur Bevölkerungsstatistik Deutschlands 1815–1871*, Band 1 (Boppard, Germany: Harald Boldt, 1980), 25-26, 183–188.

24 Posen

I. Location

The Prussian province of Posen was surrounded on the west by the province of Brandenburg, on the north by Westpreußen, on the east by the Russian Empire, and on the south by the province of Schlesien.[1] The capital city was likewise named Posen.

II. Census Enumerations in Posen

The kingdom of Preußen ruled over seven provinces in eastern Germany and two in western Germany shortly after the Congress of Vienna. All Prussian provinces were to produce and submit to the statistical bureau in Berlin annual statistical tables from 1817 to 1822 (head counts only). The schedule was then altered to require such data only every three years, but no set of strict standards guided the enumerations. City officials were to carry out the work.[2] Although the campaigns of the 1820s were designed to produce only statistics, the records of several years featured the names of heads of households.

In 1818, Posen was one of the seven eastern Prussian provinces to be grouped into a customs union. One year later, Westfalen and Rheinprovinz were formed into a western Prussian customs union. The next predictable step was the inclusion of all nine Prussian provinces in the Prusso-Hessian Customs Union founded in February 1828.

Census enumerations followed triennially and the schedule continued without interruption even after the establishment of the *Zollverein* [Customs Union] on January 1, 1834. Under the strong leadership of Preußen, the *Zollverein* required census records every three years for three full decades and the quality of those records steadily improved.

Another census was enumerated in 1867 in conjunction with the North German Confederation and all German states participated. Under the German Empire,

enumerations were done in Posen in 1871, every five years from 1875 to 1910, and finally in 1916.[3]

III. Specific Instructions to Town Officials and Enumerators

Significant new and revised instructions for Posen census campaigns have not been located, but the following regulations issued to other Prussian provinces were in effect in Posen:

1825: if significant differences are found in comparison with the results of 1822, explain the causes of those differences

1840: we are sending you the forms to be used; each page has room for sixty names; police officials should conduct the campaign; do not begin to collect the data before December 1; the work must be completed in towns by December 20 and in cities by December 25, so that the reports can be received in Berlin by December 31; you are allowed to refer to documents previously compiled, such as lists of residents; do not count travelers in inns and active military and their dependents; local residents temporarily away from home are to be counted

1843: refer to the deficiencies in the 1840 census in order to produce more reliable results; count military personnel in reserve status; where the number of enumerators is insufficient, tax officials and retired military officers may be called into service and remunerated appropriately

1846: begin the collection of data on December 3; count all foreigners employed here but not persons traveling through the town; count inmates in prisons and hospitals;

persons who own more than one dwelling should be counted where they live in the winter; do not refer to previous lists such as residential registration; in large cities, heads of households may fill out the forms themselves to save enumerators time

1852: the handwriting on the lists must be neat and orderly; should authorities at the next higher level identify mistakes in the local records, the cost of any required corrections shall be charged to the responsible authorities; owners of major estates are to count their respective populations and submit the lists to the local town authorities

1855: persons who refuse to cooperate will be fined

1858: local officials are to announce the upcoming census in the newspaper

1861: for those persons who live in one location and work in another during the week, they are to be counted in the location where they spend the night before the census day; do not count persons in inns or visiting families

1864: do not count persons who have been absent from their home town for more than one year; officials who do not carry out the census according to instructions are to be fined; an enumeration district should not include more than 600 people; non-government persons assigned to assist in the campaign may be paid a maximum of one *Thaler*; count only those foreigners who have lived here for at least one year; record the year of birth rather than the age; children in each family are to be listed in order of their birth

IV. Content of Census Records in Posen from 1822 to 1864

No images have been found as yet for the Prussian province of Posen, but the following details have been gathered from Brandenburg, Pommern, and Sachsen and represent what would have been required by the statistical bureau in Berlin for Posen as well.

	'22	'25	'28	'31	'34	'37	'40	'43	'46	'49	'52	'55	'58	'61	'64
No images available	X	X		X											
Name of each person			X				X	X	X	X	X	X	X	X	X
Name of head of household					X	X									
Married persons (by gender)			X												
Total residents			X		X	X	X	X	X	X	X	X	X	X	X
Age in years			X				X	X	X	X	X	X	X	X	X
Persons under 6 (by gender)			X		X	X									
Persons 7–9 (by gender)			X		X	X									
Persons 10–14 (by gender)			X		X	X									
Persons 15–60 (by gender)			X		X										
Persons over 60 (by gender)			X		X	X									
Lutherans			X		X	X							X	X	X
Catholics			X		X	X							X	X	X
Jewish (with citizenship status)					X	X							X	X	X
Persons 15–16 (by gender)						X									
Males 17–20						X									
Males 21–40						X									
Males 41–60						X									
Males over 60						X									
Females 17–45						X									
Females 46–60						X									
Females over 60						X									
Total females over 14						X									
Total males						X									
Total females						X									
Reformed Lutherans						X									
Mennonites						X									X
Comments			X						X	X	X	X	X	X	X
Status or occupation							X	X	X	X	X	X	X	X	X
Religion							X	X	X	X	X	X			
Blind												X			
Deaf												X			
Greek Orthodox															X
Dissidents															X
Other religions															X
Handwritten column titles			X		X										X
Pre-printed pages						X	X	X	X	X	X	X	X	X	X

V. Accessibility of Census Records in Posen

The fact that this province was ceded to Poland following World War II complicates the search for original census regulations and lists of inhabitants. As part of this investigation, emails were sent to county and regional archives in what was once the province of Posen but none of those responded positively regarding census records in their collections.[4] Nevertheless, a letter written in Polish to a city, county, or regional government archive found through a search of websites might prove successful. (See Appendix A for suggestions on writing that inquiry in Polish.)

As of this writing, no census records are available in the Family History Library on microfilm and no digital images have been located on the Internet.

VI. Selected Images of Posen Census Records

As of this writing, no images of census records have been found for this province.

Notes

[1] This is a simplified representation. The changes in borders among Prussian provinces in the nineteenth century are legion but not of specific importance here.

[2] Harald Michel, "Volkszählungen in Deutschland: Die Erfassung des Bevölkerungsstandes von 1816 bis 1933," in *Jahrbuch für Wirtschaftsgeschichte* 1985/II, 85.

[3] Antje Kraus, *Quellen zur Bevölkerungsstatistik Deutschlands 1815–1871*, Band 1 (Boppard, Germany: Harald Boldt, 1980), 25-26, 207–212.

[4] The author expresses his appreciation to Magdalena Zajac, a native Polish student at the University of Vienna, who conducted an extensive campaign with archives in cities that once were in the provinces of Ostpreußen, Posen, Schlesien, and Westpreußen.

25 Reuß ältere Linie [Reuss Elder Line]

I. Location

The principality of Reuß ältere Linie (also known as Reuß-Greiz) was one of the eight so-called "Saxon duchies" within the central German region collectively known as Thüringen. One of the smallest states in Germany, Reuß ältere Linie had two smaller exclaves. Neighboring states were Reuss jüngere Linie, Sachsen-Weimar-Eisenach, the Prussian province of Sachsen to the west and the kingdom of Sachsen to the east. The only major cities in this principality in the nineteenth century were Greiz and Burgk.

II. Census Enumerations in Reuß ältere Linie

The first known census enumeration in this principality was conducted in 1828 with a second in 1833, just after the principality had agreed to join the *Zollverein* [Customs Union] and as preparation for membership therein. From 1834 through 1864, a census was enumerated in Reuß ältere Linie every three years.[1] The principality also participated in the first all-German census conducted in 1867. Under the German Empire, enumerations were done in Reuß ältere Linie in 1871, every five years from 1875 to 1910, and finally in 1916.

III. Specific Instructions to Town Officials and Enumerators

No detailed instructions for the conduct of the census in Reuß ältere Linie have been located as of this writing.

IV. Content of Census Records in Reuß ältere Linie from 1828 to 1864

Original lists have been found for only two enumeration years. However, one may assume that the content of census records in Reuss ältere Linie will be similar to that found in Reuß jüngere Linie and other states belonging to the *Zollverein* over the years.

	1828	1833	1834	1837	1840	1843	1846	1849	1852	1855	1858	1861	1864
No images available		X	X	X	X		X	X	X	X	X	X	X
Name of each resident	X												
Age in years	X												
Total number of residents	X												
Other details	X													
Name of head of household						X							
Number of residents in household						X							
Number of adult males						X							
Number of adult females						X							
Total children under 14						X							
Male children under 14						X							
Female children under 14						X							
Handwritten column titles	X												
Pre-printed pages						X							

V. Accessibility of Census Records in Reuß ältere Linie

For this study, email inquiries were sent to all major cities in the historic principality of Reuß ältere Linie. No responses were received as of this writing. It is possible that those and other towns in that province do indeed have records and carefully-worded inquiries or personal visits may lead to significant discoveries. (See Appendix A for instructions on how to write the inquiry.) One or more of the archives in the modern state of Thüringen may also have records collected from locations within Reuß ältere Linie towns over the years. Those archives are listed on the website: http://www.thueringen.de/th1/tsk/kultur/staatsarchive. No Reuß census records are currently found on microfilm in the collection of the Family History Library, but a search in that catalog by town now and then might yield new documents.

VI. Selected Images of Reuß ältere Linie Census Records

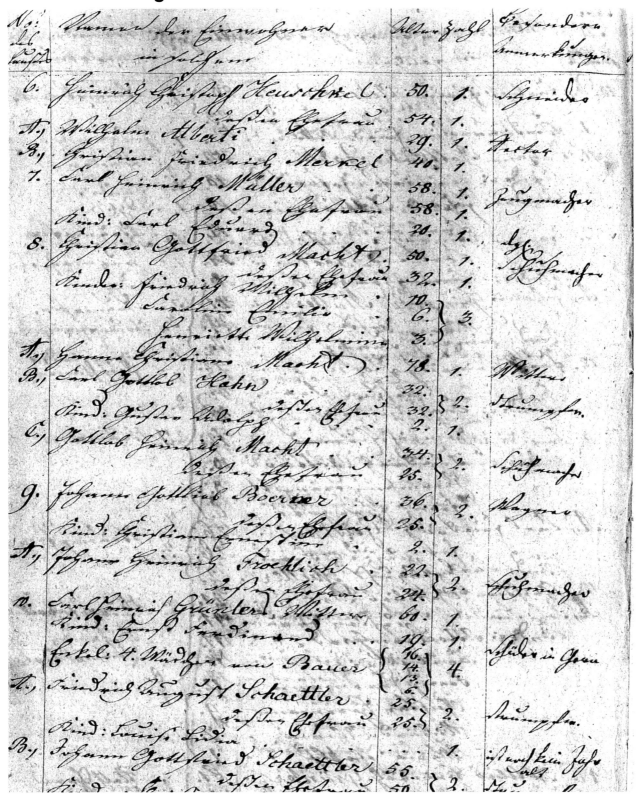

Figure 1. 1828 Census Page from Zeulenroda, Reuß ältere Linie

Column headings: number of household; name of each individual; age in years; total number of persons; other details [Thüringisches Staatsarchiv Greiz]

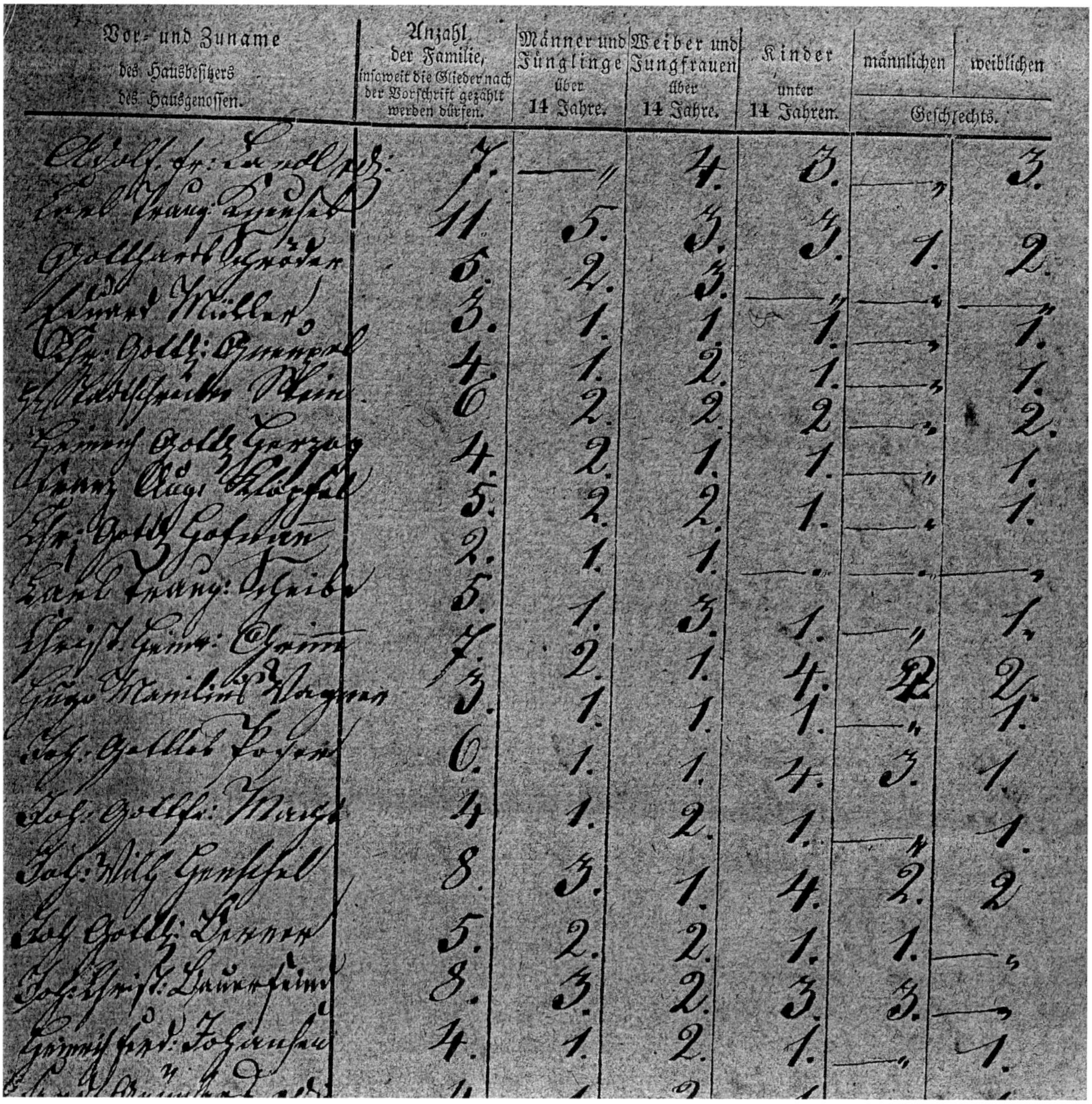

Figure 2. 1843 Census Page from Zeulenroda, Reuß ältere Linie

Column headings: name of head of household; total number of residents; males over 14; females over 14; number of children under 14; males under 14; females under 14 [Thüringisches Staatsarchiv Greiz]

Notes

[1] Antje Kraus, *Quellen zur Bevölkerungsstatistik Deutschlands 1815–1871*, Band 1 (Boppard, Germany: Harald Boldt, 1980), 30, 319–324. Beginning in 1841, population statistics were also calculated for each non-census year according to the following formula: total population in the previous year plus the number of children born minus the numbers of persons who died.

26 Reuß jüngere Linie [Reuß Younger Line]

I. Location

The principality of Reuß jüngere Linie (also known as Reuß-Schleiz) is one of the eight so-called "Saxon duchies" within the central German region collectively known as Thüringen. One of the smallest states in Germany, Reuß jüngere Linie had two exclaves. Six of the seven Saxon duchies shared borders with Reuß jüngere Linie, as did the Prussian province of Sachsen to the west and the kingdom of Sachsen to the east.

II. Census Enumerations in Reuß jüngere Linie

The first known census enumeration was conducted in 1833, just after the principality had agreed to join the *Zollverein* [Customs Union] and as preparation for membership therein. From 1834 until 1864, a census was enumerated in Reuß jüngere Linie every three years.[1] The 1867 census was conducted here as well as all over Germany that year. Under the German Empire, enumerations were done in Reuß jüngere Linie in 1871, every five years from 1875 to 1910, and finally in 1916.

III. Specific Instructions to Town Officials and Enumerators

No detailed instructions for the conduct of the census in Reuß jüngere Linie have been located as of this writing.

IV. Content of Census Records in Reuß jüngere Linie from 1833 to 1864

The form used in 1833 is likely a precursor for those used in subsequent enumerations. One may also assume that the content of census records in Reuß jüngere Linie will be similar to that of Reuß ältere Linie and other states in the *Zollverein* over the years.

	1833	1834	1837	1840	1843	1846	1849	1852	1855	1858	1861	1864
Image not available		X	X	X	X	X		X	X	X	X	X
Surname of head of household	X											
Owner or renter	X											
Number of persons in family	X						X					
Total Males	X											
Total Females	X											
Status or occupation of head of household	X											
Apprentices	X											
Journeymen	X											
Domestic servants	X											
Total persons in household							X					
Total persons in family							X					
Name of head of household or adult living alone							X					
Males over 14							X					
Females over 14							X					
Males under 14							X					
Females under 14							X					
Handwritten pages												
Pre-printed pages	X						X					

V. Accessibility of Census Records in Reuß jüngere Linie

For this study, email inquiries were sent to all major cities in the historic principality of Reuß jüngere Linie. Only one response was received as of this writing. It is possible that other towns in that province have records and carefully-worded inquiries or personal visits to neighboring towns may lead to significant discoveries. (See Appendix A for instructions on how to write the inquiry.) One or more of the archives in the modern state of Thüringen may also have census records collected from towns in Reuß jüngere Linie over the years. Those archives are listed on the website: http://www.thueringen.de/th1/tsk/kultur/staatsarchive. No Reuß census records are currently found in the collection of the Family History Library, but a search in that catalog by town now and then might yield new documents. Likewise, no such documents are known to exist as digital images on the Internet.

VI. Selected Census Images from Reuß jüngere Linie

~~Haus-nummer.~~	~~Nummer~~ der Familien.	Namen der Familien oder einzelnen selbstständigen Personen.	Ob Eigenthümer oder Hausgenosse.	Die Familie besteht: anwesenden Personen männlichen Geschlechts.	Perso[nen] weibli[chen] Geschle[chts.]
		Vacat.	Vacat.		

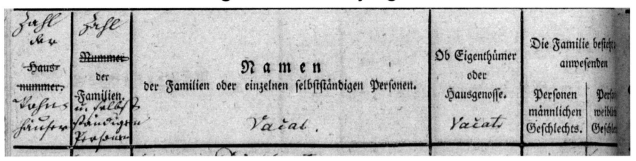

Figure 1. 1833 Census Page from Gera, Reuß jüngere Linie [left-hand page—used for statistics rather than as a normal page for personal data]

Column headings: dwelling number; household number; name of the head of household or person living alone; whether owner or renter; number of persons in the family (male and female)

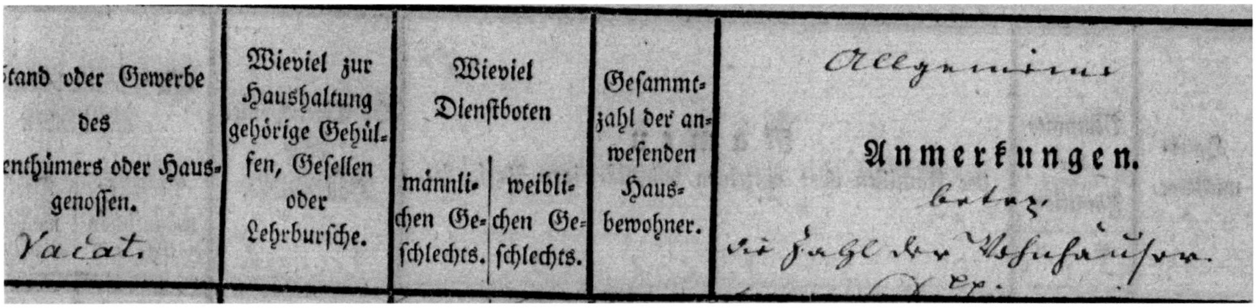

[S]tand oder Gewerbe des [Eig]enthümers oder Hausgenossen.	Wieviel zur Haushaltung gehörige Gehülfen, Gesellen oder Lehrburschen.	Wieviel Dienstboten männlichen Geschlechts.	weiblichen Geschlechts.	Gesammtzahl der anwesenden Hausbewohner.	Anmerkungen.
Vacat.					

Figure 2. 1833 Census Page from Gera, Reuß jüngere Linie [right-hand page—used for statistics rather than as a normal page for personal data]

Column headings: Status or occupation of the head of household; number of apprentices, journeymen, and domestics in the household; number of servants (male and female); total number of residents in the household; comments

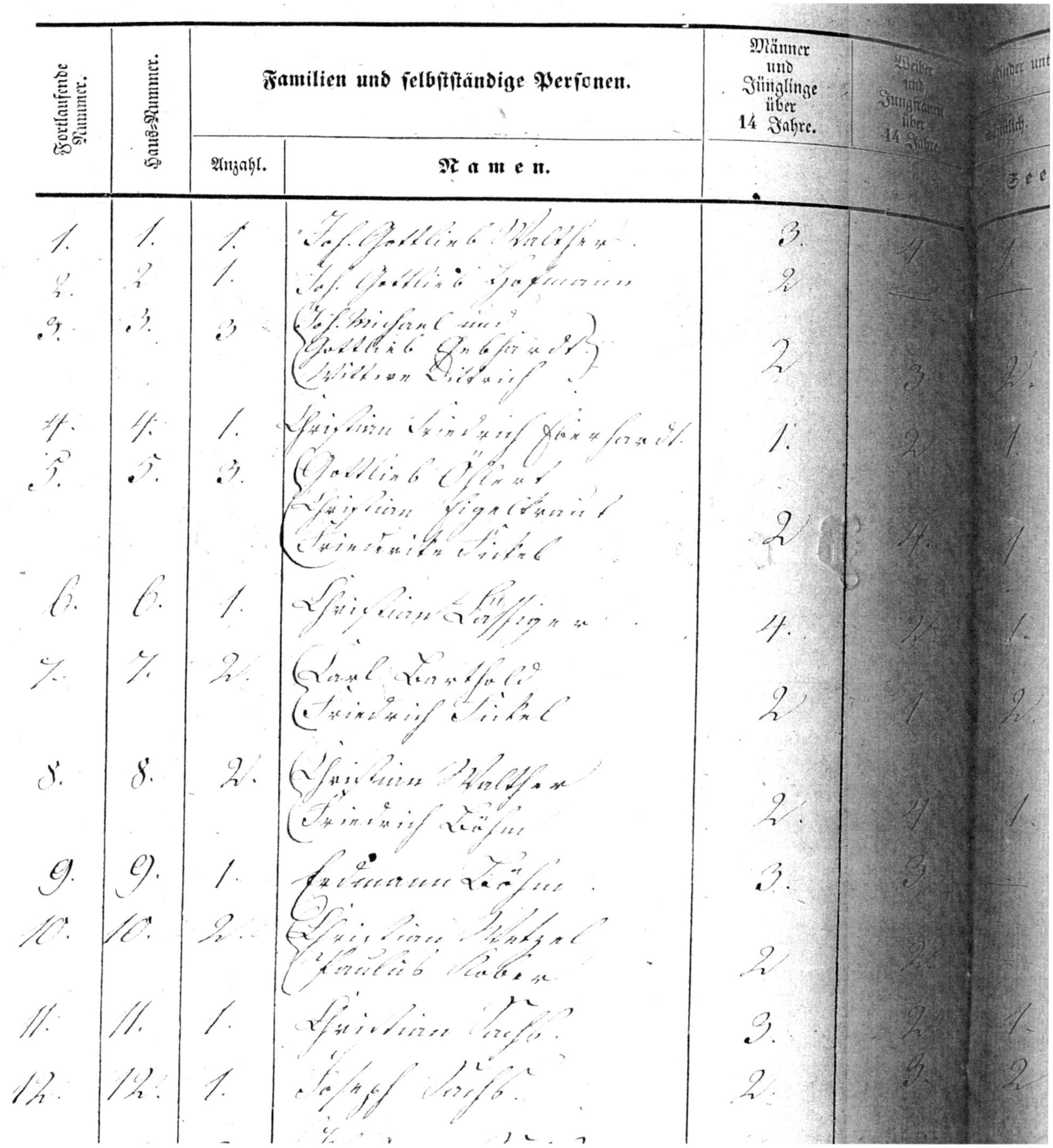

Fortlaufende Nummer.	Haus-Nummer.	Familien und selbstständige Personen.		Männer und Jünglinge über 14 Jahre.	Weiber und Jungfrauen über 14 Jahre	Kinder unter schlich.
		Anzahl.	Namen.			
1.	1.	1.	*[Joh. Gottlieb Walther]*	3.	4	1
2.	2.	1.	*[Joh. Gottlieb Hofmann]*	2.		
3.	3.	3	*[Joh. Michael ...]* *[Gottlieb ...]* *[Wilhelm Dietrich]*	2.	3	2
4.	4.	1.	*[Christian Heinrich ...]*	1.	2	1
5.	5.	3.	*[Gottlieb Oßner]* *[Christian ...]* *[Heinrich Sichel]*	2.	4	1
6.	6.	1.	*[Christian ...]*	4.	4	1
7.	7.	2.	*[Carl ...]* *[Friedrich Sichel]*	2.	1	2
8.	8.	2.	*[Christian Walther]* *[Friedrich ...]*	2.	4	1
9.	9.	1.	*[Hermann ...]*	3.	3	
10.	10.	2.	*[Christian ...]* *[... ...]*	2.	2	
11.	11.	1.	*[Christian ...]*	3.	2	4
12.	12.	1.	*[Joseph ...]*	2.	2	2

Figure 3. 1849 Census Page from Schleiz, Reuß-jüngere Linie [left-hand page]

Column headings: consecutive number of family; number of dwelling; number of household; total males over 14; total females over 14 [Thüringisches Staatsarchiv Greiz]

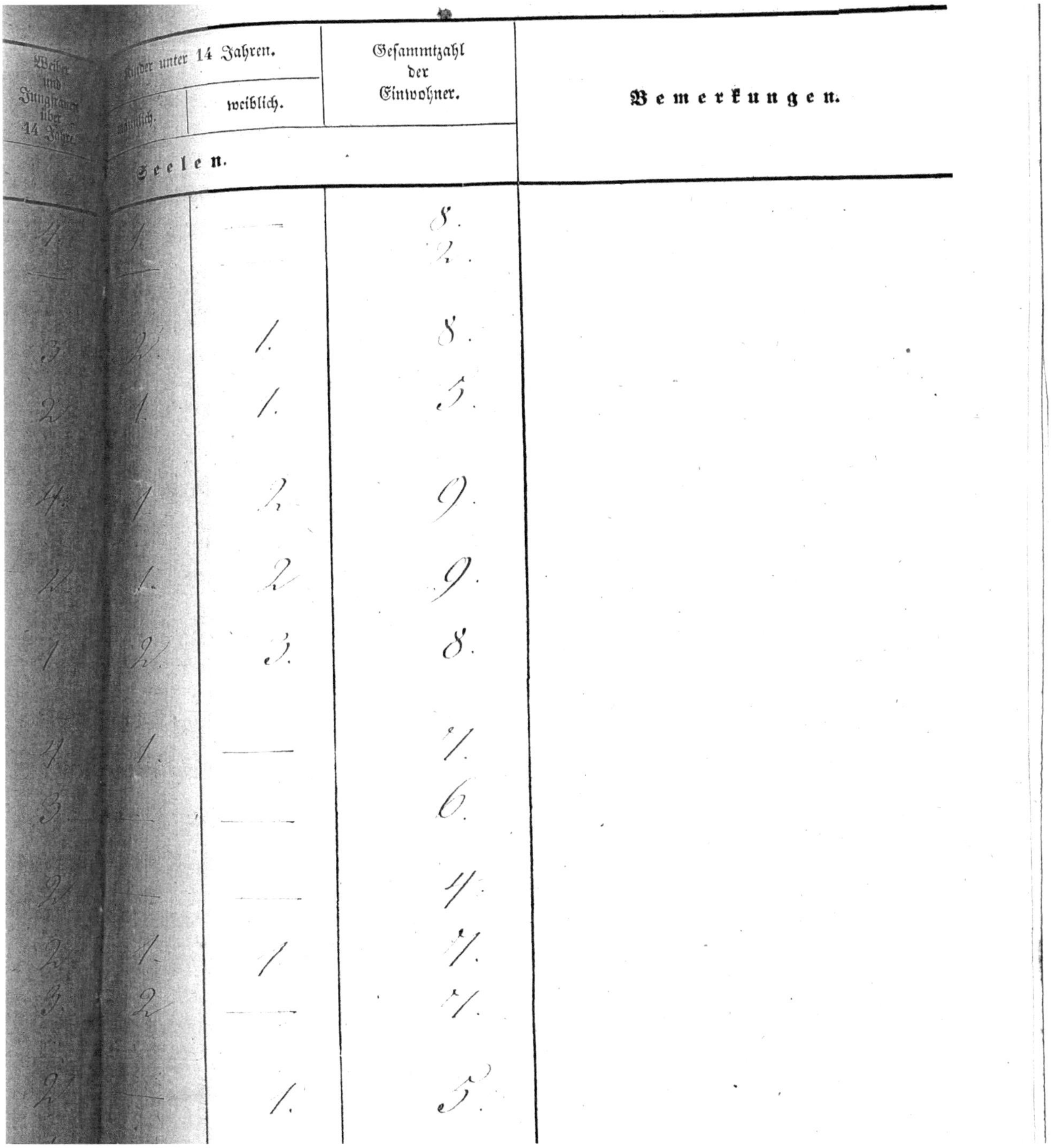

Weiber und Jungfrauen über 14 Jahren	Kinder unter 14 Jahren.		Gesammtzahl der Einwohner.	Bemerkungen.
	männlich.	weiblich.		
Seelen.				
4	1		8	
			2	
3	2	1	8	
2	1	1	5	
4	1	2	9	
2	1	2	9	
1	2	3	8	
4	1	—	7	
3		—	6	
2		—	4	
2	1	1	7	
4	2		7	
2		1	5	

Figure 4. 1849 Census Page from Schleiz, Reuß-jüngere Linie [right-hand page]

Column headings: males under 14; females under 14; total residents in household; comments [Thüringisches Staatsarchiv Greiz]

Notes

[1] Antje Kraus, *Quellen zur Bevölkerungsstatistik Deutschlands 1815–1871*, Band 1 (Boppard, Germany: Harald Boldt, 1980), 29, 313–318. Beginning in 1841, population statistics were also calculated for each non-census year according to the following formula: total population in the previous year plus the total of children born minus the numbers of persons who died.

27 Rheinprovinz [Rhineland Province]

I. Location

The state called Rheinprovinz lay in western Germany, across the border from the Netherlands, Belgium and Luxembourg to the west and France to the south. Neighboring German states in the nineteenth century were the Prussian province of Westfalen to the northeast, and Hessen-Nassau and the grand duchy of Hesse to the east, and the Palatinate (Bayern) to the south. The provincial capital was Koblenz.

II. Census Enumerations in Rheinprovinz

The kingdom of Preußen ruled over several provinces in eastern Germany, but only two of the German states in the west—Rheinprovinz and Westfalen. All Prussian provinces were to produce and submit to the statistical bureau in Berlin annual statistical tables every three years beginning in 1822, but no set of strict standards guided the enumerations. City officials were to carry out the work.[1] Although the campaigns of the 1820s were designed to produce only statistics, the records of several years featured the names of heads of households.

In 1822, Rheinprovinz and Westfalen were grouped into a western Prussian customs union. Thus it was only logical that Rheinprovinz automatically be accepted into the Prusso-Hessian Customs Union that was founded in February 1828. Census enumerations followed triennially and the schedule continued without interruption even after the establishment of the *Zollverein* [Customs Union] on January 1, 1834. Under the strong leadership of Preußen, the *Zollverein* required census records every three years for three full decades and the quality of those records steadily improved.

Another census was enumerated in 1867 in conjunction with the North German Confederation and all German states participated. Under the German Empire, enumerations were done in the Rheinprovinz in 1871, thereafter every five years from 1875 to 1910, and finally in 1916.[2]

III. Specific Instructions to Town Officials and Enumerators

The directions issued a few months before each census enumeration was to begin often featured identical wording for specific paragraphs year after year (see 1858 below). Significant new and revised instructions for Rheinprovinz census campaigns are summarized as follows:

1831: use the same form and instructions as in 1828 but strive for greater accuracy; submit results by January 15

1840: record the first and last name of each person; use the form provided; for each family, list the parents and children in order; if more than one family lives in the same dwelling, list the owner's family first; the mayor is responsible for the census campaign and must check the original lists for accuracy; he may compare the results with any other existing list to determine accuracy; officials who are not reliable must not be allowed to participate, but may be replaced by pastors and teachers

1843: every house must be visited; begin and finish the census in December; don't count military personnel; traveling salesmen and workers are to be counted in the town of their residence

1846: begin and finish on December 3; cities of more than 30,000 may need up to three days; don't count family and servants of military personnel; don't count persons in inns or visiting families; count locals temporarily away from home; persons who own more than one residence are to be counted where they are on December 3; don't take census data from any other existing lists

1855: persons refusing to cooperate are to be warned with a fine of 3 *Thaler*; in the "dissident" category, indicate to which group the person belongs [nine listed]

1858: we see no need to repeat the same seven pages of instructions issued on November 9, 1855; count retired military persons and dependents; count workers where they are employed, not where they live (if elsewhere) on weekends; each page has 25 lines—use them all, leave no lines blank, write no data between lines

1864: don't count locals who have been away from home for more than one year; in larger cities the enumerators may solicit in advance so-called "house lists" from heads of households, but must check them carefully for accuracy

IV. Content of Census Records in Rheinprovinz from 1822 to 1864

	1822	1825	1828	1831	1834	1837	1840	1843	1846	1849	1852	1855	1858	1861	1864
No images available		X	X	X	X										
Description of dwelling	X					X	X		X	X	X	X	X	X	X
Name of head of household	X					X									
Year of birth	X														
Comments	X					X	X		X	X	X	X	X	X	X
Total males						X									
Total females						X									
Total residents						X	X		X	X	X	X	X	X	X
Married males						X		X							
Married females						X		X							
Lutherans						X		X							
Catholics						X		X							
Jewish (citizenship?)						X		X							
Persons 0–5 (by gender)						X		X							
Persons 6–7 (by gender)						X		X							
Persons 8–14 (by gender)						X		X							
Total persons under 14						X									
Persons 15–16 (by gender)						X		X							
Males 17–20						X									
Males 21–25						X		X							
Males 26–32						X		X							
Males 33–39						X		X							
Males 40–45						X		X							
Males 46–60						X		X							
Males over 60						X		X							
Total males over 16						X									
Females 17–45						X		X							
Females 46–60						X		X							
Females over 60						X		X							
Total females over 16						X									
Active military						X									
Away for school or work						X									
Name of each resident							X	X	X	X	X	X	X	X	X
Age at last birthday							X	X	X	X	X	X	X	X	X
Religion							X		X	X	X	X	X	X	X
Status or occupation								X							
Gender								X							
Mennonites															X
Greek Orthodox															X
Dissidents															X
Other religions															X
Handwritten headings	X						X		X	X	X				
Pre-printed pages						X					X	X	X	X	X

V. Accessibility of Census Records in Rheinprovinz

Regional archives of the modern state of Rheinland-Pfalz have few if any census documents. Researchers should direct their inquiries to the archives of towns and counties, where excellent census records have been found. (See Appendix A for suggestions about communicating with archivists.) Census records on microfilm in the Family History Library are rare, but a visit to the catalog now and then may turn up new holdings. As of this writing, no Rheinprovinz census records are known to be available in digital form on the Internet.

VI. Selected Images of Rheinprovinz Census Records

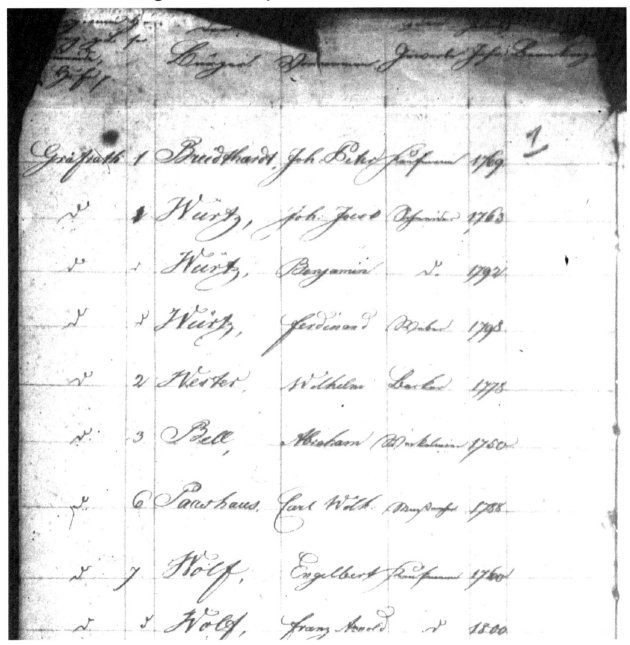

Figure 1. 1822 Census Page from Gräfrath, Rheinprovinz

Column headings: town; household number; surname of head of household; given name; status or occupation; birth year; comments [Stadtarchiv Solingen]

Haus Nummer	Name und Vorname	Stand und Gewerbe	Alter	Geschlecht		In der Ehe leben		Confession			bis zum 5. Jahre		6 bis 7 Jahre		8 bis 14 Jahre	
				männlich	weiblich	Männer	Frauen	evangelisch	katholisch	Juden	Knaben	Mädchen	Knaben	Mädchen	Knaben	Mädchen
	[illegible]	*[illegible]*	23	1				1								
	[illegible], Wilhelm	*[illegible]*	45	1				1								
	[illegible]	*[illegible]*	22	1					1							
	[illegible]	*[illegible]*	31	1					1							
	[illegible]	*[illegible]*	23	1					1							
	Laurentius, Joh. Peter	Gärtner	44	1		1			1							
	Ott, *[illegible]*	*[illegible]*	46	1			1		1							
	Junker, *[illegible]*	*[illegible]*	28	1					1							
	[illegible], Johann	*[illegible]*	31	1					1							
52	*[illegible]*	*[illegible]*	45	1					1							
	Zimmermann, *[illegible]*	*[illegible]*	65		1				1							
	Jungbluth, *[illegible]*	*[illegible]*	57	1					1							
53	Kaufmann, Karl	*[illegible]*	52	1		1			1							
	Scholl, *[illegible]*	*[illegible]*	16	1			1	1								
"2	Heinrichs, *[illegible]*	*[illegible]*	*[illegible]*	1			1		1							
	[illegible]	*[illegible]*	46	1			1		1							
	Heinrichs, Peter Jos.	"	16	1					1							
	" *[illegible]*	"	18		1				1						1	
	" *[illegible]*	"	14		1				1						1	

Figure 2. 1843 Census Page from Wickrath, Rheinprovinz (left-hand page)

Column headings: first and last name; status or occupation; age in years; males; females; married men; married women; Lutherans; Catholics; Jewish; males 0–5; females 0–5; males 6–7; females 6–7; males 8–14; females 8–14; males 15–20, females 15–20 [Stadtarchiv Mönchengladbach]

152

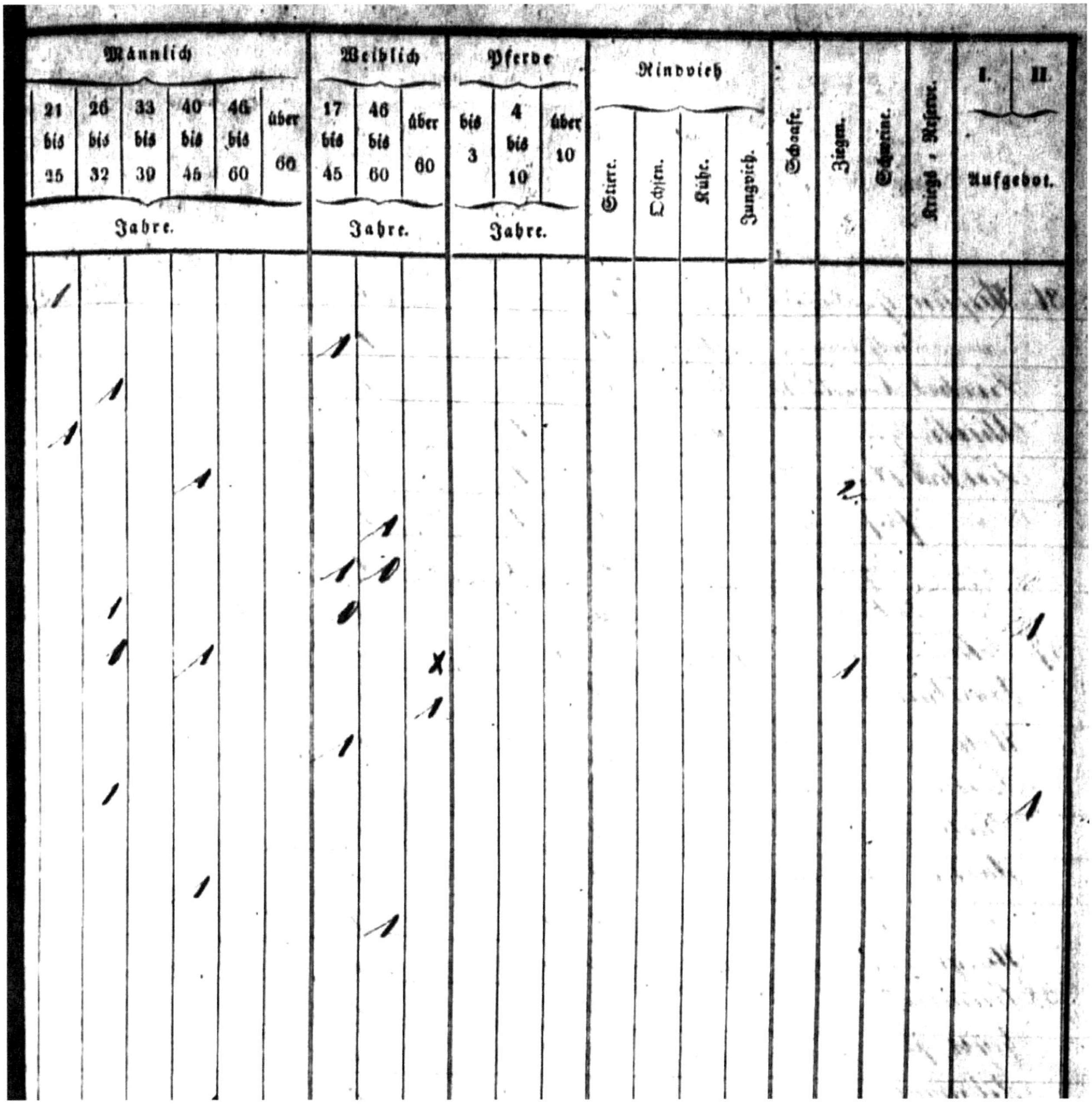
Männlich
21 bis 25 | 26 bis 32 | 33 bis 39 | 40 bis 45 | 46 bis 60 | über 60
Jahre.
Weiblich
17 bis 45 | 46 bis 60 | über 60
Jahre.
Pferde
bis 3 | 4 bis 10 | über 10
Jahre.
Rindvieh
Stiere. | Ochsen. | Kühe. | Jungvieh.
Schaafe. | Ziegen. | Schweine. | Kriegs- , Reserve.
I. | II.
Aufgebot.

Figure 3. 1843 Census Page from Wickrath, Rheinprovinz (right-hand page)

Column headings: males 21–25; males 26–32; males 33–39; males 40–45; males 46–60; males over 60; females 17–45; females 46–60; females over 60; livestock, 8 categories [Stadtarchiv Mönchengladbach]

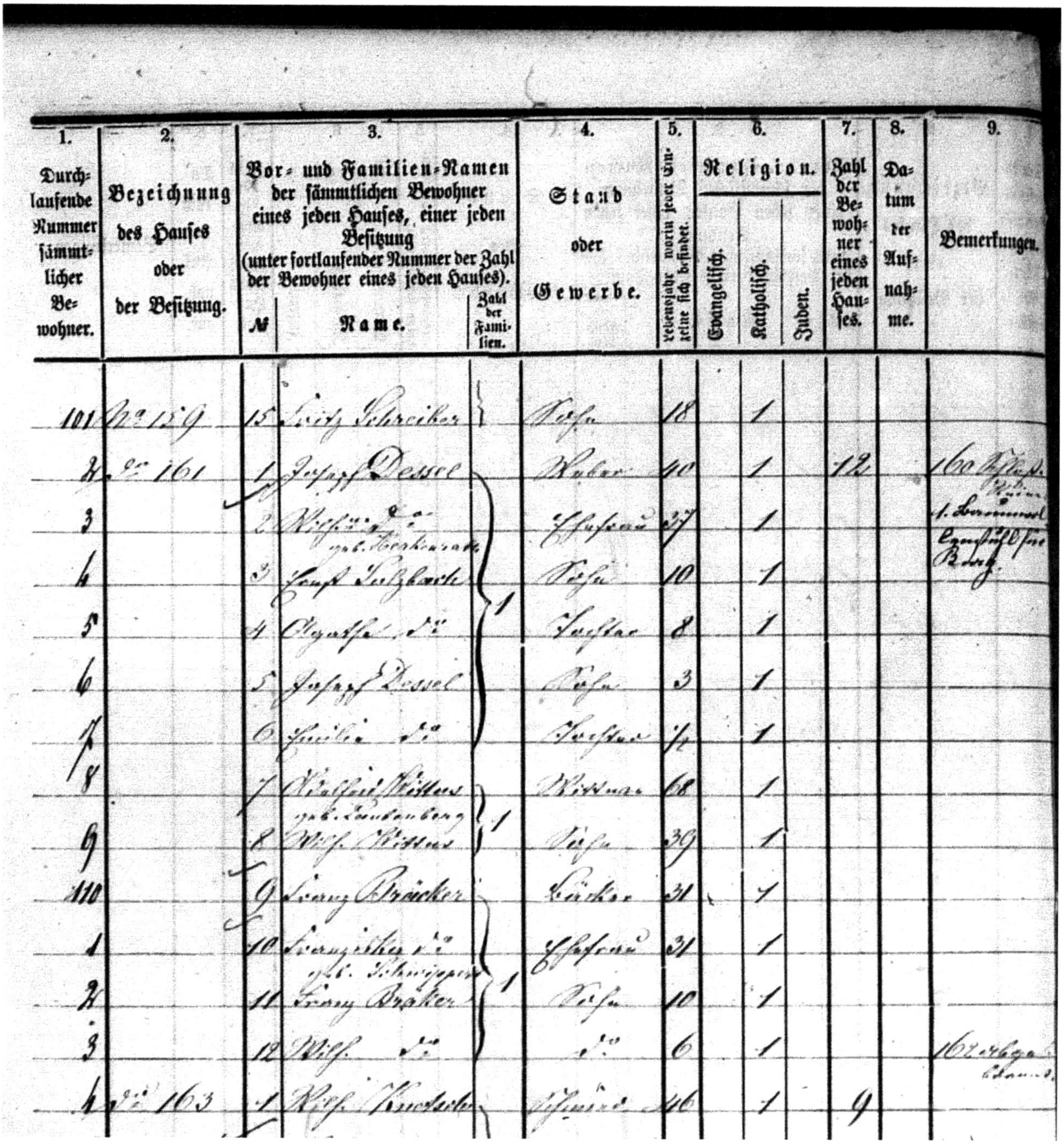

1. Durchlaufende Nummer sämmtlicher Bewohner.	2. Bezeichnung des Hauses oder der Besitzung.	3. Vor- und Familien-Namen der sämmtlichen Bewohner eines jeden Hauses, einer jeden Besitzung (unter fortlaufender Nummer der Zahl der Bewohner eines jeden Hauses).			4. Stand oder Gewerbe.	5. Lebensjahr worin jeder Einzelne sich befindet.	6. Religion.			7. Zahl der Bewohner eines jeden Hauses.	8. Datum der Aufnahme.	9. Bemerkungen.
		№	Name	Zahl der Familien.			Evangelisch.	Katholisch.	Juden.			

Figure 4. 1861 Census Page for Wald, Rheinprovinz

Column headings: description or address of dwelling; name of each resident; status or occupation; age at last birthday; Lutheran; Catholic; Jewish; total residents; date of entry; comments [Stadtarchiv Solingen]

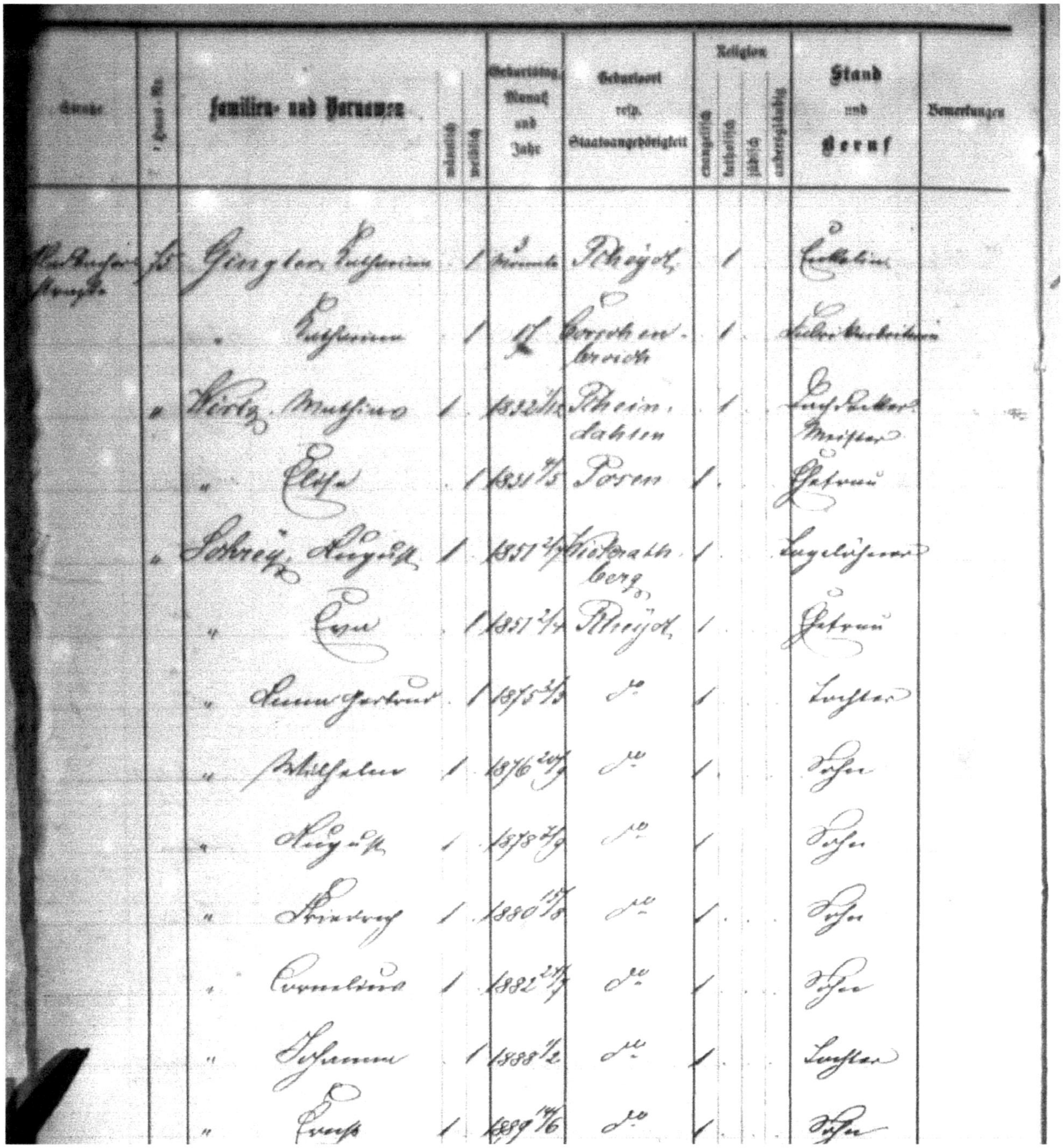

Figure 5. 1890 Census Page from Rheydt, Rheinprovinz

Column headings: street name; house number; name of each resident; males; females; birth date; birth place or citizenship; Lutheran; Catholic; Jewish; Other religion; status or occupation; comments [Stadtarchiv Mönchengladbach]

Notes

[1] Harald Michel, "Volkszählungen in Deutschland: Die Erfassung des Bevölkerungsstandes von 1816 bis 1933," in *Jahrbuch für Wirtschaftsgeschichte* 1985/II, 85.

[2] Antje Kraus, *Quellen zur Bevölkerungsstatistik Deutschlands 1815–1871*, Band 1 (Boppard, Germany: Harald Boldt, 1980), 25–26, 213–218.

28 Sachsen-Altenburg [Saxe-Altenburg]

I. Location

The duchy of Sachsen-Altenburg is one of the eight so-called "Saxon duchies" within the central German region collectively known as Thüringen. Consisting of two large separate territories, it shares borders with six of the Saxon duchies, as well as the Prussian province of Sachsen and the kingdom of Sachsen. The capital city was likewise called Altenburg.

II. Census Enumerations in Sachsen-Altenburg

Annual counts of the inhabitants of this duchy were done annually beginning in 1816, but the first known census enumerations involving the names of individuals were conducted in 1828, 1832, and 1833. The clergy carried out the program in towns and smaller communities while government officials did so in the cities.[1]

Sachsen-Altenburg joined the *Mitteldeutscher Handelsverein* [Central German Commercial Union] in 1828 but moved to the *Zollverein* [Customs Union] in 1834 when the former fell apart. As a member state of the *Zollverein*, census campaigns were conducted every three years from 1834 to 1864 and participated in the first national census in 1867.[2] Under the German Empire, enumerations were done in Sachsen-Altenburg in 1871, every five years from 1875 to 1910, and finally in 1916.

III. Specific Instructions to Town Officials and Enumerators

Available literature on instructions given to officials of towns in Sachsen-Altenburg has proved to be hard to find in this investigation; important details are:

1864: distribute the lists to all heads of households beginning on November 29 and collect them on December 3; even adults living alone count as households; directors of hospitals, prisons, etc. are to fill out the forms for their residents; if the head of household cannot fill out the form, the enumerator will do that for him

Figure 1. The literature provided to the town of Altenburg for the census of 1867 consisted of nine different publications, including 600 pre-printed household lists. [Stadtarchiv Meuselwitz AE I F 1 Nr. 1 u. 3]

IV. Content of Census Records in Sachsen-Altenburg from 1828 to 1864

Only one census record has been located during this study:

	1828	1832	1833	1835	1837	1840	1843	1846	1849	1852	1855	1858	1861	1864
No images available	X	X	X		X	X	X	X	X	X	X	X	X	X
Name of head of household				X										
Total adult males				X										
Total adult females				X										
Total children				X										
Total servants				X										
Total cattle				X										
Total sheep				X										
Handwritten column headings				X										
Pre-printed pages														

V. Accessibility of Census Records in Sachsen-Altenburg

Researchers hoping to find census records in this former duchy may find the website of the Thüringen Staatsarchiv system to be helpful: http://www.thueringen.de/th1/tsk/kultur/staatsarchive. Specific inquiries should be directed to the archive of any town or city where the persons in question are believed or known to have lived. (See Appendix A for suggestions in writing an efficient inquiry in German.) Currently the Family History Library has no census images from Sachsen-Altenburg on microfilm and no digital images are known to be available on the Internet.

VI. Selected Images of Sachsen-Altenburg Census Records

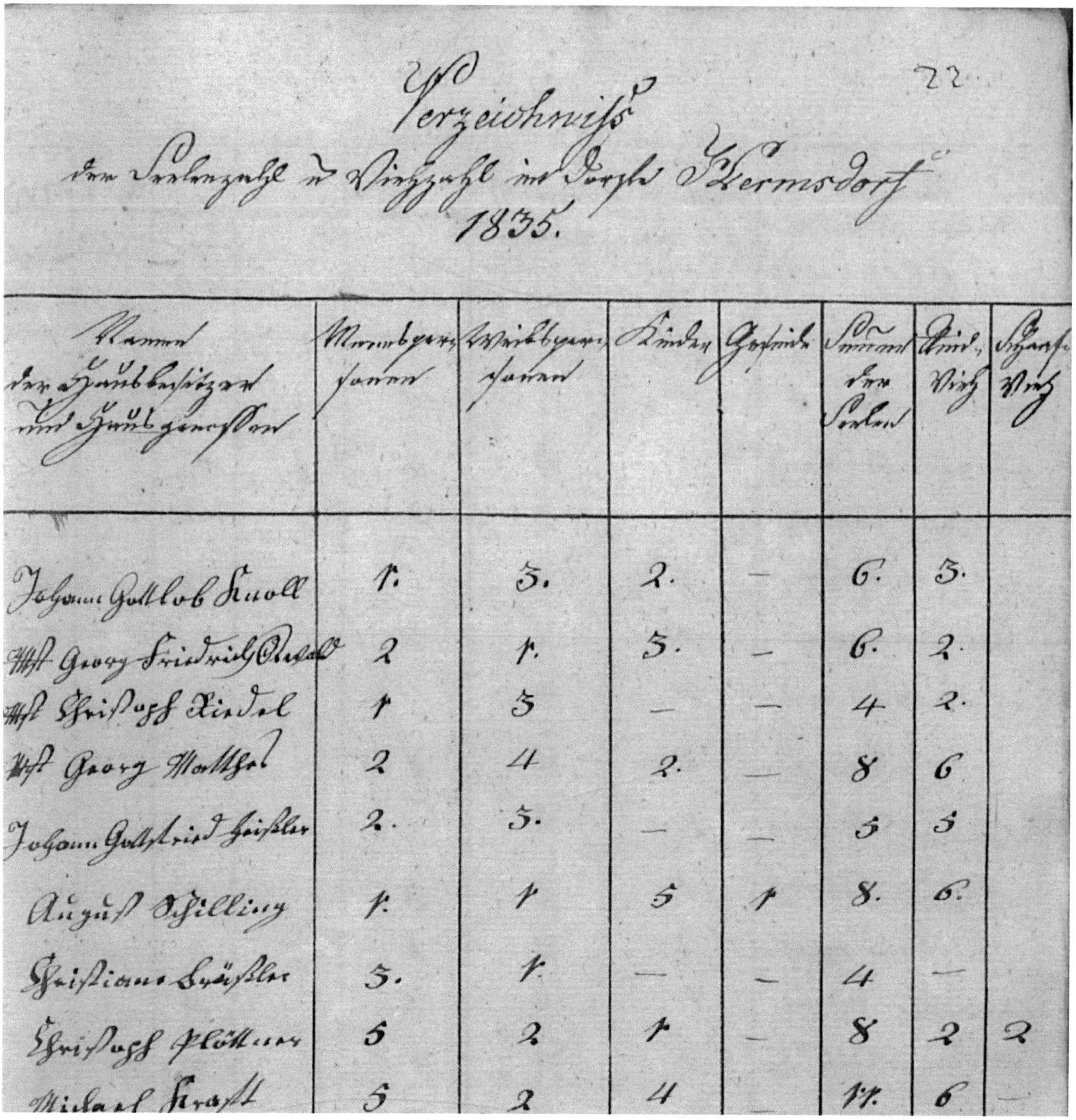

Figure 2. 1835 Census Page for Hermsdorf, Sachsen-Altenburg

Column headings: name of head of household; adult males; adult females; children; servants; total residents; cattle; sheep [Thüringisches Staatsarchiv Altenburg, Kreisamt Eisenberg, Nr. 273, Bl.22]

Notes

[1] Statistisches Bureau Berlin, "Die Volkszahl der Deutschen Staaten nach den Zählungen seit 1816," in *Monatshefte zur Statistik des Deutschen Reichs für das Jahr 1879* [2], *Die Statistik des Deutschen Reichs*, Vol. 37/2; urn:nbn:de:zbw-drsa_3721 (Berlin: Verlag des Königlich Preussischen Statistischen Bureaus, 1879), 16.

[2] Antje Kraus, *Quellen zur Bevölkerungsstatistik Deutschlands 1815–1871*, Band 1 (Boppard, Germany: Harald Boldt, 1980), 29, 301–306.

29 Sachsen-Coburg-Gotha [Saxe-Coburg-Gotha]

I. Location

The duchy of Sachsen-Coburg-Gotha is one of the eight so-called "Saxon duchies" within the central German region collectively known as Thüringen. Consisting of two large land masses and several small exclaves, the duchy shared borders with Sachsen-Meiningen, Sachsen-Weimar-Eisenach, both Schwarzburg duchies, and three large German states: Bayern to the south, the kingdom of Sachsen to the east, and the Prussian province of Sachsen to the north.

II. Census Enumerations in Sachsen-Coburg-Gotha

The first known census data were collected in the eighteenth century, but by 1816 still consisted of numbers only. The duchy joined the *Mitteldeutscher Handelsverein* [Central German Commercial Union] in 1828, but moved to the more influential *Zollverein* [Customs Union] when the former fell apart. As was required of member states of the *Zollverein*, census campaigns were conducted in Sachsen-Coburg-Gotha every three years from 1834 to 1864.[1] The national census of 1864 also included this duchy. Under the German Empire, enumerations were done in 1871, every five years from 1875 to 1910, and finally in 1916.

III. Specific Instructions to Town Officials and Enumerators

Instructions for several of the census years have been located. Similar instructions were issued by the ministry of interior in other census years several months before the designated enumeration date.

1834: As member states of the [Customs Union] we are to conduct a census of our population this year and every third year thereafter.

1846: Use the forms provided; distribute the instructions and the forms to each city official (and others selected as enumerators) by November 30; carefully describe their duties and responsibilities

1852: study the regulations issued in 1846 and 1849; use persons other than city officials only if absolutely necessary; return all unused forms and all instruction pages to this office

1861: The Zollverein has ruled that we should collect more data this year regarding livestock and real estate; each head of household is to be given a separate list on November 30 and is to return that list on December 3 to the dwelling owner, who will fill out the statistical report for that dwelling

Figure 1. The instructions for the 1846 census were issued in the name of Duke Ernst of Sachsen-Coburg-Gotha. [Thüringisches Staatsarchiv Gotha]

IV. Content of Census Records in Sachsen-Coburg-Gotha from 1816 to 1864

	1816	1831	1834	1837	1840	1843	1846	1849	1852	1855	1858	1861	1864
No images available	X	X	X		X	X					X	X	X
Name of head of household				X									
Citizenship classification				X									
Number of civilian families in dwelling				X									
Males over 14				X						X			
Females over 14				X						X			
Males under 14				X						X			
Females under 14				X						X			
Total number of civilians				X									
Same detail for military families				X									
Total persons in the dwelling				X			X	X	X	X			
Occupation groups (locals and foreigners by gender)				X						X			
Description or address of dwelling							X	X	X				
First and last name of each resident							X	X	X				
Status or occupation							X	X	X				
Age in years							X	X	X				
Religion							X	X	X				
Comments							X	X	X				
Handwritten column headings				X									
Pre-printed pages							X	X	X	X			

V. Accessibility of Census Records in Sachsen-Coburg-Gotha

For this study, the principal source of census records was the Thuringian State Archive in Gotha. Given the complexity of border changes since the days of the eight Saxon duchies, several other archives in the Thuringian system might have census records from other towns. The website is http://www.thueringen. de/th1/tsk/kultur/staatsarchive. As in other German states, email inquiries to towns and cities may yield better results. (See Appendix A for instructions on how to write the inquiry.) Sachsen-Coburg-Gotha census records in the collection of the Family History Library are few and far between, but a search in that catalog by town now and then might yield new documents.

VI. Selected Images of Sachsen-Coburg-Gotha Census Records

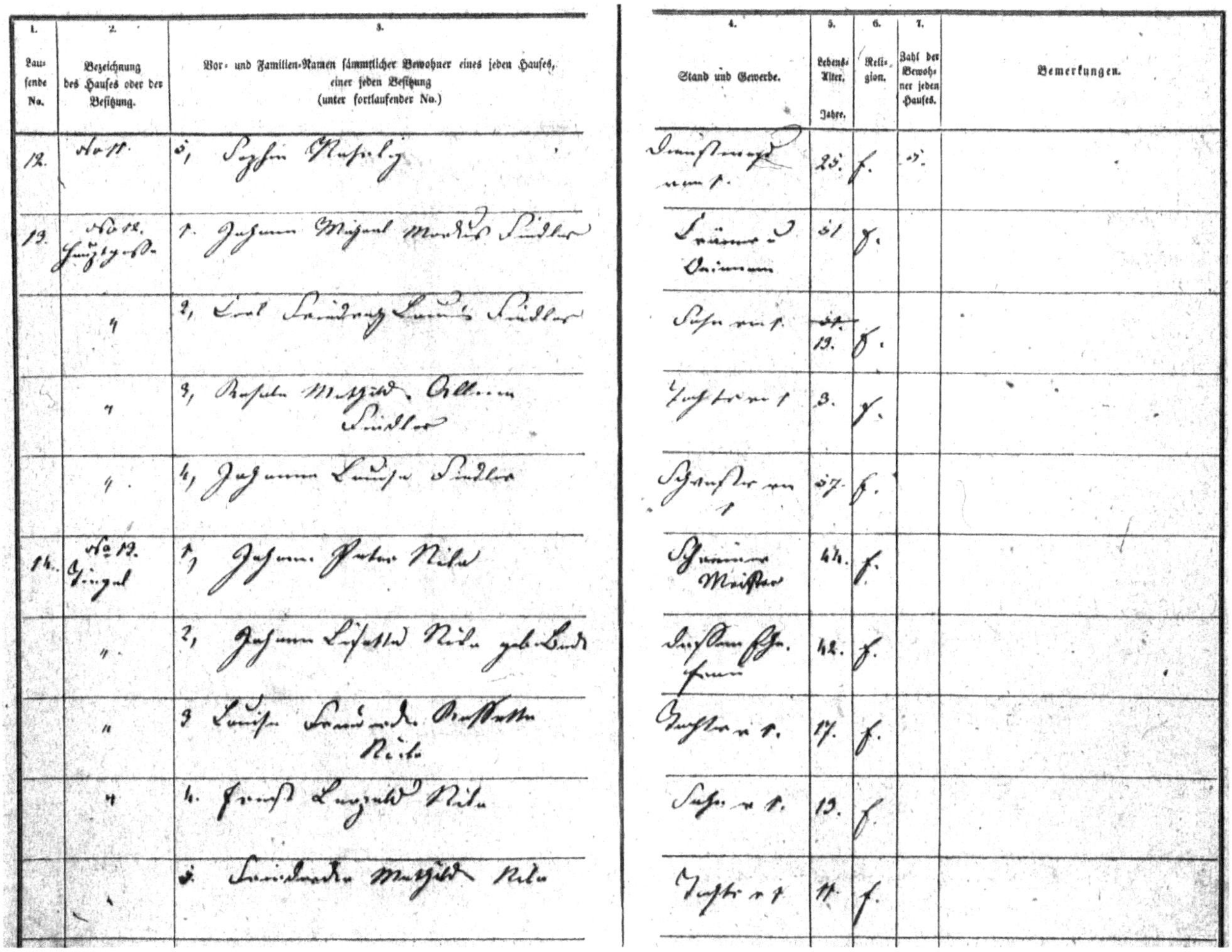

1. Laufende No.	2. Bezeichnung des Hauses oder der Besitzung.	3. Vor- und Familien-Namen sämmtlicher Bewohner eines jeden Hauses, einer jeden Besitzung (unter fortlaufender No.)	4. Stand und Gewerbe.	5. Lebens-Alter. Jahre.	6. Reli-gion.	7. Zahl der Bewoh-ner jeden Hauses.	Bemerkungen.
12.	No 11.	5, *[illegible]*	*[illegible]*	25.	f.	5.	
13.	No 11. *[illegible]*	1, Johann Michael *[illegible] Sidler*	*[illegible]*	51	f.		
	"	2, *[illegible] Sidler*	*[illegible]*	49. 19.	f.		
	"	3, *[illegible] Sidler*	*[illegible]*	3.	f.		
	"	4, Johann *[illegible] Sidler*	*[illegible]*	57.	f.		
14.	No 12. *[illegible]*	1, Johann *[illegible] Nile*	*[illegible] Meister*	44.	f.		
	"	2, Johann *[illegible] Nile geb. [illegible]*	*[illegible]*	42.	f.		
	"	3 *[illegible] Nile*	*[illegible]*	17.	f.		
	"	4. *[illegible] Nile*	*[illegible]*	13.	f.		
	"	5. *[illegible] Nile*	*[illegible]*	11.	f.		

Figure 2. 1846 Census Page from Apfelstädt, Sachsen-Coburg-Gotha

Column headings: total persons in the dwelling; description or address of the dwelling; first and last name of each resident; status or occupation; age in years; religion; comments [Kreisarchiv Erfurt]

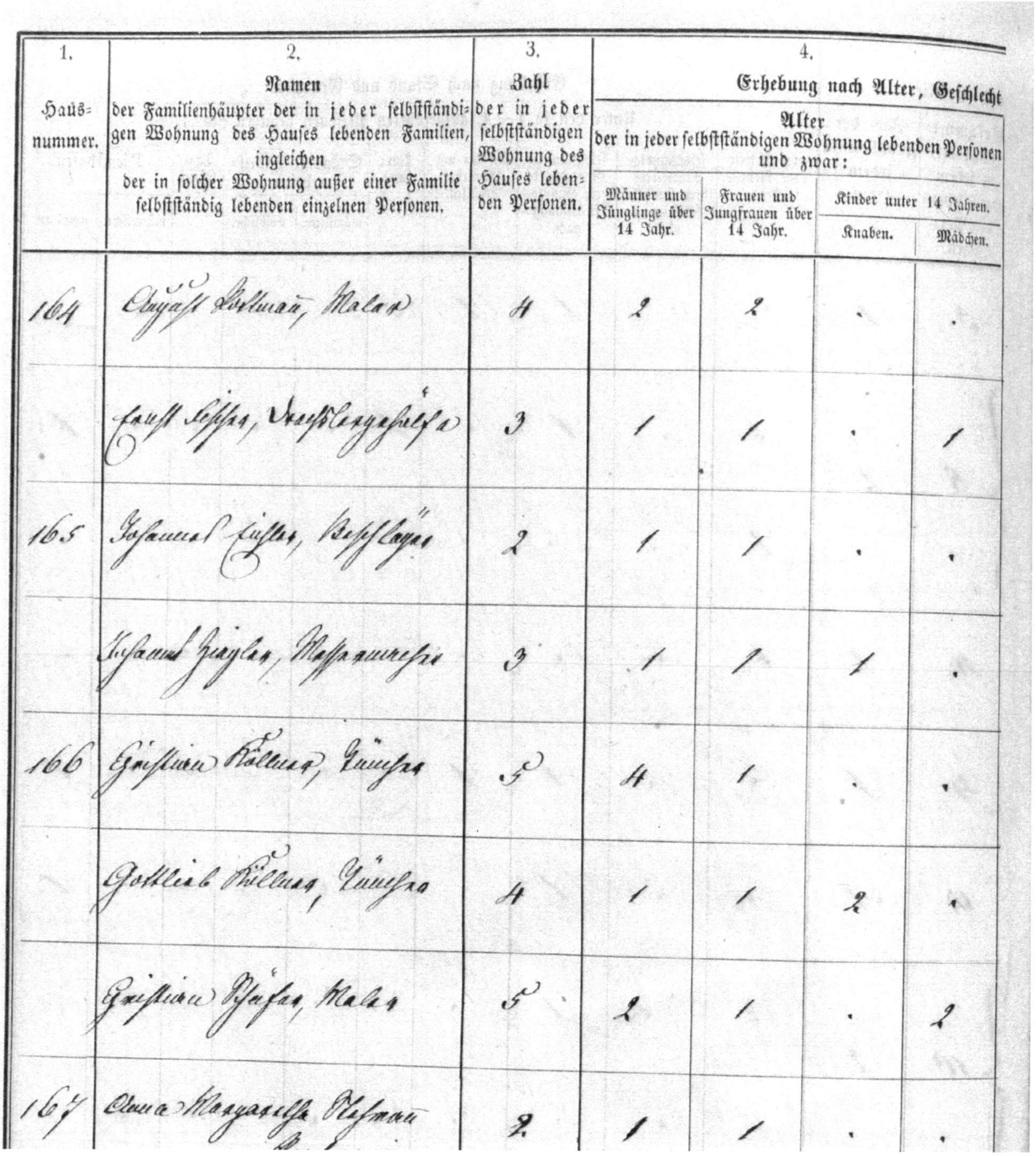

1. Haus-nummer.	2. Namen der Familienhäupter der in jeder selbstständigen Wohnung des Hauses lebenden Familien, ingleichen der in solcher Wohnung außer einer Familie selbstständig lebenden einzelnen Personen.	3. Zahl der in jeder selbstständigen Wohnung des Hauses lebenden Personen.	4. Erhebung nach Alter, Geschlecht — Alter der in jeder selbstständigen Wohnung lebenden Personen und zwar:			
			Männer und Jünglinge über 14 Jahr.	Frauen und Jungfrauen über 14 Jahr.	Kinder unter 14 Jahren. Knaben.	Mädchen.
164	*[illegible]* Gottman, Maler	4	2	2	.	.
	[illegible] Sesser, *[illegible]*	3	1	1	.	1
165	Johannes *[illegible]*, Beschlager	2	1	1		
	Johann *[illegible]*, *[illegible]*	3	1	1	1	
166	Christian *[illegible]*, *[illegible]*	5	4	1	.	.
	Gottlieb *[illegible]*, *[illegible]*	4	1	1	2	.
	Christian *[illegible]*, Maler	5	2	1	.	2
167	Anna Margaretha *[illegible]*	2	1	1		

Figure 3. 1855 Census Page from Ruhla, Sachsen-Coburg-Gotha (left-hand page)

Column headings: dwelling number; name of each head of household or adult living alone; number of persons in each household; age of each inhabitant: men and boys over 14; women and girls over 14; males under 14; females under 14 [Thüringisches Staatsarchiv Gotha I. Loc. 28 Nr. 6/186]

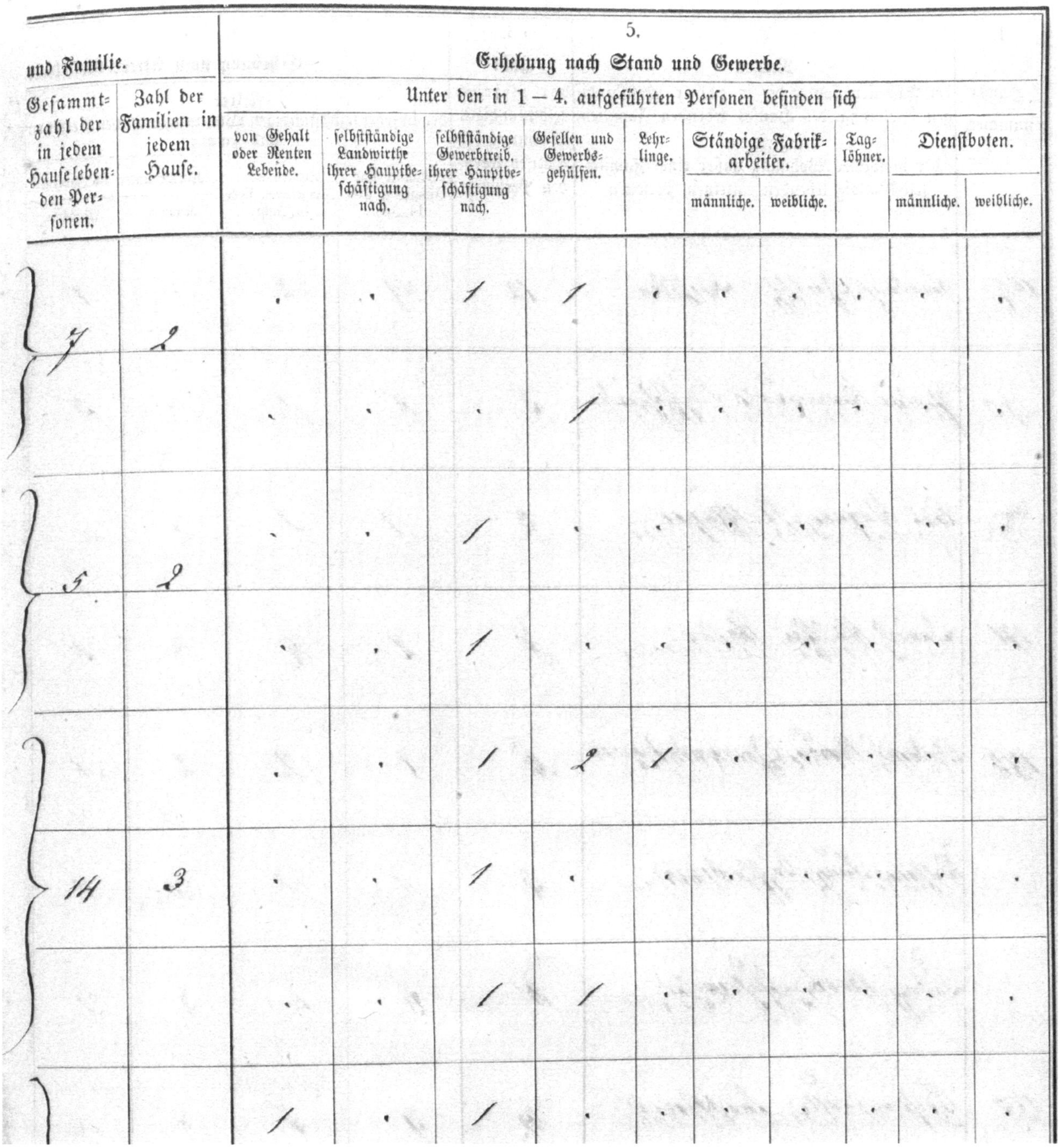

und Familie.		5.										
		Erhebung nach Stand und Gewerbe.										
Gesammt= zahl der in jedem Hause leben= den Per= sonen.	Zahl der Familien in jedem Hause.	Unter den in 1 — 4. aufgeführten Personen befinden sich										
		von Gehalt oder Renten Lebende.	selbstständige Landwirthe ihrer Hauptbe= schäftigung nach.	selbstständige Gewerbtreib. ihrer Hauptbe= schäftigung nach.	Gesellen und Gewerbs= gehülfen.	Lehr= linge.	Ständige Fabrik= arbeiter.		Tag= löhner.	Dienstboten.	
							männliche.	weibliche.		männliche.	weibliche.
7	2	.	.	1	1	.					
					1						
5	2	.	.	1							
		.	.	1	.						
		.	.	1	2	1					
14	3	.	.	1	.						
			.	1	1						
		1	.	1							

Figure 4. 1855 Census Page from Ruhla, Sachsen-Coburg-Gotha (right-hand page)

Column headings: total inhabitants in each household; number of families in the dwelling; persons supported by wages or retirement; independent farmers; independent craftsmen or tradesmen; journeyman; apprentices; male factory laborers; female factory laborers; laborers; male servants; female servants [Thüringisches Staatsarchiv Gotha I. Loc. 28 Nr. 6/186]

Notes

[1] Antje Kraus, *Quellen zur Bevölkerungsstatistik Deutschlands 1815–1871*, Band 1 (Boppard, Germany: Harald Boldt, 1980), 29, 295–300.

30 Königreich Sachsen [Kingdom of Saxony]

I. Location

Königreich Sachsen in central Germany was bordered on the west by several of the Saxon duchies (Thüringen), on the north by the Prussian province of Sachsen, on the east by Prussian Schlesien and on the south by the Austrian Empire. The capital city was Dresden.

II. Census Enumerations in Königreich Sachsen

Census enumerations were conducted in the kingdom annually from 1815 to 1830 (head counts only), then in 1832 with a renewed emphasis on reliability.[1] The first of those compilations included the names of individuals. Sachsen joined the *Zollverein* [Customs Union] in 1833 and followed the organization's guidelines regarding census campaigns every three years from 1834 through 1864.[2]

In 1867, the population of Königreich Sachsen was counted as part of a campaign carried out all over Germany. Under the German Empire, enumerations were done in Königreich Sachsen in 1871, every five years from 1875 to 1910, and finally in 1916.

III. Specific Instructions to Town Officials and Enumerators

Quite a few copies of these regulations have survived. Only new or extraordinary details are shown here:

1837: the pastor, the police, and a private scribe are to conduct the census

1840: begin the census on December 1; in small towns record the data for more than one household on the same page

1846: anyone who does not cooperate with this census will be fined 5 *Thaler*; each head of household will fill out the form before December 3; if the head of household cannot fill out the form, the enumerator will do so for him; the forms will be picked up on December 4 and each household must see to it that a person is at home until such time that the enumerator has retrieved the form

1852: fill out all forms in duplicate—one for the local office and one to be submitted to the county; be especially precise regarding place names, because this census will be used to compile a new directory of places for the kingdom; in the new form, pages 1 and 4 are for the dwelling and pages 2 and 3 for the household

1855: it must be understood that the census data will not be used for taxation purposes; residents in prisons, hospitals, etc. should be registered by the directors of said institutions

1861: count all persons, locals and foreigners; count persons who died after midnight, December 2–3, but not the children born after that time; the forms include instructions; the forms are to be distributed before December 3 and collected on December 5; if a person lives in one place and works in another, he is to be counted where he lives; count locals who are temporarily away from home; do not count travelers in inns

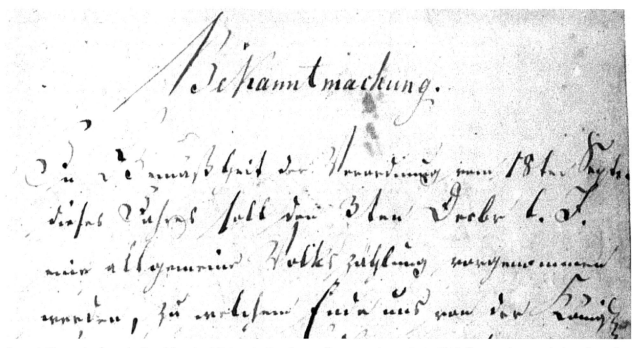

Figure 1. The notice from the Royal Interior Ministry in Dresden to all towns and counties in 1849: "In accordance with the ruling of September 18, a census will be conducted on December 3." [Kreisarchiv Brand-Erbisdorf]

IV. Content of Census Records in Königreich Sachsen from 1832 to 1864

	1832	1834	1837	1840	1843	1846	1849	1852	1855	1858	1861	1864
No images available		X	X			X	X	X	X	X	X	
Total males	X											
Total females	X											
Name of each resident	X			X	X							X
Married persons	X											X
Widows and widowers	X			X	X							X
Unmarried persons	X			X	X							X
Deaf-mute persons	X			X	X							X
Persons born blind	X			X	X							X
Age in years	X			X	X							
Religion	X			X	X							X
Status or occupation	X			X	X							X
Foreigners (3 categories)	X			X	X							
Comments	X											
Married males				X	X							
Married females				X	X							
Divorced persons				X	X							X
Married persons living apart				X	X							X
Children under 6 not of these parents				X	X							
Other persons				X	X							
Age in years or months												X
Insane												X
Employer or employee (details)												X
Handwritten column headings	X											
Pre-printed pages				X	X							X

V. Accessibility of Census Records in the Kingdom of Sachsen

In the course of this study, no regional archives were found to have collections of census documents in the historic Königreich Sachsen. Researchers should thus first search in the collection of the Family History Library where quite a few census documents have been found. During the 1980s when the Family History Library was denied permission to microfilm records of the Lutheran Church in Sachsen (then a district in the German Democratic Republic), operatives filmed documents of lesser importance in governmental archives and in that effort came across quite a few census records.

If the ancestor is known or believed to have lived in a specific town or county, inquiries should be sent to the archives of those places. (See Appendix A for suggestions about how to write efficient letters and emails). As of this writing, no digital images of census records from the kingdom of Sachsen are known to be available on the Internet.

VI. Selected Images of Kingdom of Sachsen Census Records

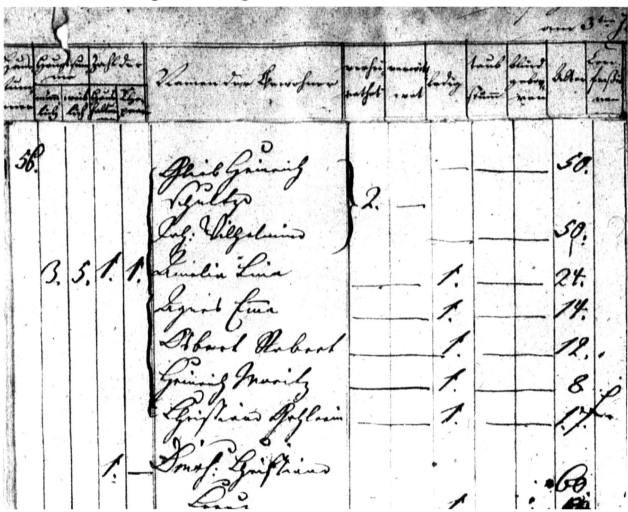

Figure 2. 1832 Census Page from Frauenstein, Königreich Sachsen (left-hand page)

Column headings: house number; total males; total females; number of households; number of married couples; name of each resident; married; widowed; unmarried; deaf-mute; blind; age; religion [Kreisarchiv Brand-Erbisdorf]

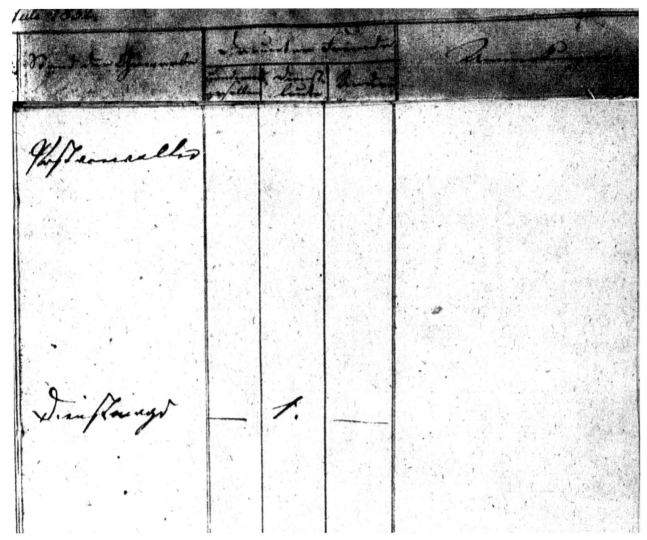

Figure 3. 1832 Census Page from Frauenstein, Königreich Sachsen (right-hand page)

   Column headings: status and occupation; foreign journeymen; foreign laborers; other foreigners; comments [Kreisarchiv Brand-Erbisdorf]

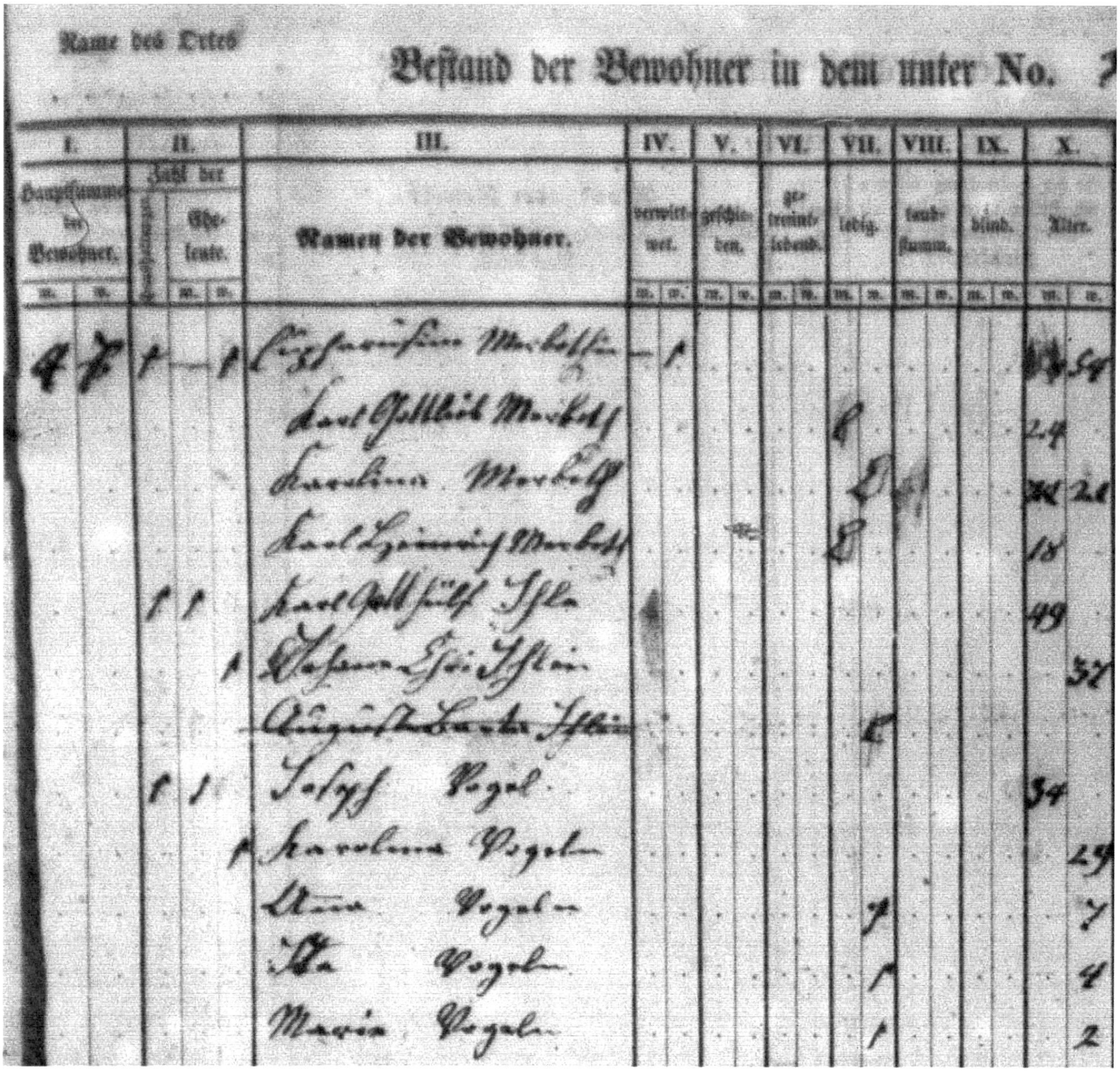

Figure 4. 1843 Census Page from Stollberg, Königreich Sachsen (left-hand page)

Column headings: total males; total females; total households; married men; married women; name of each resident; widowers; widows; divorced males; divorced females; males living apart; females living apart; unmarried males; unmarried females; deaf-mute; blind; age in years or months [Kreisarchiv Stollberg]

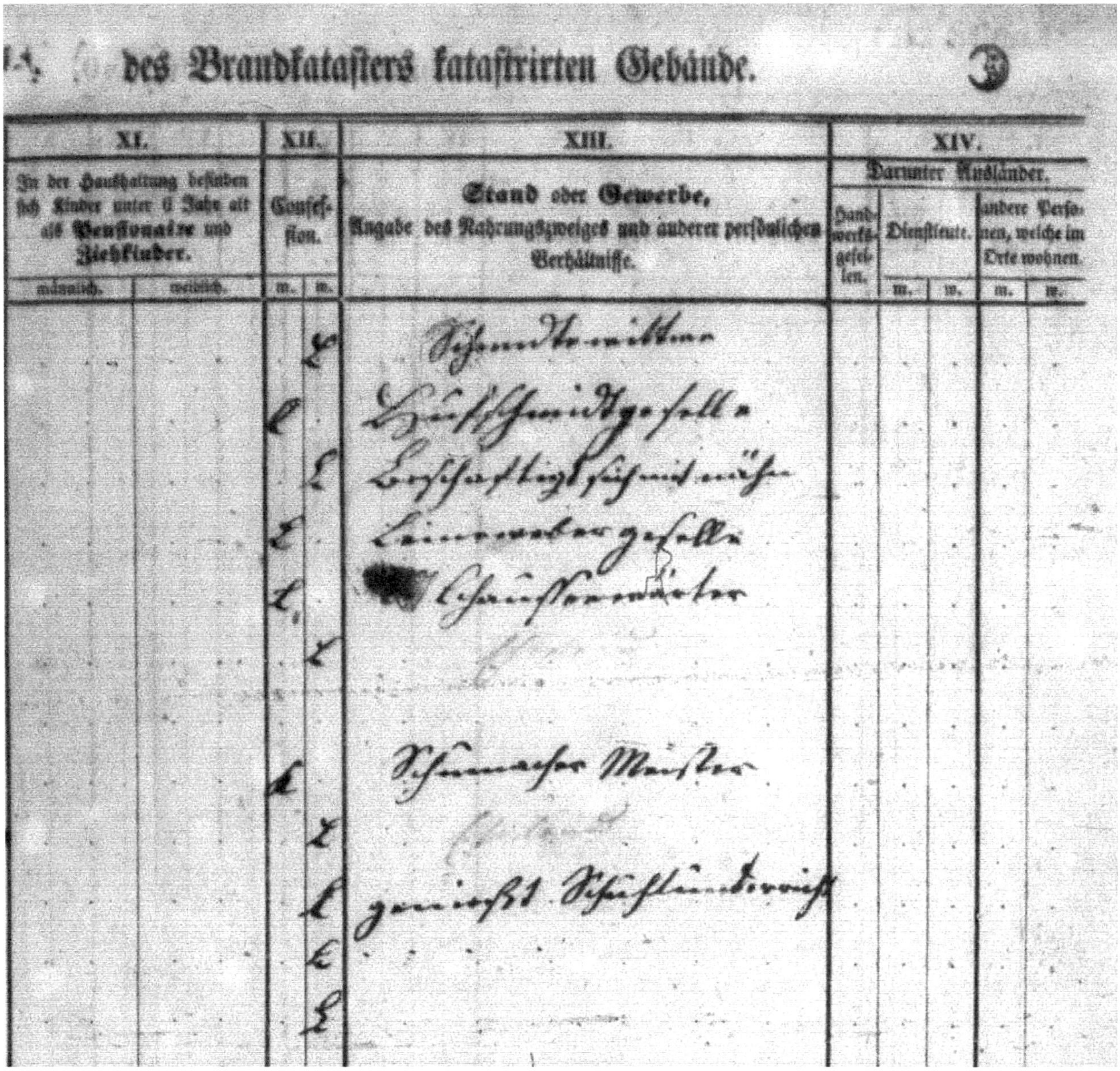
des Brandkatasters katastrirten Gebäude.

XI. In der Haushaltung befinden sich Kinder unter 6 Jahr alt als Pensionaire und Ziehkinder. männlich. weiblich.

XII. Confession. m. w.

XIII. Stand oder Gewerbe, Angabe des Nahrungszweiges und anderer persönlichen Verhältnisse.

XIV. Darunter Ausländer. Handwerksgesellen. Dienstleute. m. w. andere Personen, welche im Orte wohnen. m. w.

Figure 5. 1843 Census Page from Stollberg, Königreich Sachsen (right-hand page)

Column headings: children under 6 not born to these parents; religion; status or occupation; foreign journeymen; male laborers; female laborers; other persons [Kreisarchiv Stollberg]

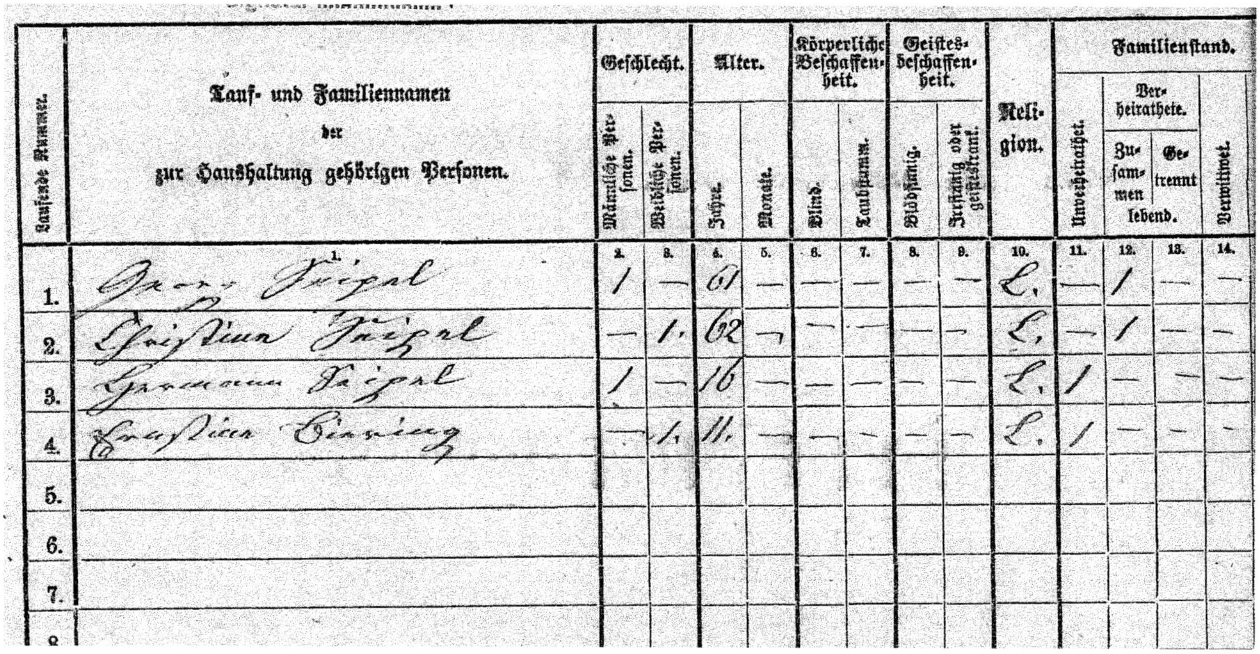

Figure 6. 1864 Census Page from Gösau, Königreich Sachsen (left-hand page)

Column headings: first and last name of each resident; male; female; age in years; age in months; blind; deaf-mute; mentally retarded; insane; religion; unmarried; married living together; married living apart; widowed [Kreisarchiv Zwickau Gös I. 74]

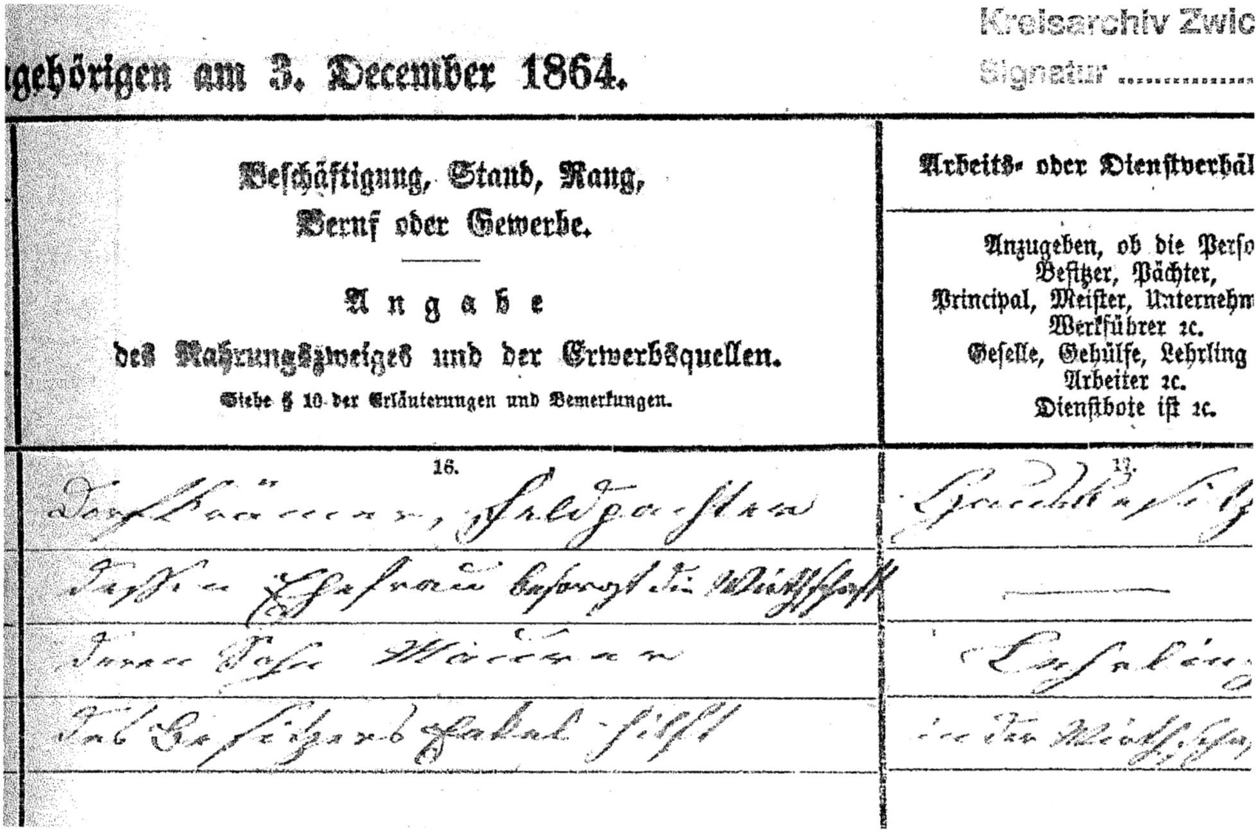

Figure 7. 1864 Census Page from Gösau, Königreich Sachsen (right-hand page)

Column headings: status or occupation (how does this person support himself?); employer or employee (details) [Kreisarchiv Zwickau Gös I. 74]

170

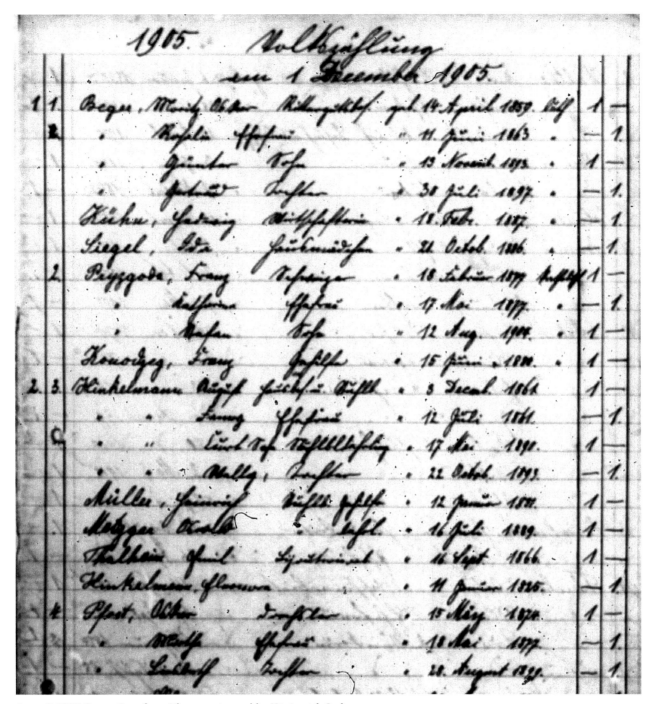

Figure 8. 1905 Census Page from Klostergeringswalde, Königreich Sachsen

Column headings: name of each resident; birth date; religion; gender [Kreisarchiv Rochlitz]

Notes

[1] Antje Kraus, *Quellen zur Bevölkerungsstatistik Deutschlands 1815–1871*, Band 1 (Boppard, Germany: Harald Boldt, 1980), 19–20, 51–56.

[2] Statistisches Bureau Berlin, "Die Volkszahl der Deutschen Staaten nach den Zählungen seit 1816," in *Monatshefte zur Statistik des Deutschen Reichs für das Jahr 1879* [2], *Die Statistik des Deutschen Reichs*, Vol. 37/2; urn:nbn:de:zbw-drsa_3721 (Berlin: Verlag des Königlich Preussischen Statistischen Bureaus, 1879), 12.

31 Sachsen-Meiningen [Saxe-Meiningen]

I. Location

The duchy of Sachsen-Meiningen is one of the eight so-called "Saxon duchies" within the central German region collectively known as Thüringen. One of the smallest states in Germany, Sachsen-Meiningen consisted of one large land mass and several very small exclaves. Six of the other Saxon duchies and the Prussian province of Sachsen were neighboring states. The capital city was Meiningen.

II. Census Enumerations in Sachsen-Meiningen

The first known census data were collected in this duchy in 1822 and 1824, but were head counts only. The enumerations in 1828 and 1833 were likely done due to the duchy's membership in the *Mitteldeutscher Handelsverein* [Central German Commercial Union] founded in 1828.[1] By 1834, the *Handelsverein* had been dissolved and Sachsen-Meiningen joined the *Zollverein* [Customs Union]. As was required of member states of the *Zollverein*, census campaigns were conducted every three years from 1834 to 1864.

Sachsen-Meiningen next participated in the national German census of 1867. Under the German Empire, enumerations were done in 1871, every five years from 1875 to 1910, and finally in 1916.

III. Specific Instructions to Town Officials and Enumerators

The following instructions were new or significantly different when issued:

1824: Only persons who have resided here for at least one year should be counted as heads of households; children residing else-where are not to be counted locally; single adults are to be counted as households; personal names must be written clearly; use the format provided

1834: conduct the campaign between December 6 and December 18; do not count active military personnel or their families; do not count locals away as journeymen

1837: count military persons stationed here; agents are to visit each house

1861: local officials will meet on November 13 to receive their instructions

1864: a census form will be delivered to each head of household from November 29 to December 1 to be filled out; data is to be valid as of December 3; enumerators will have identification papers; persons refusing to cooperate will be fined 5 *Florin*

IV. Content of Census Records in Sachsen-Meiningen from 1822 to 1864

The content of census records in Sachsen-Meiningen varies over the years perhaps more than in any other German state. As shown in the table below, some content items were used not just in consecutive enumerations, but in some cases many years later after a hiatus (as was the case in 1828 and 1861).

	1822	1824	1828	1832	1834	1837	1840	1843	1846	1849	1852	1855	1858	1861	1864
No images available	X							X	X	X	X	X			
Name of head of household		X	X	X	X	X	X							X	X
Does father live here?		X													
Does mother live here?		X													
Residents over 15		X													
Residents under 15		X													
Servants		X	X			X	X								
Other persons		X													
Total residents		X	X	X	X	X	X							X	X
Other employees		X	X										X		
Comments		X			X	X	X						X		
Males over 14			X		X								X		
Females over 14			X		X								X		
Males under 14			X		X	X	X						X		
Females under 14			X		X	X	X						X		
Lutherans			X			X	X						X	X	X
Catholics			X			X	X						X	X	X
Mennonites			X			X	X						X	X	X
Jewish (citizens)			X			X	X						X	X	X
Jewish (non-citizens)			X			X	X						X	X	X
Name of the owner of the dwelling				X											
Number of other employees (by origin and gender)				X											
Number of local military on duty away				X											
Occupation of head of household						X	X								
Males 14–60						X	X								
Females 14–60						X	X								
Males over 60						X	X								
Females over 60						X	X								
Number of married						X	X								
Name of every person													X		
Status of every person													X		
Age in years													X		
Persons absent for work															X
Blind and deaf															X
Other religions															X
Marital status															X
Property ownership															X
Handwritten pages		X		X	X	X	X						X		X
Pre-printed pages		X	X			X	X						X		

V. Accessibility of Census Records in Sachsen-Meiningen

From the correspondence conducted with archives in this former duchy, it is clear that most extant census records are found in town archives. Inquiries should thus be directed to towns where the persons in question are known or believed to have lived. For general assistance, the website of the Thüringen Staatsarchiv system may be helpful: http://www.thueringen.de/th1/tsk/kultur/staatsarchive. (See Appendix A for suggestions in writing in German to archives). The holdings of the Family History Library include census records from several towns in Sachsen-Meiningen. As of this writing, no census records in digital form or on websites have been identified.

VI. Selected Images of Sachsen-Meiningen Census Records

Hausnummer.	Namen der in jedem Hause wohnenden Familien-Häupter oder ausser einer Familie selbstständig lebenden einzelnen Personen.	Zahl der in jeder Haushaltung lebenden Familien-Glieder mit Einschluss des Familien-Hauptes, ingleichen Zahl der ausser einer Familie selbstständig lebenden einzelnen Personen.	Zahl der bei der Herrschaft wohnenden Dienstleute.	Zahl der mit der Familie wohnenden Gehülfen und Lehrlinge, Pfleglinge und andern Personen.	Männer u. Jünglinge über 14 Jahren.	Weiber und Jungfr. über 14 Jahren.	Kinder unter 14 Jahren männl.	Kinder unter 14 Jahren weibl.	Evangel. Christen.	Rom.-cathol. Christen.	Menoniten.	Juden mit Staatsbürgerrecht	Juden ohne Staatsbürgerrecht	Gesammtzahl der zur Haushaltung gehörigen Personen.	Gesammtzahl der Bewohner jedes Hauses.	Anzahl der Familien in jedem Hause.
	Heinrich Ehrlich	4	1		2	2	1	-	5	-			-)	5	5	1
		3	-		1	2	-	-	3					3	3	1
		2	1		1	2	-		3					3	6	2)
		3	-		1	1	1	-	3					3		)
	Wilhelm	7	-		2	2	3	7	7					7	7	1
		4	1		1	2	-	-	3					3	4	2)
		1			-	1	-	-	1					1		)
		6	-		1	1	3	1	6					6	13	2
	Carl	7	-	.	-	1	3	8	7					7		)
		4	-		2	2	-	-	4					4	4	1
		4	1		2	3	"	•	5					5	5	1
	Wilhelm	2			2	1	-	-	2					2	2	1
	Carl Ehrlich	7			1	1	1	4	7					7	7	1

Figure 1. 1828 Census Page from Ummerstadt, Sachsen-Meiningen

Column headings: name of head of household; number of family members; domestic servants; other employees; males over 14; females over 14; males under 14; females under 14; Lutherans; Catholics, Mennonites; Jewish with citizenship; Jewish without citizenship; total persons in the household; total persons in the dwelling; families in the dwelling [Kreisarchiv Hildburghausen]

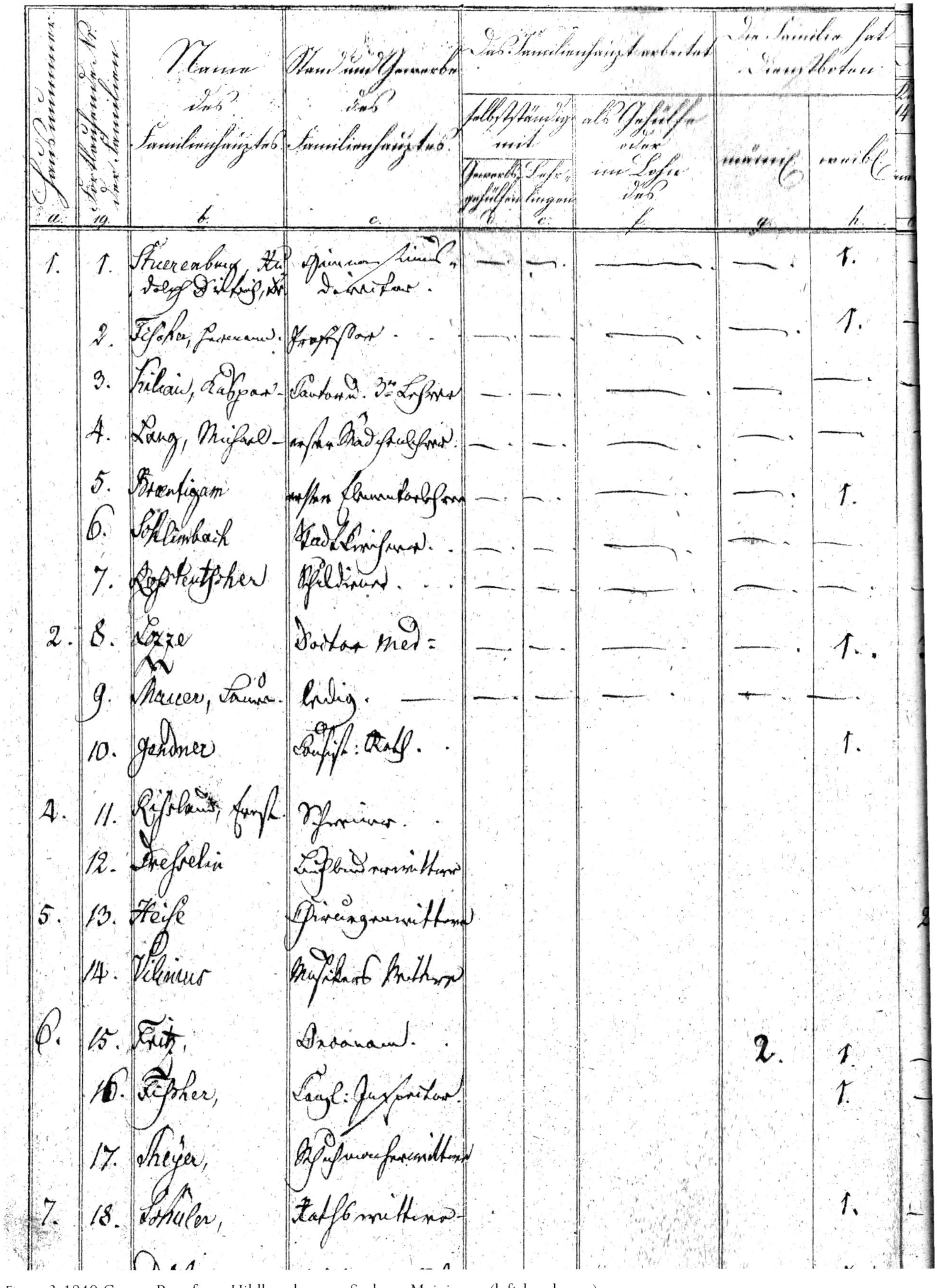

Figure 2. 1840 Census Page from Hildburghausen, Sachsen-Meiningen (left-hand page)

Column headings: name of head of household; status or occupation; status within employment; employees; servants [Kreisarchiv Hildburghausen]

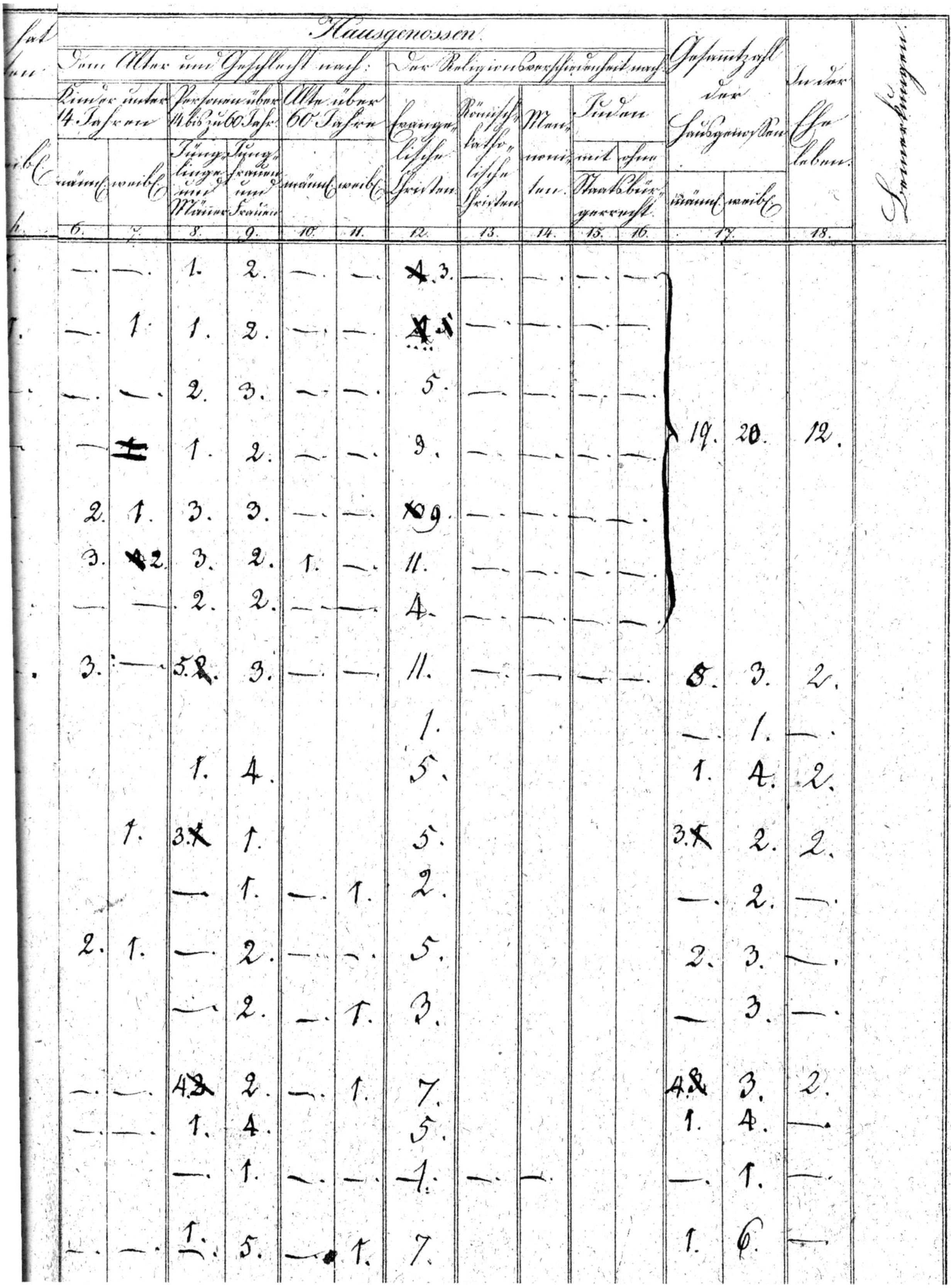

6	7	8	9	10	11	12	13	14	15	16	17 (m)	17 (f)	18
—	—	1.	2.	—	—	X 3.							
—	1	1.	2.	—	—	X X							
—	—	2.	3.	—	—	5.							
—	=	1.	2.	—	—	9.					19.	20.	12.
2.	1.	3.	3.	—	—	X 9							
3.	X2	3.	2.	1.	—	11							
—	—	2.	2.	—	—	4.							
3.	—	5 X 2.	3.	—	—	11					8.	3.	2.
						1.					—	1.	—
		1.	4.			5.					1.	4.	2.
	1.	3 X	1.			5.					3 X	2.	2.
		—	1.	—	1.	2.					—	2.	—
2.	1.	—	2.	—		5.					2.	3.	—
		—	2.	—	1.	3.					—	3.	—
—	—	4 X	2.	—	1.	7.					4 X	3.	2.
—	—	1.	4.	—	—	5.					1.	4.	—
		—	1.	—	—	1.					—	1.	—
—	—	1.	5.	—	1.	7.					1.	6.	—

Figure 3. 1840 Census Page from Hildburghausen, Sachsen-Meiningen (right-hand page)

Column headings: males under 14; females under 14; males 14-60; females 14-60; males over 60; females over 60; Lutherans; Catholics; Mennonites; Jewish with citizenship; Jewish without citizenship; total males; total females; persons married; comments [Kreisarchiv Hildburghausen]

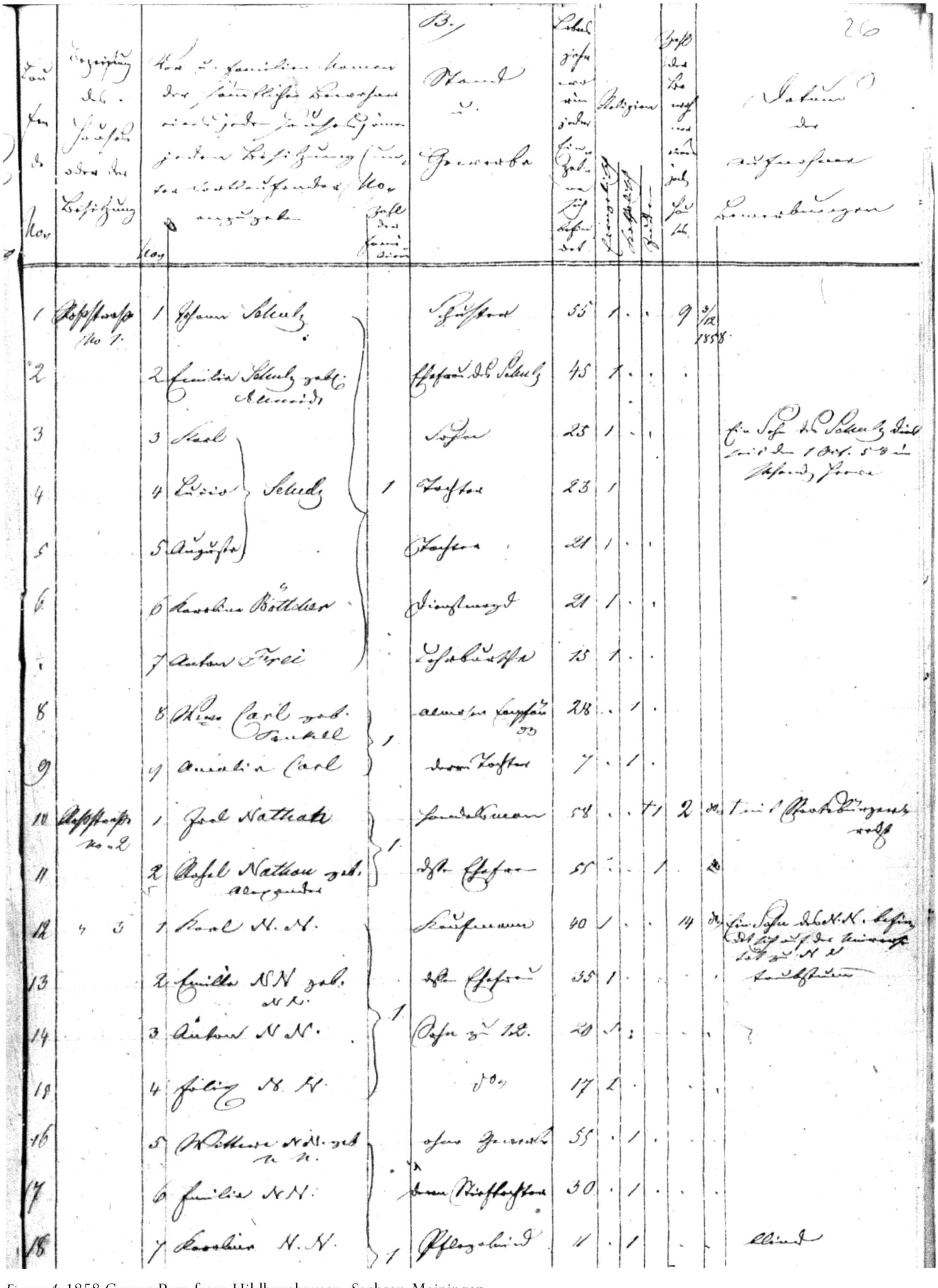

Figure 4. 1858 Census Page from Hildburghausen, Sachsen-Meiningen

Column headings: address of the dwelling; first and last name of each person; status or occupation; age in years; Lutheran; Catholic; Jewish; total residents; date of record and comments [Kreisarchiv Hildburghausen]

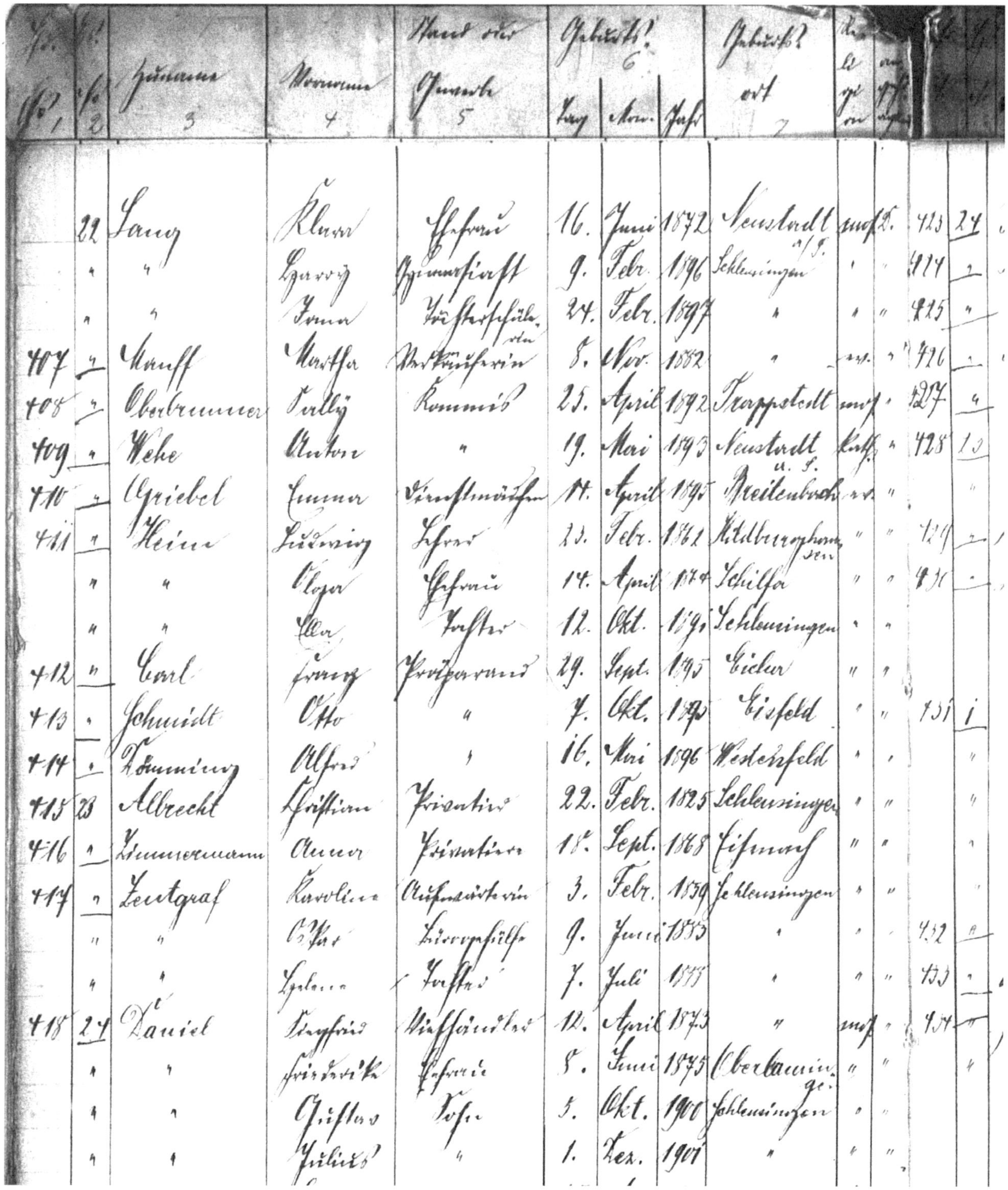

Figure 5. 1858 Census Page from Schleusingen, Sachsen-Meiningen

Column headings: dwelling number; family number; surname; first name; status or occupation; birth day; birth month; birth year; birth place; religion; citizenship [Kreisarchiv Hildburghausen]

Notes

[1] Antje Kraus, *Quellen zur Bevölkerungsstatistik Deutschlands 1815–1871*, Band I, (Boppard, Germany: Harald Boldt, 1980), 29, 301–306.

32 Provinz Sachsen [Province of Saxony]

I. Location

The Prussian province of Sachsen in north-central Germany had many neighbors—the duchy of Braunschweig to the west and the Prussian provinces of Hannover to the northwest and Brandenburg to the northeast. Other neighbors were the kingdom of Sachsen to the southeast, several of the Saxon duchies (Thüringen) to the south, and the province of Hessen-Nassau to the southwest. The capital city was Magdeburg.

II. Census Enumerations in Provinz Sachsen

Along with other provinces of Preußen, Sachsen conducted a comprehensive census in 1816 (head count only). As a provision of its inclusion in a Prussian customs union, the province collected census data every year until 1822 when a royal edict required enumerations only every third year. That schedule corresponded with the enumerations for the *Zollverein* [Customs Union] beginning in 1834 (and was likely the basis thereof).

The census of 1840 required for the first time the recording of the name of each person in the province. Census enumerations in Provinz Sachsen continued every three years through 1864.[1] With all other German states, Sachsen participated in the national 1867 census. Under the German Empire, census data were collected in the province in 1871, every five years from 1875 to 1910, and finally in 1916.

III. Specific Instructions to Town Officials and Enumerators

For many census years (especially under the *Zollverein*), instructions for enumerators in Prussian provinces were repeated in identical text. Instructions for the years 1822 through 1852 have not been identified in Provinz Sachsen locations, but they would have been similar if not identical to those provided officials in other provinces of Preußen. Significant new and revised instructions for Prussian census campaigns are summarized as follows:

1840: use the forms provided; each page has room for sixty names; police officials should conduct the campaign; do not count active duty military personnel; you are allowed to refer to such documents as lists of residents that have been previously compiled; do not begin to collect the data before December 1; the work must be completed in towns by December 20 and in cities by December 25, so that the reports can be received in Berlin by December 31

1843: refer to the deficiencies in the 1840 census in order to produce more reliable results; count military personnel in reserve status; use forms that are essentially identical to those of 1840; where the number of enumerators is insufficient, tax officials and retired military officers may be called into service and remunerated appropriately

1846: begin the collection of data on December 3; persons employed by or living in the homes of active military personnel are not to be counted; count all foreigners employed here but not persons traveling through the town; count locals temporarily employed or traveling elsewhere; do not refer to previous lists such as residential registration; in large cities, heads of households may fill out the forms themselves to save enumerator time; the work must commence and conclude on that day in most locations; in larger cities three days will be granted

1852: the handwriting on the lists must be neat and orderly; should authorities at the next higher level identify mistakes in the local records, the cost of any required corrections shall be charged to the responsible authorities; owners of major estates are to count their respective populations and submit the lists to the local town authorities

IV. Content of Census Records in Provinz Sachsen from 1822 to 1864

	1822	1825	1828	1831	1834	1837	1840	1843	1846	1849	1852	1855	1858	1861	1864
No image available	X	X	X	X	X	X									
Name of every person							X	X	X	X	X	X	X	X	X
Status or occupation							X	X	X	X	X	X	X	X	X
Age in years							X	X	X	X	X	X	X	X	X
Religion							X	X	X	X	X	X	X	X	X
Total persons in household							X	X	X	X	X	X	X	X	X
Comments									X	X	X	X	X	X	X
Blind, deaf												X			
Lutheran													X	X	X
Catholic													X	X	X
Jewish													X	X	X
Mennonites															X
Greek Orthodox															X
Dissidents															X
Other religions															X
Handwritten column headings							X	X	X	X			X	X	
Pre-printed forms							X	X	X	X	X	X	X	X	X

V. Accessibility of Census Records in Provinz Sachsen

Fortunately for family history researchers, there are many towns in Provinz Sachsen for which census records have been preserved. However, as of this writing, there are no indexes for those records. Researchers will need to send an inquiry to the town or the county archive regarding existing records. (See Appendix A for suggestions about writing an appropriate inquiry.) Archives at higher governmental levels (such as in the capital city of Magdeburg) cannot be expected to have many census records. Census records from Provinz Sachsen are available in the catalog of the Family History Library in quite a few locations for a very important reason: during the existence of the German Democratic Republic—principally in the early 1980s—the Family History Library was not allowed to copy original church records, so they copied the next-best records available. As of this writing, no digital images of census records from this province can be found on the Internet.

VI. Selected Census Images in Provinz Sachsen

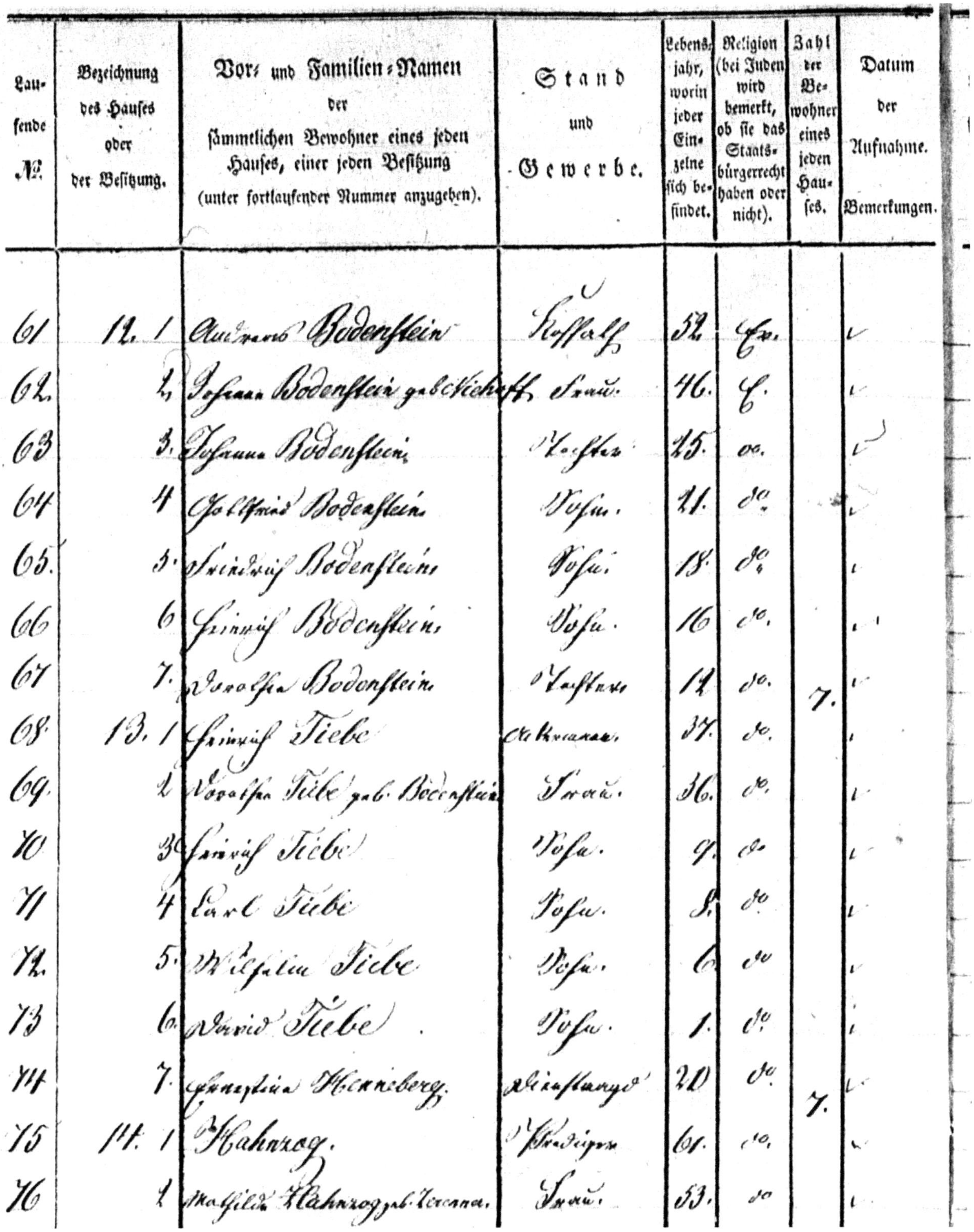

Laufende №.	Bezeichnung des Hauses oder der Besitzung.	Vor- und Familien-Namen der sämmtlichen Bewohner eines jeden Hauses, einer jeden Besitzung (unter fortlaufender Nummer anzugeben).	Stand und Gewerbe.	Lebens- jahr, worin jeder Ein- zelne sich be- findet.	Religion (bei Juden wird bemerkt, ob sie das Staats- bürgerrecht haben oder nicht).	Zahl der Be- wohner eines jeden Hau- ses.	Datum der Aufnahme. Bemerkungen.
61	12. 1	Andreas Bodenstein	Roßarth	52	Chr.		⌐
62	2,	Johanna Bodenstein geb. Nichoff	Frau.	46	C.		⌐
63	3.	Johanna Bodenstein	Tochter	25	do.		⌐
64	4	Gottfried Bodenstein	Sohn.	21	do.		
65	5.	Friedrich Bodenstein	Sohn.	18	do.		⌐
66	6	Heinrich Bodenstein	Sohn.	16	do.		⌐
67	7.	Dorothea Bodenstein	Tochter	14	do.	7.	⌐
68	13. 1	Heinrich Tiebe	Ackermann	37	do.		
69	2	Dorothea Tiebe geb. Bodenstein	Frau.	36	do.		⌐
70	3	Heinrich Tiebe	Sohn.	9	do.		⌐
71	4	Carl Tiebe	Sohn.	8	do.		⌐
72	5.	Wilhelm Tiebe	Sohn.	6	do.		⌐
73	6	David Tiebe	Sohn.	1	do.		⌐
74	7	Henriette Hennsberg	Dienstmagd	20	do.	7.	⌐
75	14. 1	Hahnrog	Prediger	61	do.		⌐
76	2	Margilith Hahnrog geb. Terrana	Frau.	53	do.		

Figure 1. 1840 Census Page from Weddersleben, Sachsen-Provinz

Column headings: consecutive number of individuals; number of dwelling; given name and surname; status and occupation; age on next birthday; religion (Jewish, whether citizens?); total number of persons in the home; date data were recorded and comments [Kreisarchiv Landkreis Harz, Gemeindebestand Weddersleben, Archivsignatur 7]

Lau- fende Nr.	Bezeichnung des Hauses oder der Besitzung.	Vor- und Familien-Namen der sämmtlichen Bewohner eines jeden Hauses, einer jeden Besitzung (unter fortlaufender Nummer anzugeben).	Stand und Gewerbe.	Lebens- jahr, worin jeder (Ein- zelne sich be- findet.	Religion (bei Juden wird bemerkt, ob sie das Staats- bürgerrecht haben oder nicht).	Zahl der Be- wohner eines jeden Hau- ses.	Datum der Aufnahme, Bemerkungen.
	Langen Bruch No. 68.				Transp.	558	
559.		1) Heinrich Trümpelmann sen.		55	ev.		
60.		2) Johanna — " — geb. Mayerstein		53	"		
61.	desgl.	3) Heinr. Trümpelmann jun.	Goldschmied	25	ev.		
62.		4) Johanna — " — geb. Helle		22	"		
63.	desgl.	5) Wwe. Auguste Hofmeister		45	ev.		
64.		6) Caroline — " —	Tochter	19	"		
65.		7) Louise — " —	do	18	"		
66.		8) Wilhelm — " —	Sohn	13	"		
67.		9) Auguste — " —	Tochter	11	"		
68.		10) Emilie — " —	do	9	"		
69.		11) Marie — " —	do	4	"		
70.	desgl.	12) Christoph Thielecke	Schuhmacher	53	ev.		
71.		13) Johanna — " — g. Börk		52	"		
72.		14) Wilhelmine Thielecke	Tochter	22	"		
73.		15) Auguste — " —	do	19	"		
74.		16) Friederich — " —	Sohn	15	"		
75.	desgl.	17) Wittwe Friedr. Voigt	Spinnerin	56	ev.		
76.		18) Carl Voigt	Tagelöhner	25	"		
77.	desgl.	19) Andreas Schildknecht	Arbeitsmann	31	ev.		
78.		20) Dorothea — " — g. Krakau		29	"		
79.		21) Wilhelm Schildknecht	Sohn	7	"		
80.		22) — " —	Tochter	4	"		

Figure 2. 1852 Census Page from Nöschenrode, Sachsen-Provinz

Column headings: consecutive number of individuals; address of dwelling, given name and surname; status and occupation; age on next birthday; religion (Jewish, whether citizens?); total number of persons in the home; date data were recorded; comments (horses, cows, calves, goats, pigs, sheep) [Kreisarchiv Landkreis Harz, Gemeindebestand Nöschenrode, Archivsignatur 7]

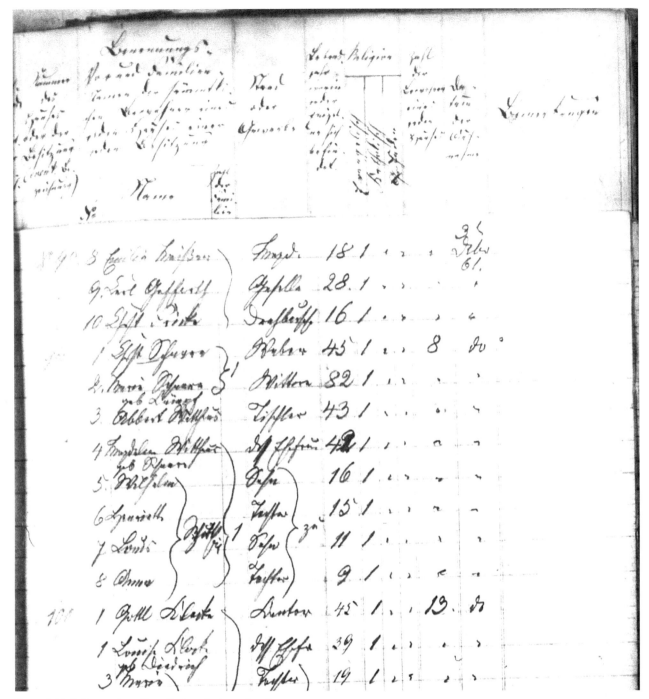

Figure 3. 1861 Census Page from Frohse, Sachsen-Provinz

Column headings: address of dwelling; given name and surname; status and occupation; age on next birthday; religion (Lutheran, Catholic, Jewish); total persons in the home; date data recorded; comments [Stadtarchiv Schönebeck]

Notes

[1] Antje Kraus, *Quellen zur Bevölkerungsstatistik Deutschlands 1815–1871*, Band I (Boppard, Germany: Harald Boldt, 1980), 25–26, 177–182. Population statistics were also calculated for each non-census year beginning in 1816 via this formula: total number of persons from the previous year plus the number of children born minus the number of persons who died; the information was usually taken from local church records.

33 Sachsen-Weimar-Eisenach [Saxe-Weimar-Eisenach]

I. Location

The grand duchy of Sachsen-Weimar-Eisenach had more neighbors among the German states than any other in the nineteenth century. Its three main territories and many exclaves were surrounded by the other seven so-called "Saxon duchies" (collectively called Thüringen), the kingdom of Bayern on the southwest, and the Prussian province of Hessen-Nassau on the west. Prussian Sachsen lay to the north and the kingdom of Sachsen to the east. The cities of Weimar and Eisenach both played governmental roles over the years.

II. Census Enumerations in Sachsen-Weimar-Eisenach

The first known census data were collected in Sachsen-Weimar-Eisenach in 1816 (numbers only) and the practice was continued annually even after the grand duchy joined with other states to form customs unions. The first of those was the *Mitteldeutscher Handelsverein* [Central German Commercial Union], founded in 1828 under the leadership of the kingdom of Hannover. Sachsen-Weimar-Eisenach joined that union along with the other seven Saxon duchies. However, the *Handelsverein* turned out to be less effective than initially designed and the grand duchy was one of several members that defected to the new *Zollverein* [Customs Union] in 1834.

Within the *Zollverein* system, census campaigns requiring personal names were collected every three years, but the work was not done in the grand duchy under official *Zollverein* directions until 1846.[1]

In 1867, the population of Sachsen-Weimar-Eisenach was counted as part of a campaign carried out among all of the German states. Under the German Empire, enumerations were done in 1871, every five years from 1875 to 1910, and finally in 1916.

III. Specific Instructions to Town Officials and Enumerators

The following regulations were new or represented revisions from previous years:

1852: target date is December 3; observe the standards published in 1846; do not count locals in employment elsewhere or military personnel; count foreigners who have been here for at least one year

1855: study the instructions carefully in order to avoid the mistakes made in 1852; each head of household is to fill out a list completely and correctly; directors of prisons, hospitals, etc. will fill out lists for persons living in their institutions; tell each head of household that the *Zollverein* pays our government 2 *Thaler* for each person correctly listed

1861: enumerators should show each head of household the instructions printed on the reverse of the form; use black ink; no pencils are allowed

IV. Content of Census Records in Sachsen-Weimar-Eisenach from 1828 to 1864

Records for only three census years have been located as of this writing. Fortunately, each of them provides the name of every resident.

	1828	1831	1834	1837	1840	1843	1846	1849	1852	1855	1858	1861	1864
Images not available	X	X	X	X	X	X	X	X	X	X			
First and last name of each person											X	X	X
Status or occupation											X	X	X
Age in years											X	X	X
Age in months											X	X	X
Birth place (country if foreigner)											X	X	X
Religion											X	X	X
Blind persons											X	X	X
Deaf persons											X	X	X
Is he/she a property owner?											X		
Marital status (four categories)											X	X	X
Total persons in household											X	X	X
Comments											X	X	X
If property owner (three classifications)												X	X
Number of males													X
Number of females													X
Relationship to head of household													X
Pre-printed pages											X	X	X

V. Accessibility of Census Records in Sachsen-Weimar-Eisenach

There are several towns in Sachsen-Weimar-Eisenach in which census records have been preserved. However, as of this writing, there are no indexes for those records. Researchers will need to send an inquiry to the town or the county archive regarding existing records. (See Appendix A for suggestions about writing an appropriate inquiry.) Recent correspondence with archives at higher governmental levels (such as in the capital cities of Weimar and Eisenach) has yielded little information about surviving census records. Census records from Sachsen-Weimar-Eisenach are available in the catalog of the Family History Library in quite a few locations for a very important reason: during the existence of the German Democratic Republic—principally in the early 1980s—the Family History Library was not allowed to copy original church records, so camera operators filmed the next-best records available. No digital images of census records in this state can be found on the Internet as of this writing.

VI. Selected Images of Sachsen-Weimar-Eisenach Census Records

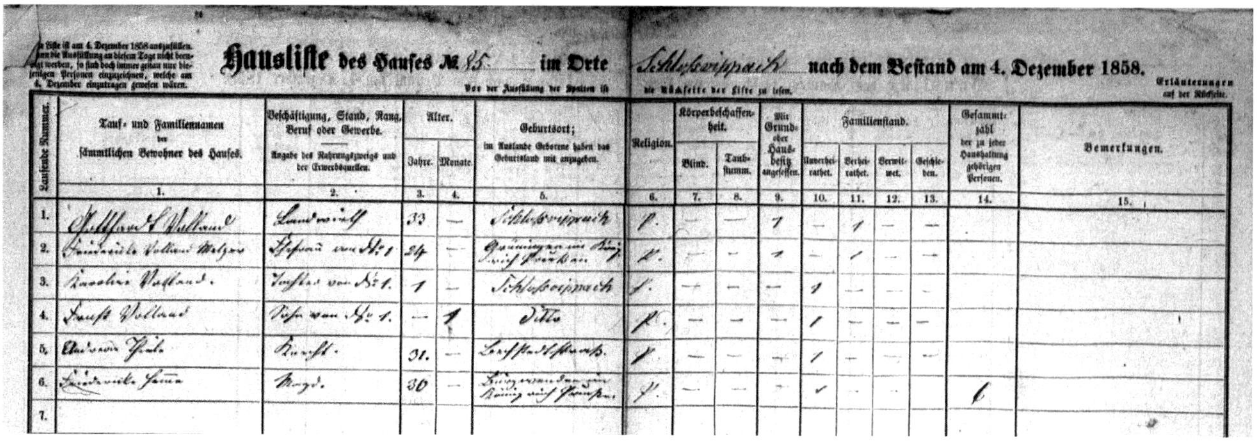

Figure 1. 1858 Census Page from Schlossvippach, Sachsen-Weimar-Eisenach

Column headings: consecutive number of individuals; first and last name of each person; status or occupation; age in years; age in months; birth place (country if foreigner); religion; blind; deaf; property owners; unmarried; married; widowed; divorced; total residents; comments [Kreisarchiv Erfurt]

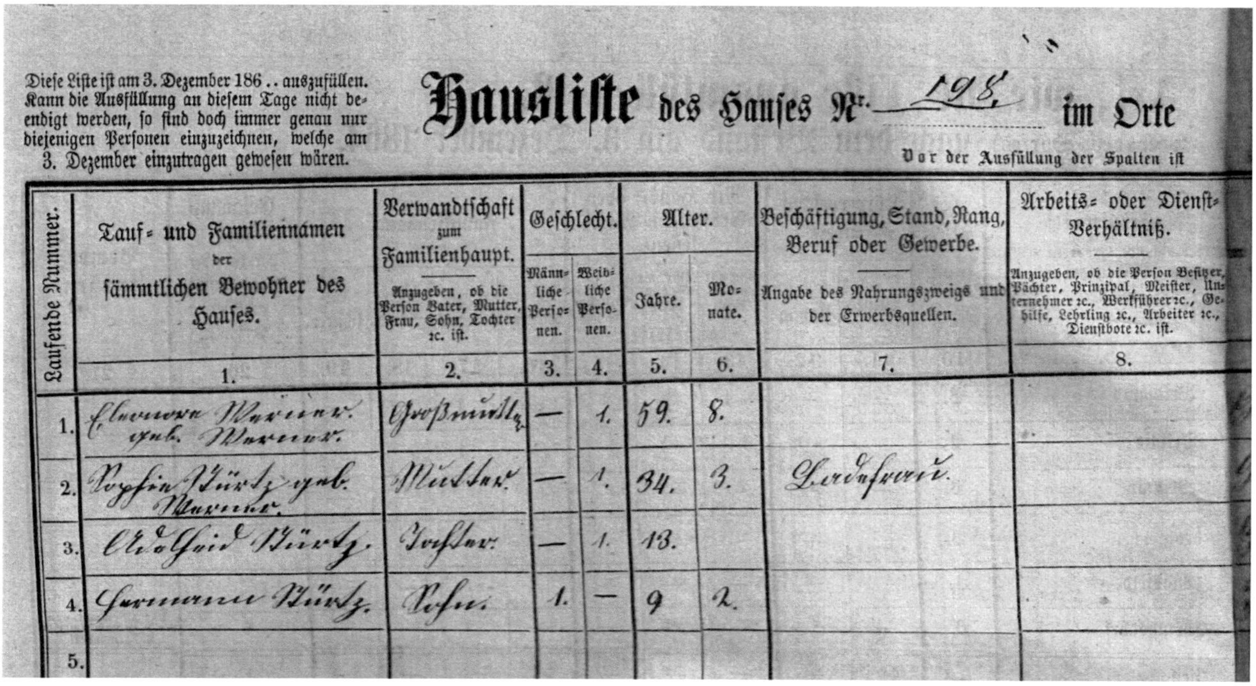

Figure 2. 1864 Census Page from Illmenau, Sachsen-Weimar-Eisenach (left-hand page)

Column headings: consecutive number of individuals; first and last name of each person; relationship to the head of household; males; females; age in years; age in months; status or occupation; employment [Thüringisches Staatsarchiv Illmenau 104025]

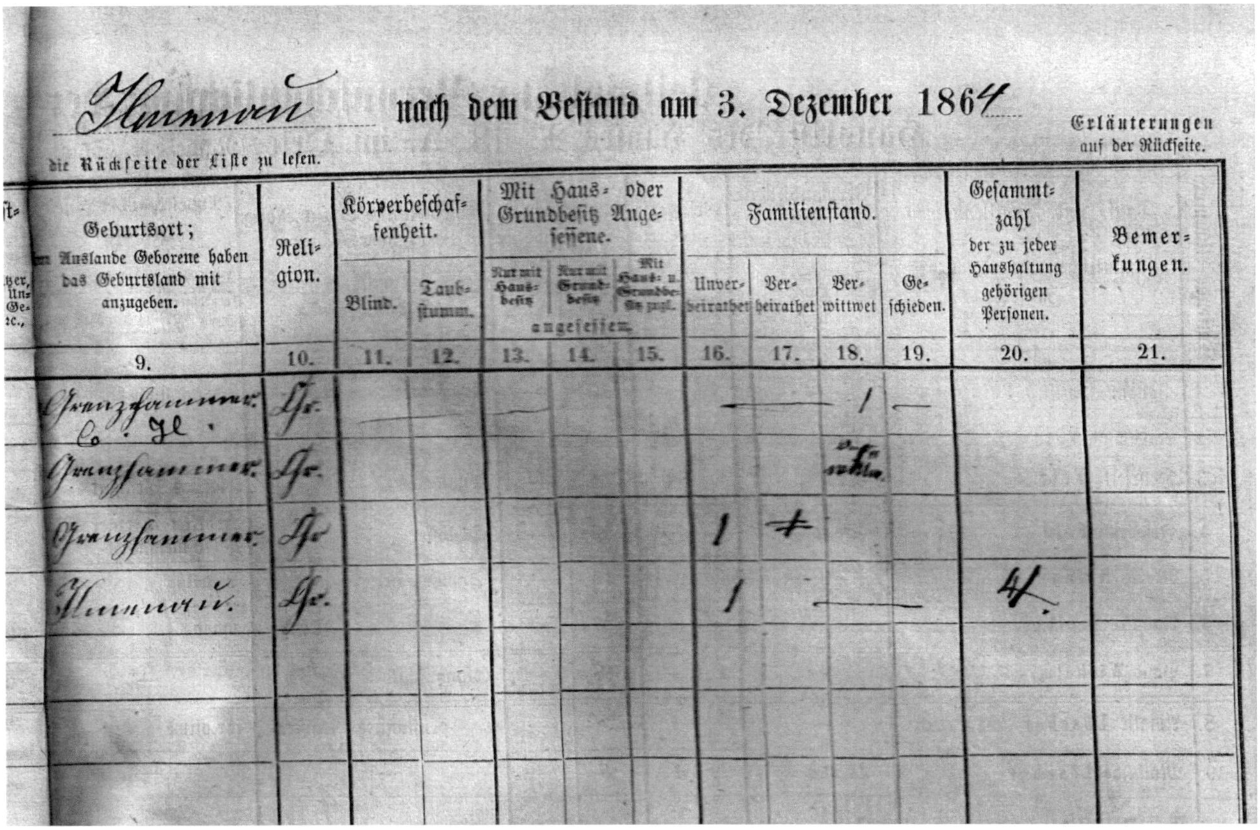

Ilmenau nach dem Bestand am 3. Dezember 1864

die Rückseite der Liste zu lesen.

Erläuterungen auf der Rückseite.

Geburtsort; im Auslande Geborene haben das Geburtsland mit anzugeben.	Religion.	Körperbeschaffenheit. Blind.	Körperbeschaffenheit. Taubstumm.	Mit Haus- oder Grundbesitz Angesessene. Nur mit Hausbesitz	Nur mit Grundbesitz	Mit Haus- u. Grundbesitz zugl. angesessen	Familienstand. Unverheirathet	Verheirathet	Verwittwet	Geschieden.	Gesammtzahl der zu jeder Haushaltung gehörigen Personen.	Bemerkungen.
9.	10.	11.	12.	13.	14.	15.	16.	17.	18.	19.	20.	21.
Granzhammer Co. Il.	Ev.			—			—	—	1	—		
Granzhammer	Ev.								[illegible]			
Granzhammer	Ev.						1	+				
Ilmenau	Ev.						1	—	—	—	4.	

Figure 3. 1864 Census Page from Illmenau, Sachsen-Weimar-Eisenach (right-hand page)

Column headings: birth place (country for foreigners); religion; blind; deaf; if owner of a house; if owner of land; owner of both house and land; total residents; comments [Thüringisches Staatsarchiv Illmenau 104025]

Notes

[1] Antje Kraus, *Quellen zur Bevölkerungsstatistik Deutschlands 1815–1871*, Band 1 (Boppard, Germany: Harald Boldt, 1980), 28, 289–294.

34 Schaumburg-Lippe

I. Location

The principality of Schaumburg-Lippe lay in northern Germany—surrounded on three sides by the kingdom of Hannover and on the west by the Prussian province of Westfalen. It consisted of two major political units represented by the cities of Bückeburg and Stadthagen.

II. Census Enumerations in Schaumburg-Lippe

The first census carried out by the principality was dated 1816, but only numbers were collected. This very small principality resisted the movement that led to the establishment of three customs unions among the German states in 1828 and made its own way through interstate economics for the next few years. The 1836 census was the first in Schaumburg-Lippe to feature the names of persons (heads of households). Two years later, the government decided to join the *Steuerverein* [Tax Union] that was led by giant neighbor Hannover and also included as of that year the grand duchy of Oldenburg.[1] Census campaigns were required by that organization every three years from 1839 to 1848.

However, the *Steuerverein* was never strong enough to compete with the Prussian-led *Zollverein* [Customs Union] and the two groups merged in 1851-52. The Schaumburg-Lippe census of 1852 was conducted based on *Zollverein* guidelines and the triennial pattern was sustained through 1864.[2] Another census was enumerated in 1867 as a joint effort that involved all of the German states. Under the German Empire, enumerations were done in Schaumburg-Lippe in 1871, every five years from 1875 to 1910, and finally in 1916.[3]

III. Specific Instructions to Town Officials and Enumerators

Instructions given to officials in Schaumburg-Lippe before 1861 have not been located as of this writing. Six full pages of regulations were provided in 1861 and were repeated with no significant revisions in 1864 (those regulations are reflective of the content of census records before 1861). The main points are these:

> The enumeration is not to begin before midnight on December 3; count all locals and foreigners whose residence is here on that day; count all students; locals working elsewhere are to be counted with their local households; persons who own two dwellings are to be counted at the location of their winter residence; military personnel and inmates in prisons are not to be counted with the local population; count retired soldiers and their families

IV. Content of Census Records in Schaumburg-Lippe from 1836 to 1864

	1836	1839	1842	1845	1848	1852	1855	1858	1861	1864
Name of head of household	X	X	X	X	X	X	X	X	X	X
Total males	X	X	X	X	X	X				
Total females	X	X	X	X	X	X				
Total residents	X	X	X	X	X	X				
Number of sons	X									
Number of daughters	X									
Number of servants	X									
Number of other relatives	X									
Persons under 7 (by gender)	X	X	X	X	X	X				
Persons age 7 to 14 (by gender)	X	X	X	X	X	X				
Persons age 14 to 25 (by gender)	X									
Persons age 25 to 70 (by gender)	X									
Persons over 70 (by gender)	X									
Married persons	X									
Widowers	X	X	X	X	X	X				
Widows	X	X	X	X	X	X				
Unmarried persons	X									
Comments	X									
Persons 14 to 20 (by gender)		X	X	X	X	X				
Persons 20 to 45 (by gender)		X	X	X	X	X				
Persons 45 to 60 (by gender)		X	X	X	X	X				
Persons 60 to 90 (by gender)		X	X	X	X	X				
Persons over 90 (by gender)		X	X	X	X	X				
Married couples		X	X	X	X	X				
Lutheran		X	X	X	X	X				
Reformed Lutheran		X	X	X	X	X				
Catholic		X	X	X	X	X				
Mennonite		X	X	X	X	X				
Jewish		X	X	X	X	X				
Civilian males over 14							X	X	X	X
Civilian females over 14							X	X	X	X
Civilian males under 14							X	X	X	X
Civilian females under 14							X	X	X	X
Same details for military and dependents							X	X	X	X
Varying formats							X	X	X	X
Handwritten column headings	X		X		X					
Pre-printed pages		X		X		X	X	X	X	X

V. Accessibility of Census Records in Schaumburg-Lippe

Of the thirty-eight German states featured in this book, the one with the most complete and accessible census records is—by a wide margin—the small principality of Schaumburg-Lippe. From the first enumeration in 1836 to the emergence of the German Empire in 1871, every page of every census for every location in the principality has been preserved. The entire collection can be read on microfiche in the state archive in Bückeburg.[4] Unfortunately, the quality of the microfiche is rather poor, in that the pages are substantially under-exposed. Nevertheless, the majority of the names of the heads of household are legible. Inquiries regarding specific towns may be directed to the archive (see Appendix A for instructions on writing such inquiries). As of this writing, no digital copies of these records are available on the Internet and the Family History Library has none of them in its collection.

VI. Selected Images of Schaumburg-Lippe Census Records

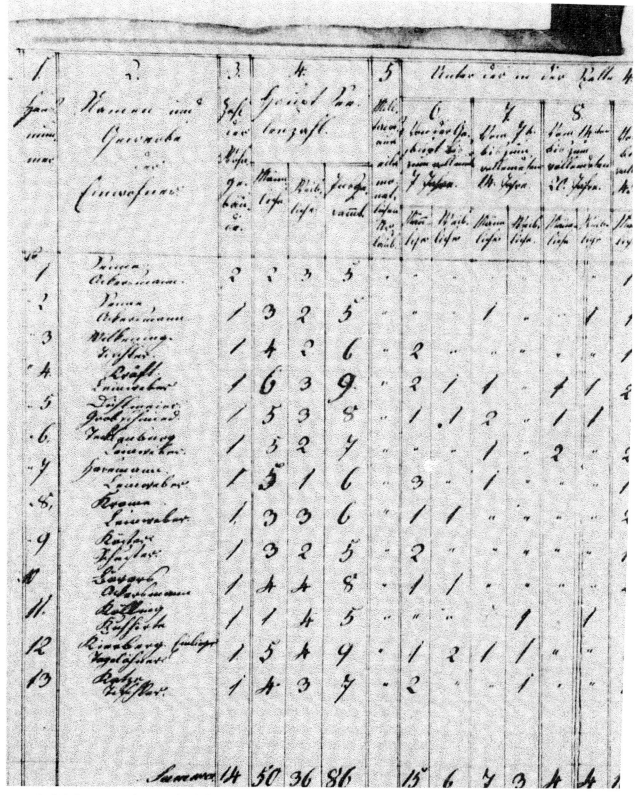

Figure 1. 1848 Census Page from Niedernholz, Schaumburg-Lippe (left-hand page)

Column headings: name of head of household; number of dwellings; total males; total females; total residents; number of soldiers in reserve status; males under 7; females under 7; males 7–14; females 7–14; males 14–20; females 14–20 [Niedersächsisches Landesarchiv Bückeburg Bf Nr 737e fol 40-89]

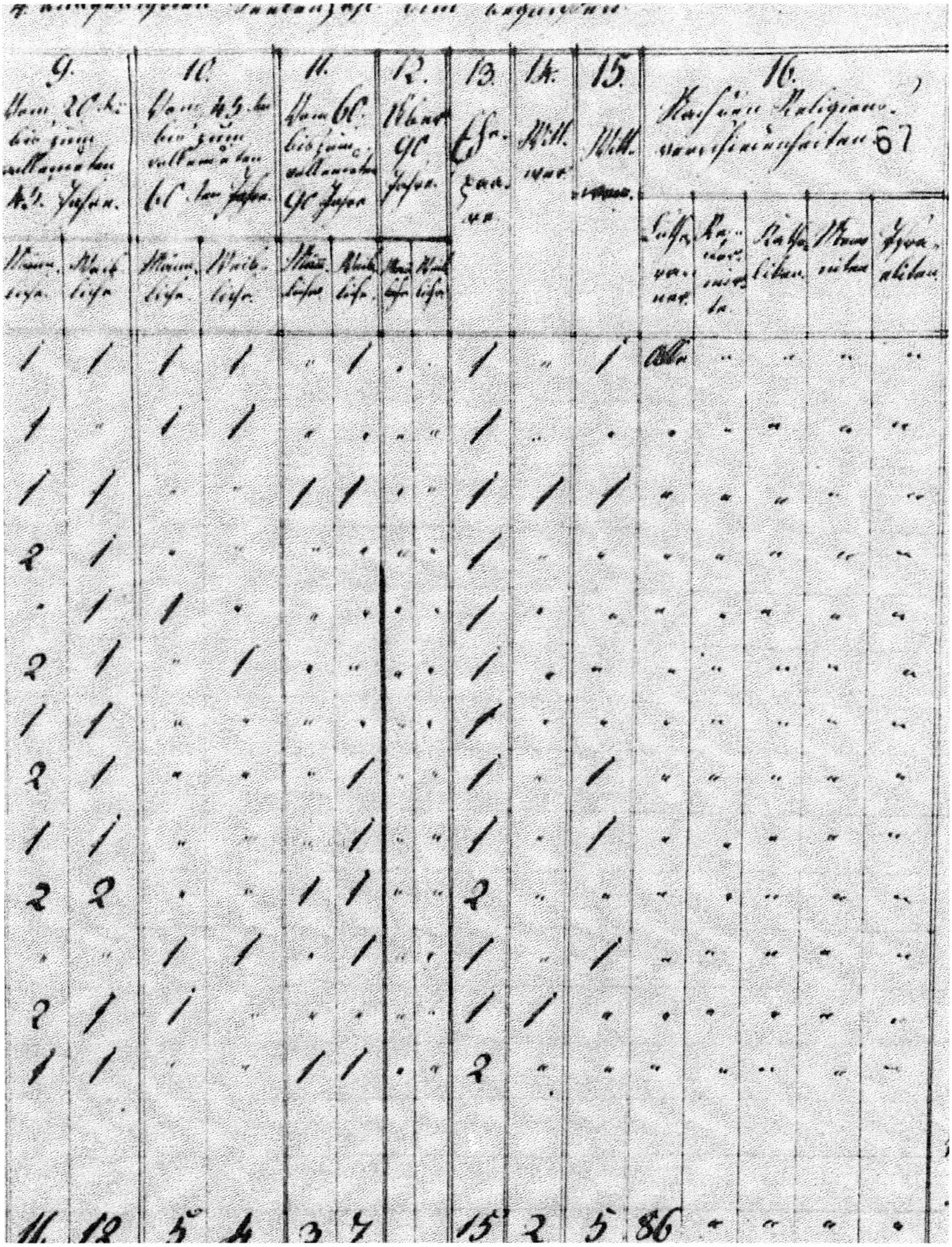

Figure 2. 1848 Census Page from Niedernholz, Schaumburg-Lippe (right-hand page)

Column headings: males 20–45; females 20–45; males 45–60; females 45–60; males 60–90; females 60–90; males over 90; females over 90; married persons; widowers; widows; Lutherans; Reformed Lutherans; Catholics, Mennonites; Jewish [Niedersächsisches Landesarchiv Bückeburg Bf Nr 737e fol 40-89]

№	Namen der [Haus...]	I. Nach den Ortserhebungen über den Civilstand.					
		Anzahl der Familien	Männer und Jünglinge über 14 Jahre	Weiber und Jungfrauen über 14 Jahr	Kinder unter 14 Jahren männlich	Kinder unter 14 Jahren weiblich	Anzahl der Einwohner vom Civilstande
					Seelen		
	[...]	14	15	6	11	8	69
	[...]	2	4	3	5	1	15
8	[...]	3	3	4	4	2	13
9	[...]	1	1	3	2	·	6
10	[...]	1	3	1	·	1	5
11	[...]	2	4	4	·	·	8
12	[...]	1	1	1	2	·	4
13	[...]	2	3	4	3	2	12
14	[...]	3	4	3	3	3	13
15	[...]	1	2	2	·	·	4
16	[...]	1	2	3	2	·	7
17	[...]	3	5	4	1	6	16
18	[...]	1	5	1	·	·	6
19	[...]	1	2	3	1	·	6

Figure 3. 1864 Census Page from Oberwöhren, Schaumburg-Lippe (left-hand page)

Column headings: name of head of household; number of families in dwelling; males over 14; females over 14; males under 14; females under 14; total civilian residents (military residents are counted on the right-hand page) [Niedersächsisches Landesarchiv Bückeburg L3 Bf Nr 7k fol 65-118]

Notes

[1] W. O. Henderson, *The Zollverein* (London: Frank Cass, 1959), 214-215.

[2] Otto Klingelhöffer, "Der Zollverein im Jahr 1865" in *Zeitschrift für die gesamte Staatswissenschaft*, v. 19 (1863), 96.

[3] Antje Kraus, *Quellen zur Bevölkerungsstatistik Deutschlands 1815-1871*, Band 1 (Boppard, Germany: Harald Boldt, 1980), 26, 231-236.

[4] Niedersächsisches Landesarchiv Bückeburg. The link to the catalog of the archive's collection is www.arcinsys.niedersachsen.de/arcinsys/start.action.

35 Schlesien [Silesia]

I. Location

The Prussian province of Schlesien was bordered by sister provinces: Sachsen to the west, Brandenburg to the northwest and Posen to the north, and the kingdom of Sachsen to the southwest. International neighbors were the Russian Empire to the east and the Austrian Empire to the south. Breslau was the capital city.[1]

II. Census Enumerations in Schlesien

The kingdom of Preußen ruled over seven provinces in eastern Germany and two in western Germany shortly after the Congress of Vienna. All Prussian provinces were to produce and submit to the statistical bureau in Berlin annual statistical tables from 1817 to 1822. The schedule was then altered to require such data only every three years, but no set of strict standards guided the enumerations. City officials were to carry out the work.[2] Although the campaigns of the 1820s were designed to produce only statistics, the records of several years featured the names of heads of households.

In 1818, Schlesien was one of the seven eastern Prussian provinces to be grouped into a customs union. One year later, Westfalen and Rheinprovinz were grouped into a western Prussian customs union. The next predictable step was the inclusion of all nine Prussian provinces in the Prusso-Hessian Customs Union founded in February 1828.

Census enumerations followed triennially and the schedule continued without interruption even after the establishment of the *Zollverein* [Customs Union] on January 1, 1834. Under the strong leadership of Prussia, the *Zollverein* required census records every three years for three full decades and the quality of those records steadily improved.

Another census was enumerated in Schlesien in 1867 and all German states participated in the campaign. Under the German Empire, enumerations were done there in 1871, every five years from 1875 to 1910, and finally in 1916.[3]

III. Specific Instructions to Town Officials and Enumerators

Significant new and revised instructions for Schlesien census campaigns have not been located, but the following regulations issued to other Prussian provinces were in effect in Schlesien:

1825: if significant differences are found in comparison with the results of 1822, explain the causes of those differences

1840: use the forms provided; each page has room for sixty names; police officials should conduct the campaign; do not begin to collect the data before December 1; the work must be completed in towns by December 20 and in cities by December 25, so that the reports can be received in Berlin by December 31; you are allowed to refer to documents previously compiled, such as lists of residents; do not count travelers in inns and active military personnel and their dependents; local residents temporarily away from home are to be counted

1843: refer to the deficiencies in the 1840 census in order to produce more reliable results; count military personnel in reserve status; where the number of enumerators is insufficient, tax officials and retired military officers may be called into service and remunerated appropriately

1846: begin the collection of data on December 3; count all foreigners employed here but not persons traveling through the town; count inmates in prisons and hospitals; persons who own more than one dwelling should be counted where they live in the winter; do not refer to previous lists such as residential registration; in large cities, heads of households may fill out the forms themselves to save enumerators time

1852: the handwriting on the lists must be neat and orderly; should authorities at the next higher level identify mistakes in the local records, the cost of any required corrections shall be charged to the responsible authorities; owners of major estates are to count their respective populations and submit the lists to the local town authorities

1855: persons who refuse to cooperate will be fined

1858: local officials are to announce the upcoming census in the newspaper

1861: for those persons who live in one location and work in another during the week, they are to be counted in the location where they spend the night before the census day; do not count persons in inns or visiting families; for persons living in one location and working in another, count them where they are on the night of December 2–3

1864: do not count persons who have been absent from their home town for more than one year; officials who do not carry out the census according to instructions are to be fined; an enumeration district should not include more than 600 people; non-government persons assigned to assist in the campaign may be paid a maximum of one *Thaler*; count only those foreigners who have lived here for at least one year; record the year of birth rather than the age; children in a given family are to be listed in order of their birth

IV. Content of Census Records in Schlesien from 1822 to 1864

No census images have been found as yet for the Prussian province of Schlesien, but the following details have been gathered from Brandenburg, Pommern, and Sachsen and represent what would have been required by the statistical bureau in Berlin for Schlesien as well.

	'22	'25	'28	'31	'34	'37	'40	'43	'46	'49	'52	'55	'58	'61	'64
No images available	X	X		X											
Name of each person			X				X	X	X	X	X	X	X	X	X
Name of head of household					X	X									
Married persons (by gender)			X												
Total residents			X		X	X	X	X	X	X	X	X	X	X	X
Age in years			X				X	X	X	X	X	X	X	X	X
Persons under 6 (by gender)			X		X	X									
Persons 7–9 (by gender)			X		X	X									
Persons 10–14 (by gender)			X		X	X									
Persons 15–60 (by gender)			X		X										
Persons over 60 (by gender)			X		X	X									
Lutherans			X		X	X							X	X	X
Catholics			X		X	X							X	X	X
Jewish (with citizenship status)					X	X							X	X	X
Persons 15–16 (by gender)						X									
Males 17–20						X									
Males 21–40						X									
Males 41–60						X									
Males over 60						X									
Females 17–45						X									
Females 46–60						X									
Females over 60						X									
Total females over 14						X									
Total males						X									
Total females						X									
Reformed Lutherans						X									
Mennonites						X									X
Comments			X						X	X	X	X	X	X	X
Status or occupation							X	X	X	X	X	X	X	X	X
Religion							X	X	X	X	X	X			
Blind												X			
Deaf												X			
Greek Orthodox															X
Dissidents															X
Other religions															X
Handwritten column headings			X		X										X
Pre-printed pages						X	X	X	X	X	X	X	X	X	X

V. Accessibility of Census Records in Schlesien

The fact that this province was ceded to Poland following World War II complicates the search for original census regulations and lists of inhabitants. As part of this investigation, emails were sent to county and regional archives in what was once the province of Schlesien but none of those responded positively regarding census records in their collections.[4] Nevertheless, a letter written in Polish to an archive found through a search of city, county, or regional government websites might prove successful. (See Appendix A for suggestions on writing that inquiry in Polish.) As of this writing, no census records from Schlesien are available in the Family History Library on microfilm and no digital images have been located on the Internet.

VI. Selected Images of Schlesien Census Records

As of this writing, no images of census records have been found for Schlesien.

Notes

[1] This is a simplified representation. The changes in borders among Prussian provinces in the nineteenth century are legion but not of specific importance here.

[2] Harald Michel, "Volkszählungen in Deutschland: Die Erfassung des Bevölkerungsstandes von 1816 bis 1933," in *Jahrbuch für Wirtschaftsgeschichte* 1985/II, 85

[3] Antje Kraus, *Quellen zur Bevölkerungsstatistik Deutschlands 1815–1871*, Band 1 (Boppard, Germany: Harald Boldt, 1980), 25–26, 207–212.

[4] The author expresses his appreciation to Magdalena Zajac, a native Polish student at the University of Vienna, who conducted an extensive email campaign with archives in cities that once were in the provinces of Ostpreußen, Posen, Schlesien, and Westpreußen.

36 Schleswig-Holstein

I. Location

The duchies of Schleswig and Holstein are located between the North Sea and the Baltic Sea, with the kingdom of Denmark on the north, the Prussian province of Hannover to the southwest, and the Mecklenburg grand duchies to the southeast. The free Hanseatic cities of Hamburg and Lübeck are also neighboring states.

II. Census Enumerations in Schleswig-Holstein

Independent of (but claimed by both) Denmark and the German Confederation during much of the nineteenth century, Schleswig-Holstein did not join any customs union when the movement was so popular in the late 1820s and 1830s. However, the census history of the duchies suggests a closer connection to Denmark, because enumerations were carried out at the same time (1835, 1840, 1845, 1855, and 1860) with the same detail as in Denmark.[1]

Another census was conducted in Schleswig-Holstein for unknown reasons in 1864, but the duchies' alignment with the *Zollverein* [Customs Union] soon thereafter resulted in participation in the 1867 census that included all of the German states.[2] Under the German Empire, enumerations were done in Schleswig-Holstein in 1871, every five years from 1875 to 1910, and finally in 1916.

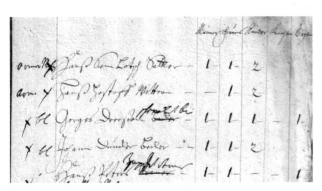

Figure 1. One of the earliest census records found in this study was compiled in 1720 in Heide, Schleswig-Holstein; it shows the head of household, the number of males, females, children, and servants [Stadtarchiv Heide].

III. Specific Instructions to Town Officials and Enumerators

Instructions issued by the ducal government for the conduct of the census have been found for the years 1835 and 1840. Those dated 1864 were printed on the reverse of the pages distributed to heads of households.

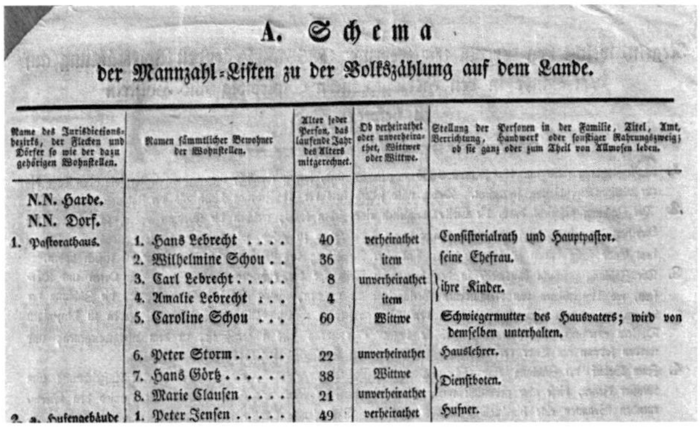

A. Schema

der Mannzahl-Listen zu der Volkszählung auf dem Lande.

Name des Jurisdictionsbezirks, der Flecken und Dörfer so wie der dazu gehörigen Wohnstellen.	Namen sämmtlicher Bewohner der Wohnstellen.	Alter jeder Person, das laufende Jahr des Alters mitgerechnet.	Ob verheirathet oder unverheirathet, Wittwer oder Wittwe.	Stellung der Personen in der Familie, Titel, Amt, Verrichtung, Handwerk oder sonstiger Nahrungszweig; ob sie ganz oder zum Theil von Almosen leben.
N.N. Harde.				
N.N. Dorf.				
1. Pastorathaus.	1. Hans Lebrecht	40	verheirathet	Consistorialrath und Hauptpastor.
	2. Wilhelmine Schou . .	36	item	seine Ehefrau.
	3. Carl Lebrecht	8	unverheirathet	ihre Kinder.
	4. Amalie Lebrecht . . .	4	item	
	5. Caroline Schou . . .	60	Wittwe	Schwiegermutter des Hausvaters; wird von demselben unterhalten.
	6. Peter Storm	22	unverheirathet	Hauslehrer.
	7. Hans Görtz	38	Wittwe	Dienstboten.
	8. Marie Clausen	21	unverheirathet	
2. a. Hufengebäude	1. Peter Jensen	49	verheirathet	Hufner.

Figure 2. This sample census page was sent to officials before the 1835 enumeration [Stadtarchiv Heide].

1835: the census campaign is to begin on February 1 and finished as soon as possible; town officials are to serve as enumerators and the pastor may assist; indicate the gender of any person whose name leaves that questionable; count all those absent whose principal residence is local; count soldiers, students, etc.; number the children in each family consecutively by age

1840: all of Denmark and the duchies [of Schleswig and Holstein] are to conduct a census in 1840 and every five years thereafter, beginning on February 1;[3] conduct the campaign as described in the instructions given in 1835; civil officials are to collect the data

1864: the list is to be filled out by the owner of the dwelling; the data are to be correct as of the night of December 2-3; record the age at the next birthday; do not count current military personnel; indicate which persons are residing here only temporarily

IV. Content of Census Records in Schleswig-Holstein from 1835 to 1864

	1835	1840	1845	1855	1860	1864
Name of head of household	X	X	X	X	X	X
Community within the town or address	X	X	X	X	X	X
Full name of each resident	X	X	X	X	X	X
Age at next birthday	X	X	X	X	X	X
Marital status	X	X	X	X	X	X
Relationship to head of household or employment in the household	X	X	X	X	X	X
Birth place (country if foreigner)			X	X	X	X
Number of insane persons			X	X	X	X
Duration of insanity			X		X	X
Religion				X	X	X
Number of deaf persons				X	X	X
Number of mute persons				X	X	X
Number of persons insane since birth					X	X
Comments					X	
Age at last birthday						X
If temporary resident						X
Pre-printed pages	X	X	X	X	X	X

V. Accessibility of Census Records in Schleswig-Holstein

Nearly all of the Schleswig-Holstein census records conducted via the model of the Danish census from 1835 through 1860 have survived and can be viewed on microfilm in the Family History Library system. Researchers should look in the Library's catalog on the town or county level, because the census was done on that level—not by farming communities. As of this writing, no Schleswig-Holstein census documents are known to exist as digital images on the Internet.

VI. Selected Images of Schleswig-Holstein Census Records

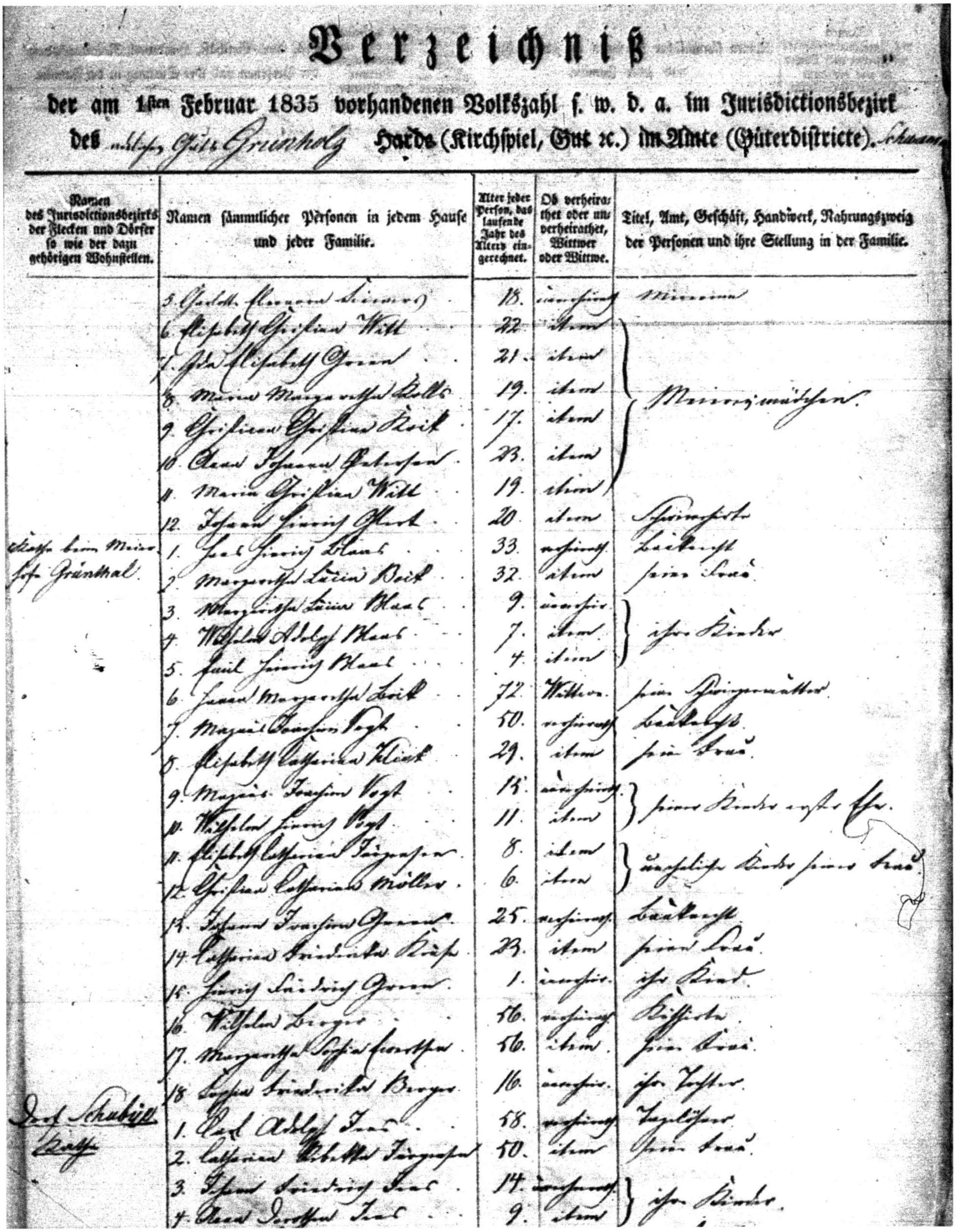

Verzeichniß

der am 1sten Februar 1835 vorhandenen Volkszahl f. w. d. a. im Jurisdictionsbezirk des ... Hards (Kirchspiel, Gut rc.) im Amte (Güterdistricte).

Namen des Jurisdictionsbezirks der Flecken und Dörfer so wie der dazu gehörigen Wohnstellen.	Namen sämmtlicher Personen in jedem Hause und jeder Familie.	Alter jeder Person, das laufende Jahr des Alters eingerechnet.	Ob verheirathet oder unverheirathet, Wittwer oder Wittwe.	Titel, Amt, Geschäft, Handwerk, Nahrungszweig der Personen und ihre Stellung in der Familie.

Figure 3. 1835 Census Page from Grünholz, Schleswig-Holstein

Column headings: name of neighborhood or address; first and last name of each resident; age at next birthday; whether married; relationship to head of household or employment therein [Rigsarkivet, København]

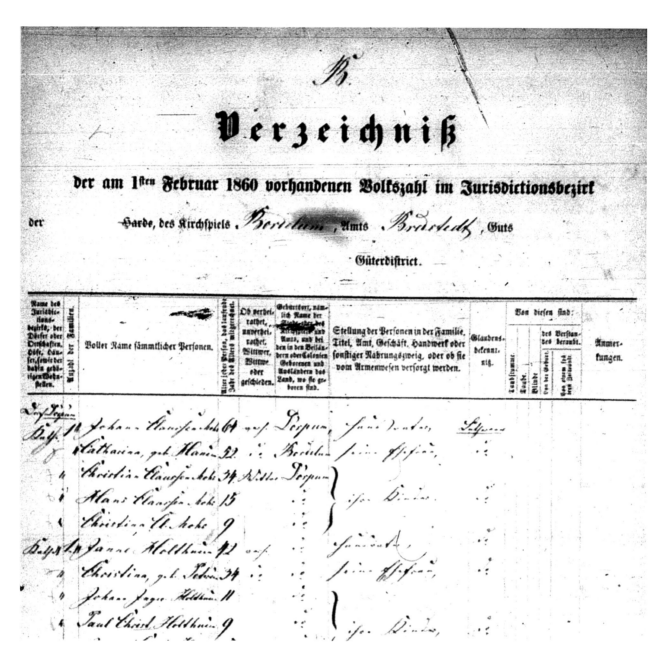

Figure 4. 1860 Census Page from Bordelum, Schleswig-Holstein

Column headings: name of neighborhood or address; first and last name of each resident; age at next birthday; whether married; birth place (country if foreigner; county if not local); relationship to head of household or employment therein; religion; insane; deaf; blind; if born insane; how long insane; comments [Rigsarkivet, København]

Notes

[1] Population counts were done in the duchies from 1816 through at least 1834 but apparently no names were recorded. See Antje Kraus, *Quellen zur Bevölkerungsstatistik Deutschlands 1815–1871*, Band 1 (Boppard, Germany: Harald Boldt, 1980), 124.

[2] Antje Kraus, *Quellen*, 24, 123–128.

[3] This study did not discover a reason why the 1850 census did not take place nor does relevant literature explain its absence.

37 Schwarzburg-Rudolstadt

I. Location

The principality of Schwarzburg-Rudolstadt was one of the eight so-called "Saxon duchies" within the central German region collectively known as Thüringen. The territory consisted of several exclaves and enclaves of various sizes. Six of the seven other Saxon duchies shared borders with Schwarzburg-Rudolstadt, as did the Prussian province of Sachsen to the north. The capital city was Rudolstadt.

II. Census Enumerations in Schwarzburg-Rudolstadt

Little is known about the first census enumerations here after the Napoleonic era, but one occurred in 1816 and another in 1822 (head counts only).[1] In 1831, census data were collected in the principality and in other member states of the short-lived *Mitteldeutscher Handelsverein* [Central German Commercial Union]. Schwarzburg-Rudolstadt moved to the more successful *Zollverein* [Customs Union] by 1834. As a member of that organization the principality conducted census campaigns every three years from 1834 through 1864. Evidence suggests that census procedures during that era were similar to those employed in her sister duchy of Schwarzburg-Sondershausen. After the founding of the German Empire, enumerations were done in the duchy in 1871, every five years from 1875 to 1910, and finally in 1916.[2]

III. Specific Instructions to Town Officials and Enumerators

Only four pages of instructions have been located regarding the procedures for census campaigns—all from the same year:

1822: compare the results of this census with the results of 1816 and explain any increase or decrease in the local population; don't count foreigners residing here only temporarily

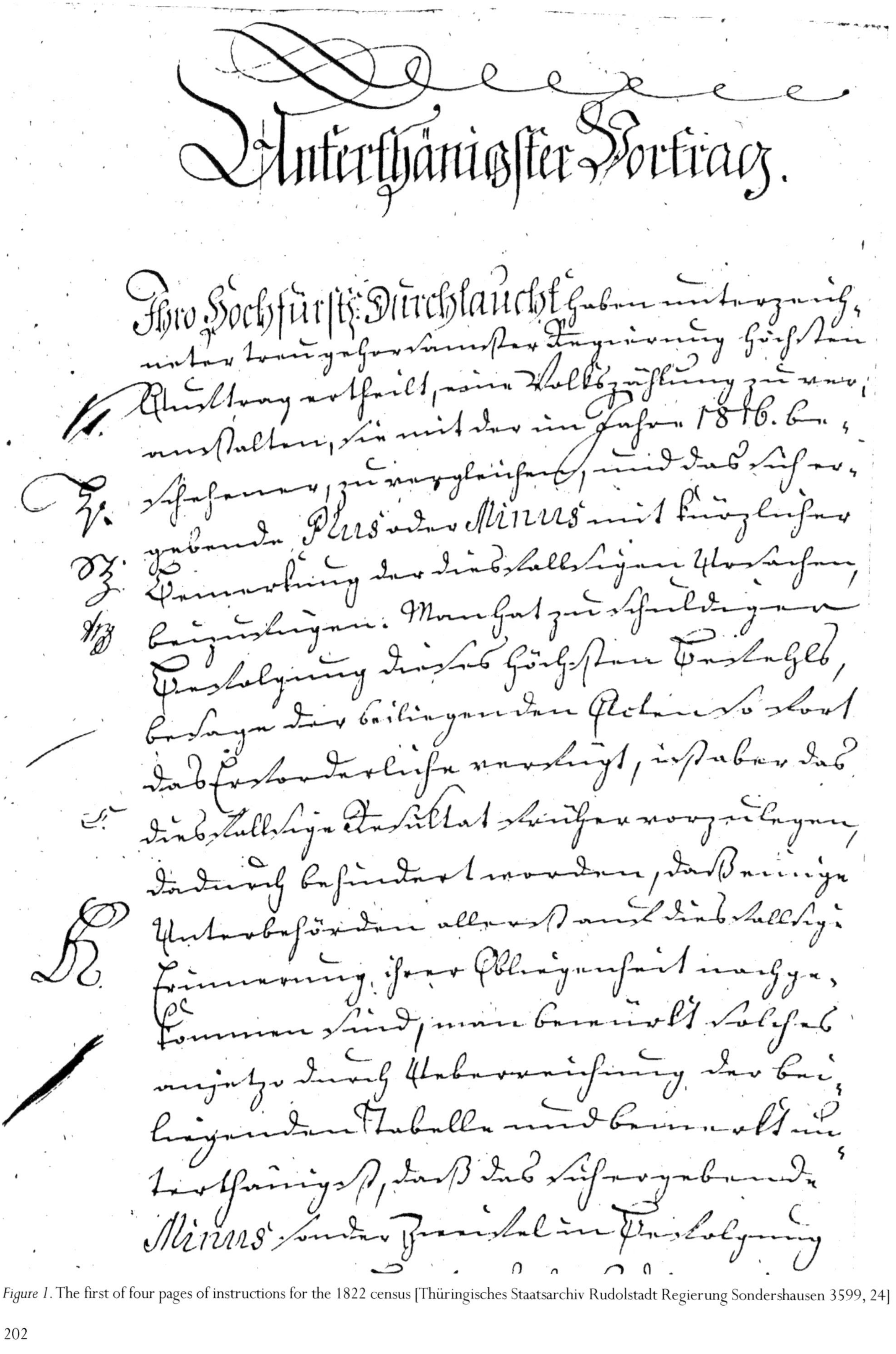

Unterthänigster Vortrag.

Ihro Hochfürstl. Durchlaucht [...]

Figure 1. The first of four pages of instructions for the 1822 census [Thüringisches Staatsarchiv Rudolstadt Regierung Sondershausen 3599, 24]

202

IV. Content of Census Records in Schwarzburg-Rudolstadt from 1816 to 1864

One may assume that the content of census records in this duchy will be similar to that found in Schwarzburg-Sondershausen and other states belonging to the *Zollverein* over the years.

	1816	1822	1831	1834	1837	1840	1843
No images available	X	X	X	X	X	X	X

	1846	1849	1852	1855	1858	1861	1864
No images available	X	X	X	X	X	X	X

V. Accessibility of Census Records in Schwarzburg-Rudolstadt

What is likely the largest collection of census records for both Schwarzburg duchies is found in the Thuringian State Archive in Rudolstadt. The catalog of the archive can be seen at http://www.thueringen. de/th1/tsk/kultur/staatsarchive.

Census records not found in Rudolstadt might still be housed in the archives of towns and cities within the historical principality (lists of those towns are included on several websites). Letters in German should be directed to local city and county archives. (See Appendix A for instructions on how to formulate such letters.) Currently there are no census records in the collection of the Family History Library in Salt Lake City, nor are Schwarzburg-Rudolstadt census records known to exist on microfilm or in digital form on the Internet as of this writing.

VI. Selected Images of Schwarzburg-Rudolstadt Census Records

No images of census records from this duchy are available as of this writing.

Notes

[1] Antje Kraus, *Quellen zur Bevölkerungsstatistik Deutschlands 1815–1871*, Band 1 (Boppard, Germany: Harald Boldt, 1980), 28, 283–288.

[2] Kraus, *Quellen zur Bevölkerungsstatistik Deutschlands,* 284.

38 Schwarzburg-Sondershausen

I. Location

The principality of Schwarzburg-Sondershausen is one of the eight so-called "Saxon duchies" within the central German region collectively known as Thüringen. The territory consisted of several exclaves of various sizes. Four of the seven other Saxon duchies shared borders with Schwarzburg-Sondershausen, as did the Prussian province of Sachsen to the north.

II. Census Enumerations in Schwarzburg-Sondershausen

Little is known about the first census enumerations here after the Napoleonic era, but one occurred in 1816 (head count only).[1] In 1831, census data were collected as required of this and the other member states in the short-lived *Mitteldeutscher Handelsverein* [Central German Commercial Union]. Schwarzburg-Sondershausen moved to the more successful *Zollverein* [Customs Union] by 1834. As a member of that organization census campaigns were conducted every three years from 1834 through 1864. Evidence suggests that census procedures during that era were similar to those employed in the sister duchy of Schwarzburg-Rudolstadt. After the founding of the German Empire, enumerations were done in the duchy in 1871, every five years from 1875 to 1910, and finally in 1916.[2]

III. Specific Instructions to Town Officials and Enumerators

Census instructions have been found for only two enumeration years, but they were sent to all towns within the principality a few months before a census was to be taken. Instructions were written by officials of the duchy's interior ministry.

1861: refer to the census standards of 1855; collect all papers on December 3; any revisions or corrections must be done according to the status of the persons on December 3

1864: do not use residential registration lists for this census, but count every individual anew; do not count persons whose home town is here but have lived more than one year elsewhere; use only the official forms provided

IV. Content of Census Records in Schwarzburg-Sondershausen from 1816 to 1864

One may assume that the content of census records in this duchy will be similar to that found in Schwarzburg-Rudolstadt and other states belonging to the *Zollverein* over the years.

	1816–1817	1831	1834	1837	1840	1843	1846	1849	1852	1855	1858	1861	1864
No images found		X		X	X	X	X	X	X	X	X	X	X
Name of head of household	X		X										
Number of adult males	X												
Number of adult females	X												
Number of males under 14	X		X										
Number of females under 14	X		X										
Number of males 15–60			X										
Number of females 15–60			X										
Number of males over 60			X										
Number of females over 60			X										
Total residents in household			X										
Comments			X										
Handwritten column headings	X		X										

V. Accessibility of Census Records in Schwarzburg-Sondershausen

What is likely the largest collection of census records for both Schwarzburg duchies is found in the Thuringian State Archive in Rudolstadt. The archive catalog can be found at http://www.thueringen.de/th1/tsk/kultur/staatsarchive.

Census records not there might however be found in the archives of towns and cities of those states (lists of those towns are included on several websites). Letters in German should be directed to local archives. (See Appendix A for instructions on how to formulate such letters.) Currently there are no census records from Schwarzburg-Sondershausen in the collection of the Family History Library in Salt Lake City, nor are any known to exist elsewhere on microfilm or in digital form on the Internet as of this writing.

Häuser	Män̄er	Weiber	Knab. im 14 Jr	Mäd
1 *[des Fürst Güth]*	28	8	3	2
2 *[Th. Förster Heil]*	2	2	1	—
3 *[der Schäfft Goda]*	5	2	—	1
4 *[Heinrich Joach Brander]*	1	1	—	1
5 *[Wd. Lindemann]*	1	1	—	1
6 *[Gastwirth Rahrbach]*	1	2	2	2
7 *[Löbner Zylmann]*	1	1	1	2
8 *[Heinrich Harbst]*	2	1	—	—
9 *[Andreas Lindenstadt]*	1	1	1	2
10 *[Johan Dörderich Jä]*	1	2	—	—
11 *[Christoff Müller]*	1	1	—	—
12 *[Andon Heil]*	1	1	1	2
13 *[Ferd Lieg]*	1	1	1	—
14 *[Wd. Johan Ernst Küster]*	1	1	—	3
15 *[Andreas Göbel]*	2	—	1	—
16 *[der Müller Dörfall]*	1	2	1	1
17 *[Wd. Wilhelm Schmid]*	2	1	2	1
18 *[Gabriel Göz]*	2	1	2	—
19 *[Wd. Johan ernst Häming]*	1	1	1	

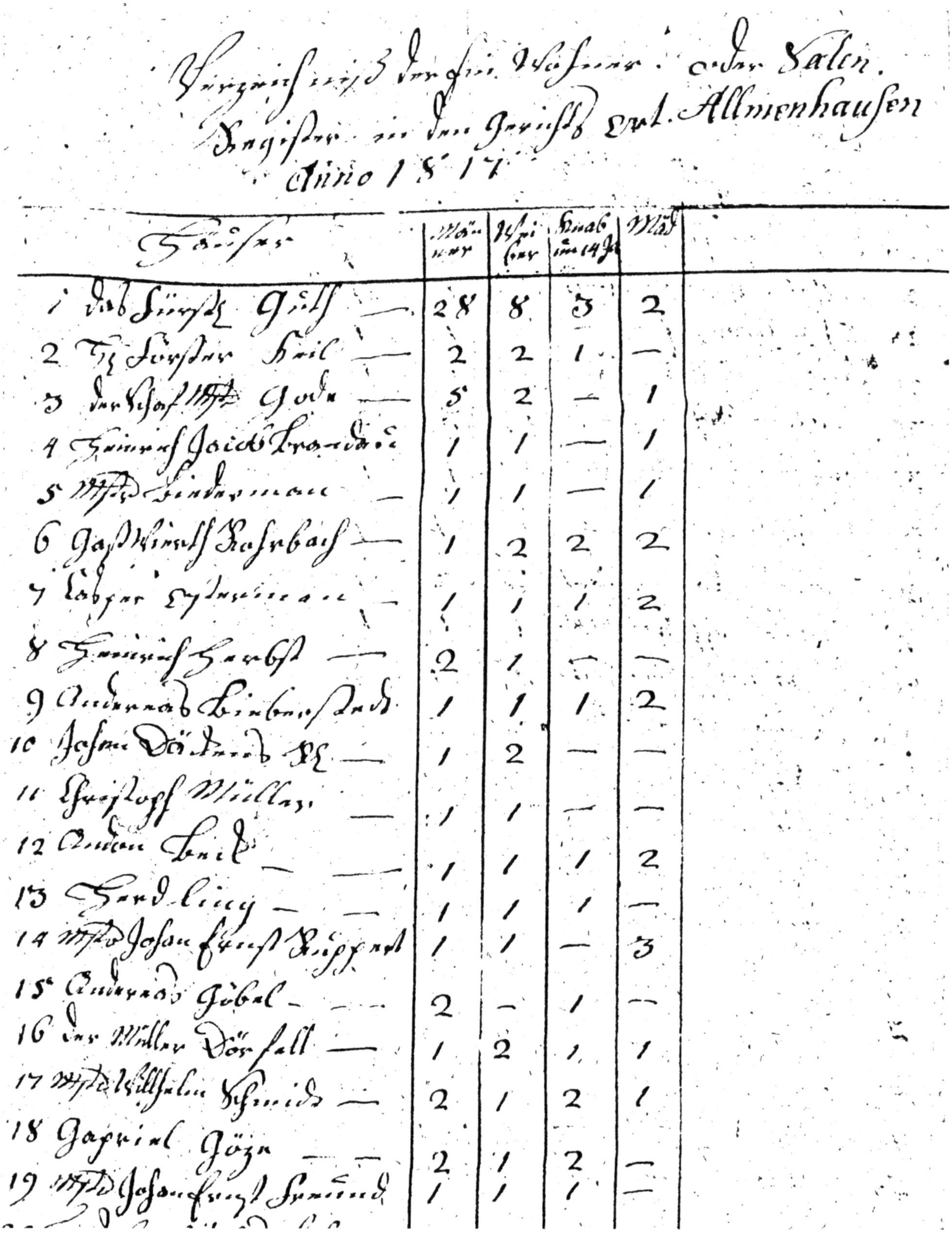

Figure 1. 1817 Census Page from Allmenhausen, Schwarzburg-Sondershausen (left-hand page only)

Column headings: head of household; adult males; adult females; males under 14; females under 14
[Thüringisches Staatsarchiv Rudolstadt, Regierung Sondershausen 3599, 24]

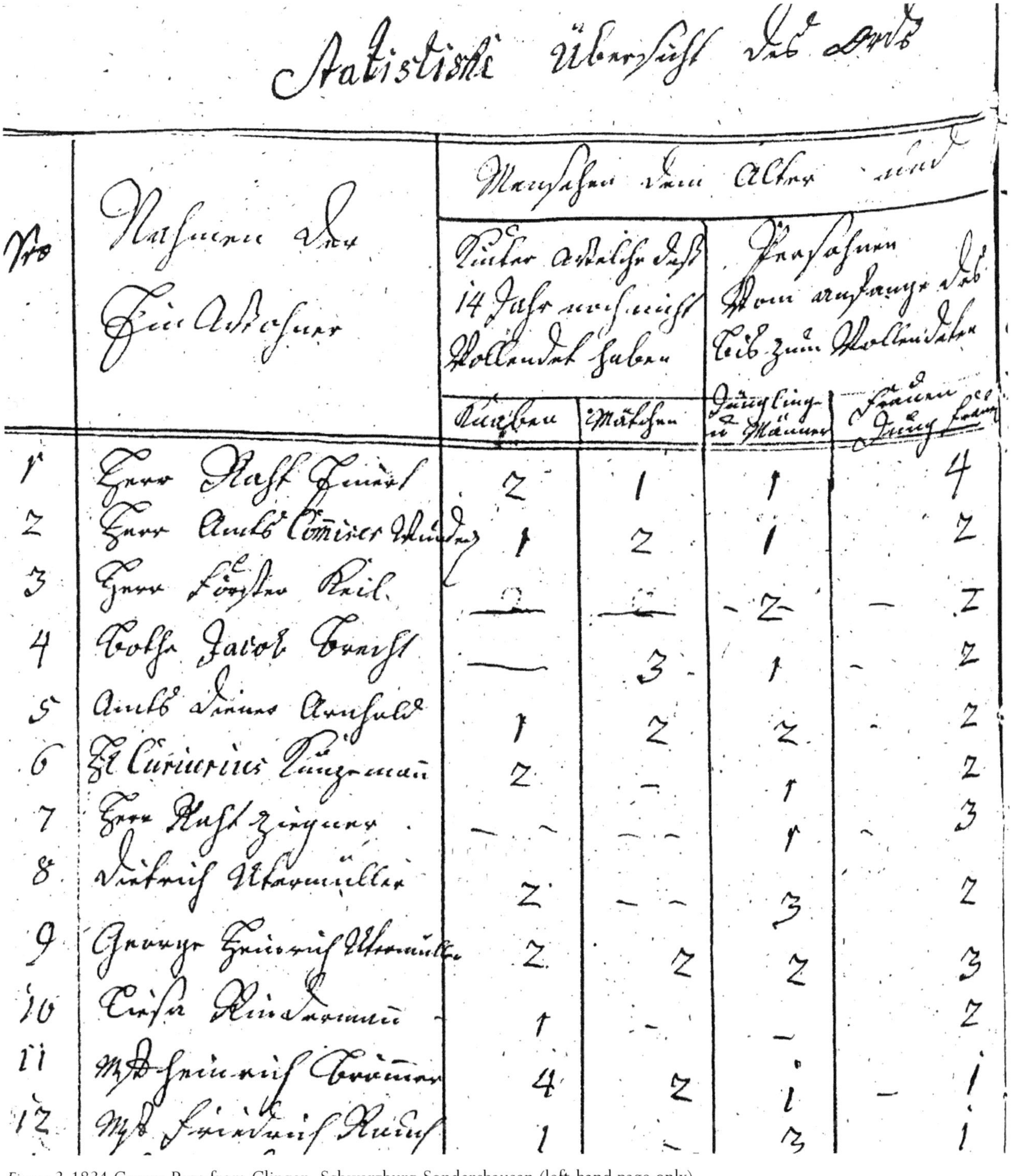

Figure 2. 1834 Census Page from Clingen, Schwarzburg-Sondershausen (left-hand page only)

Column headings: consecutive number of individuals; head of household; males under 14; females under 14; males 15–60; females 15–60 [Thüringisches Staatsarchiv Rudolstadt, Regierung Sondershausen 3599, 24]

Notes

1   Antje Kraus, *Quellen zur Bevölkerungsstatistik Deutschlands 1815–1871*, Band 1 (Boppard, Germany: Harald Boldt, 1980), 28, 277–282.

2   Kraus, *Quellen zur Bevölkerungsstatistik Deutschlands*, 278.

39 Waldeck

I. Location

The small principality and later Prussian province of Waldeck in northern Germany was surrounded by two Prussian provinces—Westfalen on the northwest and Hessen-Nassau on the southeast. The capital city was Arolsen.

II. Census Enumerations in Waldeck

As an independent member of the German Confederation, Waldeck conducted census campaigns on her own schedule, doing so as early as 1816 (head counts only). From at least 1826 until 1835, the enumerations were annual and bore the title *Seelenregister*.[1] An edict issued by the government in Arolsen in 1836 ended the *Seelenregister* schedule and specified a triennial census beginning in 1838.[2] This satisfied the requirements of the *Zollverein* [Customs Union] that Waldeck had joined in 1834.

The Waldeck county of Pyrmont was not included in census campaigns until 1843. The final census under the *Zollverein* and the first in conjunction with the North German Confederation occurred in 1867; every German state participated.[3] Under the German Empire, census data were collected in the province in 1871, every five years from 1875 to 1910, and finally in 1916.

III. Specific Instructions to Town Officials and Enumerators

Even though each census conducted from 1838 to 1864 was announced in government circulars, no instructions have survived.[4] They would likely have reflected those issued in other states belonging to the *Zollverein*.

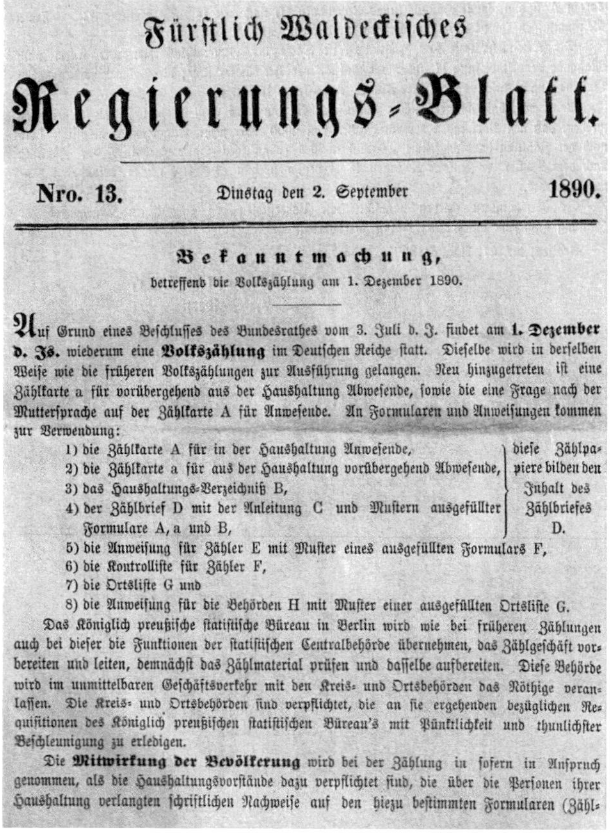

Fürstlich Waldeckisches

Regierungs-Blatt.

Nro. 13. Dinstag den 2. September **1890.**

Bekanntmachung,

betreffend die Volkszählung am 1. Dezember 1890.

Auf Grund eines Beschlusses des Bundesrathes vom 3. Juli d. J. findet am **1. Dezember d. Js.** wiederum eine **Volkszählung** im Deutschen Reiche statt. Dieselbe wird in derselben Weise wie die früheren Volkszählungen zur Ausführung gelangen. Neu hinzugetreten ist eine Zählkarte a für vorübergehend aus der Haushaltung Abwesende, sowie die eine Frage nach der Muttersprache auf der Zählkarte A für Anwesende. An Formularen und Anweisungen kommen zur Verwendung:

1) die Zählkarte A für in der Haushaltung Anwesende,
2) die Zählkarte a für aus der Haushaltung vorübergehend Abwesende,
3) das Haushaltungs-Verzeichniß B,
4) der Zählbrief D mit der Anleitung C und Mustern ausgefüllter Formulare A, a und B,
} diese Zählpapiere bilden den Inhalt des Zählbriefes D.
5) die Anweisung für Zähler E mit Muster eines ausgefüllten Formulars F,
6) die Kontrolliste für Zähler F,
7) die Ortsliste G und
8) die Anweisung für die Behörden H mit Muster einer ausgefüllten Ortsliste G.

Das Königlich preußische statistische Büreau in Berlin wird wie bei früheren Zählungen auch bei dieser die Funktionen der statistischen Centralbehörde übernehmen, das Zählgeschäft vorbereiten und leiten, demnächst das Zählmaterial prüfen und dasselbe aufbereiten. Diese Behörde wird im unmittelbaren Geschäftsverkehr mit den Kreis- und Ortsbehörden das Nöthige veranlassen. Die Kreis- und Ortsbehörden sind verpflichtet, die an sie ergehenden bezüglichen Requisitionen des Königlich preußischen statistischen Büreau's mit Pünktlichkeit und thunlichster Beschleunigung zu erledigen.

Die **Mitwirkung der Bevölkerung** wird bei der Zählung in sofern in Anspruch genommen, als die Haushaltungsvorstände dazu verpflichtet sind, die über die Personen ihrer Haushaltung verlangten schriftlichen Nachweise auf den hiezu bestimmten Formularen (Zähl-

Figure 1. Every census in the principality of Waldeck was announced several months in advance in the official government publication. This 1890 issue lists the eight types of literature (A through H) to be used in the campaign. [Stadtarchiv Korbach]

IV. Content of Census Records in Waldeck from 1826 to 1864

Surviving *Seelenregister* and census records have only been located for four years as of this writing, but pages used in other years likely resemble those used in other *Zollverein* states. In each year, the content is identical and included details on livestock owned by each family.

	1826	1832	1834	1836	1837	1840	1843	1846	1848	1852	1855	1858	1861	1864
No images available			X	X	X	X	X			X	X	X	X	X
First and last name of every person	X	X						X	X					
Age in years	X	X						X	X					
If married	X	X						X	X					
Status or occupation	X	X						X	X					
Type of real estate owned	X	X						X	X					
Type of real estate rented	X	X						X	X					
Pre-printed pages	X	X						X	X					

V. Accessibility of Census Records in Waldeck

During this study, census records were located in only two cities in the former principality of Waldeck, but inquiries may be directed by researchers to the archive of any city or town in historic Waldeck (see Appendix A for suggestions about writing such an inquiry). Currently there are no census records on microfilm in the Family History Library and no digital images of Waldeck census records on the Internet have been located.

VI. Selected Images of Waldeck Census Records

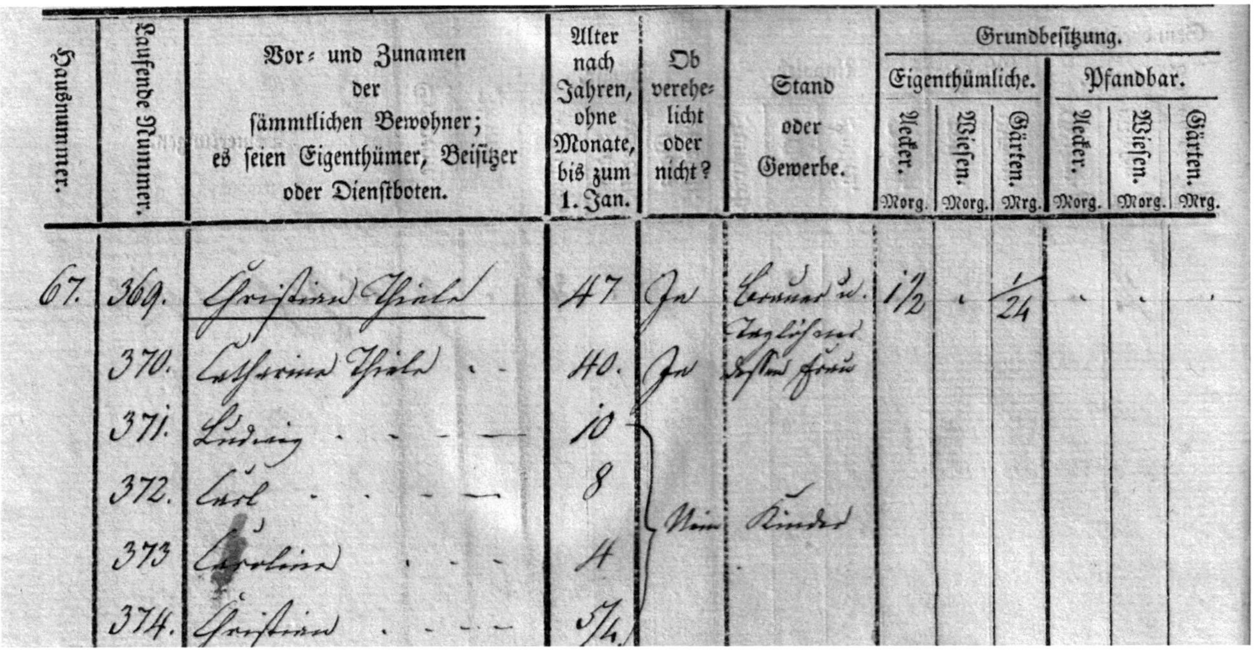

Figure 2. 1832 *Seelenregister* page from Korbach, Waldeck (left-hand page)

Column headings: first and last name of each resident; age in years; whether married; status or occupation; property owned (fields, meadows, gardens with acreage); [Stadtarchiv Korbach Abt. BIa Nr. 18]

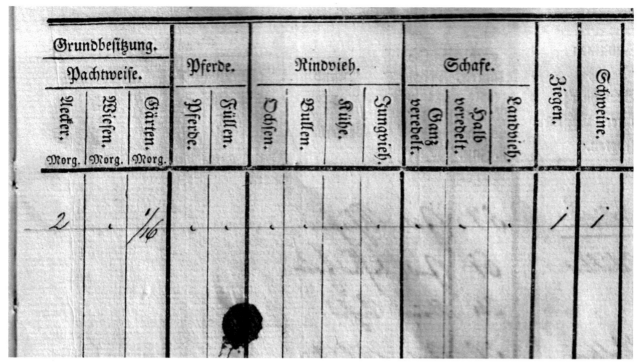

Figure 3. 1832 *Seelenregister* page from Korbach, Waldeck (right-hand page)

Column headings: properties rented (fields, meadows, gardens with acreage); horses (two categories); cattle (four categories); sheep (three categories); goats; pigs; comments (not shown) [Stadtarchiv Korbach Abt. BIa Nr. 18]

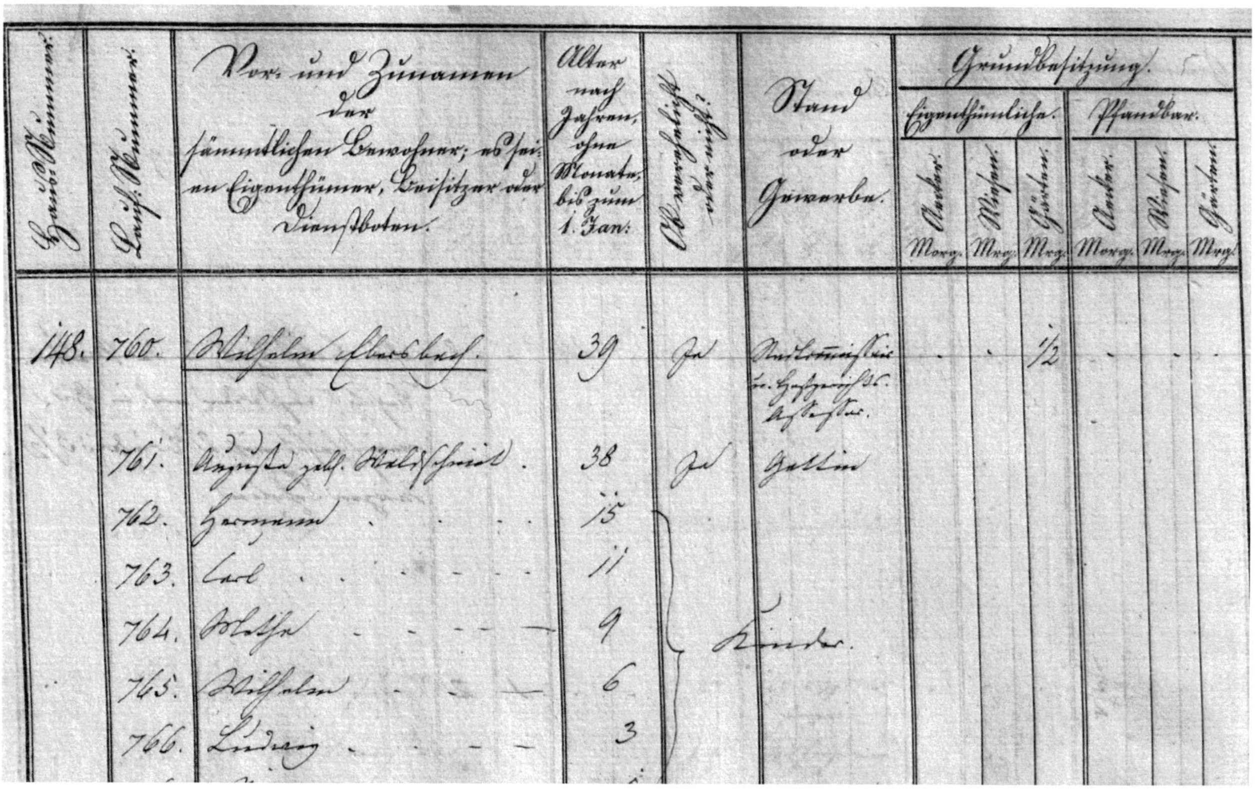

Figure 4. 1849 Census page from Korbach, Waldeck (left-hand page)

Column headings: first and last name of each resident; age in years; whether married; status or occupation; property owned (fields, meadows, gardens with acreage); [Stadtarchiv Korbach Abt. BIa Nr. 20]

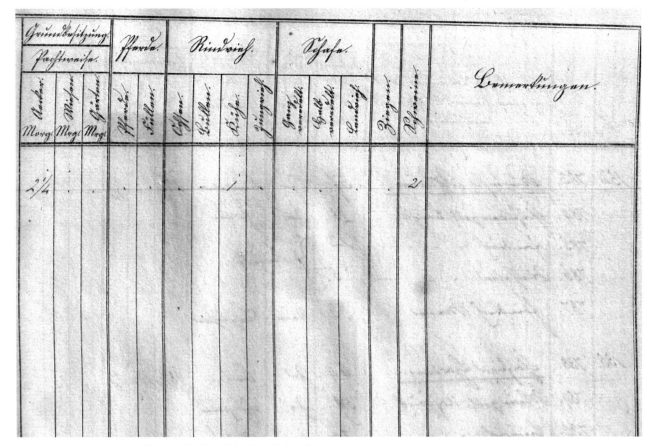

Figure 5. 1849 Census page from Korbach, Waldeck (right-hand page)

Column headings: properties rented (fields, meadows, gardens with acreage); horses (two categories); cattle (four categories); sheep (three categories); goats; pigs; comments [Stadtarchiv Korbach Abt. BIa Nr. 20]

Notes

[1] The term *Seelenregister* originated with parish priests who compiled lists of their parishioners. When used in government documents, the word simply means "list of persons."

[2] Fürstlich Waldeckische Regierung, "Verordnung wegen der Aufstellung der jährlichen Seelenregister," March 28, 1836. [Stadtarchiv Korbach 24.3 FüWaRe 1836].

[3] Antje Kraus, *Quellen zur Bevölkerungsstatistik Deutschlands 1815–1871*, Band 1 (Boppard, Germany: Harald Boldt, 1980), 27, 183–188.

[4] Those circulars are found in the holdings of the Korbach city archive.

40 Westfalen [Westphalia]

I. Location

The Prussian province of Westfalen lay in north-western Germany, across the border from the Netherlands. The Kingdom of Hannover lay to the north, the principality of Lippe and the duchy of Brunswick to the east. Sister provinces Hessen-Nassau and Rheinprovinz were neighbors to the southeast and the southwest respectfully. The capital city was Minden.

II. Census Enumerations in Westfalen

Following the Congress of Vienna, the kingdom of Preußen ruled over seven provinces in eastern Germany, but only two of the German states in the west—Westfalen and Rheinprovinz. All Prussian provinces were directed to produce and submit to the statistical bureau in Berlin annual statistical tables from 1817 to 1822. The schedule was then altered to require such data only every three years, but no set of strict standards guided the enumerations. City officials were to carry out the work.[1] Although the campaigns of the 1820s were designed to produce only statistics, the records of several years featured the names of heads of households.

In 1819, Westfalen and Rheinprovinz were grouped into a western Prussian customs union. Thus it was only logical that Westfalen automatically be accepted into the Prusso-Hessian Customs Union that was founded in February 1828. Census enumerations followed triennially and the schedule continued without interruption even after the establishment of the *Zollverein* [Customs Union] on January 1, 1834. Under the strong leadership of Prussia, the *Zollverein* required census records every three years for three full decades and the quality of those records steadily improved.

Another census was enumerated in Westfalen in 1867 in conjunction with all of the German states. Under the German Empire, enumerations were done in this province in 1871, every five years from 1875 to 1910, and finally in 1916.[2]

III. Specific Instructions to Town Officials and Enumerators

Significant new and revised instructions for Westfalen census campaigns are summarized as follows:

1840: the full name of each person is to be recorded; existing lists, e.g., lists of residents, may serve as a guide for this enumeration; use the forms provided; if two or more families inhabit the same dwelling, label them as a, b, c, d, etc.; local government officials are to carry out the process beginning on December 1; don't count travelers or active military personnel and their families; count locals temporarily away from home; count foreigners only if they have lived here for more than one year

1843: count inmates in hospitals and prisons

1846: if the city is very large, pass out the forms a few days in advance to be filled out by the heads of households and picked up by city officials on December 3; do not refer to other existing lists when compiling the census data

1858: if significant changes in the statistics since 1855 are determined, explain the basis for such changes

IV. Content of Census Records in Westfalen from 1822 to 1864

	1822	1825	1828	1831	1834	1837	1840	1843	1846	1849	1852	1855	1858	1861	1864
No images available	X	X				X						X			X
Name of house*			X	X	X		X								
Total residents			X	X	X		X	X	X	X	X		X	X	
Males under 14			X	X	X										
Females under 14			X	X	X										
Male young adults			X	X	X										
Female young adults			X	X	X										
Male adults up to 60			X	X	X										
Female adults up to 60			X	X	X										
Males over 60			X	X	X										
Females over 60			X	X	X										
Males 26–32			X	X	X										
Males 33–39			X	X	X										
Married males			X	X	X										
Married females			X	X	X										
Lutherans			X	X	X								X	X	
Catholics			X	X	X								X	X	
Jewish			X	X	X										
Blind persons (by gender)					X										
Demented (by gender)															
Name of every resident							X	X	X	X	X		X	X	
Status or occupation							X	X	X	X	X		X	X	
Age at last birthday							X	X	X	X	X		X	X	
Religion (Jewish, citizens?)							X	X	X	X	X		X	X	
Comments							X	X	X	X	X		X	X	
Handwritten column headings			X	X	X										
Pre-printed pages							X	X	X	X	X		X	X	

* In some parts of Germany, houses (dwellings) had names, many of which did not correspond to the surname of the family living in that house at any given time.

V. Accessibility of Census Records in Westfalen

None of the regional archives of the modern state of Nordrhein-Westfalen have substantial collections of census documents. Researchers should direct their inquiries to the archives of towns and counties, where excellent census records have been found in a few instances. (See Appendix A for suggestions about communicating with archivists.) Westfalen census records on microfilm in the Family History Library are rare, but a visit to the catalog now and then may turn up new holdings. As of this writing, only census records from the city of Minden are known to be available in digital form on the Internet.

VI. Selected Images of Westfalen Census Records

Figure 1. 1828 Census Page from Paderborn, Westfalen (left-hand page)

Column headings: number and name of the dwelling; total residents; males under 14; females under 14; young men; adult men; young women; adult women; males over 60; females over 60; males 15–25 [Stadtarchiv Paderborn]

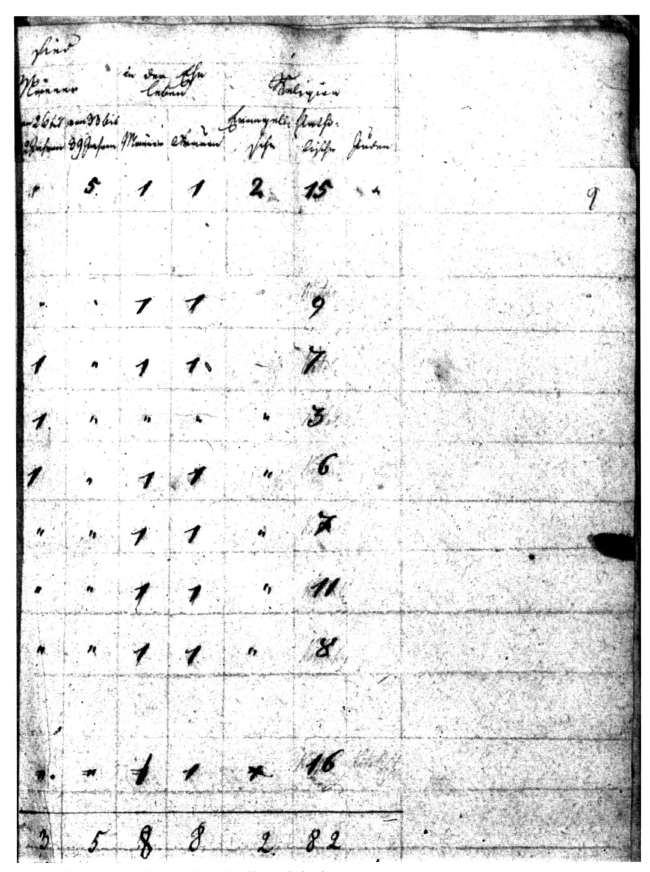

Figure 2. 1828 Census Page from Paderborn, Westfalen (right-hand page)

Column headings: males 26–32; males 33–39; males married; females married; Religion: Lutheran, Catholic, Jewish [Stadtarchiv Paderborn]

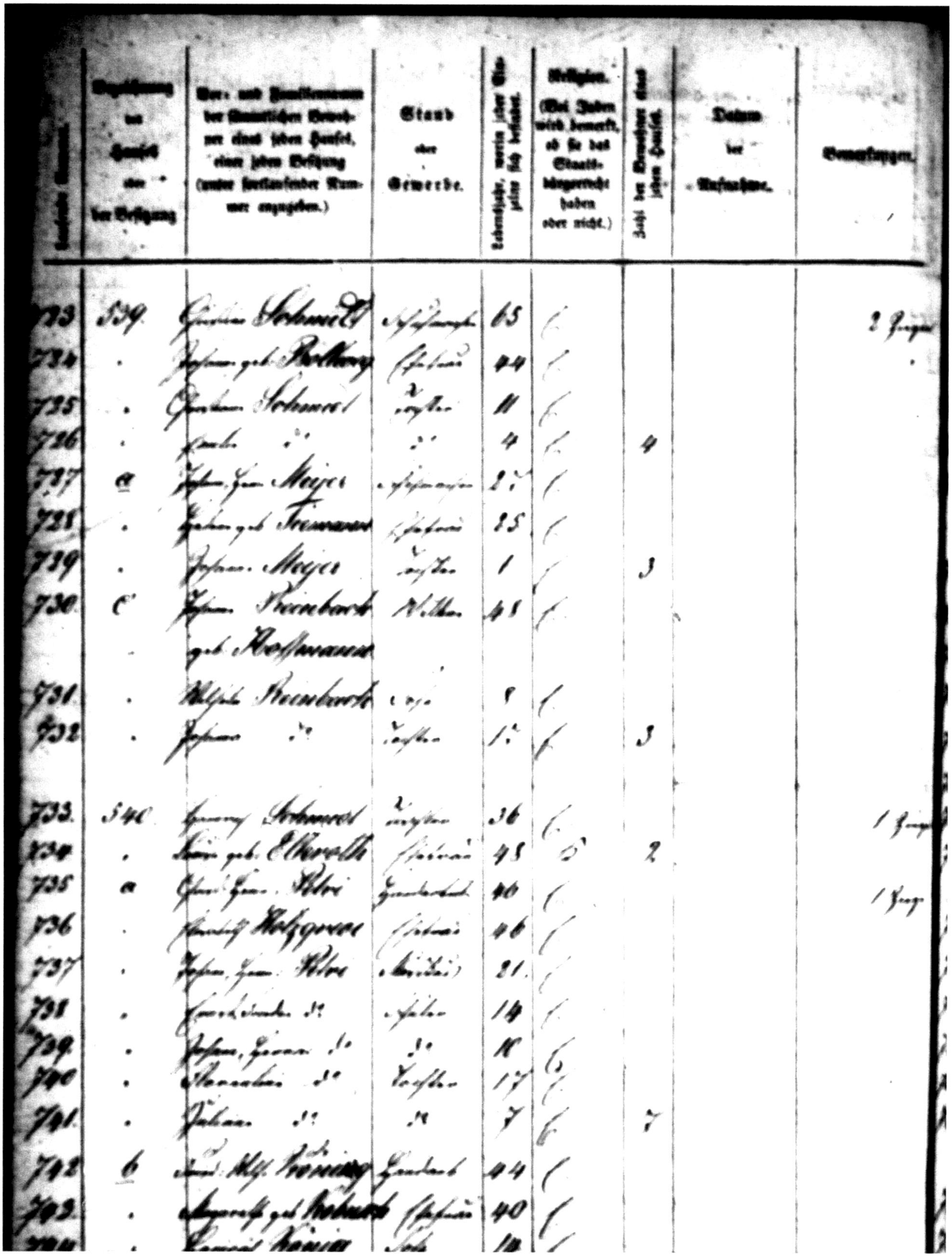

Figure 3. 1846 Census Page from Bielefeld, Westfalen

Column headings: consecutive number of individuals; number or description of the dwelling; first and last name of each resident; status or occupation; age at last birthday; religion (if Jewish, what citizenship status?); total residents; date of entry; comments [Stadtarchiv Bielefeld]

1. Durchlaufende № sämmtlicher Bewohner.	2. Bezeichnung des Hauses oder der Besitzung.	3. Vor= und Familien=Namen der sämmtlichen Bewohner eines jeden Hauses, einer jeden Besitzung (unter fortlaufender Nummer der Zahl der Bewohner eines jeden Hauses.) № Name. Zahl der Familien.	4. Stand oder Gewerbe.	5. Lebensjahr, worin jeder Einzelne sich befindet.	6. Religion. Evangelisch.	Katholisch.	Juden.	7. Zahl der Bewohner eines jeden Hauses.	8. Datum der Aufnahme.	9. Bemerkungen.
		Transport								13
1	Rabenhorst Feldmark No	1 Herman Sening geb. Niederbäumer	Schön	31	1			6. 3 Leg		
2		2 Johann Sening geb. Bönsel	Schmied daselbst	44	1					
3		3 Heinrich Bönsel	Schneider dem Knecht	22	1					
4		4 Diep. Hassenhorst	Knecht	24	1					
5		5 Heinr. Hollman	do	13	1					
6		6 Anna Roeggchen	Magd	22	1					
7	1 b	1 Herm. Hassenhorst	Haushalt	48	1			7.		
8		2 Wießlein Hassenh. geb. Steffens	Frau daselbst	50	1					
9		3 Johann Hassenh.	Sohn daselbst	20	1				1 Sohn das	
10		4 Wießlein H.	Tochter do	12	1					
11		5 Herm. Fleere	Haushalt	47	1					
12		6 Johann Fleere geb. Meyer	Frau daselbst	45	1					
13		7 Diep. Fleere	Sohn daselbst	20	1				1 Sohn das	
14	1 c	1 Herm. Krose	Haushalt	49	1			3.		
15		2 Anna Krose geb. Lindemann	Frau daselbst	45	1					
16		3 Johann Krose	Tochter daselbst	20	1				daselbst	
17	2. a	1 Herm. Deisdieckmann	Schön	40	1			5.		

Figure 4. 1861 Census Page from Herford, Westfalen

Column headings: number of person; description of dwelling; consecutive number of person in dwelling, and first and last name of each resident; status or occupation; age at last birthday; Religion: Lutheran, Catholic, Jewish, total residents; date of entry; comments [Stadtarchiv Herford]

Notes

[1] Harald Michel, "Volkszählungen in Deutschland: Die Erfassung des Bevölkerungsstandes von 1816 bis 1933," in *Jahrbuch für Wirtschaftsgeschichte* 1985/II, 85.

[2] Antje Kraus, *Quellen zur Bevölkerungsstatistik Deutschlands 1815–1871*, Band 1 (Boppard, Germany: Harald Boldt, 1980), 25–26, 207–212.

41 Westpreußen [West Prussia]

I. Location

The Prussian province of Westpreußen was surrounded on the west by the provinces of Brandenburg and Pommern, and on the north by the Baltic Sea. Two more sister provinces were neighbors— Ostpreußen to the east and Posen to the south, as was the Russian Empire.[1] The capital city was Danzig.

II. Census Enumerations in Westpreußen

The kingdom of Preußen ruled over seven provinces in eastern Germany and two in western Germany shortly after the Congress of Vienna. All Prussian provinces were to produce and submit to the statistical bureau in Berlin annual statistical tables from 1817 to 1822. The schedule was then altered to require such data only every three years, but no set of strict standards guided the enumerations. City officials were to carry out the work.[2] Although the campaigns of the 1820s were designed to produce only statistics, the records of several years featured the names of heads of households.

In 1818, Westpreußen was one of the seven eastern Prussian provinces to be grouped into a customs union. One year later, Westfalen and Rheinprovinz were grouped into a western Prussian customs union. The next predictable step was the inclusion of all nine Prussian provinces in the Prusso-Hessian Customs Union founded in February 1828.

Census enumerations followed triennially and the schedule continued without interruption even after the establishment of the *Zollverein* [Customs Union] on January 1, 1834. Under the strong leadership of Prussia, the *Zollverein* required census records every three years for three full decades and the quality of those records steadily improved.

Another census was enumerated in 1867 in conjunction with the North German Confederation and all German states participated. Under the German Empire, enumerations were done there in 1871, every five years from 1875 to 1910, and finally in 1916.[3]

III. Specific Instructions to Town Officials and Enumerators

Significant new and revised instructions for Westpreußen census campaigns have not been located, but the following regulations issued to other Prussian provinces were in effect in Westpreußen:

1825: if significant differences are found in comparison with the results of 1822, explain the causes of those differences

1840: we are sending you the forms to be used; each page has room for sixty names; police officials should conduct the campaign; do not begin to collect the data before December 1; the work must be completed in towns by December 20 and in cities by December 25, so that the reports can be received in Berlin by December 31; you are allowed to refer to documents previously compiled, such as lists of residents; do not count travelers in inns and active military and their dependents; local residents temporarily away from home are to be counted

1843: refer to the deficiencies in the 1840 census in order to produce more reliable results; count military personnel in reserve status; where the number of enumerators is insufficient, tax officials and retired military officers may be called into service and remunerated appropriately

1846: begin the collection of data on December 3; count all foreigners employed here but not persons traveling through the town; count inmates in prisons and hospitals; persons who own more than one dwelling should be counted where they live in the winter; do not refer to previous lists such as residential registration; in large cities, heads of households may fill out the forms themselves to save enumerators time

1852: the handwriting on the lists must be neat and orderly; should authorities at the next higher level identify mistakes in the local records, the cost of any required corrections shall be charged to the responsible authorities; owners of major estates are to count their respective populations and submit the lists to the local town authorities

1855: persons who refuse to cooperate will be fined

1858: local officials are to announce the upcoming census in the newspaper

1861: those persons who live in one location and work in another during the week are to be counted in the location where they spend the night before the census day; do not count persons in inns or visiting families; for persons living in one location and working in another, count them where they are on the night of December 2-3

1864: do not count persons who have been absent from their home town for more than one year; officials who do not carry out the census according to instructions are to be fined; an enumeration district should not include more than 600 people; non-government persons assigned to assist in the campaign may be paid a maximum of one *Thaler*; count only those foreigners who have lived here for at least one year; record the year of birth rather than the age; children in each family are to be listed in order of their birth

IV. Content of Census Records in Westpreußen from 1822 to 1864

No census images have been found as yet for the Prussian province of Westpreußen, but the following details have been gathered from Brandenburg, Pommern, and Sachsen and represent what would have been required by the statistical bureau in Berlin for Westpreußen as well.

	'22	'25	'28	'31	'34	'37	'40	'43	'46	'49	'52	'55	'58	'61	'64
No images available	X	X		X											
Name of each person			X				X	X	X	X	X	X	X	X	X
Name of head of household					X	X									
Married persons (by gender)			X												
Total residents			X		X	X	X	X	X	X	X	X	X	X	X
Age in years			X				X	X	X	X	X	X	X	X	X
Persons under 6 (by gender)			X		X	X									
Persons 7–9 (by gender)			X		X	X									
Persons 10–14 (by gender)			X		X	X									
Persons 15–60 (by gender)			X		X										
Persons over 60 (by gender)			X		X	X									
Lutherans			X		X	X							X	X	X
Catholics			X		X	X							X	X	X
Jewish (with citizenship status)					X	X							X	X	X
Persons 15–16 (by gender)						X									
Males 17–20						X									
Males 21–40						X									
Males 41–60						X									
Males over 60						X									
Females 17–45						X									
Females 46–60						X									
Females over 60						X									
Total females over 14						X									
Total males						X									
Total females						X									
Reformed Lutherans						X									
Mennonites						X									X
Comments			X					X	X	X	X	X	X	X	X
Status or occupation							X	X	X	X	X	X	X	X	X
Religion							X	X	X	X	X	X			
Blind													X		
Deaf													X		
Greek Orthodox															X
Dissidents															X
Other religions															X
Handwritten column headings			X		X										X
Pre-printed pages							X	X	X	X	X	X	X	X	X

V. Accessibility of Census Records in Westpreußen

The fact that this province was ceded to Poland following World War II complicates the search for original census regulations and lists of inhabitants. As part of this investigation, emails were sent to county and regional archives in what was once the province of Westpreußen, but none of those responded positively regarding census records in their collections.[4] Nevertheless, a letter written in Polish to an archive found through a search of websites sponsored by city, county, or regional governments might prove successful. (See Appendix A for suggestions on writing that inquiry in Polish.)

As of this writing, no Westpreußen census records are available in the Family History Library on microfilm and no digital images have been located on the Internet.

VI. Selected Images of Westpreußen Census Records

As of this writing, no images of census records have been found for this province.

Notes

[1] This is a simplified representation. The changes in borders among Prussian provinces in the nineteenth century are legion but not of specific importance here.

[2] Harald Michel, "Volkszählungen in Deutschland: Die Erfassung des Bevölkerungsstandes von 1816 bis 1933," in *Jahrbuch für Wirtschaftsgeschichte* 1985/II, 85.

[3] Antje Kraus, *Quellen zur Bevölkerungsstatistik Deutschlands 1815–1871*, Band 1 (Boppard, Germany: Harald Boldt, 1980), 25–26, 207–212.

[4] The author expresses his appreciation to Magdalena Zajac, a native Polish student at the University of Vienna, who conducted an extensive email campaign with archives in cities that once were in the provinces of Ostpreußen, Posen, Schlesien, and Westpreußen.

42 Württemberg [Wuerttemberg]

I. Location

The kingdom of Württemberg in southwestern Germany was bordered on the west by the grand duchy of Baden and the Prussian province of Hohenzollern, on the north by the grand duchy of Hessen, on the east by the kingdom of Bayern, and on the south by the Austrian Empire. The capital city was Stuttgart.

II. Census Enumerations in Württemberg

The first known census data was collected in Württemberg annually from 1816 to 1823.[1] In those days, the population of the current year was established by adding to the previous year's total the number of children born and subtracting the number of persons who died. The work was done by local pastors. In 1823, the frequency of census enumerations (by head count or by name) was reduced to every three years, but the annual numbers were collected until 1870.[2]

The first interstate German customs union was established by Württemberg and its neighbor, Bayern, in January 1828, but it appears that no census was conducted in connection with this treaty. Local practices simply continued. It was not until 1834, when the kingdom had joined with the much larger *Zollverein* [Customs Union], that a census was conducted under interstate guidelines.[3]

Within the *Zollverein's* system, census data were collected every three years through 1864.[4] In addition to this census, Württemberg continued to conduct its own census on a ten-year basis (1832, and 1842). A subsequent law stipulated census enumerations in 1846 and 1858. Those enumerations required much more data than those of the *Zollverein* campaigns, such as the age of the residents in eleven categories and the religious affiliation.

In 1867, the population of Württemberg was counted as part of a campaign carried out in all of the German states. Under the German Empire, enumerations were done in 1871, every five years from 1875 to 1910, and finally in 1916.

III. Specific Instructions to Town Officials and Enumerators

Instructions were sent out from Stuttgart every census year. The following were new or revised provisions:

1834: conduct the census in the last half of December

1843: begin the census on December 3 and finish the same day; larger cities may take three days; enumerators are to go to every dwelling; do not use any other existing record (such as residential registration); household forms may be distributed before the target date to be filled out by the head of household; the enumerator will pick them up on December 3; local authorities should decide who (whether civil or military) shall count active military personnel and their dependents; count all persons—local or foreign—except those staying in inns or visiting relatives; count locals who are temporarily away from home; persons who own more than one dwelling are to be counted where they live in the winter

1846: when pastors serve as enumerators, they are to be paid no more than 10 *Kreuzer* per 100 entries recorded

1855: count all residents in prisons and hospitals, as well as pupils and students in schools and training facilities of all kinds; do not count local journeymen away from home; single persons supporting themselves count as heads of households

IV. Content of Census Records in Württemberg from 1832 to 1864

	1832	1834	1837	1840	1843	1846	1849	1852	1855	1858	1861	1864
No images available	X					X			X	X	X	X
Name of head of household		X	X	X	X		X	X				
Adult males		X										
Adult females		X										
Males over 14		X	X	X	X		X	X				
Males under 14		X	X	X	X		X	X				
Females over 14		X	X	X	X		X	X				
Females under 14		X	X	X	X		X	X				
Servants and laborers (by gender)		X										
Total local residents		X										
Total locals living elsewhere in Württemberg (by gender)		X										
Total locals living in other countries (by gender)		X										
Foreigners from elsewhere in Württemberg (by gender)		X										
Foreigners from other countries (by gender)		X										
Total residents		X	X	X	X		X	X				
Comments		X										
Pre-printed pages		X	X	X	X		X	X				

V. Accessibility of Census Records in Württemberg

The main state archive in Stuttgart has a large collection of census instructions but almost no lists by towns. Fortunately, some local archives have census lists. The best tactic is to send an inquiry to the archive of the town or county where the persons in question are known or believed to have lived. (See Appendix A for suggestions on writing such an inquiry in German.) As of this writing, no census records for this kingdom have been found in the collection of the Family History Library, but a periodic search by specific location should be done as the collection increases. Currently there are no digital images of Württemberg census records on the Internet.

VI. Selected Census Images in Württemberg

111.

Haus-Nro.	Familie								Dienstboten.		Einger...
	Bewohner.	Männer.	Frauen.	Kinder.					Männliche.	Weibliche.	Männliche
				Männliche.		Weibliche.					
				über 14 Jahr.	unter 14 Jahr.	über 14 Jahr.	unter 14 Jahr.				
148.	Jos. Joseph Schädele snß		1.	2.			1.				
	Michael Stein manns snß		1.	1.	1.	1.					
	Annde Speck	1.	1.	1.		1					
	Joseph Nägele jung	1.	1.								
	phil. Spohn	1	1.		1.	1.					
149.							3				
150.	Jos. Benne müsig	1	1		1		1				1.

Figure 1. 1834 Census Page from Neckarsulm, Württemberg (left-hand page)

Column headings: house number; head of household; males; females; male children over 14; male children under 14; female children over 14; female children under 14; male servants/laborers; female servants/laborers: foreign male servants/laborers, foreign female servants/laborers (not shown) [Stadtarchiv Neckarsulm A1 9510]

Durch außerordentliche Zufälle.		Anzahl der sämtlichen Orts-Angehörigen.	Davon sind abwesend.				Dazu kommen Fremde.				Totalsumme sämtlicher im Ort befindlichen Personen.	Bemerkungen.
			In andern Orten des Königreichs.		Im Auslande.		Aus andern Orten des Königreichs.		Ausländer, die sich im Ort aufhalten.			
Männl.	Weibl.		Männl.	Weibl.	Männl.	Weibl.	Männl.	Weibl.	Männl.	Weibl.		

Figure 2. 1834 Census Page from Neckarsulm, Württemberg (right-hand page, format design)

Column headings: males here for other purposes; females here for other purposes; total local residents; males living in other places in Württemberg; females living in other places in Württemberg; males living in other states; females living in other states; males from other places in Württemberg; females from other places in Württemberg; males from other states; females from other states; total local residents; comments [Stadtarchiv Neckarsulm A1 9510]

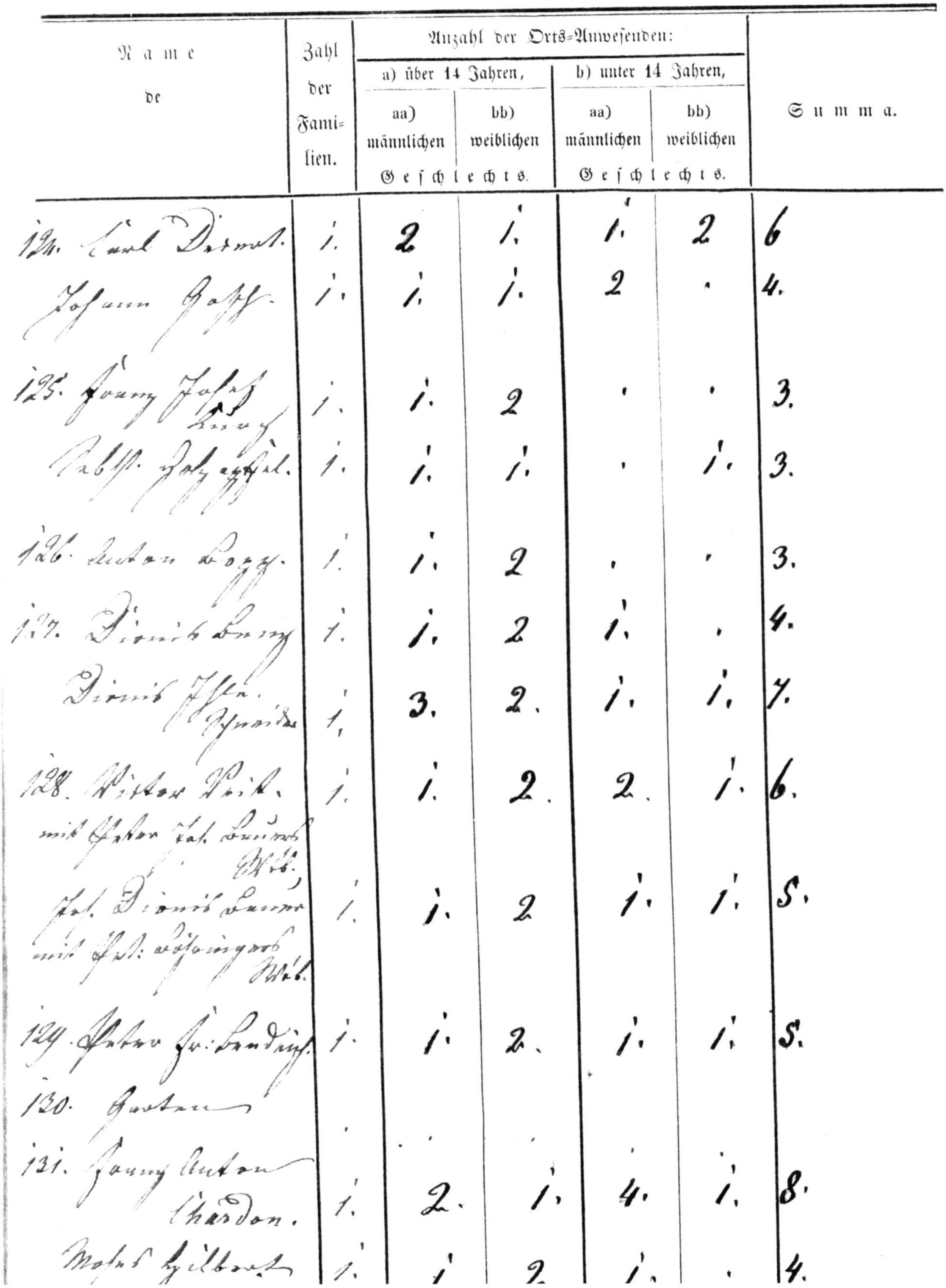

Name de	Zahl der Fami= lien.	Anzahl der Orts-Anwesenden:				Summa.
		a) über 14 Jahren,		b) unter 14 Jahren,		
		aa) männlichen	bb) weiblichen	aa) männlichen	bb) weiblichen	
		Geschlechts.		Geschlechts.		
124. Carl Diemel.	1.	2	1.	1.	2	6
Johann Roth.	1.	1.	1.	2	.	4.
125. Franz Jahs	1.	1.	2	.	.	3.
Rob. Roth ehefr.	1.	1.	1.	.	1.	3.
126. Anton Rogg.	1.	1.	2	.	.	3.
127. Dionis Burg	1.	1.	2	1.	.	4.
Dionis Hsn. Schneider	1.	3.	2.	1.	1.	7.
128. Wittwe Reik. mit Schw. Kat. Sennet Wb.	1.	1.	2.	2.	1.	6.
Kat. Dionis Laun mit Kat. Schwingod Wb.	1.	1.	2	1.	1.	5.
129. Peter Fr. Landirf.	1.	1.	2.	1.	1.	5.
130. Gurtner	.	.	.	.	.	
131. Franz Anton Chardon.	1.	2.	1.	4.	1.	8.
Matt. Hilbert	1.	1.	2	1.	.	4.

Figure 3. 1852 Census Page from Neckarsulm, Württemberg

Column headings: name of head of household; number of families; males over 14; females over 14; males under 14; females under 14; total residents [Stadtarchiv Neckarsulm A1A 9510]

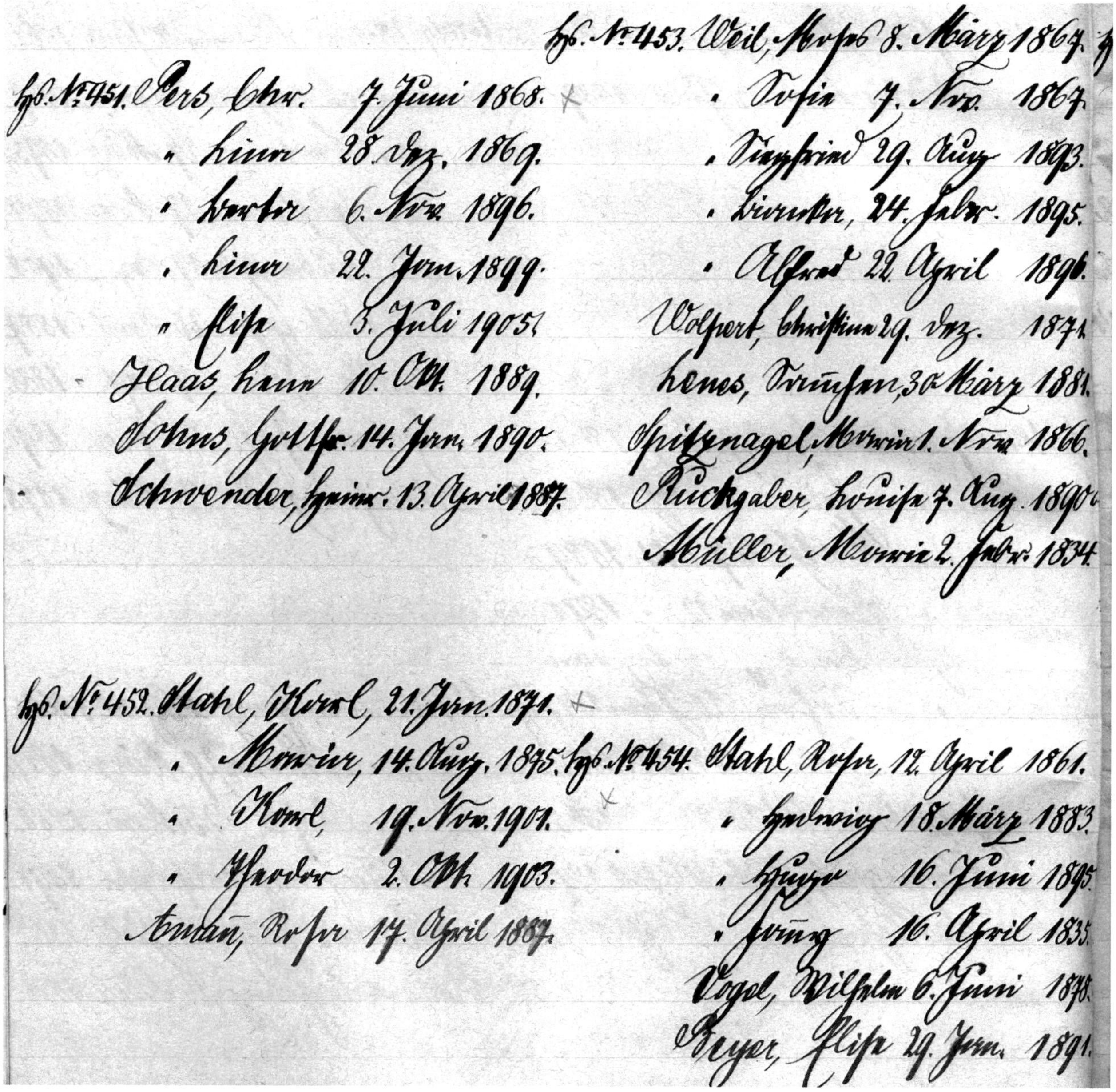

Figure 4. 1905 Census Page from Neckarsulm (extracted)

Residents of homes 451–454 in the census of 1905 in Bad Mergentheim [Stadtarchiv Bad Mergentheim, 065.02]

Notes

[1] Harald Michel, "Volkszählungen in Deutschland: Die Erfassung des Bevölkerungsstandes von 1816 bis 1933," in *Jahrbuch für Wirtschaftsgeschichte* 1985/II, 88.

[2] [anonymous], "Die Volkszahl der Deutschen Staaten nach den Zählungen seit 1816," in *Monatshefte zur Statistik des Deutschen Reichs für das Jahr 1879* [2], *Die Statistik des Deutschen Reichs*, Vol. 37/2; urn:nbn:de:zbw-drsa_3721 (Berlin: Verlag des Königlich Preussischen Statistischen Bureaus, 1879), 12.

[3] Antje Kraus, *Quellen zur Bevölkerungsstatistik Deutschlands 1815-1871*, Band (Boppard, Germany: Harald Boldt, 1980), 17-18, 33–38.

[4] Michel, "Volkszählungen in Deutschland," 88.

43 German Census Records 1816–1916: What Do We Know Now?

At the onset of this investigation into the phenomenon of census records in Germany from the Congress of Vienna in 1815 to the end of the German Empire in 1918, it was evident that American researchers of German ancestry knew very little about census records in the old country. The findings of the investigation led to the conclusion that German researchers are equally uninformed about census records. The eight questions formulated in the introduction of this book can now be answered and those answers might be informative to both groups of researchers. Indeed, perhaps researchers in other disciplines can also benefit from the results of this study.

1. *In which German states were censuses conducted?* Nearly every one of the states did populations counts that did not involve the recording of names. All thirty-eight states that became members of the German Empire in 1871 conducted census enumerations with names of persons more than once from 1816 to 1867.

2. *When were the censuses conducted?* Many states conducted census campaigns every three years beginning in 1834. Others were doing so as early as 1818. A few carried out census campaigns without strict schedules. Some states (especially the Prussian provinces) did as many as twenty-six census campaigns during the century under study.

3. *For what purposes were the censuses conducted?* The primary (and in many cases only) purpose for conducting a census that included the names of individuals was to facilitate the distribution of customs revenues collected by the unions discussed in the history section of this book. Census literature collected as part of the current investigation does not mention military or tax considerations, nor the use of population figures to determine representation in legislative bodies in the various German states (before 1871).

4. *What content did each census include?* The primary details in all census records during this period were the names of heads of households and the numbers of family members and other household inhabitants by gender. Secondary in frequency were the status or occupation of persons named, the numbers of persons in specific age categories, and details on birth dates and places. Many census enumerations also required data on inhabited structures, livestock, and even fruit trees. (Only census records featuring people are discussed in this book.)

5. *Do original census sheets exist?* The author of this book has personally seen more than 10,000 pages of original census records in many media. There are likely hundreds of thousands more in local archives, most of which have probably never been studied by genealogists. Multiple copies of such lists were rarely made during ongoing census campaigns. Unfortunately, it appears that the majority of the original lists (*Haushaltsvorstandslisten* and *Urlisten*) were destroyed soon after the statistics were collected. Some were probably discarded years later when their storage demanded too much space. Natural and man-made disasters may also have contributed to the loss of census documents.

6. *Where are original census records stored?* In 2009, Gehrmann was correct in writing the following about the loss (in many cases intentional) of original census records and the difficulties in gaining access to those that have survived: "In general, they are kept in local archives, and the central archives—and there is often more than one in each federal state—are not always informed of their existence. More research must be done in this field."[1] In general, the more local the archive, the more likely that census records will be found there. (In three humorous incidents, the author

was told by archivists that their holdings did not include census records, but within an hour in each archive, original census records were found.) Almost all original surviving census records are housed in government archives and libraries today. Some few are known to be held by historical societies. Whereas hundreds of archives contacted as part of this investigation indicated that census records are included in their holdings, hundreds more have yet to be contacted and might offer positive responses to the question.

7. *Have original census records been copied (microfilmed or digitized)?* Most original German census records have never been copied. Fortunately, the Family History Library in Salt Lake City, Utah, has produced perhaps one hundred microfilms featuring German census records (including some censuses that were compiled before 1816). As of this writing, very few German archives have produced microfilm or microfiche copies of their census records. A few repositories and commercial operations have begun to preserve census records by digital photography and the number of websites featuring such documents will certainly increase over time.

8. *How can researchers gain access to existing census records?* The Family History Library microfilms can be located in the Library's catalog under the names of the towns, counties, or provinces (https://familysearch.org/search). Nearly all of those microfilms are instantly available to patrons in the Library. With a few restrictions, microfilms can also be sent to more than 4,500 family history centers world-wide for study. Personal communication with German, French, and Polish archives can lead to information regarding what records exist and how they can be accessed (See Appendix A below for suggestions on writing such messages). Where archives have microfilmed their census records, researchers are usually not allowed to handle the original papers. Regarding the ever-increasing numbers of census images on the Internet, researchers should use tried-and-true search tactics to locate them. As with all family history research, those who don't have the time, effort, or knowledge to conduct research in German census records can engage qualified persons to do so for them. Some German archivists will do so at no cost, but most will require a modest fee. Still others will indicate that the best they can do is make the records available for visitors to study. This author has yet to find a census document that he was not allowed to copy (via camera or hand-scanner) or have copied by the archive staff (as photocopies or scans).

Notes

1   Gehrmann, Rolf. "German Census-Taking Before 1871," Restock, Germany: Max-Planck-Institut für demografische Forschung, 2009, 17.

Figure 1. Of course, a few old census records are no longer in excellent condition; this one shows fire damage.

44 Conclusions

Readers might wonder what role German census records could play in genealogical and family history research. The question is justified, given the fact that two other sources of personal information have dominated the research scene since the common man began to identify his ancestors:

1. Church records: records of baptisms, marriages, and burials began in Germany in the sixteenth century and have never been more than temporarily interrupted. The overwhelming majority of those records have been preserved.[1] Only rare church records (principally in Württemberg) feature lists of families.

2. Civil registration: government records of births, marriages, and deaths did not begin in Germany until 1874 in Preußen and 1876 in the Reich (with the exception of the Rheinprovinz, the Bavarian Palatinate, and a few northern German cities in 1798). Civil registration records for entire families are rare.

In other words, before 1874, at least eighty percent of the German population is covered only by church records. What happens then in the cases where church records no longer exist, or for those few persons (Jewish, separatists, sectarians, et al.) whose names were never recorded by local pastors? Are their genealogical data found in other records? Military rolls and lists of emigrants have such data at times, but only a small portion of the population emigrated and only men over fourteen (and relatively few of them) served in the military (where most records have not survived). Tax and land records rarely contain genealogical data and were not always preserved. Lists of citizens and voters may have sporadic dates and places, but only for certain men. In these and many other cases, the surviving census record takes on greater significance.

In the enumerations featuring entire households, the census is of critical importance. When only the head of household is listed, researchers have a chance to find him or her and thus answer the most important question in genealogical research: where did my ancestor live? Census pages that inquired about the birth places of the residents are all the more valuable.

Because this study did not discover any census regulations that required the preservation of the actual lists until 1852, it is likely that the majority of those pages were indeed discarded sooner or later. However, so many have been found that it is this investigator's recommendation that researchers consider the possibility that such pages are still kept carefully in the holdings of small archives—possibly by archivists who are unaware of the existence of those documents.[2]

If veteran genealogist Eike Pies (as quoted above) immediately recognized the potential value of extant census records, many other researchers will want to try their hands at locating records in their target locations.

The investigation that led to the writing of this book shows that census records can be difficult to find. Thus success in this regard cannot be guaranteed, but it takes little time, effort, or expense to compose and send an inquiry. Even among those researchers whose Germanic family trees are apparently complete as far back as church records support the work, one question will likely always linger: "Is there perhaps just one more record somewhere about these people?" The local census might just be that "one more record."

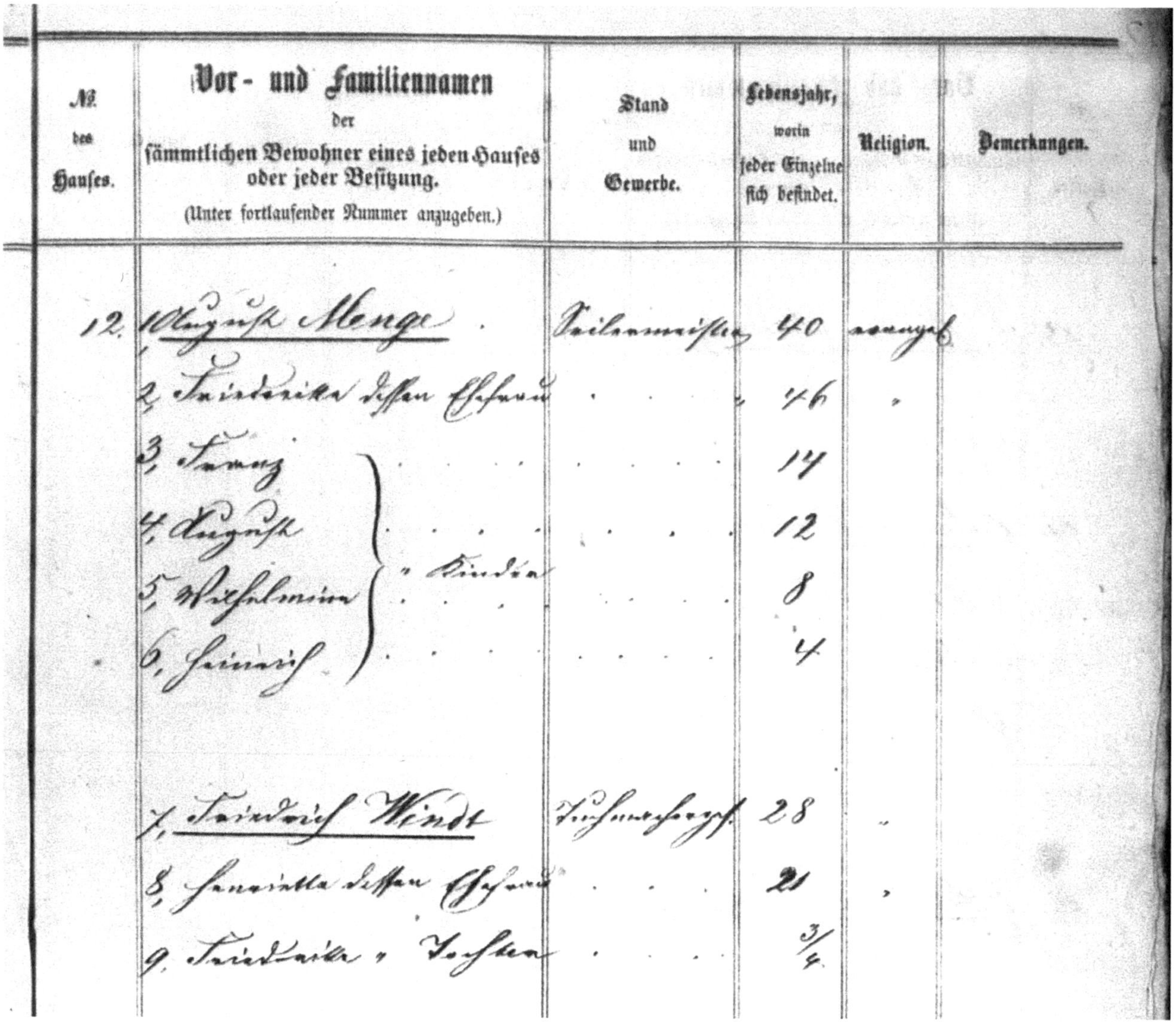

№ des Hauses.	Vor- und Familiennamen der sämmtlichen Bewohner eines jeden Hauses oder jeder Besitzung. (Unter fortlaufender Nummer anzugeben.)	Stand und Gewerbe.	Lebensjahr, worin jeder Einzelne sich befindet.	Religion.	Bemerkungen.
12.	1 August Menge	Teilenmüller	40	evangel.	
	2 Friedericke dessen Ehefrau	"	46	"	
	3 Franz		14		
	4 August		12		
	5 Wilhelmine	" Kinder	8		
	6 Heinrich		4		
	7 Friedrich Wendt	Fischerknecht	28	"	
	8 Henriette dessen Ehefrau	"	21	"	
	9 Friedrike " Tochter		3/4		

Figure 1. "Look, Howard! There was a son named Franz who didn't come to Baltimore with the family in 1853. He might have died or just stayed in Germany. We didn't know anything about him!" [1849 census for Coswig, Anhalt; Stadtarchiv Coswig]

Notes

[1] This writer's experience over forty years leads him to believe that at least 85% of the German church records ever written exist today in some medium.

[2] The author of this study was told by the directors of several archives that their collections did not include actual census lists. In each case, the author found such lists in the archive the same day.

Writing to Archives in Germany, France, and Poland

As is the case with all genealogical research in Germany, researchers need to know how to correctly and efficiently formulate letters and emails to staff members in archives on all levels of jurisdiction—public and private. In the case of census records, the archives will be entities of the governments of towns, counties, provinces, and states (depending upon the organization of archives in each of the modern states of the Federal Republic of Germany).

Conclusions may be drawn from the correspondence campaign carried out in preparation for the current book. More than one thousand letters and emails were sent and perhaps one-half of those received a response. The best responses came from city archives, while responses from archives at higher levels were progressively less satisfying. The author agrees with Gehrmann's conclusion, "In general, [census records] are kept in local archives, and the central archives—and there is often more than one in each federal state—are not always informed of their existence. More research must be done in this field."[1] This book represents such research.

You should send the first communication to the lowest possible level of archive jurisdiction. The higher one goes in the system, the less likely a positive response will be received.

External and internal German borders have undergone a great number of changes since 1916—the end of this investigation. Before writing to an archive, the researcher must determine the current geopolitical situation of the town in question. For example, the states of Lippe (Detmold), Schaumburg-Lippe, Oldenburg, and Waldeck (to name only a few) have totally disappeared from the map, having been subsumed by larger modern states formed following World War II.

The entire principality of Lippe (Detmold) is now situated within the borders of the state of Nordrhein-Westfalen. Recent inquiries to Lippe towns were forwarded to regional archives in the cities of Detmold and Minden. And the list goes on.

The first task is to determine the county and state of the target town during the years of the German Empire (1871–1918). The primary tool for that search is *Meyers Orts und Verkehrsverzeichnis des Deutschen Reichs* [Meyer's Commerce Directory for the German Empire].[2] Access to this key resource is possible through various leading genealogical websites. Once the location of the town has been identified, other websites will establish the current county and state of that town. Wikipedia will usually provide such details.

The next step is to locate the address of the town archive in question. The finest tool for this task is the Internet. To begin, use the German pattern to locate the official website of that town: www.[townname].de. For example, www.fulda.de and www.darmstadt.de will quickly take you to the official city websites of Fulda and Darmstadt.

Unfortunately, there is no common organization for city websites in Germany. Some have excellent organizational trees that will guide you to the archive's address (*Archiv* is a convenient cognate) and even provide the names of staff members. Other websites seem to disregard the existence of a town archive.

In searching for the town's archive, it will help to know these terms:

Gemeinde: city, town, community

Verwaltung(en): administration

Bürgerservice: services to residents

Ämter: offices

Personal: personnel

Kommunal: public

Öffentlich: public

Mitarbeiter: colleagues, employees

Bürgermeister: mayor

Some websites have a translation option to render the text in English.

Efficient searching or good luck or both will lead you to the archive and even the archivist. Take careful note of the name and email address of the director. If your best efforts do not lead to the discovery of the archive, you may write to the office of the mayor or the director of personnel and ask to have the message forwarded to the archive. (For regular letters, see additional instructions below.) A good default email address is info@[town name].de as in info@darmstadt.de.

The next step is to compile a message that is short and precise. You don't need to indicate the reason for your search for census documents, just give the name(s) of the person(s) in question, any genealogical data you have for that person, and—above all—the best information you have about where that person lived. Indicate in what medium you prefer to receive the documents (as photocopies or as scans), and that you are willing to pay for the service. Provide both your regular mailing address and an email address to facilitate a timely response.

For many reasons, this communication should be done in German. There are now many Internet websites that offer translation services at no fee (often limiting the text to 150 words), but some of them are not very accurate. If you use a website translation, have a qualified writer of German check out the text for mistakes that only a computerized dictionary can make. (You will often find such mistakes in the English versions of German websites—some are humorous while others inhibit communication.) The table below provides several phrases that can be used to construct your message.

While it is possible that you will receive the documents as scans without an invoice, plan on paying for the research and the copies that represent a positive response. Many archivists will not charge if they spend only a small amount of time and find nothing. Others will indicate in advance that you will owe a minimum fee (specified) even if their search is fruitless. Others will do the work and indicate that they will send the documents as soon as you have paid the invoice; this practice does not involve any risk on your part.

Waiting for a response can at times be difficult. Archivists are often overworked and understaffed. You should wait at least two weeks before sending another email. Ask for confirmation of receipt of your inquiry and keep a careful record of correspondence, including the date you sent the inquiry, the addressee, and the information requested.

Few American researchers have bank accounts in Germany, so most will need to find a way to obtain a bank check in Euro. Again, the Internet features several websites where such checks can be purchased. Remember that your personal check cannot be used in Germany. If you choose to send a bank check in dollars, add at least ten percent to the required amount to cover the conversion fee the archivist will have to pay when cashing the check at the city's German bank. If you pay by bank transfer, you will need two codes from the archive: the IBAN and the BIC. Both will be shown on their stationery. If not, you need to request those in another email.

Pay any required fee without delay; you or others will be writing to that archive again and a good relationship is most important.

Acknowledge any response from an archive with a short email. The archivists will want to know that you received the message and any documents they sent, and that attached images can be read.

If writing a letter for air mail delivery to Germany, be sure that you use the correct mailing address for the archive, including the five-digit postal code that precedes the name of the city. Check the U.S. Postal website for current air mail rates. Your letter should consist of only one page and will thus cost the minimum for international air mail.

If you receive copies of important documents and choose to publish them in articles or books, you should be aware that essentially even the smallest archive requires that you request permission before doing so. Some will want a copy of your publication while others only copies of the pages where their documents appear. Some archivists will give permission up front to use the documents without restriction, but the best approach is to have written permission in every case (which was a true challenge in the writing of this book). Of course, there is little chance that your publications will land on the desk of an archivist in a small German town and any fraudulent use thereof be discovered, so this is a matter of an author's integrity. Finally, be sure to request the official citation for any document used as an image or to which you refer in your text.

Dear Sir [archivist, mayor, etc.]	*Sehr geehrter Herr [Archivar, Bürgermeister, etc.]*
Dear Madam	*Sehr geehrte Frau [Archivarin, etc.]*
Dear Director	*Sehr geehrte Frau Direktorin, Sehr geehrter Herr Direktor*
I am looking for census documents	*Ich bin auf der Suche nach Volkszählungsurkunden …*
… for the year [1843 etc.]	*… aus dem Jahre [1843 etc.]*
… for the years [1834 to 1846.]	*… aus den Jahren [1834 bis 1846]*
The person I am looking for was…	*Die gesuchte Person hieß …**
The people I am looking for were …	*Die gesuchten Personen hießen…*
They lived in the town of [name]	*Sie wohnten in der Ortschaft [name]***
They lived in the county of [name]	*Sie wohnten im Kreis [name]*
I would like photocopies of any documents you find regarding this person.	*Ich hätte gern Fotokopien von allen Urkunden, die Sie bezüglich dieser Person finden.*
I would like scans if possible of any documents you find regarding this person.	*Ich hätte gern Scans (wenn möglich) von allen Urkunden, die Sie bezüglich dieser Person finden.*
I will be pleased to pay the usual fee for photocopies and/or scans and/or postage.	*Ich bin gern bereit, die anfallenden Gebühren für Fotokopien und/oder Scans und/oder Porto zu begleichen.*
I can send you a bank check in Euro as payment.	*Ich kann Ihnen einen Bankscheck in Euro schicken.*
My bank can transfer the money to your account.	*Meine Bank kann den Betrag direkt auf Ihr Konto überweisen.*
Please provide your IBAN and BIC.	*Teilen Sie mir bitte Ihren IBAN und BIC mit.*
Thank you for your kind assistance.	*Vielen Dank für die freundliche Hilfe.*
With best regards,	*Mit freundlichen Grüßen,*
Did you receive my inquiry of May 15?	*Haben Sie meine Anfrage vom 15. Mai bekommen?*
I am still very interested in this information.	*Ich bin immer noch sehr an diesen Informationen interessiert.*
I hope you will find time soon to help me.	*Ich würde mich freuen, wenn Sie mir schon bald weiterhelfen könnten.*

*Word processing programs have fonts that include ß (double s) and *Umlaut* characters (ä ö ü Ä Ö Ü), as well as the Euro symbol €.
** Use only the German spellings of place names (not Munich for *München* or Cologne for *Köln*).

A simple request might look like this:

Dear Director,

I am looking for census records of the years 1852 to 1864. The person I am looking for is Adam Henrich Meinert. He lived in Jeggen in Osnabrück County. I would like photocopies of any documents you find regarding this person. I will be pleased to pay the usual fee for photocopies and postage. I can send you a bank check in Euro as payment. Thank you for your kind assistance.

With best regards,
Melanie Minert Bell
[Complete mailing address]

The German version reads (in just 68 words):

Sehr geehrte Frau Archivarin,

Ich suche Volkszählungensurkunden aus den Jahren 1852 bis 1864. Der gesuchte Mann hieß Adam Henrich Meinert. Er wohnte in Jeggen, Kreis Osnabrück. Ich möchte Fotokopien von allen Urkunden, die Sie bezüglich dieser Person finden. Ich bin gern bereit, die anfallenden Gebühren für Fotokopien und Porto zu begleichen. Meine Bank kann den Betrag unmittelbar an Ihr Konto überweisen. Vielen Dank für die freundliche Hilfe.

Mit freundlichen Grüßen
Melanie Bell geb. Minert
[Complete mailing address]

Writing to Archives in France

In writing to archives in France (for a location in Germany before 1918), you may use the following version of the above letter and replace the underlined names of persons and places as appropriate:

A l'attention de l'archiviste:
Monsieur,

J'effectue des recherches concernant les recensements allemands, de 1852 à 1864.

La personne que je recherche s'appelait Franz Josef Kurscheid.

Il vivait à Bitschweiler dans le district d'Weissenburg.

Vous serait-il possible de me fournir des photocopies de tous les documents que vous puissiez trouver concernant cette personne.

Je suis prêt à payer les frais de photocopies et d'affranchissement. Ma banque peut également transférer le montant directement sur votre compte.

Je vous remercie pour votre aide.

Cordialement
Avec mes sincères salutations

Payments to French archives will be requested in Euro.

Writing to Archives in Poland

If you need to write to an archive in Poland (for a location in Germany before 1945), you may use the following message with your specific persons and places:[2]

Szanowni Państwo,

Poszukuję dokumentów ewidencji ludności stałej, dotyczących pana Friedricha Karla Kujauda z lat 1852–1864. Pan Kujaud zamieszkiwał w Wylatkowie, gmina Witkowo. Jeżeli znajdują się u państwa owe dokumenty, prosiłbym o kopię wszystkich Akt dotyczących tej osoby.

Jestem gotowy uiścić opłatę za pańską pracę, fotokopie i przesyłkę według cennika Archiwum w formie bezpośredniego Przelewu na podane przez pana konto.

Z poważaniem

Payments to Polish archives might be requested in dollars or *Zloty*. Pay precisely as requested. Use the conversion and payment methods described above for German remittances. Response times from archives in Poland tend to be a bit longer than from Germany.

Addressing Envelopes (examples)

Stadtarchiv Darmstadt	[all terms and titles in native language]
Karolinenplatz 3	[house number follows street name]
64289 Darmstadt	[postal code precedes city name]
Germany	[country of destination in English]

Archiv de Wissembourg	
11 place de la République	[not all proper nouns like *place*
67160 Wissembourg	are capitalized in French]
France	

Archiwum Panstwowe we Wrocławiu	[city name is declined for grammatical case]
ul. Pomorska 2	[*ul.* = *ulica* = street and is not capitalized]
50- 215 Wrocław	[do not use the German name = Breslau]
Poland	

Notes

[1] Gehrmann, Rolf. "German Census-Taking Before 1871," Restock, Germany: Max-Planck-Institut für demografische Forschung, 2009, 17.

[2] Gazetteers are also available for each German state of the Empire period, but they are often difficult to locate. Internet searches will likely bring good results in some cases.

[3] The author expresses appreciation to Magdalena K. Zajak for her kind assistance in the translation of communications from and to archives in Poland.

B Conducting Census Research in Archives in Germany, France, and Poland

Should you be fortunate to have the time and money to invest in a trip to Europe to pursue census records, you have a lot of work to do before you go. Finding a copy of the book *Researching in Germany* would be the best way to start, because it was written with you in mind. In general, you would do well to consider the following points:[1]

1. Begin planning your trip at least six months in advance.

2. Write out specific goals for your research.

3. If possible, study the online catalog of any archive that might have the documents you need.

4. Communicate carefully with each archive regarding your research goals.

5. Know the archive's schedule for visitors; many have different hours (or no hours) on different days of the week (and watch out for holidays). Only a very few are open on Saturdays.

6. Make appointments for every research venue (ask for a day or two more than you need).

7. Plan enough time at each venue to study everything you need to see. Moving to the next venue before you are done can be very disappointing. Returning may be impossible.

8. Order all possible files and documents in advance of your visit.

9. Bring a camera or scanning equipment in case you are allowed to copy documents.

10. Have your computer equipment in order (including flash drives and backup hardware).

11. Engage research assistants or translators/interpreters before your arrival. Archivists can generally recommend competent helpers who speak English and read the old German handwriting; the fee should be negotiated in advance.

12. You will almost always be allowed to make copies, but never do so by camera or hand scanner without specific permission. If archive personnel make the copies, you may need to exercise great patience. Filling out copy requests takes time. The copies will usually be made after you leave and will be mailed or emailed to you with an invoice several weeks later.

13. Send thank-you cards to anybody who helped you significantly.

Of course, this list deals only with things you should consider that regard archives. There are many more aspects of the trip that must be carefully addressed, such as air and ground travel, lodging, and meals. If planned well, such a trip can be the adventure of a lifetime for a family history researcher.

Notes

[1] Roger P. Minert et al., *Researching in Germany*, 2nd ed. (Provo, UT: Picton Press, 2013).

Interesting Documents Relating to German Census Campaigns

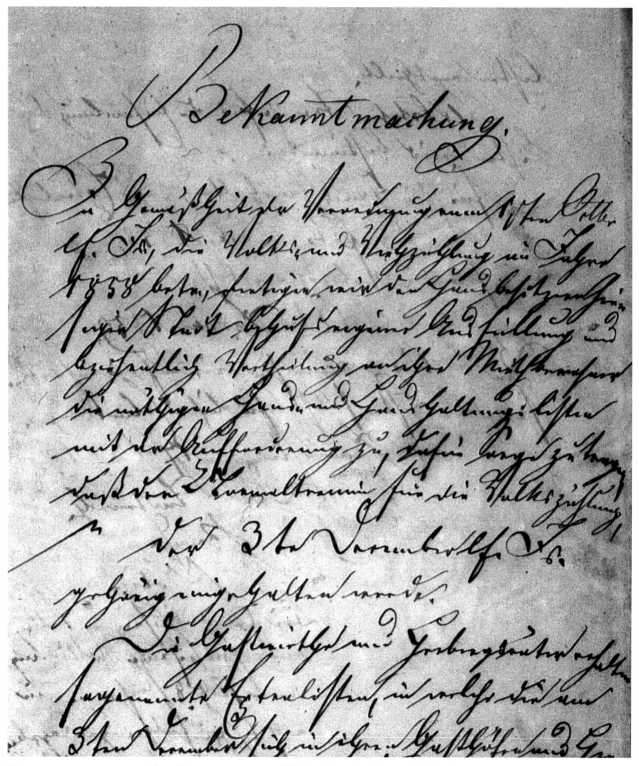

This announcement was issued from the Interior Ministry of the kingdom of Sachsen in the fall of 1858: "Proclamation! In cooperation with the *Zollverein* [Customs Union], there will be a census conducted on December 3, 1858..." [Kreisarchiv Brand-Erbisdorf]

Regierungs-Blatt

für das

Großherzogthum
Sachsen-Weimar-Eisenach.

Nummer 28.	Weimar.	10. Oktober 1895.

Inhalt: Ministerial-Bekanntmachung, betr. die Volkszählung am 2. Dezember 1895, Seite 389. — Ministerial-Bekanntmachung, betr. Wechsel in der Hauptagentur der Internationalen Unfallversicherungs-Aktien-Gesellschaft in Wien, Seite 395.

Ministerial-Bekanntmachungen.

[96] I. Nach Beschluß des Bundesrathes findet am 2. Dezember d. J. in allen Deutschen Staaten eine Volkszählung statt.

Indem das unterzeichnete Staats-Ministerium dies hierdurch zur öffentlichen Kenntniß bringt und sämmtlichen zur Leitung und Ausführung derselben im Großherzogthum berufenen Behörden diejenige strenge Sorgfalt und Gewissenhaftigkeit dringend zur Pflicht macht, welche die genannte für die verfassungsmäßigen Zwecke des Deutschen Reichs wie für die Staatsverwaltung des Großherzogthums gleich wichtige Angelegenheit erfordert, werden zugleich folgende, auf Beschlüssen des Bundesrathes und bezüglich des unterzeichneten Staats-Ministeriums beruhende Bestimmungen zur Kenntnißnahme und pünktlichen Beachtung besonders hervorgehoben.

§ 1.

Durch die Volkszählung soll die ortsanwesende Bevölkerung, das ist die Gesammtzahl der innerhalb der Grenzen der einzelnen Staaten in der Nacht vom 1. auf den 2. Dezember ständig oder vorübergehend anwesenden Personen, festgestellt werden.

1895

59

This announcement of the 1895 census was directed to all government officials in Sachsen-Weimar-Eisenach through the state's official publication. [Stadtarchiv Weimar]

Helmstedter

Kreis=  Blat.

Das Helmstedter Kreisblatt erscheint, mit Ausnahme der Festtage, jeden Montag, Mittwoch und Freitag Abend nebst wöchentlich einem Bogen Unterhaltungsblatt. — Preis vierteljährlich 25 ℊ. — Alle Herzogl. Postanstalten nehmen Bestellungen an.

Insertionsgebühr für die dreispaltige Bourgeoiszeile oder deren Raum für das Inland ½ ℊ., für das Ausland 1 Xunahme von Insertionen am betreffen Tage nur bis 9 Uhr Morgens. —diese werden franco erbeten.

№ 140.   Mittwoch, den 27. November.   1867.

Bekanntmachung.

Da in Folge der Verordnung vom 31. v. Mts.

am nächsten Dienstage, den 3. December d. J.

eine Volkszählung in hiesiger Stadt nebst Zubehör vorzunehmen ist, so werden die hiesigen Einwohner hiermit aufgefordert, den Zählern bei deren große Umsicht und Genauigkeit erheischenden, ohnehin lästigen Geschäfte jede thunliche Unterstützung zu leisten, insbesondere die von denselben über Familie und Hausgenossen verlangte Auskunft bereitwillig und gewissenhaft zu ertheilen.

Helmstedt, den 27. November 1867.

Der Stadtmagistrat.

F. Claus. Louis Löfer. C. Böwing.

Deutschland.

Berlin, 25. Nov. In diplomatischen Kreisen hält man nach wie vor die Conferenz-Angelegenheit für schwankend und das Zustandekommen für fraglich. Preußen — dies wird man mit Sicherheit annehmen können — hat sich mit der Mehrzahl der Mächte verständigt, um seinerseits die Lücke eines Programms für die Conferenz auszufüllen. Das, was man jetzt

bis zum Betrage von 50 Thlr. bereits nach dem in hußen geltenden Tarif vereinbart. In dem Vertrage mit Oreich ist stipulirt, daß dieses Verfahren von einem durch bPostverwaltungen näher zu verabredenden Termine an in Xsamkeit treten soll.

— Der Rothstand in der Provinz Preußen wächj Die Provinz steht, wenn nicht rasch und durchgreifend geholßwird, vor der Gefahr des Hungertyphus.

— An der Expedition gegen Abyssinien werden ß auch einige preußische Offiziere betheiligen.

— Die peruanische Regierung sucht zur Begründn von Colonien europäische Einwanderer anznlocken. Die Prazialbehörden sind aufgefordert worden, vor der Auswarung nach Peru dringend zu warnen.

— Vom Central-Bureau des Zollvereins ist eine gleichung der gemeinschaftlichen Zolleinnahmen im 1. und Xuartal des Jahres 1867 mit denen der ersten Hälfte ₺Worjahres aufgestellt worden. Danach beliefen sich diese nahmen im Jahre 1867 auf 11 Millionen 53,835 X im norigen Jahre aber auf 9 Mill 775.407 Thlr Mjßflt

---

The upcoming census was front-page news to the citizens in Helmstedt when the local newspaper appeared on November 27, 1867 ("Bekanntmachung"): "Announcement. Based on the ruling of October 31, a census of this city will be conducted next Tuesday, December 3, 1867. Local citizens are called upon to offer all possible support to the enumerators in this demanding and burdensome [!] task. All families and residents are requested to supply the correct information and to do so willingly. Helmstedt on November 27, 1867. The city council. F. Claus. Louis Löfer. C. Böwing." [Stadtarchiv Helmstedt]

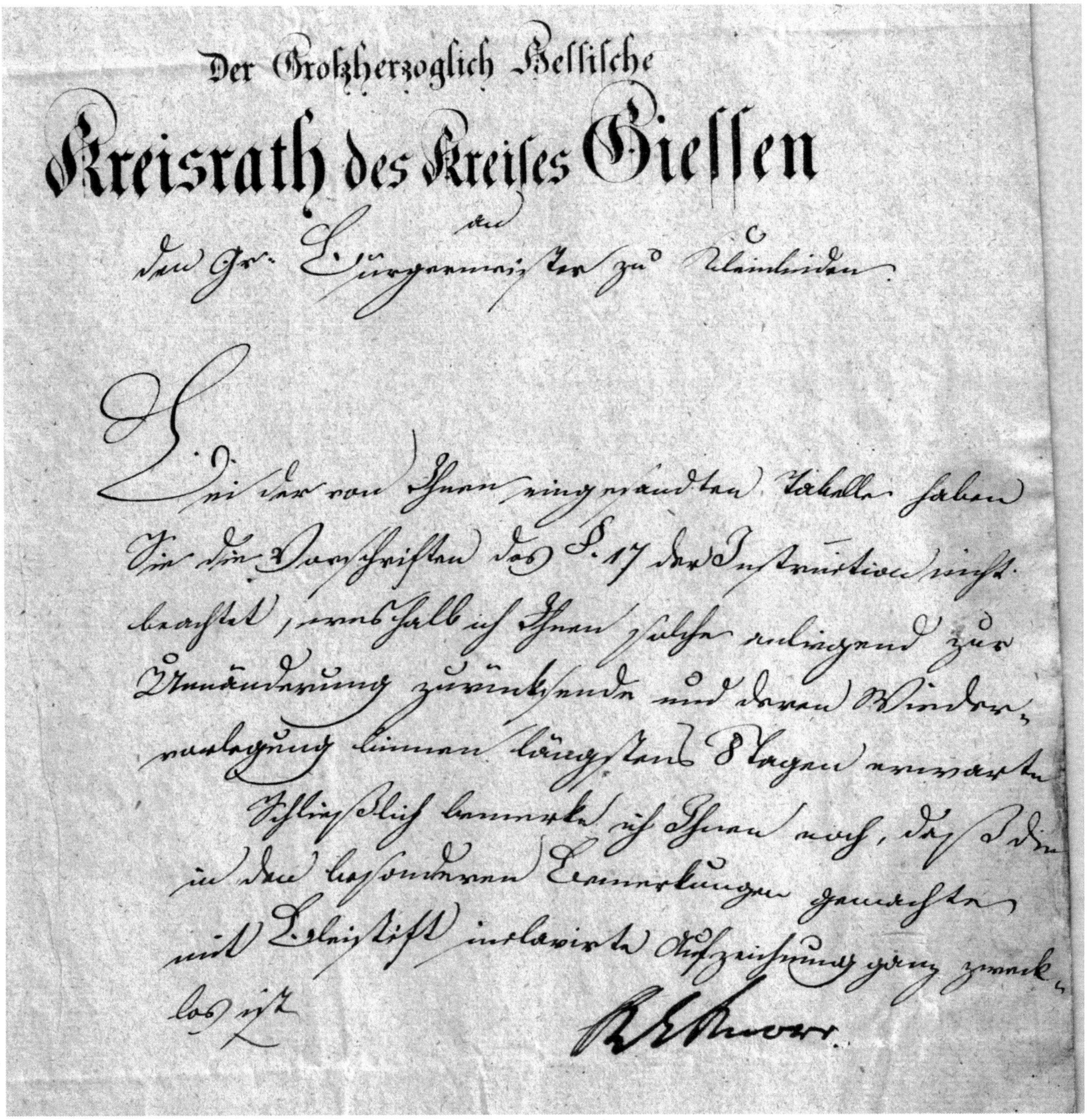

Der Großherzoglich Hessische

Kreisrath des Kreises Giessen

[handwritten letter text in German cursive script]

From an official of Giessen County, Hessen to the town of Kleinlinden following the census of 1840: "Regarding the statistical tables you submitted, you failed to observe the conditions of Paragraph 17 of the instructions. Thus I am returning the papers and expect you to make the necessary revisions and re-submit the report within one week. Please also note that what you wrote in pencil in the 'comments' column is totally meaningless." [Stadtarchiv Giessen KL23-II.2/3/2]

Da in den mit Unserm Ausschreiben vom 26. v. M. übersandten Formularen zu den Listen A. und B., die Volkszählung betreffend, der Druckfehler sich eingeschlichen hat, daß auf beiden Listen hier und da die Witwen vor den Witwern aufgeführt sind, letztere aber haben vorangestellt werden sollen; so werden die Obrigkeiten darauf mit der Anweisung aufmerksam gemacht, in dieser Beziehung die mitgetheilten Formulare nachzusehen und da, wo der erwähnte Druckfehler vorgekommen sein sollte, eine Verbesserung desselben eintreten zu lassen.

Hildesheim, den 23. November 1852.

Königlich Hannoversche Landdrostei.

Bar.

From the Royal District Office in Hildesheim, kingdom of Hannover, on November 23, 1852 (summarized): "There is a printing error on the new census form. The headings "Widows" and "Widowers" have been mistakenly reversed. Please make corrections if necessary." [Magistrat der Stadt Göttingen]

Im December d. J. findet die allgemeine Volkszählung statt. — Dieselbe muß auf das Genaueste erfolgen, um den Preußischen Staat den andern Zollvereinsstaaten gegenüber vor Verlusten zu sichern. —

Die Haus-Eigenthümer oder deren Stellvertreter werden daher hierdurch aufgefordert:

die umstehende Liste durch Aufnahme aller in ihren Besitzungen vorhandenen Seelen und des Viehstandes

am 1sten December

vollständig auszufüllen und die Richtigkeit der Angaben darunter zu bescheinigen. —

Am 3. December werden wir diese Liste in jedem Hause revidiren und abholen lassen. —

Wird die Liste gar nicht oder nicht richtig ausgefüllt vorgefunden, so tritt gegen den betreffenden Besitzer oder Stellvertreter eine Strafe von 15 Sgr. ein. —

Reicht das Formular bei einzelnen Besitzungen nicht aus, so kann noch Formular-Papier in unserer Kanzlei empfangen werden. —

Nordhausen, den 25. November 1855.

Der Magistrat.

From the county magistrate in Nordhausen, province of Sachsen, to all localities in 1855 (summarized): "Any persons who refuse to cooperate with the census campaign on December 1 this year, or who fill out the form incompletely or incorrectly will be fined 15 Groschen." [Kreisarchiv Nordhausen]

On October 6, 1880, the F. Doehl & Co. of Berlin shipped one wooden box full of census forms weighing 79 pounds bound for Duderstadt, Prussian province of Hannover. The charge was 1,40 Reichsmark. On October 8, Anton Binemann transported the box from the Herzberg Railway Station to Duderstadt (twelve miles) and charged 40 Pfennig for the service. [Stadtarchiv Duderstadt]

Der Herr Minister der geistlichen, Unterrichts- und Medicinal-Angelegen-heiten hat verfügt, daß am 1. December d. J., an welchem Tage die allgemeine Volkszählung stattfindet, der Unterricht in sämmtlichen Schulen ausfallen soll. Der Herr Minister erwartet, daß die Lehrer bereit sein werden, sich an dem Zählgeschäft mithelfend in der einen oder anderen Weise zu betheiligen. Daß Schüler dazu herangezogen werden, ist nicht statthaft.

Wir veranlassen Sie, demnach das Erforderliche in Ihrem Aufsichtsbezirke anzuordnen.

Für jeden Localschul-Inspector Ihres Bezirks erfolgt ein Exemplar dieses Ausschreibens hierneben.

Dröge.

From the Hildesheim Royal Office of Churches and Schools to the town officials in Duderstadt, Prussian province of Hannover in 1885 (summarized): "You are hereby instructed to close all schools on December 1 for the census campaign. It is expected that teachers will be assisting in the enumeration effort, but it is not appropriate to engage pupils for that purpose." [Stadtarchiv Duderstadt]

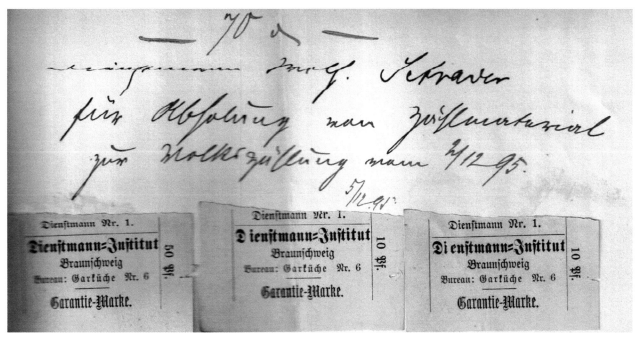

Some archivists keep everything. The archivist in Braunschweig pasted these three tickets to a paper for preservation. Each ticket authorizes the bearer to call at the address indicated to pick up additional census forms if needed. The forms were to be distributed to households on December 2, 1895. [Stadtarchiv Braunschweig D IV 1132]

Schotten, den 19 November 1910.

Betreffend: Die Volkszählung am 1 Dezember 1910.

Herrn Stadtkassier Glöck.
Hier.

Nachdem Sie von der in rubr: Sache tätigen Commission als Zähler vorgeschlagen worden sind und wir annehmen, dass Sie sich dieser Arbeit gerne unterziehen werden, bitten wir Sie, sich Freitag den 25 d. M. nachmittags 4½ Uhr im Rathaus zur Entgegennahme der Zähl-Formulare gefäll: einfinden zu wollen.

Allenfallsige Ablehnungen bitten uns sofort mitzuteilen.

Grossh: Bürgermeistrei Schotten.

Mayor Kromm of Schotten, Hessen sent this notice to city accountant Glöck on November 19, 1910 (summarized): "You have been selected as an enumerator for the census on December 1. We assume your cooperation and expect you to appear at city hall on November 25 to receive the necessary literature." [Stadtarchiv Schotten]

City accountant Glöck's reponse to the mayor of Schotten, Hessen in November 1910: "I regret to inform you that I am not able to assist with the census at this time. As the mayor well knows, the city accounting report is due soon and takes a great deal of time. I hereby request that you proceed without me." [Stadtarchiv Schotten]

The final statistical pages for the tiny duchy of Schwarzburg-Rudolstadt were so extensive that even the small Church of Jesus Christ of Latter-day Saints [Mormons] was included (eleventh column from left). There were no Mormons in the duchy that year and barely 2,000 in all of Germany at that time. [Thüringisches Staatsarchiv Schwarzburg-Rudolstadt Ministereim R. II. Abteilung (Inneres) 5748]

Rostock, den *27. Oktober* 19*0*0.

Betrifft:

Volkszählung.

Es ist *immer* mit Schwierigkeiten
verbunden gewesen, zu den Volks-
u.s.w. Zählungen die hier erfor-
derlichen 4-500 unbesoldeten Zähler
zu erlangen. Die Zahl der Einwohner,
welche sich auf Umfrage und öffent-
liche Bekanntmachung hin zur Mitwirkung bereit erklärte, deckte nur
zur Hälfte den Bedarf. Von den dann
ungefragt zu Zählern ernannten Ein-
wohnern aber reichten viele ihre
Zählpapiere unter Angabe aller
möglichen schwer zu prüfenden Hin-
derungsgründe und oftmals in letz-
ter Stunde zurück.

Das Polizeiamt gestattet sich
deshalb um baldgefällige Mitteilung

An official of the Rostock (Mecklenburg-Schwerin) Residential Registration Office wrote to the Braunschweig City Statistical Bureau on October 27, 1900: "We are having difficulties finding the 400 to 500 officials we need to conduct the census here. Only about one-half of the needed volunteers have come forward. Of those we assigned to assist, many returned the census forms to us—even at the last minute—giving all kinds of excuses that are difficult to verify. Thus we humbly ask you to respond quickly regarding how you go about finding enough enumerators. We are especially interested in knowing whether you pay your enumerators and how much. About how many agents do you engage and how many households does each agent count?" (signed H. Altvater) [Stadtarchiv Braunschweig D IV 1157.1]

The States of Germany in 1871

German	English
Anhalt	Anhalt
Baden	Baden
Bayern	Bavaria
Brandenburg	Brandenburg
Braunschweig	Brunswick
Bremen [Hansestadt Bremen]	Bremen
Elsaß-Lothringen	Alsace-Lorraine
Hamburg [Hansestadt Hamburg]	Hamburg
Hannover	Hanover
Hessen [Hessen-Darmstadt]	Hesse [Hesse-Darmstadt]
Hessen-Nassau	Hesse-Nassau
Hohenzollern	Hohenzollern
Lippe [Lippe-Detmold]	Lippe [Lippe-Detmold]
Lübeck [Hansestadt Lübeck]	Luebeck
Mecklenburg-Schwerin	Mecklenburg-Schwerin
Mecklenburg-Strelitz	Mecklenburg-Strelitz
Oldenburg	Oldenburg
Ostpreußen	East Prussia
Pommern	Pomerania
Posen	Posen
Preußen*	Prussia
Reuß ältere Linie [Reuß-Greiz]	Reuss Elder Line [Reuss-Greiz]
Reuß jüngere Linie [Reuß-Schleiz]	Reuss Younger Line [Reuss-Schleiz]
Rheinprovinz [Rheinland]	Rhineland
Sachsen-Altenburg	Saxe-Altenburg
Sachsen-Coburg-Gotha	Saxe-Coburg-Gotha
Sachsen Königreich	Kingdom of Saxony
Sachsen-Meiningen	Saxe-Meiningen
Sachsen Provinz	Province of Saxony
Sachsen-Weimar-Eisenach	Saxe-Weimar-Eisenach
Schaumburg-Lippe	Schaumburg-Lippe
Schlesien	Silesia
Schleswig-Holstein	Schleswig-Holstein
Schwarzburg-Rudolstadt	Schwarzburg-Rudolstadt
Schwarzburg-Sondershausen	Schwarzburg-Sondershausen
Waldeck	Waldeck
Westfalen	Westphalia
Westpreußen	West Prussia
Württemberg	Wuerttemberg

* Not treated in this book as a state (it was a kingdom consisting of thirteen provinces)

Bibliography

Centralbüreau des Zollvereins. "Grundsätze über die Bevölkerungs-Aufnahme in den Zollvereinsstaaten nach den Vereinbarungen vom 31. Januar 1834 und vom 23. Oktober 1845," 1. Berlin: Centralbüreau des Zollvereins, 1845.

Engel, Ernst. "Die Volkszählung im Deutschen Reiche am 1. Dezember [1871] und ihre wünschenswerthe Unterstützung durch die Presse und die Kanzel."

Gehrmann, Rolf. "German Census-Taking Before 1871." Rostock, Germany: Max-Planck-Institut für demografische Forschung, 2009.

Großherzoglich Mecklenburg-Schwerinsches officielles Wochenblatt, 1819, Achtzehntes Stück, Sonnabend, den 3ten Julii, 18.

Hahn, Hans-Werner. *Geschichte des Deutschen Zollvereins.* Göttingen: Vandenhoeck und Ruprecht, 1984. All translations from German by Roger P. Minert.

"Hauptprotokoll der Vollzugskommission in München vom 14.02.1834," Artikel 22.

Henderson, W.O. *The Zollverein.* London: Frank Cass, 1959.

Klingelhöffer, Otto. "Der Zollverein im Jahr 1865" in *Zeitschrift für die gesamte Staatswissenschaft,* v. 19 (1863).

Kraus, Antje. *Quellen zur Bevölkerungsstatistik Deutschlands 1815-1871.* Boppard am Rhein, Germany: Harald Boldt, 1980.

Michel, Harald. "Volkszählungen in Deutschland: Die Erfassung des Bevölkerungsstandes von 1816 bis 1933," in *Jahrbuch für Wirtschaftsgeschichte* 1985/II. Berlin: DeGruyter.

Minert, Roger P. *Deciphering Handwriting in German Documents: Analyzing German, Latin, and French in Historical Manuscripts,* 2nd ed. Provo, UT: GRT Publications, 2013.

_____. *Researching in Germany,* 2nd ed. Provo, UT: Lorelei Press, 2013.

Statistisches Bureau Berlin, "Die Volkszahl der Deutschen Staaten nach den Zählungen seit 1816," in *Monatshefte zur Statistik des Deutschen Reichs für das Jahr 1879* [2], *Die Statistik des Deutschen Reichs,* Vol. 37/2; urn:nbn:de:z-bw-drsa_3721. Berlin: Verlag des Königlich Preussischen Statistischen Bureaus, 1879.

Von Bismarck, Otto. Proclamation October 9, 1867 from the Bundesrat of the North German Confederation. Niedersächsisches Landesarchiv Bückeburg Dep 9C Nr 637.

Index